Doing Development Res

Doing Development Research

Edited by
Vandana Desai and Robert B. Potter

Los Angeles | London | New Delhi
Singapore | Washington DC

SAGE Publications Ltd
1 Oliver's Yard
55 City Road
London EC1Y 1SP

SAGE Publications Inc.
2455 Teller Road
Thousand Oaks, California 91320

SAGE Publications India Pvt Ltd
B 1/I 1, Mohan Cooperative Industrial Area
Mathura Road
New Delhi 110 044

SAGE Publications Asia-Pacific Pte Ltd
3 Church Street
#10-04 Samsung Hub
Singapore 049483

British Library Cataloguing in Publication data
A catalogue record for this book is available from the British Library

ISBN 978-1-4129-0284-7
ISBN 978-1-4129-0285-4 (pbk)

Library of Congress Control Number: 2005934837

Typeset by C&M Digitals Pvt. Ltd., Chennai, India
Printed on paper from sustainable resources
Printed in Great Britain by the MPG Books Group

MIX
Paper from
responsible sources
FSC
www.fsc.org
FSC® C018575

Contents

List of contributors   viii
Preface   X

PART I   INTRODUCTION   1

1   **The *Raison d'être* of *Doing Development Research***   3

PART II   STRATEGIC ISSUES IN PLANNING SOUND RESEARCH   11

2   **Doing Fieldwork in Developing Countries: Planning
     and Logistics**   13
     Tony Binns

3   **Ethical Practices in Doing Development Research**   25
     Lynne Brydon

4   **Working in Different Cultures: Issues of Race,
     Ethnicity and Identity**   34
     Caesar R.A. Apentiik and Jane L. Parpart

5   **Women, Men and Fieldwork: Gender Relations and Power Structures**   44
     Janet Henshall Momsen

6   **Working with Children in Development**   52
     Lorraine van Blerk

7   **Collecting Sensitive and Contentious Information**   62
     Margaret E. Harrison

8   **Dealing with Conflicts and Emergency Situations**   70
     Morten Bøås, Kathleen M. Jennings and Timothy M. Shaw

9   **Working with Partners: Educational Institutions**   79
     Bill Gould

10   **Working with Partners: Government Ministries**   87
     Mansoor Ali and Andrew Cotton

11   **Working with Partners: NGOs and CBOs**   94
     Claire Mercer

12   **Doing Development Research 'at Home'**   104
     Tim Unwin

PART III   INFORMATION AND DATA COLLECTION METHODS   113

(i) METHODS OF SOCIAL RESEARCH AND ASSOCIATED FORMS OF ANALYSIS

✓13   **Quantitative, Qualitative or Participatory? Which Method, for What and When?**   115
      Linda Mayoux

✓14   **Field Surveys and Inventories**   130
      David Barker

✓15   **Interviewing**   144
      Katie Willis

✓ 16 **Focus Groups**   153
      Sally Lloyd-Evans

17   **Your Questions Answered? Conducting Questionnaire Surveys**   163
     David Simon

18   **Lost in Translation? The Use of Interpreters in Fieldwork**   172
     Janet Bujra

✓ 19 **Ethnography and Participant Observation**   180
      Jan Kees van Donge

✓ 20 **Participatory Methods and Approaches: Tackling the Two Tyrannies**   189
      Harriot Beazley and Judith Ennew

21   **Diaries and Case Studies**   200
     JoAnn McGregor

(ii) USING EXISTING KNOWLEDGE AND RECORDS   207

22   **Literature Reviews and Bibliographic Searches**   209
     Paula Meth and Glyn Williams

23   **Using Indigenous Local Knowledge and Literature**   222
     Cathy McIlwaine

24 **Using Images, Films and Photography** 231
Cheryl McEwan

✓ 25 **Using Archives** 241
Michael Jennings

26 **Remote Sensing, GIS and Ground Truthing** 251
Dennis Conway and Shanon Donnelly

✓ 27 **The Importance of Census and Other Secondary Data in Development Studies** 262
Allan M. Findlay

28 **Using the World Wide Web for Development Research** 273
Emma Mawdsley

29 **Data from International Agencies** 282
Jonathan Rigg

(iii) DISSEMINATING FINDINGS/RESEARCH 295

30 **Writing an Effective Research Report or Dissertation** 297
Stephen Morse

31 **How is Research Communicated Professionally?** 310
Sally Gainsbury and Cheryl Brown

Index 320

vii

List of Contributors

Mansoor Ali, Water, Engineering and Development Centre (WEDC), University of Loughborough, UK.

Caesar R.A. Apentiik, International Development Studies, Dalhousie University, Canada.

David Barker, Department of Geography and Geology, University of the West Indies, Mona, Jamaica.

Harriot Beazley, School of Social Work and Applied Human Sciences, University of Queensland, Brisbane, Australia.

Tony Binns, Department of Geography, University of Otago, Dunedin, New Zealand.

Morten Bøås, Fafo – Institute for Applied International Studies, Oslo, Norway.

Cheryl Brown, Institute of Development Studies, University of Sussex, UK.

Lynne Brydon, Centre of West African Studies (CWAS), University of Birmingham, UK.

Janet Bujra, Department of Peace Studies, University of Bradford, UK.

Dennis Conway, Department of Geography, Indiana University, USA.

Andrew Cotton, Water, Engineering and Development Centre (WEDC), University of Loughborough, UK.

Vandana Desai, Department of Geography, Royal Holloway, University of London, UK.

Shanon Donnelly, Department of Geography, Indiana University, USA.

Judith Ennew, Centre for Family Research, University of Cambridge, UK.

Allan M. Findlay, Department of Geography, University of Dundee, UK.

Sally Gainsbury, Public Finance Magazine, London, UK.

Bill Gould, Department of Geography, University of Liverpool, UK.

Margaret E. Harrison, Department of Natural and Social Sciences, University of Gloucestershire, UK.

Kathleen M. Jennings, Fafo – Institute for Applied International Studies, Oslo, Norway.

Michael Jennings, Centre for Development Studies, University of Wales Swansea, UK.

Sally Lloyd-Evans, Department of Geography, School of Human and Environmental Sciences, University of Reading, UK.

Emma Mawdsley, School of Geography, Birkbeck College, University of London, UK.

Linda Mayoux, International Development Consultant, 61 Cheney Way, Cambridge, UK.

Cheryl McEwan, Department of Geography, University of Durham, UK.

JoAnn McGregor, Department of Geography, School of Human and Environmental Sciences, University of Reading, UK.

Cathy McIlwaine, Department of Geography, Queen Mary, University of London, UK.

Claire Mercer, Department of Geography, University of Leicester, UK.

Paula Meth, Department of Town and Regional Planning, University of Sheffield, UK.

Janet Henshall Momsen, Department of Human and Community Development, University of California, Davis, USA.

Stephen Morse, Department of Geography, School of Human and Environmental Sciences, University of Reading, UK.

Jane L. Parpart, International Development Studies, Dalhousie University, Canada; Research Fellow, London School of Economics; Political Studies, Stellenbosch University, South Africa.

Robert B. Potter, Department of Geography, School of Human and Environmental Sciences, University of Reading, UK.

Jonathan Rigg, Department of Geography, University of Durham, UK.

Timothy M. Shaw, Institute of Commonwealth Studies, University of London, UK.

David Simon, Department of Geography, Royal Holloway, University of London, UK.

Tim Unwin, Department of Geography, Royal Holloway, University of London, UK.

Lorraine van Blerk (née Young), Department of Geography and Earth Sciences, Brunel University, UK.

Jan Kees van Donge, Public Policy and Development Management, Institute of Social Studies, The Hague.

Glyn Williams, Department of Geography, King's College, University of London, UK.

Katie Willis, Department of Geography, Royal Holloway, University of London, UK.

Preface

Our intention as the editors of *Doing Development Research* has been to bring together information and guidance from start to finish that will prove invaluable to the inexperienced student or researcher embarking on research and fieldwork overseas. We realize that students cannot be totally prepared for all eventualities that might occur, but we think useful preparations can be made and some common problems avoided to maximize academic usefulness and to help ensure rewarding fieldwork. We hope to provide an overview of the major issues surrounding development research today.

From the outset, it was envisaged that the book would offer a one-stop reference guide for anyone with a practical, professional or academic interest in doing development research. The book is of particular relevance to those doing research in the fields of development studies, geography, economics, politics, sociology, social anthropology and social policy, along with NGO practitioners and those in donor agencies.

Doing Development Research recognizes the prior existence of numerous good general texts on doing research in developing countries. Our book is not in any way a standard manual. Rather, we hope to give a range of tips and sound advice to those contemplating the challenges of undertaking fieldwork in 'developing' areas. However, this book performs a unique function in bringing together a wide range of issues concerning doing research in developing countries, from the start of the process to the end of the research. As such, the book can effectively be used as a course textbook for research training, methodology courses, while, with the exercise of selective judgement, it can be treated as a source of key course readings and discussion pieces in connection with higher-level options and training courses, for example, at the Masters degree level. In order to guide both interested students and general readers who want to pursue doing research, each chapter is followed by some questions for discussion, a further reading section and a list of useful websites. It is also our hope that students will be able to use the book for the duration of their research and fieldwork and not just for one or two aspects of doing research.

Although every fieldwork context is unique, many features are common to all. *Doing Development Research* covers a wide range of issues from preparing to go into the field, the eventualities of actually working in the field, the positionality of the researcher, working with various organizations, using interpreters, or different methods to collect data, using various types of information from different sources to finally presenting the findings of the research.

The chapters are divided into two main sections, dealing respectively with the strategic issues in planning sound research, and information and data collection methods. The second section is further divided into three parts, dealing respectively with methods of social research and associated forms of analysis, using existing knowledge and records, and finally disseminating research.

One of the major strengths of the book is that it is written mostly by academics who have supervised and guided students at both undergraduate and postgraduate levels, who draw on their extensive, rich and diverse experiences of a range of research carried out in various developing countries. We have also tried to incorporate authors from around the world who are involved in development. We are thankful for their support and contributions.

We hope that our readers find doing development research an exciting and memorable life experience and not just an intellectual exercise. In essence, we see development research as a continuous learning process, and we hope this book will stimulate critical thinking.

Vandana Desai and Rob Potter

Part I

Introduction

1

The *Raison d'être* of *Doing Development Research*

The aim of *Doing Development Research* is to provide a comprehensive introduction to the process of undertaking research in the multi- and interdisciplinary field of development studies. This volume seeks, therefore, to provide the bases for a thorough initial training for anyone aiming to carry out research in, or on, developing countries. In this context, the geographical category 'developing countries' is to be interpreted in the broadest of fashions. This geographical signpost might more properly be referred to as 'overseas', referring to cases where somebody is researching in an area, region or culture other than the one in which they grew up, or with which they are now familiar. But we do not preclude doing development work in, or on, one's own country, following the premise that development is change in either positive or negative terms, and thereby occurs in all localities and regions to a greater or lesser extent (see Brookfield, 1975; Potter et al., 2004).

Having said this, although it is hoped that the volume will address the concerns of practitioners and consultants working on 'hands-on' or applied development issues, the book is primarily designed with the needs of undergraduate and postgraduate students to the fore. For generations of students, the requirement that they should prepare a dissertation or thesis has represented their first professional-academic contact with doing development research at first hand, and this represents the starting point

for *Doing Development Research*. We assume, therefore, that the person aiming to undertake development research has attended introductory courses and read the background literature (see Chapters 22 and 28) on development theory and practice. We also hope that as part of their general undergraduate or postgraduate training they will have read a little about different research methods and the ways in which data can be collected and analysed.

The volume brings together a range of experts who have extensive first-hand experience of undertaking overseas research. It starts from the premise that overseas development is a more complex, personal, professionally demanding and nuanced experience than most manuals on research methodology acknowledge. It follows that at the outset of their work, starting students need all the help and assistance they can get. *Doing Development Research* aims to bring a much-needed cross-cultural perspective to the issues surrounding working overseas.

Doing Development Research enters a field where there are already some very good books and our intention has been to complement these, both in terms of the level of treatment and the subject areas covered. For example, a very helpful volume is provided by Scheyvens and Storey (2003). Their practical guide to doing development fieldwork considers the nature of quantitative and qualitative research at the outset, before the major parts of the book deal with preparing to go into the field, the eventualities of actually working in the field and, subsequently, the issues involved in leaving the field. Overall, there is a strong and much needed emphasis on the researchers' positionality while preparing for, completing and acting on fieldwork, which will directly influence the research process and outcomes. We envisage that our readers who are strongly fieldwork-based may well progress to use Scheyvens and Storey (2003), having first consulted *Doing Development Research*. The same is true of several other books that deal primarily with the issues surrounding the completion of fieldwork in developing countries, like Robson and Willis (1997) and Devereux and Hoddinott (1992).

Several other very good books, while covering more than fieldwork logistics and methods, are distinguished by the fact that they are primarily aimed at the development practitioner – that is those professionals who are involved in implementation projects and consultancy research, etc. Laws, Harper and Marcus (2003) concentrate on topics such as quality issues in research, organizing a brief, approaches to evaluation, re-evaluating research for development work, as well as managing impacts. Mikkelson (2005) takes a very strongly participatory view of research and her book is aimed primarily at practitioners. Other books are avowedly aimed at postgraduates, as for example is the case with those by Robson and Willis (1997) and Scheyvens and Storey (2003).

In contrast, *Doing Development Research* endeavours to provide a clear overview for the beginning student – whether undergraduate or postgraduate. How can they set about their work – what published secondary data are already available? How can they make use of archives? (see Chapter 25) How can the literature on the chosen topic be reviewed? (see Chapter 22) How can they use the internet and other innovate sources such as images, films and photography to aid their research endeavours? If they are going into the field, what practical and logistical issues do they face? (see Chapter 2) What ethical factors are

to be borne in mind (see Chapter 3), and what are the special concerns of working across lines of race, ethnicity and identity? What about gender issues and the special requirements of working with children – what special considerations do these entail?

As we detail more fully in the next section, *Doing Development Research* covers more than fieldwork (logistical issues, working in different cultures, gender issues in fieldwork, using interpreters, field surveys, interviews, focus groups and questionnaires, etc.). The volume considers doing development research not only overseas in the field, but also doing development 'at home'. This is specifically covered in Chapter 12. But *Doing Development Research* also covers this important topic in respect of using data from international agencies, using the World Wide Web for development research and other secondary sources, such as remote sensing, GIS, census data, archives, indigenous literature, etc. Working with partners such as educational institutions, government departments and ministries, non-government organizations and community-based organizations is also covered under this wider remit.

Structure and content

After the brief introduction and overview of the aims and scope of *Doing Development Research* provided in this chapter, which comprises Part I of the volume, the book is divided into two principal sections (Parts II and III):

The strategic issues involved in planning and executing sound research are first surveyed in Part II of the book (see Figure 1.1). The chapters in this part cover both working in the field and working via secondary sources. It aims to introduce readers to both the practicalities and the realities of undertaking development-oriented research.

Part III then overviews the *main ways in which information and data can be collected in carrying*

4

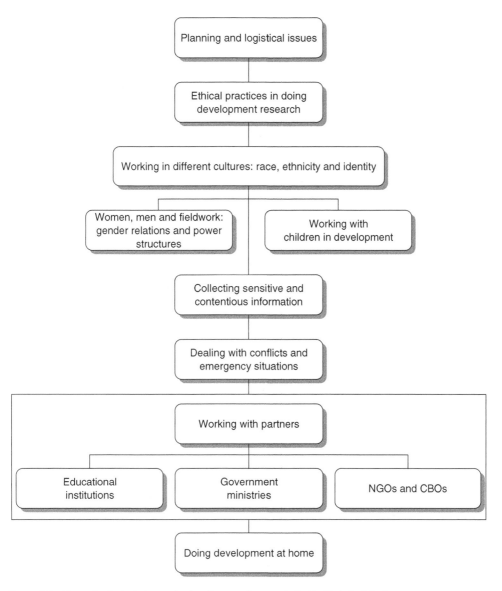

Figure 1.1 The main strategic issues in planning sound research dealt with in Part II of
Doing Development Research

out development-oriented research. This is designed to assist with selecting appropriate methods. Part III is itself split into three sub-parts:

- Section (i) deals with *methods of social research* by which data can be collected at first hand. These chapters also cover associated forms of analysis, where these are relevant. However, the primary aim of *Doing*

Development Research is not to cover statistical and other forms of data analysis. These issues are covered in far greater detail in books written for this purpose (for example, see Kitchen and Tate, 2000; Robinson, 1998).

- Section (ii) deals with *how existing knowledge and sources can be used to inform analyses of development issues.* Too often these can be

5

forgotten in the rush to collate new and relevant data. This section also makes a valuable contribution in focusing attention on up-to-date, state-of-the art innovative approaches such as those afforded by the use of the internet, using images, films and photography, and data from international development agencies such as the United Nations and World Bank.

- Section (iii), consisting of two chapters, points the way in terms of *how research can be written up effectively*, and how the results of research can be disseminated professionally. This final section is not a substitute for texts which deal specifically and comprehensively with how to write up the results of research. Such guides exist for the undergraduate (Walliman, 2004), for Masters candidates (Hart, 2004), with respect to theses and dissertations in general (Glatthorn and Joyner, 2005; Oliver, 2003; Roberts, 2004; Rudestam and Newton, 2000), and for the doctoral student (Craswell, 2004; Wellington et al., 2005). Rather, this section provides a starting point to get readers thinking about such issues and hopefully to refer to the specialist texts that exist.

Throughout, *Doing Development Research* tries to maintain a basically common-sense approach and adopts a much needed cross-cultural perspective. The book seeks to use straightforward language to guide those doing overseas research through the choice of an appropriate set of research methods, the implementation of the research, and how to communicate the findings to a range of audiences (see Chapter 30 and 31).

Doing Development Research and paradigms of development

One of the main reasons that we regard *Doing Development Research* to be so necessary is that development studies and associated research have been, and still are, characterized by a multiplicity of philosophical approaches and associated epistemologies. By an epistemology, we mean theories as to how we find out about the world. Different development agendas reflect different political, economic, social, cultural, ethical and even moral and religious goals (Cowan and Shenton, 1996; Potter et al., 2004; Power, 2003; Rapley, 1996). Thus, thinking about development has shown many sharp twists and turns over the past 150 years.

Further, the various ideas about development that have taken centre stage have not commanded attention in a strictly sequential manner. In other words, as new sets of ideas about development have come to prominence, earlier theories and models have not been totally discarded. For example, the right wing of the political spectrum have held on to free-market policies and have re-promulgated them as part of the 'New Right'. Equally, even given the near total collapse of state socialism since 1989, Marxist-inspired views and theories still pervade many areas of development thinking. So, as argued by Potter et al. (2004), theories and strategies of development have tended to stack up upon one another. Thus, Hettne (1995: 64) drew attention to the argument that theories of development in the social sciences 'accumulate rather than fade away'.

In addition, it is clear that over time different sets of thought about development have been associated with different philosophies of science and associated epistemologies. And at each stage, these different approaches have therefore been associated with different views as to how we set about finding out about the world, by means of collecting data and evidence (see Table 1.1). Naturally, this broad relationship between sets of thinking about development and linked methods has not been a perfect or mechanical one, for the reasons just explained. As we have said, old theories of development never die – in fact, they don't even seem to fade away (Potter et al., 2004). So, by extension, the approaches to finding out

Table 1.1   The broad association between philosophies of science, paradigms of development and the broad approaches covered in this book

Philosophy	Broad paradigm of development studies[1]	Broad approaches covered in this book
Empiricism	Historical approaches (pre-1950s onwards)	Field surveys Inventories Census data Data from government ministries
Logical positivism	Classical-traditional approaches (mainly 1950s/1960s)	Questionnaires Interviews GIS Remote sensing Archives
Structuralism	Radical political economy-dependency approaches (1960s onwards)	Literature reviews Indigenous literature Data from international agencies Film, images and photography
Humanism	Alternative and another development (1980s onwards)	Ethnographic approaches Participant observation Participatory research methods Focus groups Diaries and case studies

[1]*Categorization based on Potter et al., 2004: 82–120.*

that have been associated with different theories of development are also still in currency. As a broad generalization, early approaches stressed development as economic growth and therefore emphasized quantitative approaches. Later, more humanistic approaches to development saw the rise of participatory and qualitative lines of investigation, with the aim being to put fewer words into respondents' mouths and to listen more effectively (see Chapter 18).

Broadly speaking, the earliest approaches in any discipline tend to be *empiricist*. They subscribe to the view that we find out about the world by observing what has happened and how it is structured. In development studies, this has meant looking at what history tells us

about how countries and regions have developed and changed through time. As shown in Table 1.1, early and continuing approaches in the subject, therefore, have been associated with collecting data out in the field – for example, doing farm and rural surveys (see Chapters 13 and 14), urban and village assessments and inventories. Of course, just as we were arguing above, empirical data are still frequently collected as part of development research, whether collected in the field or from national censuses or data collated by government ministries or international agencies (see Chapters 27 and 29). They are often the 'staples' of basic and applied or practical research.

In most areas of intellectual endeavour, over time, pure empiricism tends to be replaced by *logical positivism.* Positivism is associated with the rise of the scientific method under conditions of modernity, subscribing to what is generally referred to as 'enlightenment thinking' (Power, 2003). Positivism basically argues that we come to understand the world by observing what has been the case experimentally. When formal ideas are tested repeatedly, this is referred to as *logical positivism.* The rise of what may be referred to as classical-traditional approaches to development (see Potter et al., 2004: Chapter 3) in the 1950s and early 1960s can be temporally associated with the rise to prominence of positivism in geography and development studies, as shown in Table 1.1. During this period, empirical data, such as numbers of hospital beds per 1,000 of the population, road network densities, were mapped to show levels of so-called modernization. And surveys were also done using questionnaires (see Chapter 17) and interviews (see Chapter 15) in order to capture data that can be tested against 'reality'. Indeed, the tenets of logicial positivism remain with us to the present day, in the form of remote sensing and GIS (see Chapter 26) and other areas of quantification and hypothesis-testing in development-oriented work.

In the 1960s and 1970s, there were two broad reactions to the general hegemony of the classical-traditional approach which stressed the salience of economic growth (Potter et al., 2004: Chapter 3). The first is referred to as *structuralism* and is principally associated with the 1960s; and the second is *humanism*, which came to prominence in the 1970s. These paradigm changes were both linked with yet further changes in epistemology and associated methodological approaches.

1   *Structuralism* is the idea that there are unseen structures and forces that guide the path of global and local events, with these often being of a political-strategic nature. This was the approach adopted by radicals in the 1960s, who argued that the global capitalist system was inherently biased against 'true'

development, and had served to accentuate extremes in wealth and inequality. This was associated with the rise of neo-Marxist and dependency approaches in the arena of development studies (Desai and Potter, 2002). Data from international agencies and indigenous Latin American and Caribbean writings became grist to the data mill during this era.

2   *Humanism* stressed the importance of the individual and ways of perceiving, thinking and doing. In development studies this was linked with the argument that the conditions under which people are living, their lifestyles, culture and their reactions are key (see Chapter 19). It is important to understand the multiplicity of perspectives that are valuable in understanding the complexities of development issues. It is also associated with thinking about empowering the voices of different groups – women, children, men, ethnic minorities, etc. (see Chapters 4, 5 and 6). This actively promotes opportunities for the less privileged to undertake research with the privileged (i.e. the researcher). The approach later came to be associated with the rise of green, environmentally oriented eco-development, broadly against a backdrop of corporate big business. The trend was accordingly towards qualitative data expressing the circumstances of people's day-to-day lives. Interviews, often of the semi-structured variety, became more important as a research methodology (Chapter 15), and in development studies participatory rapid appraisal (PRA) and associated methods were the outcome (see Chapter 20). Approaches based on indigenous literature (Chapter 23), film, images or photography also emanated from this era (Chapter 24). Focus groups, ethnographic approaches, participant observation and diaries and case studies all now have an important role to play in such studies (see Chapters 16, 19 and 21 respectively). It is essential to remember that research is a two-way process of interaction. In this process researchers need to be politically aware and need to be able to handle conflictual, sensitive or contentious information. Chapters 7 and 8 specifically hope to

raise awareness of such issues. Similarly, a lot of research is now done in collaboration or in partnership with either academics or various types of institution based in developing countries. Chapter 9, 10 and 11 specifically concentrate on educational institutes, government ministries, and NGOs and CBOs.

The important point is that approaches to data collection in development studies remain as diverse as philosophies of development themselves. And this is even more so today, in an era associated with what may be referred to as post-structuralism and postmodernity. The world is significantly more global and more complex than ever before – and it is argued that singular theories and conceptualizations are too limiting by far. Meta-theories and narratives have been replaced by a multiplicity of conceptualizations and approaches. Hence, students of development studies, defined broadly, need to be aware of the wide variety of approaches that are open to them, before embarking on their intensive work. This explains the *raison d'être* of *Doing Development Research*.

Format of chapters

Excluding this introduction, *Doing Development Research* consists of 31 short chapters. As already noted, the overarching aim is to provide a user-friendly introduction to the process of carrying out development research, covering the conceptualization of the piece of work to its write-up and dissemination.

In respect to each chapter, the authors were asked to include short summaries of the content of their chapters. The contributors were also invited to include graphics or photographs, and tables, wherever these would add considerably to the text. Likewise, boxed case studies could also be included at appropriate points in the text where they would aid understanding. It was requested that chapters should finish with a list of key items of further reading as an aid for those wishing to take topics further. In addition, authors were invited to add a maximum of fifteen additional bibliographic references. If pertinent websites exist, then it was suggested that no more than five useful sites should be listed. At the end of each chapter, approximately five questions or discussion topics are provided to act as a guide for class and tutorial discussions.

These features were all designed to try to ensure that *Doing Development Studies* is a practical learning tool for students who are setting about undertaking their first, or early, piece of development-oriented research, whether in the field, study, library or archive.

9

References

Brookfield, H. (1975) *Interdependent Development*, London: Arnold.

Cowan, M.P. and Shenton, R.W. (1996) *Doctrines of Development*, London and New York: Routledge.

Craswell, G. (2004) *Writing for Academic Success: A Postgraduate Guide*, London: Sage.

Desai, V. and Potter, R.B. (eds) (2002) *The Companion to Development Studies*, London: Arnold and New York: Oxford University Press.

Devereux, S. and Hoddinott, J. (1992) *Fieldwork in Developing Countries*, London: Sage.

Glatthorn, A. and Joyner, R. (2005) *Writing the Winning Thesis or Dissertation*, London: Sage.

Hart, C. (2004) *Doing your Masters Dissertation*, London: Sage.

Hettne, B. (1995) *Development Theory and the Three Worlds*, 2nd edn, Harlow: Longman.

Kitchen, R. and Tate, N.J. (2000) *Conducting Research in Human Geography: Theory, Methodology and Practice*, London and New York: Prentice Hall.

Laws, S., Harper, C. and Marcus, R. (2003) *Research for Development: A Practical Guide*, London: Sage.

Mikkelson, B. (2005) *Methods for Development Work and Research*, London: Sage.

Oliver, P. (2003) *Writing your Thesis*, London: Sage.

Potter, R.B., Binns, T., Elliott, J. and Smith, D. (2004) *Geographies of Development*, 2nd edn, Harlow, London and New York: Pearson/Prentice Hall.

Power, M. (2003) *Rethinking Development Geographies*, London and New York: Routledge.

Rapley, J. (1996) *Understanding Development*, London: UCL Press.

Roberts, C.M. (2004) *The Dissertation Journey*, London: Sage.

Robinson, G.M. (1998) *Methods and Techniques in Human Geography*, Chichester: John Wiley and Sons.

Robson, E. and Willis, K. (eds) (1997) *Postgraduate Fieldwork in Developing Countries: A Rough Guide*, 2nd edn, Developing Areas Research Group, Monograph No. 9, London: Royal Geographical Society and the Institute of British Geographers.

Rudestam, K. and Newton, R. (2000) *Surviving your Dissertation*, London: Sage.

Scheyvens, R. and Storey, D. (eds) (2003) *Development Fieldwork: A Practical Guide*. London: Sage.

Walliman, N. (2004) *Your Undergraduate Dissertation: The Essential Guide for Success*, London: Sage.

Wellington, J., Bathmaker, A.-M., Hunt, C., McCulloch, G. and Sikes, P. (2005) *Succeeding with your Dissertation*, London: Sage.

Part II

Strategic Issues in Planning Sound Research

2

Doing Fieldwork in Developing Countries: Planning and Logistics

Tony Binns

The value of fieldwork in Third World countries • • Selecting a fieldwork location • • Developing overseas contacts • • Finding a research assistant and/or interpreter • • Being aware of local customs and protocol • • Evaluating what you and the host community will get from the field research • • Action-based fieldwork • • Power and the control of knowledge in field-based research

Introduction

Thirty years ago, as an impressionable doctoral student, I left the UK on my first aeroplane flight to spend a year doing fieldwork in Sierra Leone, West Africa. Although I had studied a good range of geography and development courses, both as an undergraduate and postgraduate, I had received absolutely no training in 'doing fieldwork in developing countries'. I recollect that my pre-trip reading on fieldwork methodology consisted mainly of poring through manuals on conducting farm surveys and formulating and administering questionnaires. In those days (the early 1970s), there was an over-obsession with collecting mountains of quantitative data that could (often dubiously) be subjected to a gamut of statistical tests. Participatory research

had scarcely been heard of, to say nothing of the soul-searching involved in evaluating complex ethical aspects of the fieldwork experience. In retrospect, I now realize just how naïve I was about the practicalities of living and working among remote and poor communities in a tropical country. Yet at the end of the fieldwork, I was in no doubt that it had been the best year of my life. Indeed, it was an experience that provided the stimulus for me to embark on a career in teaching and researching about development issues.

In recent years, a number of authors have examined ethical issues related to 'First World' researchers undertaking fieldwork in 'Third World' countries (see, for example, Adams and Megaw, 1997; Madge, 1993, 1994; Potter, 1993; Sidaway, 1992, 1993). The coming together of the relatively rich 'researcher' with the relatively poor 'respondent' does undoubtedly raise many questions about 'power' and 'positionality', which are considered briefly later in this chapter and then in more detail elsewhere in this book. It is certainly important to be aware of such issues, but I would disagree with Bronfenbrenner (1952: 453) that the only safe way of not violating professional ethics is to refrain from doing research altogether. While some academics have expressed firm objections to research by 'outsiders' (Kobayashi, 1994), others argue that research across boundaries (of ethnicity, culture, gender, etc.) can be justified because difference is an inherent aspect of all social interactions, and we can never truly be 'insiders' or 'outsiders' in any absolute sense (Nast, 1994: 57).

I would go along with Potter (1993), in asserting that teaching about the Third World should be informed by recent first-hand field experience. Indeed, across all sectors of the education system, I firmly believe that a detailed understanding of people and environment in different parts of the Third World is essential to the development of global understanding, empathy and action. In motivating the general populace to act during humanitarian crises caused by drought, floods, famine and civil war, up-to-date media reports and evidence from the field are essential if charities such as Oxfam, Christian Aid and Save the Children are to convey the urgency of the situation.

Preparing for fieldwork

The decision to work in Sierra Leone on my chosen research topic (the relationships between food production, rural development and diamond mining), emerged from long conversations with my supervisor, who had worked in the University of Sierra Leone during the 1960s. In the absence of personal computers, the internet and email, communication with Sierra Leone was very difficult in the early 1970s, other than through expensive telephone calls and painfully slow letters. Today, the internet provides an invaluable tool for discovering a wealth of information about a proposed location for fieldwork. Affordable long-haul and exotic travel were also in their infancy in the 1970s – trips to Africa were still the preserve of the wealthy. My air ticket to Sierra Leone in 1974 cost £750 (well over £1000 at today's prices), whereas 30 years later it is only about £600. Other useful sources that are now available include travel guides such as the *Rough Guide* and *Lonely Planet* series.

Irrespective of whether your fieldwork is in a rural location, I would strongly recommend that you read Robert Chambers's classic book, *Rural Development: Putting the Last First* (Chambers, 1983). Although published over twenty years ago, it still provides a splendid introduction to some of the key issues concerning rural research in poor countries. Other valuable sources are *The Oxfam Handbook of Development and Relief* (Eade and Williams, 1995) and *Development Fieldwork: A Practical Guide* (Scheyvens and Storey, 2003).

In considering the logistics of fieldwork, you need to ask: *why? where? when?* and *how?* In answering the question '*why* do fieldwork?', this will be determined largely by the nature of your research project, its key objectives and the methodology you have chosen. Formulating the methodology can take some time, but it is particularly important that you allow for a degree of flexibility in your fieldwork plans. From experience, interview schedules and other data collection methods often need to be fine-tuned when you are actually in the field, perhaps after conducting a small pilot study. In considering *where* you should undertake fieldwork, it is likely that a specific location is a key aspect of the research topic, for example, 'The sustainability of artisanal fishing practices in the Kenyan sector of Lake Victoria'. But in deciding where to do fieldwork, you should also be aware of such factors as the willingness of local elders and community leaders to support your research, local transport and travel arrangements, the accessibility of the research area, where you might live, the safety and security situation in your proposed location, and health aspects.

The timing of your fieldwork can be quite crucial and should be based on local knowledge that you have managed to acquire. For example, undertaking fieldwork during the rainy season can be difficult and uncomfortable. But if you avoid the rainy season you could actually miss much of the farming activity, when people are working at their hardest, when food may be in short supply (the so-called 'hungry season'), and when community health and welfare are often under considerable pressure. For example, the incidence of malaria and other diseases is generally greater during the rainy season. Chambers is critical of what he calls 'dry season bias', since field research undertaken entirely in the dry season, although perhaps logistically more straightforward, fails to appreciate the annual seasonal pattern and the pressures which exist at specific times of the year. Key aspects of rural poverty can be missed by not doing fieldwork in the rainy season (Chambers, 1983). In timing your fieldwork you should also consider cultural factors, such as the timing of religious festivals. For example, fieldwork undertaken in Muslim countries during the month of Ramadan can be interrupted by the obligation for Muslims to pray at certain times, and respondents may be tired or irritable due to not eating or drinking between sunrise and sunset. Understandably, the early evening meal, taken after the daily fast is broken, is an important social occasion and not a good time to conduct interviews.

While postgraduates will nowadays normally receive training in field-based survey methods, and are also generally introduced to issues concerning the ethics and protocol of undertaking fieldwork in Third World countries, for many undergraduates there could be a limited induction in these aspects. Those who have already travelled overseas, or have worked on gap year programmes are at an advantage, but before setting off on fieldwork, it is essential that all fieldworkers should discuss their proposed study with someone who has had recent practical experience, preferably in the area where you propose to base your study. Some universities organize field courses in Third World countries that provide a useful insight to the nature of possible field research and the different field-based methods that might be used (Binns, 1992; Robson, 2002).

A good contact in the country where you plan to undertake your fieldwork can play a key role in advising on the practicalities of research and, if necessary, assisting with obtaining research permission. In the last decade, I have been involved in establishing three collaborative higher education links through the British Council with universities in Nigeria, Sierra Leone and South Africa. These links have proved invaluable in gaining research permission (where necessary) and in providing a supportive framework for both students and myself who are undertaking field research in these countries. It may not actually be necessary to obtain research permission if you are undertaking collaborative fieldwork with local researchers. Short periods of fieldwork might also be undertaken with a tourist visa, but where extended field research is planned, such as for a doctoral thesis, it is advisable to obtain official approval. This can actually take some time, but can be expedited with the assistance of a local university or NGO, which is familiar with the application procedure and can write in support of the application.

Before embarking on fieldwork, you may need to complete an 'ethical clearance' form for your own institution, in addition to undertaking a 'risk assessment' of your proposed fieldwork. This involves going through a series

15

of steps, such as identifying potential hazards, examining how they might affect you, evaluating the risk, and deciding on what precautions you should take to avoid risk. The risk assessment should then be under constant review during your time in the field, with contingency arrangements in place should problems occur. Most higher education institutions and professional bodies publish guidelines for fieldwork risk assessments, many of which are available on the internet. The UK government's Health and Safety Executive (HSE) also issues advice on formulating risk assessments (http://www.hse.gov.uk) (see Box 2.1).

Box 2.1   Checklist: Preparing for fieldwork

- Consult the internet, *Rough Guide* (http://www.roughguides.com/) and/or *Lonely Planet* (http://www.lonelyplanet.com/) for country information – currency, climate, visa requirements, international and local travel, accommodation, etc.
- The UK Foreign and Commonwealth Office (FCO) website (http://www.fco.gov.uk) gives up-to-date travel advice – details on safety and security aspects in specific countries.
- For health advice (vaccinations, malaria prophylaxis, etc.), there are various websites, for example MASTA (http://www.masta.org/).
- For information on field expeditions and expedition planning, contact the Royal Geographical Society Expedition Advisory Centre (http://www.rgs.org). See also Pawson and Teather (2002).
- Wherever possible, establish links with local individuals and/or institutions in the country you will be visiting. A local university or college, a non-governmental organization (NGO), the British Council, or your country's embassy or high commission can be useful contacts.
- It is vital that you obtain good travel insurance for yourself and your possessions for the duration of your time overseas. This should include comprehensive health cover, with repatriation by 'air ambulance' should that be necessary.
- Undertake a risk assessment and review it regularly.

Concerning what clothing and personal items you should carry during your field research, Table 2.1 is a tried and tested 'kit list' for tropical countries, which may be helpful.

Into the field

On arrival in the country where you will be doing fieldwork, you should first make contact with the individuals and institutions with whom you have been corresponding. Hopefully, they will provide you with a base on arrival, probably in the capital city. If it is your first visit to that country, you should allow yourself some time to settle in and develop your networks further. Don't be in too much of a hurry to get into the field. You should visit government offices, NGOs and higher education institutions, where individuals can probably supply you with useful perspectives on your research, as well as providing reports ('grey' literature) and statistics that may be unobtainable outside the country. You will also need to talk about the logistic arrangements for your fieldwork. On the basis

Table 2.1 Fieldwork kit list for tropical areas

Clothing	Medical and toiletries	Other items
towel	first aid book	passport
underwear	Elastoplast/ Band Aid	ticket
shirts – preferably cotton	anti-diarrhoea tablets	traveller's cheques, cash,
socks	re-hydration powders	debit/credit cards
trousers/shorts	lip salve	insurance certificate
(smart) shoes	analgesic tablets	camera
training shoes, sandals	malaria tablets	spare batteries
lightweight walking boots	sterile needles	films
plastic slip-on sandals	antihistamine tablets	vaccination certificates
swimming costume	insect repellent	address book
pullover or fleece	wet-wipes	calculator
waterproof jacket	toothbrush	string (for clothes-line, etc.)
hat	toothpaste	washing powder/liquid, pegs
belt	deodorant	luggage keys
glasses/sunglasses	soap	coathangers
	shampoo	sheet sleeping bag
	flannel	penknife
	razor & razor blades	small rucksack
	shaving soap	water bottle
	comb/hairbrush	scissors
	sun protection cream	radio (short-wave)
	multi-vitamins	clock
	ear plugs	torch
	tissues	mirror
	other personal items	pens, pencils, notebook, maps

of up-to-date information from local experts, it may then be necessary to modify your plans, for example if there is a security risk in a particular area, or if the road is impassable due to heavy rain.

Another very important matter that you will need to resolve is who will actually accompany you on your fieldwork. It is likely that you will not be fluent in the local language(s), but even if you do regard yourself as competent linguistically, I would strongly advise that you should be accompanied on fieldwork by at least one local person. In the past, I have undertaken fieldwork with colleagues from local universities, and with local undergraduate or postgraduate students. It is

always useful to be able to 'bounce ideas off' someone else, and a local person will also be more aware of safety issues and protocols that could affect the success of your fieldwork. The opportunity to live and work with local people will add much to your fieldwork experience and should help you to discover so much more about the country. While working with local students, I have been able to discuss their own research and career interests; while with academic colleagues we have considered our joint plans for future research and publication, curriculum development and their reciprocal visits to UK. Being accompanied in the field by local people is also vital in the context of helping to build up rapport and trust with potential respondents in the communities where your fieldwork is based.

University or NGO staff should be able to advise on who would be the best person to act as your interpreter and/or research assistant, and what payment they would expect for the work. University students are often keen to perform such a role, in return for having an opportunity to work closely with someone from overseas. It may not be necessary to pay them a wage as such, but it would be both polite and reasonable to cover their travel, accommodation and subsistence expenses, and to make a gift to them when the work has been satisfactorily completed. I have invariably found the fieldwork to be the most interesting and enjoyable phase of all my research projects. But the success of your fieldwork will depend on many things, most notably gaining the confidence, interest and support of the communities where you are working, and developing a good relationship with your interpreter/field assistant.

Before embarking on fieldwork you will need to find somewhere to live during the field-based investigation. This may be a guesthouse, possibly owned by the community or an NGO, or alternatively you may choose to live with a local family. There is much to be gained from the latter, as the family will be able to learn more about you and your research, and you will be able to learn about family life and local customs. You should make an allowance in your budget to pay the family for their hospitality. It is a good idea to have your own room, so that you can retire to rest and reflect, and also to allow both your hosts and yourself to 'have your own space'. It is important that you have a comfortable place to live while undertaking fieldwork. You should also take particular care of your health and nutrition, since ill-health could jeopardize your entire research project. Your host family may be keen for you to eat with them. Take care that you have a well-balanced daily food intake. You should take advice on

whether it is safe to drink the local water, and if in any doubt, you should drink boiled water or bottled mineral water, which is now available worldwide.

Ideally, you should try to make a short reconnaissance trip to your field location, to introduce yourself and explain the objectives. You should carry some form of identification, and preferably a letter of introduction from a local university or NGO. It is important to gain the interest and support of the community elders for your work. In most African communities, an audience with the chief at an early stage is an essential prerequisite for successful field research. Sometimes this will involve an exchange of gifts – you should take advice on what is expected. Understandably, the researcher will probably be asked by community leaders what the community is likely to gain from the research. This is always a difficult question to answer, but you should be prepared for this. Realistically, published books and journal articles, which are usually the principal outputs of most research projects, will have very little positive bearing on the lives of poor people in the Third World (Edwards, 1989: 123). It is important not to promise anything that you cannot deliver. As Sidaway observes: 'Particularly when the outsider is perceived as relatively powerful/rich (or even not), it is surprisingly easy for her/him to be drawn into commitments and promises that one may not be in a position to fulfil' (Sidaway, 1992: 406). Community members are often interested that the research will discover more about their community, which may or may not lead to some form of development intervention. Field researchers should be prepared to arrange regular feedback sessions, at which local people can ask questions and hear about progress in the research.

Well before commencing fieldwork, you should think carefully about your objectives and strategies for collecting data, and how these are likely to impact on individuals, families and the community as a whole. There has been much discussion in the past of whether research in Third World countries is 'parasitic', or may be characterized as 'data mining'. The field researcher should give careful thought as to how the community might be repaid for their help. You will need to take advice on whether respondents should be paid for giving their time and knowledge to the project. Arrangements vary from one location to another, and could be influenced by precedents created by earlier research projects. If you do not intend to pay respondents, then you should make this clear at the outset when discussing your project with community leaders. Rather than giving to individuals, it is a good idea to identify and give support to a community project that will benefit more people – for example, the local school or clinic. In Sierra Leone recently, after a successful period of field-based data collection, my research assistant decided it would be a good idea to give some funds for a local carpenter to construct a set of desks and benches for the local school – a gesture which was greatly appreciated by the community.

Elsewhere in this book there is much reference to different types of research strategy. Fortunately, the obsession with questionnaires in the 1960s and early 1970s has faded, though in the right place and at the right time questionnaires can still be useful. But the trend in recent years towards utilizing more participatory field-based research strategies has been a great step forward. If handled sensitively, such methods can play a key role in fostering a positive relationship between the researcher(s) and the individuals and communities being studied. Field researchers must be constantly aware of their position *vis-à-vis* the local people. As Adams and Megaw observe:

We come from outside the village. We speak other languages and follow arcane practices (socio-economic research), and we seem to have powerful friends because we bring letters of introduction. ... Above all, we can come and go: we are not committed. (Adams and Megaw, 1997: 219)

The issue of power and control of knowledge is of concern here, in the context of the capabilities and ethics of 'outsiders' who are conducting research on, and ultimately speaking about 'others'. Ake (1979) describes the power of Western knowledge as 'academic imperialism', while Minh-ha (1989) suggests that Third World research is mainly a conversation of 'us' with 'us about them'. While undertaking fieldwork, it is essential to reflect constantly on how you as an outsider should relate to local people. The issue of 'positionality' has been raised, particularly in the context of men researching women, but is also of relevance when working with such groups as poor people and children. Howard (1994) warns that the positionality of the researcher can affect an interview, because there is often a tendency for respondents to tell the researcher what they believe he or she wants to hear, especially when there is a marked power inequality between the two.

It is important to ask yourself how relevant your research is to the local community. So many lengthy field-based data collection exercises merely end up as conference papers which are then subsequently published in books and journals. I believe there is a real opportunity for field-based development researchers to get involved in so-called 'action research', in which they might actually play a role in improving conditions in the communities where they are working. For example, one of my doctoral students, undertaking research recently among a poor farming community in Eastern Cape Province, South Africa, discovered that selling their impressive vegetable crop was proving to be a major constraint on economic upliftment. Nobody in the community owned a telephone, and there was only one rather unreliable public telephone nearby. Since South Africa has relatively good mobile phone coverage, the researcher

19

decided to buy two (inexpensive) mobile phones for the community's agricultural project leaders. This enabled producers to liaise with wholesalers regularly, to alert the latter when produce would be ready for sale, and to make the necessary transport arrangements to get the produce to market. In the same community, a large debt had been accumulated for electricity to drive the water pump that irrigated the fields. The researcher was suspicious of the electricity account statement that the project leaders had received, so he arranged a meeting at the headquarters of the electricity company, in which he acted as a mediator between the electricity company officials and the project leaders. The meeting was successful and boosted the confidence of the project leaders. The company officials agreed to change the electricity tariff, such that the amount owed by the community was reduced considerably. In addition to delivering tangible benefits to the community, action research can also strengthen relationships between the community and the researcher. However, some caution is needed, since there is a fine dividing line between a researcher helping the community to deal with a specific problem and the community then looking to the researcher to solve all their problems. Megaw's involvement with an NGO in Ghana provides some useful lessons for those who may be considering more active involvement with their host communities (Adams and Megaw, 1997).

In relation to studying women, there has been some debate about whether men should actually interview women, but Scheyvens and Storey suggest that the key thing is that researchers are 'informed of and sensitive to local socio-cultural contexts' (Scheyvens and Storey, 2003: 170). However, in certain circumstances it is possible only for women to talk with women. In northern Nigeria, for example, a strict form of Islam exists, under which Hausa women of childbearing age are in seclusion. I have been involved in a number of collaborative projects with Nigerian academics in this region, and in a field study which evaluated the incidence of urban agriculture, it was necessary to have a team of women researchers who went into households to talk with women who were growing fruit and vegetables inside the walls of their compounds. Without this team of women researchers, the Hausa women's quite significant horticultural activities would have been completely ignored. In sharp contrast to this, in South Africa, where women are generally more empowered and articulate, I recollect some very lively focus group meetings with both men and women, where women dominated the discussion.

In recent years, children have, somewhat belatedly, become an important focus of research in Third World countries. When working with children, it is important to explain the purpose of the research in simple and straightforward language and to use child-friendly and less intimidating data collection strategies such as drawing, story writing and role play (Scheyvens and Storey, 2003: 174). Matthews and Tucker are concerned that research with children should not misrepresent them, or be embarrassing or harmful (Matthews and Tucker, 2000).

The key point to bear in mind while conducting research in Third World communities is that during your fieldwork you are a guest in that community, and how you relate to individuals and groups will be likely to affect the responses you receive, and can ultimately determine the success of your entire research project. Above all, you should respect local customs and make a determined effort to be unobtrusive, polite and deferential. At the end of your fieldwork you should report back on your findings to the community, explaining how you intend to follow up the fieldwork after you have left (see Box 2.2).

Box 2.2   Checklist: Into the field

- On arrival in the overseas country you should discuss your study and fieldwork logistics with local experts.
- Take advice on who would be best to accompany you as an interpreter/field assistant and discuss remuneration at an early stage.
- Investigate local travel and accommodation arrangements.
- Undertake a short reconnaissance trip to your fieldwork area, to meet community leaders and to conduct a small pilot survey.
- In the light of experience gained on your reconnaissance and pilot survey, you should consider carefully your field research objectives and methods.
- Remember that when you are in the field you are a guest of the local communities. Be polite, friendly and business-like in your work.
- Plan carefully your leaving the field. Ensure you have all necessary data and consider the best way to give feedback to communities and individuals.

Leaving the field

Leaving the field is often not easy and requires careful planning. If fieldwork has gone well, it can be difficult to withdraw from a situation where you may have lived and worked for some time (Scheyvens and Storey, 2003: Chapter 10). It is often the case that you have just one opportunity to collect field data for your project, so it is vital that you leave with all the necessary data, since funding and time constraints may preclude a return visit. There is too often a tendency among field researchers to 'take the data and run', but it is important to reflect on how much time others have given to your fieldwork enquiries. Without their help, data collection would probably have been impossible.

It is particularly difficult to leave interpreters and field assistants, with whom you have developed a close relationship. Keeping in touch with communities and individuals with whom you have worked should be a high priority. In my own case, I have managed to maintain strong links with people I met in Sierra Leone during my doctoral field research thirty years ago, despite the political instability and civil war which have afflicted

the country and its people. In the intervening period, I have supported a community member through his education, and have maintained strong links with my former research assistant, who is now Dean at the university. On my recent return to the communities where I had lived in 1974, I took a series of laminated photographs that I had taken as a research student, and presented these to the community elders. The photos provided a valuable archive of the pre-war community.

Rather than abandoning local contacts after the fieldwork, it is important to involve them as far as possible in the data analysis and writing-up phases of projects, though there may be practical difficulties in doing this. For many Third World academics, research may be low on their personal agendas, primarily because of practical difficulties. As Porter so rightly points out: 'the difficulties of obtaining a livelihood have made sustained research problematic for most indigenous academics' (Porter, 1995: 140). While a lack of electricity, water, transport and fuel are everyday problems, inadequate salaries and impoverished libraries further militate against research by academics in many Third World countries. The UK Department

21

for International Development (DfID) 'Higher Education Links Scheme', managed by the British Council, has provided me with a valuable opportunity to collaborate with colleagues in Nigeria, Sierra Leone and South Africa. The Scheme has supported visits in both directions, which have enabled field-based data collection and joint publication. The formulation of research grant applications and the facilitation of research student supervision have also developed through these links. We have purposely targeted international journals for publication, a strategy that has strengthened the capacity and achievement record of African colleagues.

Returning to the field with the final results of your work may be difficult logistically, but local collaborators can usually assist in reporting back to the communities. It is useful for community leaders to have some clear policy recommendations emerging from the fieldwork that might lead to concrete action. Local collaborators can also make contact with government and NGO officials to report on the study's main findings and to identify ways of taking these forward. In the written output from the project, you should consider carefully whether it is best to maintain anonymity, in case there could be repercussions on specific individuals where sensitive issues are involved (see Box 2.2).

Conclusion

Fieldwork in Third World countries is usually enjoyable, but there will undoubtedly be moments of exhilaration and despair, often in the same day. The important thing is to try to stay calm and do not be afraid to ask for help. You will need to take regular breaks from the fieldwork, to 'recharge your batteries', and to reflect both on what you have achieved and where you go next. Use these 'time-out' periods to possibly spend a weekend away from your field location, or alternatively to devote time to socializing with your host family and community. Teaching English to children or adults, chatting informally in the marketplace, or playing sport with schoolchildren, should help you to relax and at the same time strengthen rapport with the community.

It is likely that memories of your fieldwork will stay with you throughout your life. Share your experiences with others, and consider carefully how your fieldwork relates to your broader studies, perhaps exemplifying more theoretical statements on development issues. Preparing for fieldwork might be a daunting experience, but actually doing fieldwork and reflecting on it afterwards can be highly pleasurable.

QUESTIONS FOR DISCUSSION

1. Examine the arguments 'for' and 'against' undertaking fieldwork in Third World countries.
2. What are the key factors involved in choosing a location for field research?
3. How can you ensure that the results of your fieldwork are reported back to the communities where you collected data?
4. What specific strategies would you adopt in undertaking field-based data collection with marginalized and/or disadvantaged groups, e.g. women, children, disabled, poor, ethnic minorities?
5. To what extent is it necessary that the outcomes of field-based research should be relevant to planning future development trajectories in local communities?

Further reading

Devereux, S. and Hoddinott, J. (eds) (1992) *Fieldwork in Developing Countries*, Hemel Hempstead: Harvester Wheatsheaf.

Eade, D. and Williams, S. (eds) (1995) *The Oxfam Handbook of Development and Relief*, Oxford: Oxfam.

Robson, E. and Willis, K. (eds) (1994) *Postgraduate Fieldwork in Developing Areas: A Rough Guide*, Developing Areas Research Group, Monograph No. 8, London: Royal Geographical Society and the Institute of British Geographers.

Scheyvens, R. and Storey, D. (eds) (2003), *Development Fieldwork: A Practical Guide*, London: Sage.

References

Adams, W.M. and Megaw, C.C. (1997) Researchers and the rural poor: asking questions in the Third World, *Journal of Geography in Higher Education*, 21 (2): 215–229.

Ake, C. (1979) *Social Science as Imperialism: The Theory of Political Development*, Ibadan, Nigeria: Ibadan University Press.

Binns, T. (1992) The role of fieldwork in teaching development geography: some African perspectives, in R.B. Potter and T. Unwin (eds), *Teaching the Geography of Developing Areas*, Developing Areas Research Group, Monograph No 7, pp.113–129, London: Royal Geographical Society and the Institute of British Geographers,

Bronfenbrenner, U. (1952) Principles of professional ethics: Cornell studies in social growth, *American Psychologist*, 7: 452–455.

Chambers, R. (1983) *Rural Development: Putting the Last First*, London: Longman.

Eade, D. and Williams, S. (eds) (1995) *The Oxfam Handbook of Development and Relief*, Oxford: Oxfam.

Edwards, M. (1989) The irrelevance of development studies, *Third World Quarterly*, 11 (1): 116–135.

Howard, S. (1994) Methodological issues in overseas fieldwork: experiences from Nicaragua's northern Atlantic coast, in E. Robson and K. Willis, (eds), *Postgraduate Fieldwork in Developing Areas: A Rough Guide*, Developing Areas Research Group, Monograph No. 8, pp. 19–34, London: Royal Geographical Society and the Institute of British Geographers.

Kobayashi, A. (1994) Coloring the field: gender, 'race' and the politics of fieldwork, *Professional Geographer*, 46 (1): 73–80.

Madge, C. (1993) Boundary disputes: comments on Sidaway (1992), *Area*, 25 (3): 294–299.

Madge, C. (1994) The ethics of research in the 'Third World', in E. Robson and K. Willis (eds), *Postgraduate Fieldwork in Developing Areas: A Rough Guide*, Developing Areas Research Group, Monograph No. 8, pp. 91–102, London: Royal Geographical Society and the Institute of British Geographers.

Matthews, H. and Tucker F. (2000) Consulting children, *Journal of Geography in Higher Education*, 24 (2): 299–310.

Minh-ha, T.T. (1989) *Woman, Native, Other: Writing Postcoloniality and Feminism*, Bloomington: Indiana University Press.

Nast, H.J. (1994) Opening remarks on 'women in the field', *Professional Geographer*, 46 (1): 54–66.

Pawson, E. and Teather, E.K. (2002) 'Geographical Expeditions': assessing the benefits of a student-driven fieldwork method, *Journal of Geography in Higher Education*, 26 (3): 275–289.

Porter, G. (1995) 'Third World' research by 'First World' geographers: an African perspective, *Area*, 27 (2): 139–141.

Potter, R. (1993) Little England and little geography: reflections on Third World teaching and research, *Area*, 25 (3): 291–294.

Robson, E. (2002) An unbelievable academic and personal experience: issues around teaching undergraduate field courses in Africa, *Journal of Geography in Higher Education*, 26 (3): 327–344.

Scheyvens, R. and Storey, D. (eds) (2003) *Development Fieldwork: A Practical Guide*, London: Sage.

Sidaway, J.D. (1992) In other worlds: on the politics of research by 'First World' geographers in the 'Third World', *Area*, 24 (4): 403–408.

Sidaway, J.D. (1993) The decolonisation of development geography? *Area*, 25 (3): 299–300.

3

Ethical Practices in Doing Development Research

Lynne Brydon

What do we mean by 'ethics'?   Informed consent   Funding and funders   Power   Change   Contexts and their importance   Doing research: 'before, during and after'   Deviations from the 'ideal'!

This chapter is in two main sections, the first looks at what is meant by 'ethics' in development research, the practices of 'doing ethical research', and is further divided into subsections. The second section is shorter and more personal and shows how textbook-derived research plans and ambitions can go awry, how research 'on the ground' is a much finer-grained complex of quick thinking and responsiveness and, in some cases, the abandoning of the rules. A good and ethical researcher (the distinction is made in the earlier part of the paper) has to be readily responsive to any situation that might come up.

Ethical research

What do we mean by 'ethics'?

What do we mean by 'ethics' in the writing – and doing – of development research? Why is it important to make sure that research plans

and practices are 'ethical'? Thinking about ethics, to paraphrase Grix (2004), involves a heavy reliance on the idea of 'ought'. What *ought* we to do when carrying out development research or writing? Is 'ethical' research practice, whether fieldwork, analysis or writing and presentation, the same thing as 'incisive' fieldwork or analysis, or 'brilliant' writing and presentation?

There are, of course, no short answers here. Brilliant or incisive fieldwork may gouge out the 'truth', warts and all, of a range of social situations, but it may leave behind social chaos, breakdown and conflict in the field. Books, articles or reports may attract flattering attention from audiences outside the 'field', but if they reflect only *very* 'partial truths' (Clifford, 1986), or gloss over gaps and problems, then they are seriously flawed. Perhaps in the early days of development research, when top-down models and modernization ideas prevailed, and the 'subjects' of the research were not even considered to have a voice, when the developers were there to 'develop' the less- or under-developed and 'obviously' knew best, what was considered to be good was also considered ethical in the sense that this was what development research ought to be. But with more than fifty years of development research and practice behind us now, it has become clear that any such earlier ideas about ethical research have proved inadequate. Not only have notions of what constitutes appropriate and 'good' development research changed radically, but also the significance of ethical research has also moved from what was formerly, in effect, a background assumption, to an overt planning strand in the very forefront of research projects and practices.

So, in the past ten to fifteen years in research contexts in the North, the idea of *ethical* social research has grown hugely in importance. This is partly as a response to criticism of earlier research that ignored local practices or had a covert goal, for example, of gathering information on security issues or to promote insurrection or to foster support for a particular political party or candidate, in addition to an overt 'research' objective, say, to investigate local needs in respect, perhaps, to water supplies, education or health. It is also in accordance with changing contemporary ideas about the standards expected in all kinds of social research, whether of accountability and transparency or, more generally, in recognition of the rights of the 'researched'. The significance of the ideas about ethical research and best practice have come to the foreground (through the 1990s) to such an extent that all research agencies or university departments, in addition to the funders, are now expected to have formal *codes of practice* relating to the ethics of research carried out under their auspices. Researchers are expected to sign up to these codes of practice when they undertake their research projects. Perhaps a simple way to remember this is that, say, thirty years ago, it was common to write of the people among whom we carried out

research as (even sometimes) the *objects* of research, let alone *subjects* of our research. Now the emphasis is on collaboration, facilitation and participation, where the people among whom the research is being carried out are involved not only in the 'data collection' phase of the research (as passive 'subjects'), but also in formulating key questions in, and foci of, the research, in the design phase of the research, as well as in the analysis and evaluation of the findings.

I cannot hope completely to cover the range of factors covered by the term 'ethical' research in so short a space. What follows is a discussion of several key (and personally idiosyncratic) features to be taken into account.

Informed consent

The term 'informed consent' has come to the forefront over the past ten years as ethical concerns have grown in importance, and what this means is that we may carry out our research, ask our questions, organize focus groups, participate in community projects and so on, only after we have explained to the people in the community why we are doing this and what are the intended outcomes, both for ourselves and for them. Only after this informed consent has been obtained do we begin to carry out the research. In any case, we may achieve results only if the people are willing to participate in it and work with us. Where there are sensitive issues at stake – reproductive or contraceptive practices or finance, for example – then informed consent will probably at least entail promises of anonymity. But even research on less sensitive topics, information that might seem at first sight to be uncontroversial and unthreatening, 'pure information', such as census-type or demographic details, can also be felt to be potentially threatening as the results may be seen by, for example, tax authorities, land registraries or other local official bodies, and may be used in some way to the detriment of the original participants. Since we cannot control the readership of our final reports or papers, anonymity is often seen to be very important to participants in research. Local landowners cannot expel disgruntled tenants if they don't know whose response is whose; women cannot be threatened with violence or some form of public disgrace if no one knows to whom specific remarks on family planning, girls' education or working women can be attributed.

Funding and funders

All development work, whether research or 'doing' development, costs money. Even where we are undertaking academic research that we conceive to be unbiased and concerned with the 'real' issues on the ground, unless the results we write up and publish are in line with the views of sponsors, whether relatively small bodies or vast multilateral agencies, it is quite possible that we should be unlikely to gain access to further funding from this source, a fact that may hinder our future work (and possibly the development of our careers). However 'charitable' the source of funds, if our results conflict with the source's ideologies and principles, then we are unlikely either to get further funding, or any facilities for the wide dissemination of our work. This poses an immediate dilemma for us: do we 'publish and be damned', conveniently forget about the aspects of the research that are going to cause us problems, or do we manage to 'fudge' the results so that the problematic data are no longer a problem?

Fortunately, in most development research, as opposed to development projects and plans, the sums of money involved are relatively small and the funders are more likely to be 'Western' research councils or government agencies rather than either multinational companies or local government-controlled agencies. If a Western research council is the sponsor, then 'publish and be damned' is unlikely to have any

serious consequences for the researcher, although it may have longer-term consequences for those living in the research context. Fudging the results is never an answer, nor is the invention of convenient memory lapses. Where results are unexpected, the first thing to do is to consult, on the ground, in the research context. Solutions that are most beneficial to 'the researched' can then be addressed. In any case, unexpected results at worst mean that there have been some problems or mistakes in the research process and that these can be worked out, but at best can open up new avenues, can trigger new research and new ways of thinking.

Power

Power is a critical dimension in a research project in both its design and implementation. Any research context is riddled and crosscut by relationships of power, from those between the sponsors of the research and the researcher, and between the researcher and the researched, to power relationships within the culture of the research setting, relationships between classes and clans, landholders and landless, educated and illiterate, elders and juniors, women and men, rich and poor. In spite of the continued existence, in ideal terms anyway, of the quantitative chimera that social research and, by implication, the role of the researcher in it is 'value neutral', 'unbiased' or minimally standing aloof from the research context, researchers, whether they are administering surveys and censuses or facilitating focus groups or conducting open-ended one-to-one interviews, invariably have an agenda of their own. This can range from a genuine interest in wanting to find out what is happening in the research context (like unpeeling the layers of an onion and seeing how they fit together), to a positively held belief or wish to 'show' or 'demonstrate' a particular phenomenon or outcome of some development intervention. The 'oughts' here should be obvious. An ethical researcher should, in addition to being mindful of the standard twin goals of validity and reliability, be context-sensitive, honest and 'up front' about her/his own interests and how they affect the research and the kinds of relationship s/he has with members of the research(ed) community.

Development research, however, tends also to be short-term. Development researchers tend not to stay in research communities for long enough to be able to get to grips with local nuances of power. They may well go to the field armed with a thorough knowledge of Chambers's (1983) development research blindspots, but knowledge of undercurrents in social organization cannot be gleaned from interviews from random samples of local people, from focus groups of 'key' categories of informants or from in-depth interviews with a select few. This is a real problem with 'development research'. Unless the researcher can spend time – a number of months at least – in a research context, then s/he cannot hope to begin to understand the power relationships informing respondents' contributions to the research. Development research, in addition to being relatively short-term, tends also to rely on local intermediaries. Local intermediaries who act as translators, gatekeepers and interpreters are fine up to a point, but it is crucial to remember that they too have their own status either within the research context or with members of a research community: they have power relations and 'positions' of their own and these have also to be taken into account if our research is to be as 'good' as it *ought* to be.

Change

The outcomes of development research have at least the potential to provide information that might underpin changes. The information can lead to changes that range from the immediately technical/instrumental – the provision of a well or borehole, for example, or the provision of electricity – to the more obviously complex – something like the setting up of schemes for women's production and marketing of either processed food or crafts, for instance. The introduction of easily available and clean water in a community, for example, means perhaps that women and children have new 'spare' time because they do not have to walk to streams or queue at intermittently working pumps, or that women have more time (and money) because children suffer much less often from diarrhoea and stomach upsets. Children with new spare time may either go to school or stay awake at school, a feature that can mean significant future changes; women with new spare time may produce more on the farm, produce new crops or handicrafts to sell, or even (a more nebulous 'change' in terms of its possible outcomes) have time to meet and talk with other women (and even men) about their lives and work, their community. The introduction of electricity to rural communities has enormous implications, from the more obvious like the provision of light, opening up the evenings to a wider range of activities, the availability of refrigeration for food storage, or the possibility of using power tools, in building or carpentry on one hand to hair-dryers and sewing machines on the other. The introduction and use of such appliances and tools is a huge change in itself, but then there are questions about who pays for the tools, whose responsibility is the supply and maintenance of the electricity and the wires: all of these issues have implications for power relations in communities, between parents and children, youth and elders, men and women (see, for example, Mensah-Kutin, 2002).

Development projects and plans, and research about them, lead to changes. Some changes are anticipated, expected. Others, however, may be completely unanticipated. Some anticipated changes that appear to have obvious benefits for a community (the provision of clean and easily available water or electricity, for example) in the sense that women's lives become less onerous, or children have time to go to school, may be felt by some in the community to be problematic rather than beneficial: women have time to gossip and talk, to make trouble, for example, children spend time playing rather than learning the discipline(s) of their elders, the landless might move into craft production releasing them from their dependence on landowners and causing landowners new headaches over labour. While these changes can at the very least be said to have double-edged 'benefits', as ethical researchers we cannot just condemn the views of landowners as 'exploitative' or 'capitalistic', just as we cannot stigmatize out of hand the views of husbands and fathers, or male and female elders, as sexist or ageist. We have to think through the possible consequences of our research, pointing them out, and try to work out ways of dealing with them, from the viewpoints and power perspectives of the widest possible range of community members.

Contexts and their importance

It is crucially important in all research that involves social interaction, the recording by whatever means of social events, interviews of any kind, focus groups or participation, to realize that there is no perfect formula, no absolutely 'right' way of doing things. There is a range of different strategies that are good or appropriate, and what is good or appropriate will vary according to the 'context'. There are also strategies and practices that are regarded as 'bad' and that may involve the acquisition of biased or wrong information because of inappropriate research strategies or the failure to be open and honest about both the aims and objectives of the research or the presentation of results. A good social/development researcher *ought* at least to be aware of the importance of contexts, the appropriateness of particular research methods and openness and honesty both in the field and in the

presentation of results, and to try to avoid the pitfalls or minimize their impact.

Doing research: before, during and after

Before...

Doing research (and doing ethical research) needs careful preparation. Even if you are going to the field only for a week or two it is worthwhile learning about wherever it is you are going: contemporary politics, significant figures, whether statesmen or revolutionaries, writers, artists, musicians. If you are preparing for more extensive fieldwork, then it is worthwhile delving into the past literature of the country and/or area. With the major search engines and the web, this has become much easier in the past ten years. It is only polite to be able to understand, and, in time, participate, when people tell you about their history, their customs, their staple foods, their festivals and their crises.

Religion is also an important component of understanding and participating. For example, don't expect there to be much work on Fridays in largely Islamic states, Saturdays where research concerns Jews, or Sundays where populations are born-again Christian. Dominant religious ideas can also influence wider issues, for example, dress. There may be strict modest dress codes for women in Islamic states, for instance, but even in non-Islamic states check with Embassy or High Commission websites for dress codes for both women and men. In the 1960s and 1970s mini-skirts, for example, were considered immoral and even banned by some African governments (Kenya, Tanzania, Burkina Faso). There were mirrors at even the remotest of Burkina Faso's border outposts, to check whether women's knees were visible and that skirt lengths were appropriately modest. States in what we still call the Third World also often prescribe very elaborate levels of respect for interviews or commonplace interchanges between researchers (usually young and

29

inexperienced) and interviewees (usually older and with more experience).

During...

When you get to the field, and bearing in mind basic behavioural standards, you will often find it useful to try to affiliate with, or have at least some informal contact with, local universities or NGOs. While there may be a formal fee for university affiliation (allowing, perhaps, use of the library), universities and other institutions are often chronically short of up-to-date information: books, journal articles, reports, maps, visual data, for example. Any access to these that you can provide, from photocopies to subscriptions will be very welcome. There would, of course, be no research without the people to whom the researchers talk, the people who give their time and information for the study. In my experience, rather than try to pay each interviewee, or give them a gift, and particularly if interviewees come from a relatively small number of communities, then I have found it better to give a gift to the community so that everyone can benefit from it: bags of cement or aluminium roofing sheets for a building project; textbooks for a local school; even repairs to or spare parts for a handpump. Gifts are problematic cross-culturally: I found that my Christmas presents in the field to my friends ranged from things like tinned evaporated milk, tinned fish or sugar to supplying formal black men's tailcoats and toy British policemen's helmets for pageants and durbars and other ceremonial occasions.

After...

Telephones are wonderful. Even twenty years ago it might take six weeks to two months to hear any news from a research site, or send information to them (presuming the packet wasn't opened and trashed). Now researchers can usually phone the nearest town or telephonically equipped village and send messages to people from the 'field', not to mention asking forgotten questions and hearing news and developments there. Where there is a reasonable electricity supply and phone lines there may also be the possibility of email contact. The coverage for mobile phones has also grown enormously in the last two to three years. Where you are writing a report for a funder or organization, then you may be able to check it with people from the research communities before you go public. Where you are undertaking research for a degree, then at the very least you should send the communities involved a copy of your dissertation. Sending dissertations and publications to local university libraries is also a good idea and will be happily received.

Deviations from the 'ideal'!

This section could (perhaps flippantly) be titled 'Ten (or at least a few) bad things I know about my research!' Having set out some of the pros and cons of working towards ethical research practices, in the second part of this chapter I want to recount some of the ways in which best-laid research plans and strivings towards doing what might seem appropriate in ethical terms can come unstuck or emerge as problematic in completely unexpected ways during the course of research and writing.

I should state at the outset that although much of my field research and writing could happily be fitted under the heading 'development', my disciplinary background and training is in anthropology. The first example stems from the dilemmas that I experienced (and I think other new researchers can experience) when confronted, probably for the first time, by an unexpected and/or unwelcome event, something that brings them face to face with the realities of 'doing research'.

I had been 'in the field' for about three months. I had spent most of my time language learning and practising, getting to know people and having people get to know me. I had been to any 'event' that was going on in the village: meetings, any kind of ritual ceremonies and also a couple of funerals. The funerals I had been to were 'after the event'. The people had died and been buried weeks or months before the funeral was held, but it had taken the families time both to get themselves together and the wherewithal to hold the funeral celebration: keeping wake, hiring and feeding the village band and choir(s), cooking for visitors coming to pay respects. I had noted down the public displays of grief and, more privately, who did what and when. But then, one morning I heard a wailing from a nearby house and saw a group of women weaving/dancing around the village shaking calabash rattles and singing mourning songs: it was the first time that someone I had known had died. An elderly man, it's true, but he had been perfectly well the previous day, he had just collapsed and died early that morning.

A fine drizzle set in. I walked to the compound not having a clue what to do: the man's wife and daughters, together with other women relatives were there, ululating and singing the mourning songs, but talking together. I couldn't interrupt them: I didn't know how or to whom to talk, and I didn't want to: I felt awkward and out of place. The drizzle continued through the day. Noises from the carpenter's workshop resulted in the production of a coffin. Young male relatives were sent to dig a grave. The pastor arrived, as did relatives and neighbours to listen to the short funeral service. I felt totally out of place, an intruder. What was I doing here, dripping wet, feeling miserable, trespassing on these people's lives, not to mention their grief and upset? I was wretched and turned to slip away. But a nephew of the dead man stopped me: 'Where are you going? You can't see what's happening from there. You must stand nearer to see and hear what is going on.'

'But I shouldn't be here, I'm in the way.'

'Nonsense! You've come here to write our history and customs. You need to see

everything if you're going to do that. Everybody knows who you are. It's fine.'

Of course thirty years after the event the conversation has to be a paraphrase, but the gist of his remarks were: if you're going to do what you're supposed to be doing here, get on with it and forget these finer feelings – basically, a ban on self-indulgent navel-gazing ten years *avant la lettre*. And a reassurance that making myself generally known to people, getting the approval of chiefs and elders in the community, walking around greeting people and making the most ridiculous mistakes in the language learning process had been seen positively: I had been open and 'transparent' with them – it was an early and effective sign of approval of my research.

I do not have the space to discuss other field 'disasters' in detail: the humiliation I felt at the public refusal of a local chief's court to allow me to take notes of a case involving 'my' people, and the other side's insistence that I should leave the proceedings (the possibility of my presence prejudicing/influencing an outcome); the slow realization, in a later 'development' project in a different area, that the project agenda and implementation plans that I was dealing with had not either been thought out by the women's group themselves or was necessarily underpinned by their best long-term interests (hidden gender consequences); the vociferous and insistent assertion by 'informants' that they wanted their names to be included, rather than to be anonymous (what was the point of telling me things if their names weren't going to be known?).

My final anecdote here is a salutary warning to researchers to be honest and accountable! The ritualization of staple crop cultivation is widespread in rural communities. I had not seen these particular rituals before as they took place only once a year. This was going to be my only chance to see them in my 18 months in the field. The presence of women of menstruating age, however, was

31

anathema to the gods in whose names the rituals were performed. Not to worry, said the priests, I could have a special dispensation to attend the rituals (which involved a journey to a sacred place in the bush, libation pouring and prayers there, and a joyful return to the village with the assurance of a good harvest for the current year), as long as I wasn't actually menstruating at the time. Well, of course, I was. But I decided to go anyway. It was fascinating: the rituals performed on the way, the consecration of pre-pubertal girls to the gods; the accession to the sacred place, the centrality of the prayers and rituals there, the journey back to the village, and the reception at the shrine in the village.

About a month later my slides came back from processing: finally the pictures to complement my notes. None, not even one, of the slides from the ritual had 'worked': none was in focus, every one was blurred and its contents indistinct. So this was the result of my deception! The Western rational social science explanation might be that I was feeling so embarrassed at being there and taking photographs when I had promised that I wouldn't go and pollute the ceremonies, that I did not hold the camera steadily enough to take the photographs, but another part of me suspects that perhaps the gods had something to do with it and I was merely being punished for my unethical behaviour!

QUESTIONS FOR DISCUSSION

1. Imagine a range of situations that you are familiar with, for example the planning of an event to raise money, an outing or a party for which you need to plan and organize. Work out the consequences of particular kinds of behaviour and the roles of members of the planning group, and the organization and coping with publicity that might follow the event. Whose agenda belongs to whom? What happens if agenda(s) clash?
2. How, if at all, do you think that development projects can 'plan' change? As a development researcher, try to think what you might do if there were unanticipated, 'unplanned' changes?

Further reading

Martyn Denscombe's *The Good Research Guide* (Open University Press, 1998, 2003) is an all-round guide to doing small-scale research, but there are several sustained discussions of ethical problems throughout the book.

Marlene de Laine's *Fieldwork, Participation and Practice: Ethics and Dilemmas in Qualitative Research* (Sage, 2000) is a longer and more complicated, although more nuanced read, and contains an entire chapter specifically devoted to 'ethical dilemmas'.

Melanie Mauthner et al.'s edited collection, *Ethics in Qualitative Research* (Sage, 2002) consists of detailed accounts of ethical problems in social research, primarily derived from British public policy and social work settings.

References

Chambers, R. (1983) *Rural Development: Putting the Last First*, London: Longman.

Clifford, J. (1986) Introduction: partial truths, in J. Clifford and G.E. Mascus (eds), *Writing Culture: The Poetics and Politics of Ethnography*, London and Berkeley: University of California Press, pp. 1–27.

Grix, J. (2004) *The Foundations of Research*, Basingstoke: Palgrave Macmillan.

Mensah-Kutin, R. (2002) Gendered experiences of access to electric power: the case of a rural electrification programme in Ghana, PhD thesis, University of Birmingham, Birmingham.

4

Working in Different Cultures:
Issues of Race, Ethnicity and Identity

Caesar R.A. Apentiik and Jane L. Parpart

● ● Power gradients ● ● Shifting and negotiating
identities ● ● Preliminary visits ● ● Language ● ● Before going to
the field ● ● Communication in the field ● ● Advisory tool kit

Introduction

Race, ethnicity, class, gender, religion, marital status and other non-demographic characteristics, including one's worldview, often define the position and identity of the researcher in relation to the researched community. These factors can influence the quality and character of development research, particularly because so much of this work occurs in the 'developing world' and is undertaken by non-members of the researched communities (Scheyvens and Storey, 2003).

One of the main criticisms of 'outsider' research is its tendency to produce knowledge or interpret societies from a position or location of power and privilege, and in most cases without sufficient input from the local people. This criticism is part of an old debate about the advantages and/or disadvantages of 'insider' or 'outsider' status (see Agar, 1980;

Grafanaki, 1996). However, we believe this dichotomy ignores the complex nature of development research. At the same time, the issues facing researchers working in different cultures need to be addressed.

Recognizing that fieldwork is full of surprises, with myriad dilemmas and complicated power gradients, our aim is not to provide 'cook book' solutions for researchers working across different cultures, but rather to offer guidelines and suggestions for dealing with issues that arise in fieldwork contexts across difference – whether generated by cross-cultural misunderstandings or internal divisions.

Power gradients

Whether working across cultures, or within one's own culture, power imbalances between the researcher and the researched are commonplace, especially in the global South. At one level these power differentials are real, as the researcher (whether an insider or outsider) often has more access to resources and privileges (e.g. money, education and knowledge and power) than members of the researched community. At another level, which is not mutually exclusive, people may be hostile because of negative experiences with insensitive and arrogant researchers in the past, whether academics, government or non-government officials. Recognizing these various factors helps the researcher to avoid or minimize behaviour that might arouse old hostilities and reinforce feelings of inferiority or powerlessness on the part of the researched. The researcher can try to create comfort zones during interviews and day-to-day interactions. Be prepared for personal blunders, but these should not paralyse you. Always reflect on such blunders and take the necessary steps to make amends.

Socio-cultural, economic and political hierarchies also shape power relationships within the researched community. Even relatively egalitarian communities have some individuals, families, clans and lineages, and even organizations who act as gatekeepers. These privileged individuals and groups control access to and power over certain resources, knowledge and information. Moreover, in some countries, government departments control research access, which can inhibit frank discussions and analysis. Dealing with these hierarchies raises ethical and accountability issues as well (see Box 4.1).

Another sensitive issue is the selection of interpreters or research assistants. Gatekeepers and other power brokers often pressure researchers to hire a person of their choice and this can sometimes be difficult to refuse. Local knowledge is important, but other factors, such as reliability, position in the local community and research experience, are also crucial. A good assistant can make or break one's research and one's relations with the community, even for local researchers.

35

Box 4.1   Gatekeepers and the researcher (scenario)

Sam is conducting research on development projects' impact on agricultural productivity in a rural district. He needs a place to live, but discovers the government rest house is fully booked. He remembers a university classmate comes from the area. He calls his friend, who welcomes him warmly and offers him the guest-house in his parents' compound.

Sam goes to the village and is warmly welcomed by his friend's parents, grandparents and other kin. He settles into the comfortable guest-house, feeling lucky to have found such hospitable people. As he starts his research he quickly realizes his friend's family, the Mapomas, is very prominent in the area. His friend's father offers to introduce him to the people in the community to whom he should talk. Even the District Commissioner and the local agricultural officers seem eager to help a friend of the Mapoma family. Sam soon discovers that the Mapoma family not only has unusual access to development projects and other government programmes, they also exert considerable influence on the access of others.

One day Sam is approached by a Mr Mbazi, the former treasurer of the local agricultural co-operative. Mbazi had been fired by Mr Mapoma when he (Mbazi) discovered

(Continued)

(Continued)

that the Mapoma family was embezzling funds from the co-op and giving unsecured loans to their friends. Mr Mbazi offers to introduce Sam to other people who could tell him more about how things are really run in the district. A few days later, Mr Mapoma sees Sam talking to Mr Mbazi and warns him that Mr Mbazi is a 'bad character'.

Sam struggles with his conscience and decides that the information about the family must be collected and made public. He meets secretly with Mr Mbazi and his friends. He mails these notes to his family in the city. After completing his research, he returns to write up his research, including the material about the Mapoma family. When it is published it causes a sensation. Sam is praised for exposing corruption and abuse of power, although he loses the goodwill of the Mapomas. Sam receives a generous two-year postdoctoral fellowship at a prestigious Canadian university. While in Canada he hears that Mr Mbazi has been arrested on trumped up charges and several members of his family have been harassed and lost their jobs.

1   What are the ethical and methodological issues in this scenario?
2   Do you agree with how Sam handled the situation? Why?
3   What would you have done in Sam's situation?

Shifting and negotiating identities

In the practical world of data collection, whether as an insider or outsider, the researcher's positions and roles are negotiated and renegotiated by both the researcher and the researched community throughout the research process. Fieldwork in development research thus involves professional, social and personal relationships between the researcher and the researched. These relationships are affected by many factors. The identity assigned to researchers on the basis of race, nationality, age, gender and other fixed identities are largely outside the control of the researcher, although their impact can sometimes be anticipated in advance. For example, Devereux and Hoddinott (1992) note that in some societies, age brings status and power. In such societies, young researchers may have difficulties collecting certain types of information, whereas older researchers could make young

informants uncomfortable and inhibit frank discussion. Being aware of these sensitivities helps researchers to adapt different strategies, such as hiring older people to conduct interviews with senior informants or employing a mature interpreter.

However, sometimes differences can arouse mutual curiosity, which, if properly managed, can build rapport with the researched community. Foreign researchers, especially during the initial stages, may encounter resistance to their questions. At the same time informants want to know about the outsider's world, just as the researcher is curious about their world. This mutual curiosity can provide avenues for interaction, learning and knowledge exchange. Foreign researchers can build rapport by telling informants about their own countries, lifestyle, food, etc., and asking informants about their way of life. Indeed, Apentiik (2003) discovered that people from his own community preferred being interviewed by his foreign co-researcher, who was regarded as a novelty and not a threat, whereas many locals worried about confidentiality when speaking to him.

The lifestyle, attitudes and behaviour the researcher adopts in the field can also influence the researched community's reactions to him/her. For example, clothing that is 'normal' in Europe and North America may be seen as provocative in the developing world. Wearing mini-skirts or trousers can lead to female researchers being labelled as 'loose women', even prostitutes. This identity would affect both who would speak to her and what they would say. Researchers need to understand the consequences of such behaviour on their identity in the field and be willing to adapt their lifestyles and attitudes to the situation. Equally important, attitudes towards the researcher will generally improve if he/she shops in the local markets and eats local food. Generous compensation for local research assistants and sympathy with community concerns also help (Grafanaki, 1996).

Involvement in the cultural, economic and political life of the community can also affect attitudes towards foreign researchers. To what extent should a researcher become involved in the social life of the community? Certainly some involvement is better than none. However, the appropriate level will depend on the nature of the community, the issues being addressed and the diplomacy of the researcher. Participation in social events such as local festivals, religious ceremonies and non-partisan political meetings can offer unique opportunities to observe practical social interactions and relationships within the community. Rituals and other celebrations can reveal aspects of past and contemporary social, cultural and spiritual practices which are rarely discussed, seen as normal or simply explained as 'our customary or grandfathers' way of doing things'. Participation in community social life can also increase trust and rapport with the researcher.

However, the legitimacy and extent of researcher involvement in community life can be problematic. What the researcher may consider abusive or unacceptable behaviour may have a different value in the researched community. As Wilson (1993) notes, working in a different culture does not necessarily require abandoning one's personal code or values. The researcher still has a duty and responsibility to help address injustices. However, interventions, if appropriate, must be undertaken with the utmost caution and diplomacy, backed by a well-informed understanding of the situation. The researcher has to tread a thin line between research and political action (advocacy) and the methodological imperative of academic objectivity (Devereux and Hoddinott, 1992).

When undertaking development research projects, the researcher should be aware that many communities will perceive him/her as a representative of either a national or international donor agency. The many government and non-government agencies involved in development research and projects around the world have contributed to the general perception that research projects usually come with (or have the potential to offer) tangible development benefits. This belief is particularly strong in communities with long histories of involvement with NGOs and other development projects and activities. In such communities, informants – especially the youth – are inclined to provide ideal answers or exaggerated responses to questions, particularly to 'outsiders', in hopes of attracting development projects to their localities. As a result, informants' evidence sometimes dramatically contradicts observed practices on the ground. This gap can affect the quality of the research, particularly its policy relevance. Thus foreign and local researchers must pay attention to past research and development activities, and their potentially harmful impact on the research process (see Box 4.2).

Box 4.2   Preparing for the field

- Investigate current and past histories of development projects and activities in the proposed researched community. This information can reveal power imbalances (both real and perceived) between the researcher and the researched, and help to shape the identity and role of the researcher in the researched community.

  o Has the community been linked to regional and national government as well as missionaries and other development agencies (NGOs)?

  o Have there been any conflicts within the community, or between the community and government and non-government agencies?

  o What are the perceptions of the community (young and old, rich and poor, women and men) towards the district, regional and national government representatives, as well as their own local or traditional leaders?

  o What are the memories about Europeans and colonial histories (e.g. colonial officials' attitudes towards local cultures, practices, knowledge systems and development in general).

- Investigate current and past development and other research projects in the community.

  o Are current and past research projects purely academic undertakings, or are they policy-grounded research by the government and NGO agencies?

  o Are current and past research projects part of larger research projects, independent or in partnership/collaboration with regional and national agencies or NGOs?

- How have you been introduced to the community – through an academic supervisor, an individual or a friend from the community, a government or NGO development agency?

  o What is the perception and attitude of the community towards this second party or gatekeeper?

  o What are the typical attitudes of the community towards stranger researchers in terms of race, marital status, social and economic status, class, and age?

- How do community members perceive ethnicity and how do they interact with other ethnic groups?

- Does the research entail formal or informal involvement with and participation in the life and activities of the community?

Divide the class into groups. Ask members in each group to identify the important factors they will take into account when defining their identities:

(a) They should try to relate their discussions to issues of identity formation, particularly the impact of ethnic and national identities for development research in different cultures.

(b) Ask students to reflect on and discuss some potential cultural misunderstandings they have experienced in their interactions with people from different cultures, race, ethnic or nationalities.

(c) Discuss concepts of time, respect and other cultural values and norms in different cultures/societies.

(d) Compare the impact of race and ethnicity on different cultural practices, perceptions and behaviours.

Preliminary visits: knowing the research community

If possible, the non-resident or stranger researcher should pay a preliminary visit to the intended community of his/her research. Besides helping to clarify questions about research design and strategies, such a visit helps to overcome the initial fears of researchers working in different cultures for the first time. It also provides an opportunity to overcome anxiety about the gap between preparing for the field and the exponential leap into the field itself.

In situations where this is not possible, as with many students and even some faculty, the researcher should conduct intensive baseline historical, socio-cultural and economic studies of the target communities. This background information is crucial for understanding the culture and histories of the groups being researched. It helps to minimize erroneous perceptions as well as helping researchers to identify (and treat with caution) people bent on pushing their own version of 'reality'. Although some perceptions about the researcher are difficult to correct, especially for Europeans working in former colonies, it is important for researchers from such backgrounds to understand their own historical location and the perceptions, privileges and hostilities associated with it. Westerners working in non-Western societies and former colonies, should be aware of certain strong perceptions about the superiority and privileges of Western 'white person's knowledge', since some of these historical perceptions tend to define his/her identity for the researched community (Finlay, 2002; see also Box 4.2). Countering these assumptions by adopting more open and respectful behaviour can assist the research process and smooth researcher–community relations.

Baseline studies and preliminary visits also help the researcher to understand how certain factors, such as roles of authority, individualism, communality, competition, security,

social, economic and political relations, space, and even humour, shape everyday life and help to define group and individual identities in the researched location. Experience from preliminary visits and background information also help to sharpen and redefine the research agenda (both the proposal and other logistics) as well as providing a better understanding of inter- and intra-group relationships. Understanding these dynamics helps to avoid over-generalizations about the homogeneity and/or heterogeneity of the researched community.

Language: vehicle of communication, experience and education

Language is as important as race, nationality and ethnicity for defining one's identity. Language, both verbal and non-verbal (signs and body language), is one of the most effective tools for interaction and for understanding others' intentions, needs and way of life. Language permits discussion and debates on some of the major themes in development research. Effective communication between the researcher and the researched can increase understanding, not only improving acceptance of the researcher, but also uncovering essential evidence for the research project. Moreover, familiarity with the language increases the researcher's understanding and appreciation of subtle differences in the researched community. Even just greetings and daily courtesies, as a sign of respect, can shape the community's perceptions of the researcher and his/her identity as foreigner (or friend). Basic language skills also help the researcher to ask questions in an effective manner, since asking the wrong questions or even asking the right questions in the wrong manner can easily betray the researcher and may confirm certain negative perceptions the community has about him/her (see Box 4.3).

Box 4.3   Hints on communication in the field

- The processes through which people agree and disagree – 'yes' or a 'no' – varies in different cultures. In some African and Asian societies, depending on the age, race and social status of the researcher, informants may not explicitly say 'no' or 'yes', but will pretend to agree to what the researcher says.
- The researcher should be aware that how people agree or disagree can differ widely from culture to culture, not just in terms of verbal responses but also in terms cultural subtleties and body language.
- The researcher may encounter signs, both verbal and or non-verbal, in the researched community that are seen as hostile or 'difficult' in his/her own culture. However, it would be a serious mistake to respond to these 'signs' in the same way as you would in your own culture.
- Many societies in Africa (e.g. Ghana, Tanzania and Kenya) do not use the left hand when giving or receiving items like a business card or gift.
- Time and patience can be deceptive and slippery in different cultures. Patience is seen as a virtue in many societies, so be patient if a delay or interruption occurs.
- In many African, Latin American, Asian, and some Hispanic and First Nations cultures young people are not permitted to look adults and elders in the eye. This is viewed as defiant and rude. Failure to make eye contact or avoiding direct eye contact in these societies does not imply dishonesty, but rather a sign of respect.
- Many societies consider it rude to ask direct questions about a person's family or age.

Development researchers must pay attention to body language as well as this can signal very different things in different cultures. Instead of interpreting body language in terms of one's own cultural rules and norms, researchers should cross-check the meaning of non-verbal or body language with knowledgeable members of the society and key informants. As much as possible researchers should withhold judgement until they are absolutely sure they understand the implications of particular practices. This requires tolerance, since many misinterpretations and breakdowns in communication between researchers and respondents are due not only to poor communication, but also to impatience on the part of researcher. Remember – 'seek first to understand before being understood'.

However, we also recognize that the need for local language skills depends on the length of time and nature of the research, rather than being a universal requirement. In multilinguistic communities, especially in urban centres, learning the local language(s) is often impossible, especially when students and even professors often have limited time in the field. Nevertheless, learning (and using) basic greetings and courtesies is essential.

Conclusion

In conclusion, development researchers working across difference, whether across cultures or within them, need to pay attention to a number of issues if they are going to succeed in the field. First, they need to be aware of power gradients, both between the researcher and the researched communities and within the communities themselves. Second, they need to pay attention to the identities being assigned them on the basis of more fixed positions, as well as more fluid characteristics such as worldview, lifestyle and personality. Where possible, preliminary visits to the research community are important, but where impossible, baseline studies and intensive 'book learning' about the field site are essential. Familiarity with basic elements of the language, socio-cultural values and practices as well as past and current experiences of development activities in the target society can greatly assist the development researcher working across differences. Attention to these issues provides essential tools for negotiating and renegotiating one's identity in a positive way and for enhancing the quality of data collection and analysis. Development research across difference can be frustrating, but it is worth the effort, offering life-changing rewards for the researcher and, hopefully, the researched communities as well.

Box 4.4   Advisory tool kit

- Ask colleagues or members of the university community who are familiar with your proposed region for advice.
- Avoid getting caught up in internal politics of the community.
- Remember that the person who speaks the best English in the researched community may get your attention, but may not be the best resource person or the real leadership in the community.
- Respect for culture (etiquette, values and protocol, especially thanks for assistance) and cultural diversity encourages mutual understanding and minimizes misunderstanding.
- Focus on understanding the rules and values of the community (not conceding to them). Doing so helps you to ask appropriate questions and have meaningful conversation with interviewees.
- Look out for cultural diversity and status hierarchies among the researched.
- Address with patience the myths, stereotypes and cultural differences that interfere with the full contribution of members.
- Learn to communicate clearly and fairly because how you say something may be more important than what you say.
- Listen for what is really being said, not what you want to hear.
- Test for understanding. Ask questions, to be certain you understand what is being said.
- Know the person with whom you are communicating (young, old, elder, traditional leader, government official, male or female) and adapt your communication style to fit the situation. Try to be explicit and communicate clearly.
- Use language that fosters trust and alliance. Be calm and positive when asking or answering questions.
- When conflicts arise, strive for understanding. It is important to delay reactions, feelings and assumptions until you are *really* sure they are appropriate.
- Before reacting to sensitive issues, check your understanding in confidence with a number of people in the researched community.
- Review, revise and revisit your main objective to be certain the content is clear.

(Continued)

41

(Continued)

- Appreciate and accept both commonalities and differences as part of the essential tools for effective working relationships.
- Continue to revisit the various components of your research that address aware-ness, understanding, communication and nurturing.
- Encourage and support discussion among people in the community on the meaning of the topic you are researching.
- Demonstrate ethical commitment to fairness and to the elimination of discrimination in all its forms within and outside the group.
- Be open to belief modifications and actions based on feedback. Emphasize the good things about their cultural practices and assumptions.
- Remember that even after some cross-cultural training people still tend to interpret other cultures' behaviour by the rules and norms of their own culture.
- Develop a strategy for communicating successfully with translators.

QUESTIONS FOR DISCUSSION

1. Discuss some of the hierarchical ethical and accountability issues that may arise while doing fieldwork in small villages or close-knit communities in the developing world?
2. Discuss why it is important to pay close attention to past research and development activities in your proposed research location.
3. Discuss what background information is needed in understanding culture and histories of the research community, before you embark on fieldwork.
4. Discuss the impact that race and ethnicity can have on different cultural practices, perceptions and behaviours.

Further reading

Emerson, R.M., Fretz, R.I. and Shaw, L.L. (1995) *Writing Ethnographic Fieldnotes*, Chicago: Chicago University Press.

Francis, E. (1993) Qualitative research: collecting life histories, in S. Devereux and J. Hoddinott (eds), *Fieldwork in Developing Countries*, Boulder, CO: Lynne Rienner.

Laws, S. Haper, C. and Marcus, R. (eds) (2003) *Research for Development: A Practical Guide*, London: Sage.

Narayan, U. (1997) *Dislocating Cultures: Identities, Traditions, and Third-World Feminism*, New York: Routledge.

References

Agar, M. (1980) *The Professional Stranger: An Informal Introduction to Ethnography*, London: Academic Press.

Apentiik, R. (2003) Ethnoecology of Bulsa land use: implications for sustainable development. PhD dissertation, University of Calgary, Calgary.

Devereux, S. and Hoddinott, J. (1992) The context of fieldwork, in S. Devereux and J. Hoddinott (eds), *Fieldwork in Developing Countries*, Boulder, CO: Lynne Rienner.

Finlay, L. (2002) Negotiating the swamp: the opportunity and challenge of reflexivity in research practice, *Qualitative Research*, 2 (2): 209–230.

Grafanaki, S. (1996) How research can change the researcher, *British Journal of Guidance and Counselling*, 24 (3): 329–338.

Scheyvens, R. and Storey, D. (2003) Introduction, in R. Scheyvens and D. Storey (eds), *Development Fieldwork: A Practical Guide*, London: Sage.

Wilson, K. (1993) Thinking about the ethics of research, in S. Devereux and J. Hoddinott (eds), *Fieldwork in Developing Countries*, Boulder, CO: Lynne Rienner.

5

Women, Men and Fieldwork: Gender Relations and Power Structures

Janet Henshall Momsen

Gender issues • Power structures • Ethical
issues • Field methods • Participatory fieldwork

In order to construct a broader more totalizing science we need to cross frontiers of policy, culture, personality and academic discipline and approach our work in the field with open minds. This is especially difficult when we are working in environments different from those which are familiar to us, and even when the fieldworker is a national of the country being studied they are usually separated from the local population by education, class, and appearance. These differences create unequal power relations between researcher and researched which must be recognized and compensated for in various ways.

In this chapter I consider this problem of power relations in the field, especially in relation to gender, and discuss various methods of dealing with this situation. I look first at the type of knowledge we are trying to learn about and understand, and the barriers limiting our ability to do this. These barriers may be at the personal level of the body, or be linked to nationality, race, class and gender. All involve ethical issues. Reflexivity is not always adequate but awareness helps. I look at participatory approaches to field research as a way of overcoming power relationships and the problems involved in achieving true participation. Then I consider various field methods which may help to overcome some power relationships, but not all.

Local knowledge is rich and complex, and is organized and practised at various scales. There is no 'average' person's perspective, but rather *different* knowledge types varying by gender, age and household and community roles. The complex local landscape is made up of niches that are distinguished by the characteristics of resource users and their differential power within local structures. Only by triangulating information from several sources, including men and women, young and old, educated and non-educated plus supplementary data from key informants knowledgeable about specific topics, can one begin to appreciate the complexity of local knowledge.

Gender issues

Sex refers to universal biological differences between men and women but gender concerns male and female behavioural norms which are learnt, are different in different societies, may change over time and vary from generation to generation. Until recently, researchers, who were usually men, ignored women's knowledge, considering that because they were less educated than men and had less power they had little to contribute to an understanding of local knowledge. Nowadays, however, women are increasingly seen as keepers of traditional knowledge, protectors of biodiversity and as having distinctive and special information about their environment (Gururani, 2002; Momsen, 2004). Despite this relatively recent appreciation of women's special knowledge, it is often very difficult to tap into this knowledge. Even when women are included in community-level decision-making they have often been seen as token representatives on committees with a passive role and few real responsibilities.

It is important to develop a project design that is aware of gender issues and allows for recognition of women's and men's needs, priorities and constraints (DFID, 2002). In order to carry out a gender-sensitive stakeholder analysis, a development project should ensure that:

- participatory consultation with women as well as men in beneficiary groups occurs;
- women's groups are actively involved in both consultation and decision-making processes;
- the range of women's views is adequately represented;
- research teams and implementation teams should include women as well as men.

Power structures

Post-development writers such as Escobar (1995) criticize the way in which development discourse has been constructed to legitimize the voices of Western 'experts' while marginalizing those of local people. More specifically, England (1994) questions how we can incorporate the voices of 'others' without colonizing them in a way that reinforces domination. Long-overdue debates are now emerging on the role of Western researchers in representing other people's cultures in development planning (Scheyvens and Storey, 2003). Power relations do not disappear when women are interviewed separately. In many cases women continue to behave as if their husbands were present.

The field researcher, whether male or female, inhabits a particular space created by the local community, which it may take some time for the researcher to appreciate. The researcher's positionality (in terms of race, gender, nationality, age, economic status and sexuality) may influence the data gathered (Madge, 1993). In situations where the investigator is a foreigner they may be recreated in the field as non-gendered. If a woman is tall and has short hair, she may be seen as more similar to men than women in an indigenous village in the Andes. This ambiguous position allows the researcher entry to local male and female space and thus access to a wider range of information than would otherwise be available.

In some countries women are not used to being asked their opinions. This is particularly true where women are less well educated than men and are allowed less mobility. Thus, this problem may be found more in Asian field areas than in African ones, where women tend to have more economic independence than in Asia. Detailed information on financial aspects of a household is often difficult to obtain in Western societies because it is feared that the interviewer is seeking information that may be passed on to the government and so cause problems for the interviewee. However, in former and current socialist and centrally planned countries such information is readily given, but requests for personal opinions or ideas are seen as threatening. Thus it is necessary to be aware of national power structures as well as community and household ones.

Box 5.1   Giving voice to male and female in the household

In most societies patriarchal controls make it difficult to obtain responses from males and females which are independent. In two very different societies I overcame this. Working on a rural poverty project in south-west China among minority peoples, we found women were often shy and did not want to talk to us but we found different ways of involving them. While interviewing a male household head in front of his house we asked him if we could also speak to his wife. He called her to come out and talk to us. She did not want to, but his elder daughter replied as well. She was educated and worked in a factory in a nearby town so was more outspoken. She did not come outside but shouted answers to the questions through the door and her father deferred to her and agreed with her answers. In another minority community in the same region the society was matriarchal. Foreign visitors were not usually allowed to enter this village as the Chinese government disapproved of its social system. We were told we could not ask questions about family structure. In one household, a man was sitting by the fire relaxing while his wife was cooking in the kitchen and issuing orders for the running of the farm. We asked the man information about the seasonal calendar and who did the work on the farm. He gave us some vague answers so we then asked the woman. She started out by saying that her partner knew nothing as he did nothing! She confirmed that she was in charge and made all decisions. Our official Party interpreter translated this before he realized what she was saying. After that we were bundled out and not allowed to speak to any more women! However, trained observation of daily activities helped us to understand a lot about this society, even without talking to both genders.

On a project in a Mayan village in Mexico to look at the possibilities for tourism development there, we interviewed men and women together at home. In every case we got the stereotypical answer: the men did all the outside work on the farm and women only looked after the children, cooked and cleaned the house. A little digging did get the men to admit that women did most of the seed saving but they assured us that they, the men, did the collecting of wood and water for the household. Since we had observed even elderly women carrying bundles of firewood we were dubious about the responses to our questions. The Maya are usually considered to be a relatively gender-equal society and we were not satisfied with the constant repetition of the same story. So we asked the community leaders if we could hold a focus group just for women. In the focus group the women told us that the men did very little and women did most of the work, including working in the *milpa,* or farm. They also complained that the men had decided that any financial benefits from the tourism project were to go to improving the road to the

(Continued)

(Continued)

village and were to be paid directly to the male head of household. The women said that they wanted the money to be spent on a health clinic and improving the school in the community. Consequently, it was not surprising that the women were lukewarm about the tourism project, both because of its demands on their time and because of their lack of input into the distribution of benefits. Again, observation and experience made us wary of accepting responses at face value.

Ethical issues

Fieldwork in developing areas can lead to a complex array of ethical dilemmas relating to knowledge generation, ownership and exploitation (Scheyvens and Storey, 2003 and see Chapter 3 of this volume). These dilemmas are usually linked to the relative power of researcher and researched. There is also a moral imperative to do no harm and hopefully to do good and, especially in feminist studies, to involve empowerment in the community studied. The research process must protect the individual's dignity, privacy and basic rights, including the right to withdraw from the project at any time. The power gradients between researcher and researched must also be treated with sensitivity. Sometimes these are related to the body, where a white researcher is dealing with non-white subjects or where a white subject assumes the researcher holds the same racist views about the local black majority population. The researcher may find it difficult to remain neutral in the face of such viewpoints but in order to complete the interview may feel that he/she has to keep silent. In other cases, age differences, as between a young researcher and an elder in the society under study, or between an older researcher and children as research subjects, may cause problems not immediately apparent to the investigator. Clothing, or lack of it, may also cause difficulties for both researcher and researched, requiring considerable sensitivity and awareness to overcome this.

Truth and deception in terms of the self-presentation of the researcher as married or not is also an ethical issue (Wolf, 1996). In general, it is dangerous to begin the research with a lie, although in some cases the suggestion of a partner in the background may increase the safety of women fieldworkers. Often the presence of children in the field with the researcher provides a common interest and helps to break down barriers (Oberhauser, 1997: 170). Efforts to overcome hierarchical relations between researcher and researched require constant reflexivity and the continual reassessment of one's positionality and assumptions as a researcher. Using a range of field methods (Box 5.2) in addition to or instead of quantitative surveys may make ethical issues easier to deal with.

47

Box 5.2   Field methods for gender awareness

Alternative methods of data-gathering can overcome gender differences and improve problem identification (Feldstein et al., 1994; Thomas-Slaytor et al., 1993).

(Continued)

(Continued)

1 **Wealth ranking**: Get four or five community informants to sort cards with family names into piles according to the informant's notion of the household's relative level of well-being and then discuss the characteristics associated with each pile. This allows the researcher to interpret patterns of local socio-economic stratification. It also makes sure that the poorest households, which may remain invisible to the outsider because they do not attend meetings, are included in project design.

2 **Focus group discussions**: These can provide a forum for in-depth discussions of issues which arise in interviews as well as clarification of the range of perceptions and opinions found in the community. Having separate focus groups for men and women allows gender differences to be openly expressed.

3 **Gendered perceptions of institutions**: Asking men and women separately to rank the importance of the role of institutions such as church, school, clinic, and NGOs in the community and the links between these institutions enables the researcher to judge the relative gendered influence of these institutions.

4 **Participant observation undertaken by accompanying respondents as they carry out their daily activities**: This can range from participating in factory work to working side by side with respondents in the house and/or field. This illuminates resource constraints and interaction between individuals.

5 **GPS measurement of use of space**: This can be done by following respondents in their daily activities using GPS recorders to measure spatial movement of respondents during their daily activities. In this way, actual use of space, which may be different from reported use, by different ethnic groups and both genders within a community, is revealed.

6 **Sketch mapping**: Asking respondents to draw resource maps of their communities can show different gendered use of areas of forest, or restrictions on use by a particular group based on identification of areas as sacred, and so help researchers to understand gendered constraints on resource use. These maps may also be used to identify different gendered views of local soil types.

7 **Gendered seasonal calendar**: This allows the recognition of periods of labour shortage by gender. It may also reveal gendered tasks in relation to particular crops.

8 **Gender analysis of utilization of individual plants**: This can reveal different uses of particular cultivated and wild plants by men and women. In this way the researcher can learn about problems affecting women and men differentially, such as loss of access to certain plants through such changes as deforestation.

9 **Life histories**: Individual life histories can reveal changes in access to resources, relationships within and between communities and in community skills and facilities within one generation.

10 **Non-quantitative measurement of relative inputs**: In illiterate communities, studies of food intake and food taboos for pregnant or nursing mothers may be established by using piles of seeds or pebbles to represent basic elements of the local diet. Having identified past diets, units can be moved from piles and new piles added to show modern diets, food taboos and loss of wild food items.

Participatory fieldwork

Participatory, or 'bottom-up', approaches to development planning are now usually considered the most appropriate strategies and as such are strongly encouraged by donor agencies (see Chapters 19 and 20). However, such approaches, although theoretically and ideologically popular, are often difficult to operationalize in the field (Bell and Brambilla, 2001). In addition, '[t]he risks of participatory methods include their potential use to manipulate or control power and the creation of false confidence' (Rocheleau, 1995: 4). Concepts of active participation by local people in governance may be encouraged by outsiders but the extent to which this really occurs may be hidden. It is essential to question power relations in a community as they are usually more complex than appears at first sight. Time needs to be spent in a community to ascertain the true level of shared governance and to arrive at a satisfactory level of confidence in community relations. Use of many of the field methods listed in Box 5.2 will help in reaching this goal. In particular, life histories, sketch maps and documentation of use of space are useful sources of knowledge. Allowing individuals to reflect on and to analyse their own reality may also contribute, where this is an acceptable activity for respondents.

Researchers usually need to obtain permission from local leaders in order to enter a community and thus are seen as allied with these leaders. Local leaders may try to 'help' by suggesting the individuals to whom the researcher should talk. Attempts to carry out a random sample survey may raise questions within the community as to why certain households or individuals are excluded from the survey, so that in order to appease local feelings the researcher may be forced to interview additional households. These extra households may later be excluded from the survey analysis and used as more general sources of information.

In many cases community leaders are male and so may be unaware of issues affecting women and may not consider that women have anything to contribute to the problem being studied. This lack of awareness may mean that researchers are either allowed access to women without any problem or are prevented from talking to women. On the other hand, active participation by outside researchers may bring about unexpected results. A focus group for women may lead to consciousness-raising and the grassroots decision to start a women's group (Momsen, 2002). Even in situations where both community leaders and researchers are female and of the same nationality, class and educational differences may also create barriers to mutual understanding. Such barriers are often even more difficult to notice than those based primarily on gender differences (Momsen, 2002). This type of problem may arise in fieldwork among indigenous communities in developed countries such as the USA, Canada, Australia and New Zealand, where the majority population is often unaware of indigenous cultural understandings of gender relations and use of land and sacred sites. In these situations it is essential to have local indigenous research assistants who can bridge the cultural gap.

Participatory research must also involve the return of research findings to the community in a form which is meaningful to them. Wherever possible the researcher should plan to hold workshops with participants to enable them to provide feedback on the research findings and, through this, it also becomes possible to correct mistaken assumptions by the outside researcher. Providing reports to local authorities and/or publishing results in local newspapers or journals, or giving radio talks also help to return knowledge to the research area. If this is not done, research can be seen as imperialist and as done merely so that the researcher can get a postgraduate degree or write papers so they can get promotion in

49

academia or further consultancy positions. On the other hand, a commitment to participatory research may enable the researcher to become aware of previously invisible groups, such as the landless, female-headed households and the elderly. For fieldwork to be successful the investigator must be sensitive to the customs and mores of local society and treat respondents not as animals in a laboratory but as fellow human beings.

QUESTIONS FOR DISCUSSION

1. How far do you agree that academics have failed to explore adequately the power relations, inequalities and injustices upon which differences between ourselves and those we research are based? Discuss in relation to specific case studies.
2. How does the gender of the researcher affect their fieldwork?
3. Discuss the relations between ethics and postcoloniality in the field.
4. How do cultural and educational differences in different countries and communities affect the choice of field methods?
5. What are the problems and benefits of using participatory methods in the field?

Further reading

Robson, E. and Willis, K. (eds) (1997) *Postgraduate Fieldwork in Developing Countries: A Rough Guide*, Developing Areas Research Group, Monograph No. 9, London: Royal Geographical Society and the Institute of British Geographers.

Scheyvens, R. and Storey, D. (eds) (2003) *Development Fieldwork: A Practical Guide*, London: Sage.

Warren, Carol A.B. (1988) *Gender Issues in Field Research*, Qualitative Research Methods Series 9, London: Sage.

Wolf, D.L. (ed.) (1996) *Feminist Dilemmas in Fieldwork*, Boulder, CO: Westview Press.

References

Bell, E. and Brambilla, P. (2001) *Gender and Participation: Supporting Resources Collection*, BRIDGE Report, Brighton: Institute of Development Studies.

Department for International Development (DFID) (2002) *Gender Manual: A Practical Guide for Development Policy Makers and Practitioners*, London: Social Development Division, DFID. Also available at: http://www.genie.ids.ac.uk/gem/index_implementatation/gendermanual.pdf

England, K. (1994) Getting personal: reflexivity, positionality and feminist research, *Professional Geographer*, 46 (1): 80–89.

Escobar, A. (1995) *Encountering Development: The Making and Unmaking of the Third World*, Princeton, NJ: Princeton University Press.

Feldstein, H., Sims, J. and Jiggins, J. (eds) (1994) *Tools for the Field: Methodologies Handbook for Gender Analysis in Agriculture*, West Hartford, CT: Kumarian Press.

Gururani, S. (2002) Construction of Third World women's knowledge in the development discourse, *International Social Science Journal*, 173: 313–323.

Madge, C. (1993), Boundary disputes: comments on Sidaway (1992), *Area*, 25 (3): 294–299.

Momsen, J.H. (2002) NGOs, gender and indigenous grassroots development, *Journal of International Development*, 14: 859–867.

Momsen, J.H. (2004) *Gender and Development*, New York and London: Routledge.

Oberhauser, A.M. (1997) The home as 'field': households and homework in rural Appalachia, in J.P. Jones III, H.J. Nast and S.M. Roberts (eds), *Thresholds in Feminist Geography: Difference, Methodology, Representation*, New York: Rowman and Littlefield, pp. 165–182.

Rocheleau, D. (1995) Gendered environments, gendered methods: landscapes, lifescapes, livelihoods and life histories, in M. Schmink and S.L. Russo (eds), *Innovations and Partnerships: Working with Natural Resource Management, Gender and Local Communities in the Tropics. Report of 44th Annual Latin American Studies Conference, 31 March–1 April*, Gainesville, FL: University of Florida, pp. 1–4.

Scheyvens, R. and Storey, D. (eds) (2003) *Development Fieldwork: A Practical Guide*, London: Sage.

Thomas-Slaytor, B., Esser, A.L. and Shields, M.D. (1993) *Tools of Gender Analysis: A Guide to Field Methods for Bringing Gender into Sustainable Resource Management*, Worcester, MA: International Development Program, Clark University.

Wolf, D.L. (ed.) (1996) *Feminist Dilemmas in Fieldwork*, Boulder, CO: Westview Press.

6

Working with Children in Development

Lorraine van Blerk

Theoretical considerations Children-centred research: a participatory process Methodological choices and challenges Disseminating research: for and with children

Children represent over 40 per cent of the world's population, with 90 per cent of those aged under 18 located throughout Africa, Asia and Latin America (Ansell, 2005). This means an increasing volume of development studies research, which seeks to explore issues of social relevance, must focus on, or at least include, children. However, until recently this important group has largely been ignored in development research agendas (Scheyvens et al., 2003).

Despite this, there has been some exceptional work with children in a development context, and this has helped to stimulate interest and create a platform for academic and student researchers to consider issues relevant to children's lives. This chapter will therefore explore why it is necessary to research with children both from theoretical and practical perspectives. In particular, the chapter will focus on the research process, from ensuring children-centredness in research, to highlighting some of the methodological challenges

students might face when undertaking fieldwork, to involving children in the dissemination of findings.

Working with children: theoretical considerations

In order to work with children it is necessary to consider what it means to be a child and how childhood is perceived as a defining entity. This has been attempted both biologically, in relation to age, but also in different ways historically and culturally. Within Western societies, much previous social scientific thought on childhood has drawn on the premise that children are less-than-adult, that they are not yet full members of society because of limited biological and psychological capacities. This less-than-adult construction has also informed popular interpretations of childhood. Children are viewed as innocent and in need of protection from the evils of the adult world (the Apollonian vision of childhood), or as wicked, needing discipline and correction from their own corrupting influences (the Dionysian vision of childhood) (Jenks, 1996). Both views are prevalent in contemporary society, illustrating children as incomplete beings that need to be shaped by adults. In contrast to this, more recent academic writing, collectively referred to as the 'new social studies of childhood', has re-focused our understanding of childhood experiences by demonstrating childhood as socially, and therefore politically, culturally and economically, constructed and children as active agents in processes affecting their lives (for more detailed information, see Holloway and Valentine, 2000; James et al., 1999). The new social studies of childhood is therefore one key influence for research with children, illustrating the need to consider diversity in childhood experience, an aspect that is especially crucial for students embarking on overseas research.

A further influence that has relevance for students undertaking development research refers to the globalized notion of childhood, where Western conceptions of children have been translated to policies across the world through legislation and international organizations. In contrast to the new social studies of childhood, the global notion of childhood envisages an 'ideal' childhood experience and clearly demarcates children from adults based on biological and psychological features, and positions children as weaker members of society who are characterized by the things they cannot (rather than can) do. This has consequences, both socially and economically, for many young people in Africa, Asia and Latin America who increasingly fall outside this model and are subsequently defined as abnormal by society (see Bourdillon, 2004).

The global notion of childhood has had implications for research with children, for example, leading to the use of less appropriate research tools and research design. The model assumes that it is not necessary to identify children's needs because the global notion of childhood already knows what is *best*. Further, because the approach assumes that children lack full 'adult' capacities, research has been undertaken *with* adults *about* children (Boyden and Ennew, 1997). However, it is important to recognize that despite the prevalence of this global model, it is merely an idea rather than a 'truth' (Boyden and Ennew, 1997). By drawing on the claims made by the new social studies of childhood, it is possible through research to gain real insight into the valuable and meaningful experiences of all children.

This outline of the historical and theoretical basis for conducting research with children highlights three key points that we need to consider in our exploration of 'doing' research with children. First, much previous research regarding children's lives was undertaken with adults, excluding the very cultures and social interactions that are unique to children. There is a clear need to think through how research projects could be adapted to include children. Second, research with children presents a special challenge because of the power adults have over children. In many contexts foreign adults can be especially intimidating. Finally, children's cultures are often difficult for adults to interpret, particularly in a cross-cultural context. Therefore, children must be included throughout the research process from inception to dissemination (Boyden and Ennew, 1997).

Children-centred research: a participatory process

Children's voices are seldom heard in research and yet it is important to know what they think and do in order to plan effective interventions. (Boyden and Ennew, 1997: 16)

In order to overcome the (usually Western-based) adultist assumptions of childhood it is important to do research *with* children rather than *on* children. Therefore research has to be children-centred. This does not mean that

53

research with children has to be *qualitatively* different from working with other groups (Punch, 2002) but merely that there are special considerations which must be reflected upon.

One such consideration is ensuring children's participation in research (rather than simply using participatory techniques) as this enables children to put forward their own views, thereby re-shaping the research process both in terms of the methods used and the content of discussions. When working in a development context, children will be best placed to select not only what is of interest to them but also what is most appropriate culturally. However, as a student undertaking a research project, it is often difficult to achieve a level of participation where children are able to have significant input into the research design or the chosen methods. This is because departmental approval processes require a project plan with clear aims and methods before students go into the field. It is possible, however, to recognize the expertise children have and to discuss your plan with a group of key informants. This will raise interest in the research and allow you to identify important topics (possibly ones previously excluded) and modify the methodology to involve children as co-researchers. As Bourdillon (2004) points out, this has been shown both to benefit children, through growth in self-confidence, and to provide much needed, but often neglected, information on children's issues in local communities. It is worth pointing out that involving children in the research process in this way does not detract from the academic input and analysis that researchers also bring to the project based on their training and experience.

Methodological choices and challenges

It is often (inaccurately) assumed that ensuring children's participation in research can be adequately achieved only through the use of innovative techniques, with traditional social science research methods being seen as 'adultist'. Although innovative approaches have been heralded by some as more children-centred, they have also been critiqued as being patronizing, separating children from adults as inherently different (Punch, 2002). This can be overcome by carefully considering the groups you are researching and, if possible, working with them to select methods that are both appropriate to the research aims and to the contexts in which they live. Rather than advocate one approach over another (and indeed using both traditional and innovative methods has proved extremely fruitful), the benefits and problems of both are considered here.

Traditional social science research methods and working with children

Traditional social science methods in research with children have been critiqued in several ways, not least because they ignore the power imbalances between adults and children. Such approaches can project the authoritative stance of researchers, which may result in intimidation. This can be overcome by training children as researchers, so that they not only help to design the questions, but also carry out their own interviews and focus groups. Using a dictaphone both to record information and as a microphone can enable focus groups to take control over facilitation. For instance, the recorder can be passed from one to another when asking and answering questions (see Plate 6.1) (Young and Barrett, 2001a).

A second relevant issue relates to sensitivity towards language and culture, as children may be less confident in articulating themselves verbally in interviews and in writing questionnaires. This is particularly important when working with younger children or those who have had limited access to education. It can also be exacerbated where children are asked to work in a second language (such

Plate 6.1   Street children in Uganda facilitating their own focus group discussion
(photograph: L. van Blerk)

as English). For students who may not have time to learn a new language, working through an interpreter can prove beneficial. Questionnaires produced in dual languages allow participants to select their preference for understanding and answering. This can raise issues regarding the accuracy of translation, but participants do need to feel comfortable during the research process. Children also do not express themselves through language in the same way as adults. Therefore, it is important to involve children when developing questionnaires and interview schedules, so that they are written in familiar language and are easy to understand. When working across cultural and language barriers the involvement of children in designing the research tools will help to ensure that words used in translation do not have different meanings. In one research project regarding children's migration in southern Africa (van Blerk and Ansell, 2004), the researchers had difficulty finding terms that neatly fitted with their definitions

of migration. Although initially problematic, informal discussions with participants prior to their completion of the questionnaire meant that appropriate terms and meanings could be identified.

A further problem that may arise when using traditional methods is that respondents may provide answers they 'think you want to hear' rather than their own feelings and opinions. This is especially the case as such methods can seem like 'school', especially when accessing children through educational establishments. This can be overcome by involving children as co-researchers and by conducting questionnaires at the end of the research process, when there has been sufficient time to introduce the research fully and develop rapport. Although there are several concerns that need to be addressed when using traditional research methods with children in a cross-cultural context, by thinking through the kinds of issue aired here, rich information can be obtained.

Innovative approaches for research with children

There are a number of more innovative methods that are appropriate for researching with children. They include written methods (diaries and posters), action methods (drama and role play) and visual methods (drawing, mapping and photographic diaries). Although these methods are sometimes critiqued for separating children out as different, they do create stimulating and fun research environments. What is important is to ensure that the methods chosen are socially and culturally appropriate for those children taking part. For example, it may be more appropriate to ask children with low levels of literacy to draw pictures of their daily duties, rather than to write them down in diaries.

Awareness of literacy levels among participants provides a cautionary note for using written methods, although children with good literacy can often express themselves extremely well through stories and diaries. Where children have poor written expression, action methods provide alternative opportunities to make research fun. Drama and role play are also expressive, but are more difficult to record, unless you have access to a video camera. However, such approaches have other benefits when used in conjunction with more traditional methods. For example, Hecht (1999) created a radio role play as part of his interviewing strategy. In this work, pairs of children interviewed each other about topics relevant to the research, with one acting as the DJ and the other as the guest. This is useful when discussing very sensitive topics such as family problems or the impacts of HIV/AIDS. Drama can be used to highlight the key issues or problems faced by children without directly stigmatizing individuals.

Visual methods have gained credence in recent years with drawings, maps and photographs now used as important means of data collection. They have been found to have great benefits, but it is also necessary to think carefully before engaging in their use. In particular, it is important to remember to retrieve explanations from children about what they have drawn, photographed or mapped and why. Punch (2002) did not ask for explanations for the drawings she collected as she felt the images produced were self-explanatory. This created problems during analysis as it became difficult to distinguish between, for example, houses and schools. Interpreting images is further complicated where cultural groups differ in their ways of reading pictures. Here explanations help to minimize misinterpretation by the researcher.

An advantage of using visual methods is their usefulness in aiding the collection of verbal information as it helps to focus their discussion. Dodman (2003) used photographs as a method for discovering young people's human–environment interactions in Kingston, Jamaica. He was interested in identifying the different ways young people from varied social backgrounds experienced the city. Through asking them to take pictures and using these images as a tool for subsequent discussion, he elicited a unique insight into such interactions. Dodman (2003) found that photographic representation was a particularly useful tool for avoiding the perpetuation of the very social inequalities that can often be continued by relying solely on verbal techniques. A further advantage of using photographs in research is that this method can directly empower participants as they have control of the research activity. Street children commented on the positive benefits of feeling trusted by a researcher who was willing to give them a camera (Young and Barrett, 2001a). Finally, using photographs allows the researcher to access places and activities that they may not otherwise be able to enter, or where their presence would change the situation to such an extent that a true representation could not be gained (Young and Barrett, 2001c).

Ethical issues in working with children

The ethics of undertaking social research are complex but are particularly so when working with children. In the UK, many universities now require students to gain ethical approval and departmental authorization for research involving children and students should identify these procedures prior to undertaking fieldwork. Additionally, in a cross-cultural setting, perspectives on dealing appropriately with moral obligations may vary (see Chapter 3 for more detail on ethical practices). There has to be an element of caution here to avoid imposing Western perspectives on ethical issues that arise in other cultures, while maintaining our moral stance and responsibilities as researchers. Some of the key considerations for working with children can be considered from two perspectives: avoiding harm and issues of power. First, it is important to ensure that as researchers we do not create situations that may cause harm to those we work with. This does not mean that we should avoid all research that may cause distress, but that we, as researchers, should take responsibility for the effects of the research and be prepared to deal with distress (Boyden and Ennew, 1997; Robson, 2001).

Obtaining informed consent is important for all research projects, but when dealing with children it is necessary to think through how this is achieved. It is important that the research is explained clearly and simply so that the implications of taking part (including issues of confidentiality, anonymity and data ownership) are understood. This may involve using local languages in written and verbal communication to avoid misunderstandings. It is also necessary to think about from whom consent should be sought. Regardless of children's abilities to make informed decisions, adults also have obligations to their own children and to those who have been entrusted to their care. This means that consent may be required from family members, employers, community leaders, teachers and non-related carers. Where consent is gained from such adult gatekeepers, it is important to ensure that the children themselves are able to decide whether or not they take part. In order to avoid situations where children feel they *must* participate because, for example, their teacher has agreed to the research, it is preferable to ask children to opt *in* rather than opt *out*.

Finally, when considering doing no harm, it is necessary to think about child protection issues. Within the UK, if a child discloses abuse, researchers have a legal obligation to inform the authorities. However, given the diverse nature of childhood experience, it is appropriate to recognize that unique approaches to such situations may be required, especially given that in many places, reporting abuse does not necessarily guarantee a sensitive response (Laws et al., 2003). For example, research with street children in Uganda highlighted the difficulties associated with disclosing abusive behaviour towards street children, because often the abusers held positions of power as society's protectors. This raises questions over how abuse should be reported and to whom (Young and Barrett, 2001b). In order to avoid perpetuating situations of harm, researchers should involve children in seeking appropriate solutions and channels for reporting incidents. Often they know what is required but may need support in actioning the decision.

This latter point touches on the impacts of uneven power relations between adults and children. In many instances research students will be foreign adult researchers from relatively wealthy backgrounds who have travelled overseas to conduct research with children from more impoverished communities. This can raise expectations that there will be physical (and immediate) benefits for those who participate. It is important to be clear about the research outcomes prior to engaging in the research process and not to foster ideas that the research will be directly linked to project work (unless the research is being done collaboratively).

A related issue concerns whether to offer compensation to participants for their time. There is some debate among the research community as to whether this is appropriate, but when drawing your own conclusions there are several factors to bear in mind. First, if you decide to remunerate, can you be sure that the activity of paying will not affect the information you collect? Is it appropriate to give money to children when they may use it to feed unhealthy habits such as smoking cannabis? Under such circumstances there may be other methods of providing compensation. Possible ideas include providing food, throwing an end-of-project party, or investing in developing some tangible outputs to the research. On the other hand, some children may be engaged in employment for family or personal survival. In such cases, it may be more appropriate to compensate with cash, particularly when there is a loss of earnings as a direct result of participation.

Working with hard-to-reach groups

Some groups of children, including child workers, street children, domestic workers and young sex workers, have childhood experiences that are unfamiliar to overseas students. Researching with such groups poses particular practical challenges. It can be difficult to gain access to children in hard-to-reach groups, because they are less likely to attend school and many work in hidden occupations. Identifying organizations that support such children can help researchers access participants. It is also important to be aware that there may be non-traditional gatekeepers (such as employers, friends and gang/group leaders) from whom informed consent may need to be obtained. This will help to diffuse any suspicion over the intended purpose of the research and should be done in direct consultation with participants (Young and Barrett, 2001c).

Further difficulties of access relate to children's abilities to participate and remain engaged in research. When children are engaged in labour or work activities identifying a suitable time and place to conduct research may not be easy. For example, Laws et al. (2003) illustrate how researchers had problems engaging factory workers in Vietnam in discussions and diagramming activities because they were under constant supervision and did not have regular breaks. Many also lived too far away for home visits to be practical and this resulted in a complete revision of the research plan. Although not all situations will be as extreme as this, it is important to respect children's work and negotiate with them what are suitable times and places for research activities to occur. Similarly, lower attention spans (especially if due to the use of intoxicants) and limited literacy levels may mean that activities need to be carefully tailored to suit particular groups. This can be exemplified through research exploring street children's use of space in Uganda, where photographic diaries proved to be an extremely useful tool. The activity involved street children taking disposable cameras for 24 hours and snapping scenes from their daily lives. As they did not have to devote a specific period of time to the research, this helped to minimize the effects of low attention spans. Similarly, through the use of a visual method, high-level verbal and written skills were not necessary, and instead of undermining children's capacities this increased their self-confidence.

Disseminating research: for and with children

Dissemination is an important part of all development research (see Chapters 30 and 31 for more details) but there are two important issues when researching with children: (1) how do researchers disseminate to children and (2) is it possible for children to participate in the dissemination process? Providing a copy of

58

your dissertation or report to participants is one method of dissemination that is readily used by most students. However, when children have participated, more often than not the report is sent to the school or organization that provided access rather than to the children themselves. Although the reports could also be given to children, in most cases it is not appropriate, particularly if they are written in academic language.

If the researcher is able to return to the field, then holding discussion groups to present the findings is one useful dissemination strategy. This is beneficial in that it encourages participants to reflect and comment on the findings and how their views have been represented. If, as with many student projects, there are not funds to make return visits, discussions can still be held at the end of the fieldwork phase to discuss the research process and preliminary results. Posters could also be produced (with the children's help), presenting the results in a clear, straightforward manner. This also helps to create closure to the research, especially where the researcher and participants have developed close trust relationships. Disseminating the findings from home can also be done by creating a website (if participants have access through school, for instance) as this

will enhance feedback dialogue. Alternatively, fact sheets documenting the main findings and taking into account the literacy and language capabilities of participants can provide valuable feedback to children.

In circumstances where children have taken a major role in designing and informing the research, it may be appropriate to involve them more directly in disseminating the findings. Often participants are better placed to inform their communities and peers of the key issues raised. Presentations at school assemblies, posters for schools or organization offices/ meeting rooms are methods where children can take a leading role. Similarly, children's messages can be captured and taken to workshops and conferences. The case study presented in Box 6.1 illustrates that not only can children prove valuable in local dissemination but, through drama, they can also participate internationally, thereby overcoming complications of cost and time away from home and school. This is not to devalue the training and expertise of researchers in data analysis, and there will be some circumstances where researcher-led dissemination is more appropriate, such as writing formal or academic reports, while still representing the voices of children in the manner in which they were expressed.

Box 6.1   Young people 'doing dissemination'

In a research project exploring children's migration in response to AIDS in southern Africa, young people were involved in disseminating the findings. They highlighted the problems children face when they have to move due to the effects of AIDS in their families and communities. The researchers met with the children and presented the findings. They then discussed and ranked the findings (regarding the most pressing problems and how they could be reduced by families, communities and organizations). Following this, the children developed short dramas as a means for communicating the research and prompting discussion. They performed the dramas and carried out discussion with other children in the schools to raise awareness. Some of the children also

(Continued)

(Continued)

planned to perform their dramas at a whole-school assembly, to which parents and relatives are invited. In addition, the dramas were filmed and, with permission, shown at workshops held with NGOs and government officials seeking to develop policy recommendations. This example demonstrates how drama can be used in a non-threatening way to take research messages into wider society. In this instance, drama enabled the young people to better express their thoughts, feelings and desires regarding the problems they faced and facilitated dialogue among a wider audience (Ansell and van Blerk, 2004).

Conclusion

This chapter has outlined some of the key theoretical, methodological and ethical issues that need to be considered when working with children in a development context. Principally, the chapter advocates research with children to be handled sensitively and appropriately through the inclusion of children in all aspects of the research process. If you are able to achieve this in your research, then it is possible to yield insights into previously neglected issues that are central to development studies.

QUESTIONS FOR DISCUSSION

1. What are the key issues for ensuring children's participation in research? Previously children were either missed out of research altogether or subsumed within family or household research. Think about how you might avoid this by carefully considering how children can be involved.
2. How do you identify research methods that are appropriate for children? This chapter has demonstrated that it is important to select methods that are appropriate for the particular group of children you are researching. Think through the benefits and problems of using different research methods with (1) school children, (2) street children and (3) rural farm workers.
3. What ethical issues might you need to overcome when researching with hard-to-reach groups? The principal tenet of undertaking research is that it should do no harm. Consider how ethical issues might be made more complicated because of children's working conditions, family situation or community environment. What strategies would you need to put in place to ensure that you are able to deal will difficult situations, should they arise?

Further reading

Bourdillon, M. (2004) Children in development, *Progress in Development Studies,* 4 (2): 99–113.

Laws, S., Harper, C. and Marcus, R. (2003) *Research for Development: A Practical Guide,* London: Sage.

Punch, S. (2002) Research with children: the same or different from research with adults? *Childhood*, 9 (3): 321–341.

Young, L. and Barrett, H. (2001) Adapting visual methods: action research with Kampala street children, *Area*, 33 (2): 141–152.

References

Ansell, N. (2005) *Children, Youth and Development*, London: Routledge.

Ansell, N. and van Blerk, L. (2004) Young AIDS migrants in southern Africa: dissemination, unpublished report for the Department for International Development.

Bourdillon, M. (2004) Children in development, *Progress in Development Studies*, 4(2): 99–113.

Boyden, J. and Ennew, J. (1997) *Children in Focus: A Manual for Participatory Development*, Stockholm: Radda Barnen.

Dodman, D. (2003) Shooting in the city: an autophotographic exploration of the urban environment in Kingston, Jamaica, *Area*, 35(3): 293–304.

Hecht, T. (1999) *At Home in the Street?: Street Children of Northeast Brazil*, Cambridge: Cambridge University Press.

Holloway, S. and Valentine, G. (2000) *Children's Geographies: Playing, Living, Learning*, London: Routledge.

James, A., Jenks, C. and Prout, A. (1999) *Theorising Childhood*, London: Routledge.

Jenks, C. (1996) *Childhood*, London: Routledge.

Laws, S., with Harper, C. and Marcus, R. (2003) *Research for Development: A Practical Guide*, London: Sage.

Punch, S. (2002) Research with children: the same or different from research with adults? *Childhood*, 9(3): 321–341.

Robson, E. (2001) Interviews worth the tears? Exploring dilemmas of research with young carers in Zimbabwe, *Ethics, Place and Environment*, 4(2): 135–141.

Scheyvens, R., Scheyvens, H. and Murray, W. (2003) Working with marginalised, vulnerable or privileged groups, in R. Scheyvens and D. Storey (eds), *Development Fieldwork: A Practical Guide*, London: Sage.

van Blerk, L. and Ansell, N. (2004) Imagining migration: placing children's understanding of 'moving house' in Malawi and Lesotho, manuscript under review.

Young, L. and Barrett, H. (2001a) Adapting visual methods: action research with Kampala street children, *Area*, 33(2): 141–152.

Young, L. and Barrett, H. (2001b) Ethics and participation: reflections on research with street children, *Ethics, Place and the Environment*, 4(2): 130–134.

Young, L. and Barrett, H. (2001c) Issues of access and identity: adapting research methods with Kampala street children, *Childhood: A Global Journal of Child Research*, 8(3): 383–395.

61

7

Collecting Sensitive and Contentious Information

Margaret E. Harrison

• • A definition of sensitive and contentious information • • Cultural differences
and their influence on the data collection process • • The role and position of
the researcher in the data collection process • • Data sources and the
significance of critical analysis • • Some practical considerations before
attempting to collect sensitive and contentious information

Introduction and definitions

As part of the research process, and in particular while undertaking fieldwork, a researcher will probably ponder how to ask the most important questions. According to Pratt and Loizos (1992), these questions often go unasked because the researcher does not know how to tackle the topic, which may be too sensitive or highly contentious. This chapter is written to help the researcher think through the what, why, how, who, when and where of collecting sensitive and contentious information. For example, what is this information and why is it sensitive and contentious? How does one access such information sensibly, if indeed one should? And does what is deemed sensitive and contentious vary in time and space?

To answer these questions, in the context of development research, we need to attempt

a critical examination of cultural differences, review power dynamics, consider the sources of information and think about certain practices. These issues influence and impact on the work of the development researcher, are interrelated and connected to other strategic issues, such as ethics, researcher identity and gender relations. However, before focusing on some of these issues, a working definition of sensitive and contentious information is required.

Sensitive information is material that is delicate and could be personal, political, economic, social or cultural in nature. It can range from matters connected to national security, to personal emotions and feelings, to taboo topics which would not be shared with an outsider. Sensitive information could place the researched or researcher in a vulnerable position, and it could be used to manipulate people and possibly undermine authority. Contentious information implies that different people hold different views about a particular issue. This may result in a lack of agreement over what is right or wrong. For example, a person's views about race and sex can be quite contentious. It is possible that what is said by those being researched may conflict with the researcher's own views.

As researchers we should justify why we want to collect sensitive or contentious information, and consider how the information is to be analysed even before we attempt to collect it. Will the assemblage of highly sensitive, emotional or controversial information enhance and improve any research findings or merely sensationalize our work? In addition, how far should the researcher go to obtain information? A review of cultural differences, and in particular values and motives, is fundamental to the process of data retrieval and should help identify and clarify what may or may not be delicate and controversial material worthy of collection.

Cultural differences: values and motives

Development research must be culturally sensitive and researchers should attempt to understand the culture where they work and tease out any similarities and differences from their own. At the same time, researchers must be aware of the cultural baggage they bring with them to their work. Cultural baggage can be understood as ethnocentrism: cultural bias and believing that one's own culture and values are superior. It is essential not to judge those we study by our own values and standards (Scheyvens and Storey, 2003). It is particularly important that '[t]he researcher should be sensitive to the rights, beliefs and cultural context of the researched, as well as their position within patriarchal or colonial power relations' (Cloke et al., 2004: 165). Through the passage

of time, the relationship between the researcher and researched will most probably develop and deepen such that a sense of trust and mutual understanding is fostered. This will enable the researcher to discern what is important, delicate and controversial, and to appreciate how sensitive and contentious information can vary in different cultural settings.

Sensitivity to cultural differences is a principal ethical guideline in development research. Four other guidelines are equally important and relate to the research alliance between the researcher and researched. They are privacy, informed consent, harm and exploitation (Hammersley and Atkinson, 1995). As researchers, we should all endeavour to keep to these guidelines. Nevertheless, in the process of undertaking fieldwork and reflecting on it, we can re-evaluate our efforts at cultural sensitivity and may question whether our presence challenges or threatens the community we are studying. A researcher may recognize and realize that what started out as sensitive and appropriate action was actually quite the opposite. For example, Madge (1997) completed fieldwork in the Gambia in the early 1990s, but over time she realized the choices she had made and actions she had taken about her living arrangements and practices were insulting to the community – they set her apart and thus the development of a rapport with people was constrained by her own sense of privacy. Once she changed how she lived in the community she was treated differently. This example may seem slightly removed from the issue of collecting sensitive and contentious information, but if one considers how the research process can alter researcher actions, then researcher understanding of and access to sensitive and contentious information can be altered. If this occurs, the researcher may need to re-examine certain ethical guidelines, such as informed consent, harm and privacy.

Research motive is a difficult topic. What motivates the researcher to want to collect certain pieces of information and what motivates the researched to provide such information? A critical, reflexive analysis of the ethics and morals of undertaking research in the developing world should form an essential part of any research training (Hay and Foley, 1998). Questions about the extractive or parasitic nature of research in developing countries and whether researchers have any right to 'mine' these countries for information should be interrogated. The possession of research information has the potential to destabilize society. Ethical development research may result in the researcher realizing that there is a time and place when sensitive and contentious information should and should not be collected, and that there is no exact truth but partial truths or truths for specific moments in time or situations. The motives for giving information to the researcher may be based on the belief that the researcher is in a position to influence others for good or bad. This helps to explain why information may be given or withheld, and can be seen as part of the power dialectic in development research.

Position of power

A key issue for 'foreign' researchers, and by that I mean anyone who is not of the area or community under investigation, is that they are, by virtue of their work, education and background, in a position of power (Sidaway, 1992). However, as Scheyvens and Leslie (2000: 126) point out: 'The reality is that researchers rarely hold all of the power in the research process.' In fact those who live in developing countries should not be cast as powerless. As subjects of research they are in a powerful position. They can withhold information, supply partial information and possibly dictate the way any research is conducted. The power relationship between the researcher and researched can be seen as a

continuum and not as an either/or situation. Research is negotiated and may well display features of when either is 'in control'.

Consider an account of conducting research in the Solomon Islands and the use of language by the residents to control what information was given to the researcher:

[I]n the Solomon Islands, where there are approximately 70 local languages, Scheyvens (1995) typically used the lingua franca, pigin, to ask questions of groups of women. Women would then discuss their response in their own language, often for several minutes, before delivering back their 'official', often one line, answer in pigin. In such cases, it may be that the women actually felt some comfort that Scheyvens did not speak their language, as this allowed them to express themselves freely without their views being officially recorded. Then, if they wished, they could deliver a sanitised, or otherwise altered, version of their actual opinions. (Scheyvens and Leslie, 2000: 126)

In this example, the women of the Solomon Islands obviously felt in control of the situation. Sensitive and contentious information could be filtered out if necessary to protect themselves. This supports the view of Hoggart, Lees and Davies (2002: 193) that research 'information collected is not "fact" but a particular response to a specific social situation'. Through a position of power, the researcher could possibly ask inappropriate questions which respondents feel obliged to answer and thus obtain sensitive and contentious information. Gaining access to such information might make the researcher feel superior and reinforce his/her position of power. A guiding principle in development research is that the researcher should attempt to minimize or eliminate any sense of superiority.

As already illustrated, those who are researched can withhold information, refuse to answer questions or decide not to cooperate with the researcher. Or, as Fortuijn (1984) found, when undertaking fieldwork in Venezuela, while respondents were glad of the attention given to them and they were generally helpful, gaining access to high-level policy makers and bureaucrats was difficult. Respondents can tell you how it is, or what they think you want to hear, or what in their culture is socially correct and acceptable given the age, sex or status of the researcher with respect to the respondents. In the case of collecting information about family planning issues, respondents will vary their replies depending on who is asking the questions. Therefore, establishing what is credible and reliable information requires an element of judgement by the researcher. The researcher faces the dilemma of verifying responses, which should be undertaken with great care and with due regard for cultural differences. This may be particularly problematic if the information is sensitive and contentious. Through a process of cross-referencing and data triangulation information can usually be verified.

Sources of data and criticality

Sensitive and contentious information may come from both primary and secondary data sources. While interviews and questionnaires may appear to be the principal primary data collection method, other methods, such as personal and participant observation, may prove fruitful. The ethics of covert participant observation may challenge the researcher if, in the process of observation, particularly sexist, racist or reactionary material is uncovered which is contrary to the researcher's own morals and values.

With primary data collection there is a danger of privileging the words and stories of the researched, especially if respondents have become friends during fieldwork (Madge, 1997). They are giving information voluntarily; they are expressing their opinions

or perspectives on particular issues. In some societies, oral histories and memory may be the principal means of conveying information. Through the passage of time, sensitive and contentious issues may lose their notoriety and informants may be more amenable to discussing such issues, but memory recall, however good, may lead to exaggeration or bias. Pratt and Loizos (1992: 3) caution the researcher to remember that 'neither experts nor locals are always right, nor always wrong'. In some societies there exists a notion that only certain individuals are qualified to speak out in public (Scheyvens and Leslie, 2000). These individuals are the gatekeepers of information sources and it is vitally important that a researcher attempts to establish their political position in society.

When undertaking fieldwork, many researchers take photographs of people and places as part of their primary data collection method. Their photographs and images are used to show others what their research area is like and to support the written account of research findings. In some countries there are still restrictions on what objects may be photographed, and people have specific attitudes and ideas about what constitutes a suitable photograph. Robson (1997) discovered this to be the case when working in Nigeria and, as a result, her use of the camera altered over time. Inappropriate action by the researcher can lead to the production of sensitive visual information; or attempts to photograph a contentious issue, such as illegal commerce, can put the researcher in danger. Take the case of covert research. Routledge (2002) explains how his undercover work in Goa to obtain access to commercially sensitive information placed him at some personal risk. By adopting an activist approach in his research, he supported the views of one group of people in Goa and purposefully set about securing information from the opposition. Routledge (2002: 447) recognizes that through his work he entered the 'jungle of problematic ethical

65

and power relations'. He does question the value of the data he collected, and he considers that while taking sides he did so in a critical way.

Research that focuses on what is widely acknowledged as an illegal activity can increase the vulnerability of both the researcher and researched. Information on illegal activity will invariably be highly sensitive and the researcher needs to safeguard the security and confidentiality of any respondents. Equally important is the researcher's own safety, as well as any information he/she may collect. Illegal activity may include informal sector trading, poaching, trafficking in people, drugs and commodities, abortions and generally any activity that is contrary to the laws of the country being studied. Silberschmidt and Rasch (2001) outline how they gained access to adolescent girls in Dar es Salaam who had undergone an illegal abortion. Their work was conducted according to strict ethical guidelines: all adolescents gave verbal consent to participate in the study and anonymity and confidentiality were protected at all times.

Researchers are taught to be critical of secondary data sources: 'just because information which comes with an official seal of approval does not mean that researchers can take it simply at face value' (Cloke et al., 2004: 61). The researcher should ask why were the data collected, for what purpose and to what end? Issues of data ownership, authorship and authority must be reviewed. Bias exists in all information sources and in the case of contentious information extreme views and even misinformation may be presented. Learning how to analyse this information critically is an essential part of the research process. A researcher may know that data exists, for example confidential figures relating to economic sales, health records, or military spending, but access is denied. The challenge for the researcher is to identify alternative ways of obtaining similar information and, at the same time, acknowledge that there will always be restricted access to certain data sources. For example, in the late 1970s when undertaking research in Brazil[1] on inequality, I did not even attempt to access government health data at the level of the smallest census unit because officers of the census bureau who were my co-workers politely told me it would be impossible. In hindsight I could have challenged their suppositions and attempted to obtain the data but, as a raw postgraduate, I was eager to fit in, not put myself in any danger or abuse my position.

Practical considerations

There are a number of practical matters that need to be reviewed when aiming to collect sensitive and contentious information. The following are just some of the personal qualities a researcher may require at different points in time when working in the field: patience, persistence, tolerance, confidence, commitment, honesty, humility, trust, discernment, an open mind, diplomacy, and an acceptance that some questions may never get answered. A flexible research methodology should allow you to get closer to your chosen topic and have questions answered, but ultimately you need to be a realist. You have to recognize that however long you stay in the field, you will only ever have a partial knowledge of the situation.

The researcher needs to consider and evaluate his/her language and behaviour when in the field, and appreciate the socio-cultural context. For example, the age of the interviewer can be crucial. In some countries interviewees younger than the interviewer will give positive answers because it is considered rude to offer a negative answer to someone senior. In other cultures, such as the Buid in the Philippines, respondents will avoid giving direct answers. All this can make for challenging circumstances when trying to collect information.

Vital to the researcher is the personal quality of discernment, knowing when to ask probing questions and recognizing that what an interviewee tells you in confidence is for your ears only. This of course leads on to what the researcher does with confidential material once it has been acquired. For example, a high-ranking official may permit access to personal medical records but in the process of analysing the data the researcher detects some irregularities, such as a high incidence of death in children in certain districts. Disclosure may be politically dangerous and jeopardize the research. However, does the researcher have a moral duty to tell the official? Injudicious use of confidential information can be harmful to a person, a family or household or the community. A researcher also needs to adopt a measured approach to all that he/she does; he/she should avoid being overly emotional or aloof when asking interviewees to 'open up' and share sensitive and contentious information. Sollis and Moser (1991) have recognized that women researchers are better at obtaining sensitive information about and from other women. From my own research in Mexico about the role of female health workers in public health, I have found that women willingly, and at times eagerly, replied to my questions. They have 'opened up' and allowed me into their lives in ways I would not have imagined, and this has caused me to reflect on my own position and role in research (Harrison, 2000). Scheyvens and Leslie (2000: 124) consider that 'restricted access to certain domains should certainly not deter men from engaging in sensitive research projects in which consulting women on their ideas, knowledge and experiences is vital'. Nonetheless, it is probably true that male and female researchers will gain access to different worlds.

Another practical consideration is what contacts the researcher has in the country. These contacts may enable the researcher to collect sensitive or contentious information. The Western researcher may find him/herself living and operating near the top of the social hierarchy (Sidaway, 1992), and may have relatively easy access to politicians, ministers, industrialists and other influential people. As a result, they may provide access to a wealth and wide range of data sources. A researcher may find it useful to take stock and review his/her relationship with informants and authorities, remembering that not all will have equal access to research reports and findings. This should cause the researcher to think through how any sensitive or contentious information is used. All research is political and has the power to change people's lives. The researcher who sensationalizes research by dipping in and out of people's lives and providing 'juicy' stories does more harm than good and is not respected.

Concluding thoughts

If as part of the complex research process we do endeavour to collect sensitive and contentious information, we need to be absolutely certain why we are undertaking such work. Do we collect such data for the purpose of verification of other information, or to attempt some form of balance, avoidance of bias and representation of our complex but 'ordinary' real world? In our quest for such information do we push at the boundaries of conventional research practice, and do we challenge existing structures? Whatever the researcher is doing, Scheyvens and Leslie (2000) stress that, in the process of development research, the researcher should be politically aware of and sensitive to the context and topic in question.

If collecting sensitive and contentious information is problematic, so too is how it is interpreted. How one gives the voiceless a voice, given the nature of the information, is challenging. Through analysis of the information, one tries to identify what lies behind the data. As researchers we attempt to uncover the social, economic, cultural and political relationships in any situation. We appreciate that there may be ambiguities in the information, but the key task is knowing how to validate and analyse any information. Researchers should be aware of their responsibilities to the researched, and have cognizance of their position in the research process as either an insider or outsider.

Finally, we need to remind ourselves that in social science development research we are dealing with people. We must be culturally sensitive, go carefully, and continually reflect and review our actions. We should be self-critical, reflexive, accountable and avoid romanticizing developing countries. In our global world the research process should be a two-way one – we should learn how to give as much as we gain from those with whom we work. We should give ourselves time to hear and see what people are saying. I am reminded of what someone said after visiting southern Africa. She saw lots of young people and thought everything was vibrant and optimistic. What she did not see was what went on behind closed doors where many people were dying from AIDS and AIDS-related illnesses. She did not see the pain, suffering and sorrow of people – these are sensitive and contentious issues.

Note

1. Brazil in the 1970s was still officially a dictatorship, and democracy was re-established there only in the 1980s.

QUESTIONS FOR DISCUSSION

1. How might a definition of sensitive and contentious information change through time and in different places?
2. What are the principal guidelines in development research which relate specifically to the collection of sensitive and contentious information?
3. Why is an understanding of power relationships essential to a researcher when collecting sensitive data?
4. What are the 'acceptable' risks a researcher can take to obtain sensitive and contentious data?
5. Which personal qualities are particularly important when attempting to obtain sensitive and contentious information? And why?

Further reading

Cloke, P., Cook, I., Crang, P., Goodwin, M., Painter, J. and Philo, C. (2004) *Practising Human Geography*, London: Sage.

O'Leary, Z. (2004) *The Essential Guide to Doing Research*, London: Sage.

Pratt, B. and Loizos, P. (1992) *Choosing Research Methods: Data Collection for Development Workers,* Oxfam Development Guidelines No. 7, Oxford: Oxfam.

Scheyvens, R. and Storey, D. (eds) (2003) *Development Fieldwork: A Practical Guide*, London: Sage.

References

Cloke, P., Cook, I., Crang, P., Goodwin, M., Painter, J. and Philo, C. (2004) *Practising Human Geography*. London: Sage.

Fortuijn, E.D. (1984) The failure of ethics in practice: cultural and institutional barriers of research project in Venzuela, *Institute of Development Studies*, 15(4): 59–69.

Hammersley, M. and Atkinson, P. (1995) *Ethnography: Principles in Practice,* 2nd edn, London: Routledge.

Harrison, M.E. (2000) Identity and experience: a study of selected female physicians in five provincial states of Mexico, *Salud Pública de México*, 42(3): 208–216.

Hay, I. and Foley, P. (1998) Ethics, geography and responsible citizenship, *Journal of Geography in Higher Education*, 22(2): 169–183.

Hoggart, K., Lees, L. and Davies, A. (2002) *Researching Human Geography*. London: Arnold.

Madge, C. (1997) Ethics of research in the Third World, in E. Robson and K. Willis (eds), *Postgraduate Fieldwork in Developing Areas: A Rough Guide*, 2nd edn, Developing Areas Research Group, Monograph No. 9, London: Royal Geographical Society and the Institute of British Geographers. pp. 113–124.

Pratt, B. and Loizos, P. (1992) *Choosing Research Methods: Data Collection for Development Workers*. Oxfam Development Guidelines No. 7, Oxford: Oxfam.

Robson, E. (1997) From teacher to taxi driver: reflections on research roles in developing areas, in E. Robson and K. Willis (eds), *Postgraduate Fieldwork in Developing Areas: A Rough Guide*, 2nd edn, Developing Areas Research Group, Monograph No. 9, London: Royal Geographical Society and the Institute of British Geographers. pp. 51–74.

Routledge, P. (2002) Travelling east as Walter Kurtz: identity, performance and collaboration in Goa, India, *Environment and Planning D: Society and Space*, 20: 477–498.

Scheyvens, R. (1995) A quiet revolution: strategies for the empowerment and development of rural women in the Solomon Islands. PhD Thesis, Massey University, Palmerston North.

Scheyvens, R. and Leslie, H. (2000) Gender, ethics and empowerment: dilemmas of development fieldwork, *Women's Studies International Forum*, 23(1): 119–130.

Scheyvens, R. and Storey, D. (eds) (2003) *Development Fieldwork: A Practical Guide*, London: Sage.

Sidaway, J.D. (1992) In other worlds: on the politics of research by 'First World' geographers in the 'Third World', *Area,* 24(4): 403–408.

Silberschmidt, M. and Rasch, V. (2001) Adolescent girls, illegal abortions and 'sugar-daddies' in Dar es Salaam: vulnerable victims and active social agents, *Social Science and Medicine*, 52(12): 1815–1826.

Sollis, P. and Moser, C. (1991) A methodological framework for analysing the social costs of adjustment at the micro-level: the case of Guayaquil, Ecuador, *IDS Bulletin*, 22(1): 23–30.

8

Dealing with Conflicts and Emergency Situations

Morten Bøås, Kathleen M. Jennings and Timothy M. Shaw

How can development research be made conflict-sensitive? ••• Understanding
conflict situations and economies ••• Developing a human security
agenda for conflict zones ••• The coping strategy approach ••• Ethics for
development research and work in conflict and emergency situations

The post-Cold War world continues to experience a multitude of conflicts. These 'new' conflicts – a misleading label, as most have either been ongoing or are rooted in events that precede the collapse of the Cold War system – are often labelled intrastate wars. This, too, is misleading, for while many of the conflicts begin locally, they increasingly spread nationally and regionally, thus multiplying their direct and secondary effects and exposing the limitations of national governments and the international community in mitigating or resolving them (see Mychajlyszyn and Shaw, 2005; Shaw, 2003).

Yet despite the prevalence and endurance of these complex conflicts and emergencies, almost no one has recognized and confronted the myriad issues that arise around whether, when, and how to undertake development research in such situations.[1] Crucial questions must be asked and answered: What methodology(-ies) are most efficient in conflict situations,

and how can insights from other disciplines, such as security studies or public health, be used effectively? How can development research be made more conflict-sensitive, so as to ensure that the work does not exacerbate or undermine a vulnerable situation by, for example, empowering select people with resources and/or authority? How should development workers interact with other actors in the field, both local citizens and other national and international actors from different sectors, especially given the multiplicity of actors and mandates in post-conflict areas, as evidenced by the sign leading into the Wilson Internally Displaced Persons (IDP) camp in Liberia (see Figure 8.1)?. And how can development research be done safely and ethically in a conflict or unstable post-conflict zone? These questions matter because development and security are no longer mutually exclusive zones – if ever they were – but are, in practice, becoming gradually more interconnected and interwoven.

Figure 8.1 The sign leading in to the Wilson IDP Camp, outside of Monrovia on the road towards Klay Junction, Liberia, January 2004
Photo: Morten Bøås

The standard approach to the provision of development assistance to countries in conflict used to focus solely on humanitarian assistance and emergency relief. Governments, aid agencies and donor institutions took the view that assistance could save lives but not improve livelihoods in zones of ongoing conflict: a developmental approach has been seen as a waste of resources. This response makes sense if conflicts end quickly. However, many current conflicts are characterized by their longevity: certain zones of conflict face seemingly chronic instability and insecurity.[2] Reflecting this reality, the view that development work should not be attempted in conflict areas seems to be changing – to the benefit of vulnerable populations, but to the increasing complexity and, perhaps, danger of development workers.

A much greater level of interaction, co-operation, and collaboration is also now coalescing between development and security. The increasing intertwining is known as the security–development nexus and constitutes a major element of security sector reform, an undertaking of particular importance to OECD donors.[3] Both on the ground and in national and international bureaucracies, security and development are becoming more inclusive, if not fully integrated.

It is clear, therefore, that for the sake of their work's quality, rigour and effectiveness, development researchers and workers must familiarize themselves with the characteristics of the conflicts in which they may be working, and adapt their assumptions, hypotheses and research methods accordingly. Doing so will improve the quality of development research and work through the formulation of more conflict-sensitive methodologies; enable a better understanding of the unconventional elements of complex emergencies and conflicts; improve researchers' ability to ensure their own safety in the field; and facilitate practical connections and the formulation of best practices between the development sector and other actors, particularly security.

This chapter will begin by outlining some common characteristics of complex conflicts and the basics of the human security agenda, which takes a ground-up, human-centric approach rather than the top-down, state-focused method favoured by traditional security studies. It will then introduce conflict-sensitive methodology(-ies) that can be applied in conflict or vulnerable post-conflict areas. Finally, there is a section with practical advice on ethics and safety for researchers and workers in conflict and unstable post-conflict zones, in which we emphasize that all work in conflict zones should be conducted in accordance with the principle of 'do no harm'. People living in these situations are already vulnerable; they do not need researchers to make their lives even more complicated and dangerous.

Complex conflicts and the human security agenda

Current conflicts tend to originate as localized, intrastate conflicts. With a few notable exceptions, conflicts are now fought primarily between forces *within* a state. At the same time, however, the effects of conflict are increasingly dispersed, affecting citizens in neighbouring countries even if the governments of those states are not at war. Particularly in areas with porous or arbitrary borders, it is no surprise that conflicts spill over, either through direct combat or through indirect conflict effects such as refugee flows.

These secondary effects of conflict are exacerbated by other disturbing aspects of complex conflicts, such as the use of child soldiers and forced conscription, the widespread or wholesale criminalization of economic life – including the trafficking of humans, drugs and arms – and, in some conflicts, prevalent sexual assault and the spread of HIV through the civilian population. The impact of complex conflicts therefore tends to differentiate little between combatants and civilians, or even between children and adults, as glimpsed in the accompanying photo of a Liberian youth (see Figure 8.2).

Two of the major factors in the causation and continuation of complex conflicts are the role of resources – particularly natural resource extraction and trade – and the changing nature of government and the state. These factors are connected.

The potentially destructive role of natural resources and illicit economic activity in sparking or sustaining conflicts has been brought to the fore by the 'greed versus grievance' debate. The greed faction's argument, in its simplest form, is that the initiation and/or continuation of war and violence is the consequence of a struggle to control natural resources and trade networks (Berdal and Malone, 2000); in this view, the grievances typically ascribed to non-state armed groups are secondary, and may in fact be little more than rhetoric used to justify conflict or for the purposes of recruitment and fundraising (Collier, 2000). Although essentially reductionist, the argument has nevertheless performed an important task, highlighting the fact that natural resource exploitation can provide combatants with the incentives and ability to sustain conflict, even if economic factors were not determinative to the conflict's outbreak.

Conflict economies can be seen as alternative networked economic systems depending for profitability on the informalization of the state and its structures. This brings us to a second major factor in current conflicts, the changing nature – in particular, the recession – of government and the state. Recession of the state describes a situation in which governments exercise marginal control over many parts of society, but exert predatory control over resources. Citizens in turn are marginalized by the lack of resources and opportunity

Figure 8.2   The spread of disease is an often-encountered secondary effect of war. Women and children are especially vulnerable. This picture depicts a polio-stricken boy in Rick's Institute IDP Camp, outside of Monrovia on the road towards Klay Junction, Liberia, January 2004
Photo: Morten Bøås

provided by the recessive state. Nevertheless, political authority (as represented by government) is coveted, as it represents one of the few avenues of resource accumulation, even though most decisions about distribution and redistribution actually take place outside and in between official state structures (Reno, 1998). In short, many new and ongoing conflicts erupt in states where power relations are characterized by a small, dominant elite, sustained by informal power and resource networks, presiding over a large, poor, often youthful, disenfranchised and marginalized majority (Bøås, 2004a).

The field of security studies is increasingly evolving to reflect the fact that state-centric approaches useful during the Cold War era are not helpful in navigating an increasingly fragmented and incoherent world. This scholarship – commonly referred to as critical security studies – sees the state as increasingly challenged from above by global economic, cultural, religious and environmental dynamics, and from below by ethnic and religious fragmentations. On another level, it also challenges the belief that insecurities occur naturally. To this end, recent work has focused on the social construction of security and the cultural production of threats, danger and security crises. Human security has also been instrumental in challenging the centrality of the state in security discussions by focusing on other referents, such as individuals, households and livelihoods (Hentz and Bøås, 2003).

An important strand of the human security agenda is dedicated to examining the lived realities and unique sociality of conflict zones. We have argued elsewhere that focusing only on conflict's destructive capacity, while obviously immense, does not capture the entire reality: conflict zones represent not only the disruption and destruction of previous or existing social systems, but also the creation of new systems (Bøås, 2003). This argument essentially inverts the normal modes of thinking around the societal impacts of conflict, which tend to focus on social breakdown while ignoring the reality that the conflict zone is also a site for innovation that can reorder the social, economic and political life for individuals and households (Bøås, 2004b). Conceptualizing security in this way requires that research focus on understanding agency and the means by which agents reproduce themselves and the structures (constraints and opportunities) in which they live; and places debates about state and non-state actors – providers of security or insecurity – in the context of lived social realities. This conceptualization of conflict zones as social space is key to understanding how people and societies adapt in vulnerable situations, and underpins a conflict-sensitive methodology based upon coping strategies.

A conflict-sensitive methodology: the coping strategies approach

Because violence, insecurity and conflict occur in a specific context that predicates and shapes the way people living in those situations cope and make decisions, development researchers operating in countries in conflict must understand the local context and coping strategies in order to design and implement their study effectively. In other words, they must proceed on the basis of a sympathetic consideration and assessment of the totality of the available coping strategies that shape and contextualize people's choices and behaviour. Without an understanding of why and how people and communities in conflict zones choose and act as they do, research will at best be disconnected and incomplete, and at worst wilfully ignorant and potentially harmful.

The coping strategy approach essentially describes a method of investigating the conflict zone as inhabited and understood by individuals, households and communities. It captures the reality that security is elusive, and that what is security for one individual may be insecurity for another. As noted above, it starts from the assumption that people have agency. Thus, local communities and individuals living in zones of prolonged conflict don't just passively accept their lot; rather, they actively engage in the creation of new social systems and modes of behaviour and adaptation in their efforts to develop ways to cope with their environment. These purposeful ways of acting – 'coping strategies' – help them survive and endure, if not overcome, the direct and secondary effects of conflict.

Coping strategies

The ways in which people define and design their coping strategies are determined by both pragmatic concerns – like the level of available human and financial resources and skills and the strength of local social networks – and subjective considerations, such as how people interpret their contextual surroundings and previous experiences. Analytical work has shown that people's coping strategies can be diverse and durable, yet adaptive (see, for example, Pedersen and Sletten, 2003). The following framework for examining coping strategies focuses on actors and the relationship between actors in various networks. It consists of a set of states, effects and events, how these may be influenced by coping strategies, and how coping strategies, in turn, may be influenced by the overall social context and policies towards regions, communities or households.[4]

The first state considered is that of 'risk exposure'. This entails, for example, living in an area exposed to cattle raiding or an area of rebel activity. Households have a number of coping strategies that may change risk exposure, such as moving away from insecure areas. Government policies, such as increased security presence, may also influence a household's exposure to risk. Four important research questions are associated with the issue of risk exposure: (1) the types of risk faced; (2) the distribution of risks between households; (3) the strategies households use to reduce risk; and (4) the influence on risk by policies at the local, regional or national levels.

The second state is that of 'vulnerability'. The vulnerability of a household or individual can be seen as the potential effect an unfortunate event may have. This varies between households depending on their resources, the insurance they have, and to what extent they depend on a single resource that may be destroyed by the event. For example, a household that experiences the death of the male breadwinner may be thrown into destitution if the surviving spouse cannot work, but a single-parent household where the breadwinner is killed is much worse off. The research questions pertaining to vulnerability are: How do households differ in vulnerability? What and how many resources do households depend on? How are households insured against mishaps, either on an individual or collective basis? And how do local-, regional- and national-level policies affect vulnerability?

The third state captured by the framework is the actual shock: the occurrence of a harmful event. In a conflict, the entire situation may be conceived as a shock. Nevertheless, it is crucial to keep in mind that households have different experiences. Therefore, a key research question is the distribution of shocks across households.

The outcome, in terms of actual lived security for households and individuals, is the result of the above-mentioned factors of risk exposure, vulnerability and shock. There then comes the question of how households adapt to the shock after it has occurred, which may also depend on policy responses to the shock (such as emergency aid or food-for-work

programmes). The important research questions pertaining to outcomes are: what are the outcomes in terms of indicators related to security, including health, nutrition and displacement? What adaptations do households have? And what types of policy response exist at the various levels of governance?

A key dimension in this framework is therefore that it allows for the analysis of both household and individual adaptations and strategies, and the institutional framework allowing for risk mitigation, 'insurance' or coping. The framework is also amenable to the integration of perspectives from other disciplines, such as public health or psychology, in dealing with the unconventional challenges that arise from, for example, the use of child soldiers.

Finally, in applying this methodology development actors must be mindful of the maxim 'Do no harm'. This is particularly important in conflict or vulnerable post-conflict areas, where struggles over resources, power and identity are even more contested than elsewhere. By virtue of whom they choose to work with and listen to, development actors are privileging certain experiences and narratives at the expense of others, an exercise that may have innocuous intent but serious and unintended repercussions. Development researchers must be aware of and plan for this contingency because, as discussed below, the first priority of any development actor must be to do no harm.

Ethics and safety

The basic rule for doing research in a conflict situation is 'do no harm'. This should be self-evident, but unfortunately it is easy to bend or even break this rule in conflict situations. Although it may be easy to justify breaking this rule due to the importance of the research, we must constantly remind ourselves of the obligation to protect our informants. We can leave, they cannot. This means that in certain situations we may, in fact, have to protect our informants by choosing not to utilize some of the material we have obtained from them.

The same obligation to protect exists with regard to field assistants and other people who provide service or assistance. When we pay for services or give other kinds of favour in return for services, we must be cognizant that it may be hard for people to say no to requests that we make, even if they believe that doing so may put them at risk. Lacking a comprehensive understanding of the situation, a researcher may unintentionally push people into situations that can place them in danger. This can happen no matter how prepared and knowledgeable we are, but clearly it is a greater danger for those not fully informed. This is a moral dilemma that people who work in these kinds of situation must find a way to live with. However, trust and a sense of humility will make it easier for field assistants and others to tell you if you are asking them to do something they would otherwise not do, because it may expose them to a higher level of risk than they normally would be prepared to accept.

Concerning personal safety, the first rule is to know your field, but simultaneously accept that other people may have better information. Talk to ordinary people, not just officials in national and international bureaucracies in capitals. The broader the spectrum of people you receive information from, the better estimates you can make about the security situation. The second rule is simple: if you feel uncomfortable in a certain situation, leave. There is no point in pushing beyond your limits. People are willing to accept different levels of risk, and even if another researcher finds the security situation to be acceptable, it may not be so to you. In that case, you should leave that particular area. If you are constantly afraid, you are not likely to do good field research and, by being afraid, you may end up making decisions that break the 'do no harm' maxim. Even if you are working in a team, do not be afraid to tell your colleagues that the security situation is

unacceptable to you. Securing your safety is brave and responsible; trying to cope with what you cannot cope with is not.

Related to these two issues is the question of how to deal and/or work with security and military actors, such as peacekeeping forces or coalition forces, national armed forces, and even militia forces. This is an important issue for several reasons: security actors are obviously prevalent in conflict zones; they constitute one of the most potentially problematic relationships for development researchers and workers; and the evolving security–development nexus entails that more interaction will occur between these two sectors. The push for integrated missions – exemplified by the UN Mission in Liberia, the first UN mission to be fully integrated in its humanitarian, political, development and security aspects from the start – demonstrates the increasing importance of the development–security relationship.

It is important to realize that these two arenas have different objectives and methods that never will fully meet, even if greater integration is achieved. There may be both pros and cons of working with security actors: on one hand, tapping into potentially greater access and resources versus, on the other, possibly compromising your role and therefore both scaring people off and increasing risk exposure. We do not believe this to be a nexus in which integration should be sought at all cost. Rather, it is important for development researchers to retain principles of transparency and accountability to people from all segments of society, and the distinctiveness of the role of development actor. This means that, in some cases, the right thing to do is to say 'no' to security actors, even if they could help facilitate access to a certain field and/or guarantee your security while doing fieldwork. The pitfalls are as many here as in the two other issues discussed above. Again, the main guideline in dealing with security actors is to preserve our integrity by constantly adhering to the principle of 'do no harm'.

Conclusion

Given the complexities of conflict situations, it is imperative that we rethink established 'disciplinary' approaches and recognize that the number of actors and issues challenge comfortable positions developed in the ivory tower of academia. These present profound methodological challenges and problems of research that cannot be solved by any single discipline or methodology. In such an environment, research methods must be plural, pragmatic, and conducted with empathy towards people on the ground – characteristic of the ground-up, human-centric approach focusing on coping strategies. Such a method is conflict-sensitive and allows for the analysis of both households and individual adaptations, while the framework allows for integration from a wide range of perspectives to deal in a pragmatic manner with the unconventional challenges that arise from work in conflict and emergency situations.

Notes

1. One of the very few exceptions is Carolyn Nordstrom and Antonius Robben's collection from 1995, *Fieldwork under Fire*.
2. For example, Central Africa and the Great Lakes Region, West Africa, the Middle East (e.g. Palestine/Israel), Afghanistan and the Ferghana Valley in Central Asia, and the Andean Region in Latin America. While the number of armed conflicts has dropped since the early 1990s, of those that continue 66 per cent were more than five years old in 1999 and 30 per cent were more than 20 years old. In addition, many conflicts that were suspended in the 1990s – not least in Europe, the Middle East and Central Asia – have not been resolved (see Smith, 2001).
3. On the security–development nexus, see for example Hurwitz and Peake (2004); on security sector reform, see OECD (2004).
4. The following framework is an adapted version of the framework suggested by the World Bank (2000).

77

QUESTIONS FOR DISCUSSION

1. Identify concrete conflict and emergency situations and discuss the relationship between security and development.
2. How can research and development work be conducted in a conflict-sensitive manner?
3. Why is it important to give agency to those who live in conflict zones?
4. How can one in a practical manner operationalize 'risk exposure'? Discuss possible implications both for yourself as a researcher/development worker and for those who permanently live in a conflict situation.
5. How would you prepare for work in a conflict or emergency situation?

Further reading

Nordstrom, Carolyn and Robben, Antonius C.G.M. (eds) (1995) *Fieldwork under Fire: Contemporary Studies of Violence and Survival*, Berkeley: University of California Press.

Richards, Paul (1996) *Fighting for the Rain Forest: War, Youth and Resources in Sierra Leone*, Oxford: James Currey.

Weissman, Fabrice (ed.) (2004) *In the Shadow of 'Just Wars': Violence, Politics and Humanitarian Action*, London: Hurst & Company.

References

Berdal, Mats and Malone, David M. (eds) (2000) *Greed and Grievance: Economic Agendas in Civil War*, Boulder, CO: Lynne Rienner.

Bøås, Morten (2003) Conclusion: the task is always to revise, in James J. Hentz and Morten Bøås (eds), *New and Critical Security and Regionalism: Beyond the Nation State*, Aldershot: Ashgate, pp. 203–212.

Bøås, Morten (2004a) Africa's young guerrillas: rebels with a cause? *Current History*, 103(673): 211–214.

Bøås, Morten (2004b) Uganda in the regional war zone: meta-narratives, pasts and presents, *Journal of Contemporary African Studies*, 22 (3): 283–303.

Collier, Paul (2000) Doing well out of war: an economic perspective, in Mats Berdal and David M. Malone (eds), *Greed and Grievance: Economic Agendas in Civil War*, Boulder, CO: Lynne Rienner, pp. 91–111.

Hentz, James J. and Bøås, Morten (eds) (2003) *New and Critical Security and Regionalism: Beyond the Nation State*, Aldershot: Ashgate.

Hurwitz, Agnés and Peake, Gordon (2004) *Strengthening the Security – Development Nexus: Assessing International Policy and Practice since the 1990s*, New York: International Peace Academy.

Mychajlyszyn, Natalie and Shaw, Timothy M. (eds) (2005). *Twisting Arms and Flexing Muscles: Humanitarian Intervention and Peacebuilding in Perspective*, Aldershot: Ashgate.

Nordstrom, Carolyn and Robben, Antonius C.G.M. (eds) (1995) *Fieldwork under Fire: Contemporary Studies of Violence and Survival*, Berkeley: University of California Press.

OECD (2004) *Security System Reform and Governance: Policy and Good Practice*, Paris: OECD (DAC Guidelines and Reference Series).

Pedersen, Jon and Sletten, Pål (2003) *Coping with Conflict: Palestinian Communities Two Years into the Intifada*, Oslo: Fafo.

Reno, William (1998) *Warlord Politics and African States*, Boulder, CO: Lynne Rienner.

Shaw, Timothy M. (2003) Regional dimensions of conflict and peacebuilding in contemporary Africa, *Journal of International Development*, 15 (4): 487–498.

Smith, Dan (2001) *Trends and Causes of Armed Conflict*, Berlin: Berghof.

World Bank (2000) *World Development Report 2000/2001: Attacking Poverty*, New York: Oxford University Press.

9

Working with Partners: Educational Institutions

Bill Gould

The importance of schools and schooling • Practicalities: administrative formalities, accommodation, acculturation • Schools as a source for community-based studies: key informants and sampling frames • Schools as mirrors of 'development': sites of nation-building and resistance • Schools for education research: teaching and learning, and pupils' questionnaires • School-based partnerships: identity and positionality

Since formal education assumes very great importance in the aspirations of the mass of people in developing countries, formal educational institutions – schools, colleges, universities – are very prominent features of the physical and cultural landscape. In most states schooling is a primary means of individual social mobility and economic achievement, a widely accepted filter for economic and social advance. Education systems in developing countries are therefore major items of public and, increasingly with 'cost recovery' components in structural adjustment programmes, of private finance (i.e. higher user fees). They therefore command enormous political attention at all scales, from the national parliament to the local bar or marketplace. Each educational 'institution', from the local *madrasa* (Islamic religious class) up to the premier national university, has its own rules

and objectives (set within the educational system), staff (the teachers), clients (the learners). The wider civil society will have its own expectations of schools, in terms of learning outcomes and exam results, and also in their broader contributions to society and economy.

Educational institutions therefore have the very obvious potential to be a highly appropriate and convenient physical and social focus for 'doing development research'. Some of these reasons are highly practical; others are more related to what the schools are or are seen to be as agencies to promote development, how they work, and what they seek to achieve; others are more directly focused on the education and schooling that is provided, the immediate objectives of the schools. This discussion will consider all three of these – the practical, the developmental, and the educational – and will illustrate how development researchers can take advantage of what educational institutions can offer them, developing partnerships to mutual advantage, and will identify some of the potential dangers on the way.

Some formalities and practicalities: accommodation and acculturation

Foreign researchers in any country will normally be required to develop official contacts, characteristically in establishing a link with a local university, often coupled with any research permission granted through government. In some countries, establishing a formal link with a partner institution of higher education or a research institute is a condition of having that research permission. This should be seen not merely as an administrative inconvenience, with a financial cost – often of hundreds of dollars – to be paid to the university in question, but as a positive opportunity to enter into the culture and context of academic scholarship and concerns in the host country.

Among other benefits, formal affiliation entitles researchers to use local libraries. In most universities in the South, the general book and journal stocks are well below those expected even in small colleges in Northern countries, for largely financial reasons, but their major attraction to researchers is often in their specialist national materials, often unavailable elsewhere. These include theses and dissertations written by local students for undergraduate dissertations and for postgraduate degrees, and these can be a major source of background – and even foreground – material for beginning new work in an unfamiliar geographical region. Formal affiliation will also allow the researcher to make contacts with a wide range of staff and students, many of whom can become key academic informants and collaborators.

Participating in the broader culture of a host university – meeting other researchers, having a beer in the staff club in the evening, sharing an informal lunch or snack during the day, living in a student hall of residence or a guest flat on campus (most universities in the South are campus universities) – is important for much development research. Through such activities, just being there, foreign researchers will absorb a great deal of a general nature on life and livelihoods, on attitudes and politics in its broadest sense, and very quickly.

However, this must not be taken as one-way traffic. Researchers will be expected to share knowledge and ideas with local colleagues, and will certainly benefit enormously from this interaction. Giving a public seminar in a host department early in a research visit is a classic way of making valuable – perhaps unexpected – contacts. Any visitor should go prepared to say 'yes' to being immediately asked on arrival to give a seminar! My own experience in several university campuses in Africa, South Asia and the Caribbean is of a generous welcome from staff and students, and a genuine concern to share experiences and jointly develop knowledge and ideas.

However, universities are very specialist educational institutions. More generally, other educational institutions can provide important practical assistance to the researcher, and not only to a foreign researcher. Furthermore, the poorer the country, the more likely it is that a field researcher will look to a school or college in the field area for a range of practical supports. The most obvious of these will be accommodation. Fieldwork, especially in rural areas in economically marginalized regions with poor populations, and therefore intrinsically attractive to researchers, can present serious problems in finding secure and comfortable accommodation within easy access to a field area for an extended period of time. Since schools are widespread, even among poor populations, and teacher or other housing is often provided for staff (many teachers in poor regions will typically not be from the local area), many researchers have found it convenient to seek accommodation with teachers and sharing the costs, or in accommodation arranged through the teachers.

Developing good social and practical relationships with teachers is a familiar and very effective strategy for immediately 'finding your feet'. Teachers are relatively well educated and will be fluent in the national language, the language of instruction in the schools, even if it is not their own first language. This should normally be the working language of the researcher: the colonial European languages (English, French, Spanish or Portuguese) in the majority of countries in the South, but Arabic in Middle Eastern countries, Bahasa in Malaysia and Indonesia, Swahili in Tanzania, etc. Living and daily interacting with teachers would be a particular learning benefit to researchers where fluency in these national languages needs to be acquired.

These practical advantages of being identified in the community with the daily lives of teachers will be matched by social and cultural advantages (Robson, 1994). The researcher will be more likely to be accepted socially as well as professionally, and to be exposed to a wider range of experiences from which broad background and contextual material, as well as individual cases, can be used in the research. Through the teachers, the researcher will seek to be able to make and extend a network of local contacts, including local 'big men' or leaders of public opinion and gatekeepers for access to sources of information.

But there needs to be a note of caution here. The ease with which integration into the lifestyles and daily activities of teachers can facilitate any research activity in developing countries can in a few cases prove counterproductive. Such a case might be where teachers are themselves held in some suspicion and/or contempt by the local community. This may be because they themselves are seen as 'outsiders', at least socially if not

ethnically, in a context where there may be some local antipathy to education and schooling or the institutions of the state in general. Teachers in these circumstances may be seen to be the agents of an unpopular government imposing an unwelcome schools system, and with it a new and unfamiliar set of values (e.g. with respect to girls' education). It may also be because the teachers, though usually poorly paid in national terms, and certainly in international terms, can be among the most affluent in very poor communities, with patterns of expenditure and relations with local people that do not encourage their being easily accepted as part of that local community.

Generally, however, becoming socially integrated within the daily life of a school or college greatly facilitates progress along any learning curve in a new research context. Teachers may have a 'bad press' in many countries – lazy, unprofessional, prone to absenteeism, abusing children in their charge – and sometimes with some justification. However, these normally represent the minority. Most teachers are professional in their attitudes to colleagues and children, aware of the broader contexts in which they work, and thus helpful sources for researchers.

Schools as a source for community-based studies

There are two particular respects in which schools and colleges can be used by researchers for local community-based studies: (1) as a forum to identify key informants about the community; and (2) as a basis for deriving a sample for further study of some aspects of its development.

Schools are usually seen by the communities themselves to be important to them, and key figures in the community – government officials, leading businessmen or women, traditional 'big men' such as tribal elders – are often involved in the life of the school. This

81

may be through involvement in parent/ teacher associations, or in fundraising groups, or in work parties, and so being part of the school life can facilitate access for a researcher to such local leaders on a formal 'key-respondents' basis or, less formally, in more general conversations about the community. The school as a key feature of civil society offers the opportunity for the researcher to be exposed to perspectives on the community by its 'movers and shakers', well beyond the narrow bounds of the educational objectives and efforts of the school. Within the school itself, the leadership role of a head teacher may well extend beyond the school. Teachers, and particularly head teachers, are typically figures of respect and authority, but also often of insight into the social and economic processes that make the community what it is. They will usually be able to identify to the researcher key individuals and sources of information or alternative views, as well as themselves being key in-formants for the researcher.

One of the classic technical problems for the field researcher working at the community scale is having a systematic baseline and population or household universe for deriving a community sample. House lists or electoral rolls may be available that can be used as a base population for individual or household sampling. In other contexts, however, such civil universal databases may not exist, or for some reason be incomplete or inaccessible to the researcher. In these circumstances the school population, directly or, more conveniently, through the school register, can provide a valuable alternative basis for fairly representative household sampling.

School registers tend to be carefully kept and are normally fairly up to date, identifying the names of those enrolled by grade so that they are easily traced to their homes locally. In some cases these registers may even be available for earlier years, archived in the school. Registers can be most effectively used as a sampling frame where there are high

enrolment rates, and thus almost all eligible households can be identified. Where there are high rates of drop-out from the schools system, a register of the earliest grade will clearly be more likely to be representative of the whole community, given that incidence of drop-out, especially at primary school level, tends to be strongly associated with household socio-economic status. Schooling can quickly become a key basis for social and economic exclusion in countries where schooling is neither universal nor compulsory, and where any legal compulsion is not enforced. With these provisos, a school register-based sample can be broadly representative of the whole community.

In other contexts, the school register can be used more purposively. In a recent study of the relationships between HIV/AIDS and schooling in Tanzania, for example, and in particular how HIV/AIDS was affecting the social demand for schooling and hence the incidence of drop-outs, a sample was drawn from the registers in 12 schools in two regions, each with rural, 'roadside' and urban schools, identifying equal numbers of 'regular attenders', 'irregular attenders', 'drop-outs' and never attenders (Huber and Gould, 2003). This last group was purposively identified by teachers after the register-based sampling as they, by definition, had not attended school and had not been included. The objective here was not to have a representative sample of the whole community, or to estimate the proportions of children and young people in these various attendance groups, but to be able to compare the characteristics of the four attendance groups.

Schools as mirrors of broader processes of development

There is a long tradition in the social sciences of using schools as a surrogate for describing broader changes at the local scale. A classic of this genre is Thabault's *Mon école* (1971), a description of community/school relations in rural France through a period of over 100 years, from an isolated village before the coming of the railways and easy road transport to a community well integrated into the wider regional economy, and how the life of the school, its teachers, the aspirations of its pupils reflected these broad social changes. The school and its learning experiences were in part responsible for engineering these broader changes – but generally only in part, for schools reflect the wider currents in society much more than they generate them.

Schools are normally places of coherence and consensus, places that communities and broader society, including government, look to for leadership and innovation. The curriculum usually reflects wider political objectives, and curriculum change of a major kind is often a key feature of wider development policies. Classically, just after independence in African countries, there were major curriculum revolutions. These were not merely in content, although this was important (e.g. changing the history curriculum from the colonial British experience – or even English history, the Tudors and Stuarts – to a history of the colony and the struggle for independence). There were also changes in direction and emphasis, with more practical education in many countries, such as the education for self-reliance as part of Julius Nyerere's *Ujamaa* experiment in Tanzania from 1967 to the late 1970s, or the very strong emphasis on expansion in the number and quality of vocational schools in the East Asian Newly Industrializing Countries, notably South Korea, from the 1960s, as a necessary component of the broader structural changes to an export-based manufacturing economy, or the key role of the implementation of the National Unified School (Escuela National Unificada) programme in Chile in the downfall of the Allende government in 1973 (Farrell, 1986).

There were also changes in the overall shape of the system, with a greater emphasis on primary school education and achieving national or international targets, most recently the Millennium Development Goal of Universal Primary Education by 2015, rather than on secondary or higher education, reflecting a broader equity and inclusive strategies. Schools systems have themselves been directly affected by structural adjustment programmes that typically reduced resources allocated by governments to schooling, with a presumption of passing some of the costs through higher school fees to the users, children and public at large.

Schools can also be the focus for broader national objectives in nation-building, often epitomized by policies concerning the language of instruction. In many former colonies, where education systems originally used the colonial language, developing national identities at independence raised major policy controversies over whether and to which language school instruction would change. In many countries with a variety of ethnic backgrounds and languages, the colonial language was retained, in schools and also the language of government, as a 'neutral' solution between competing, often antagonistic, local language choices. In Kenya, for example, English was retained as the principal language of instruction, although local languages may be used (learning materials in these languages are used at lower levels of primary school) and Swahili is widely taught as a second language. In neighbouring Tanzania, by contrast, Swahili is vigorously pursued as the national language, with no materials available in schools or any instruction in local ethnic languages, of which there are many, as a deliberate policy of asserting national Tanzanian rather than local identity.

However, schools can also be places of resistance. In a few contexts, for example. in El Salvador in the 1980s (Hammond, 1998), the schools system may be at the heart of revolution. More typically, however, studies of the ways in which schools do or do not follow a national curriculum or other innovations may be important as symptoms of broader patterns of resistance. Whether by teachers or school heads (e.g. in implementing national language policies across the curriculum), or by the students, or by communities in reducing or even completely abandoning any support for the schools, whether financial or in providing labour or land for buildings, etc., there are many ways in which national policies and local implementation can diverge, and a researcher working in a school can begin to understand some of the roots of resistance. Sites of resistance are even more apparent for universities and higher education colleges, where students are most likely to be politically active and where there is a long history of suppression of student activity in many states.

If researchers can be secure in their assumption that schools will reflect many issues in contemporary or past development, then they offer an ideal and practical entrée into an examination of a wide range of local development problems, from problems of attitudes to farming and local livelihoods to wider government policies for social integration.

Schools for education research

Clearly schools and other institutions must be the primary basis for research in education directly: in-school studies of learning and achievement; studies of curriculum and learning materials; studies of the aspirations and expectations of students; studies of teachers' classroom performance; studies of schools as social environments. National education systems have been much researched by local and international scholars, the subject of a voluminous literature by international advisory agencies, such as UNESCO, and funding agencies, notably the World Bank. Some of that is based on primary data collected through in-school studies; others are based on the data routinely collected in the schools. This secondary data comprises not only statistical data on school enrolments and attendance, teacher qualifications and examination performance, but also on such aspects as learning materials, buildings and infrastructure. Each school and each school district at the lowest level will collect data, of highly variable quality, to which a researcher working in partnership in a school can gain easy access. At the primary school level, the range of such material will be much less than for the more complex institutions at the higher levels.

Probably the most frequently collected primary data of researchers in a school is derived from the whole-class questionnaire – students completing a questionnaire as a class in class time. This is a very easy and rapid method of collecting a lot of data, with many cases: 40 completed questionnaires of perhaps 10–15 questions completed in a 40-minute class lesson period. To conduct a class questionnaire usually requires the permission of the principal of the institution, and perhaps even its board of management or governors, giving them sight of the questionnaire instrument in advance. The class teacher should be involved too, if possible to review and comment on the questions in advance, to identify any possible words or terms that will need to be explained. One alternative would be to have a postal or take-home questionnaire based on the class register, but such a strategy would lose the advantage of the immediacy of the classroom situation.

However, the advantages of quantity can be substantially outweighed by the disadvantages of uncertain but generally poor-quality data, and only on a limited range of aspects. Whole-class questionnaires have to be seen as being 'quick and dirty', most usefully restricted to gathering factual data – on the students' own biological (age, gender) and directly measurable social characteristics (e.g. number of brothers and sisters, home environment), but being aware of questions where there is possible ambiguity (e.g. in polygamous societies the concepts of 'household' and 'brother/sister'). The researcher will need to be present to explain each question, and would normally need to explain the purpose of the questionnaire in terms that the students, of whatever age, might understand and then be disposed to offering cooperation. It should not be assumed that students will automatically cooperate and, even if they do, that their responses will necessarily be accurate!

A widely used second-stage strategy after the whole-class questionnaire is to sample within the class for a much more detailed one-to-one interview/questionnaire, based or a random or a purposive sample. Then the researcher can develop detail of the individual student's background, life rhythms, achievements, expectations and aspirations, the standard material that researchers typically seek in the currently burgeoning work on children in development. These interviews can be done in school, or in the student's home or in some other 'neutral' place, such as an eating-place or a sports venue. This is equally applicable for samples of students at higher levels of the hierarchy, particularly university students, who are often used as a key barometer of social trends.

A major source for identifying current research results on education and development, usually containing details of research strategies to obtain these results, is the Department For International Development-supported web source, ID21 (www.id21.org/education). This is a very large site, which is regularly updated to constitute a major source on the relationships between education, knowledge and schooling, mainly by UK-based researchers, and identifying a range of studies which are institution-based. The January 2005 pages, for example, report generally on a range of research into achieving the Millennium Development Goal of UPE by 2015, but also report on a Panos Institute study on sexual violence in schools, with discussion of school-based strategies for dealing with the problems. It also provides associated links.

School-based partnerships clarify identity and positionality

There is much to be gained by a researcher by working in, with and/or from a school or any other educational institution. The gains are direct by facilitating direct access to data and informants. They are likely also to be indirect, but no less important, by facilitating access to a broader understanding of social and economic processes in an unfamiliar environment. Being identified with a school by students, teachers and by the community at large immediately gives the researcher an identity, placing him or her in a context to which the subjects of the research can relate. This will also give the researcher an enhanced sense of his or her own positionality, a greater sense of being an active contributor to the life and aspirations of the broader community in the field area.

85

QUESTIONS FOR DISCUSSION

1. In which respects and to what extent can the 'view from the school' permit a participatory rather than 'top-down' research strategy?
2. How can a school-based research strategy be designed to study the poorest and most marginalized groups in rural areas?
3. How much can schools and schooling change the economic, social and cultural contexts of any particular society? How much do they merely reflect these broader contexts?
4. Has public higher education in developing countries been primarily a subsidy to the benefit of the national elites? How can you tell? How can this be altered?

Further reading

Gould, W.T.S. (1993) *People and Education in the Third World*, Harlow: Longman.

Website

ID21: www.id21.org/education

References

Farrell, J.P. (1986) *The National Unified School in Allende's Chile: The Role of Education in the Destruction of a Revolution*, Vancouver: University of British Columbia Press.

Hammond, J.L. (1998) *Fighting to Learn: Popular Education and Guerrilla War in El Salvador*, New Brunswick, NJ: Rutgers University Press.

Huber, U. and Gould, W.T.S. (2003) *Primary School Attendance in Tanzania: How Much Is It Affected by Orphanhood?* Papers presented at the Annual Conference of the British Society for Population Studies, Newcastle, 2002.

Robson, E. (1994) From teacher to taxi-driver: reflections in research roles in developing areas, in E. Robson and K. Willis (eds), *Postgraduate Fieldwork in Developing Areas: A Rough Guide*, Developing Areas Research Group, Monograph No. 8, London: Royal Geographical Society and the Institute of British Geographers.

Thabault, R. (1971) *Education and Change in a Village Community: Mazières-en-Gâtine, 1848–1914*, London: Routledge and Kegan Paul.

10

Working with Partners: Government Ministries

Mansoor Ali and Andrew Cotton

Governments, ministries and their working ∙ The role of researcher in working with government ministries ∙ The significance of research for governments ∙ Uptake of research and issues ∙ Lessons from experience

Introduction

Those who have worked with governments and politicians have two conflicting points of view. One view is that decision-makers hate to be well informed as it makes the process of arriving at decisions more complicated and difficult. The second view is that government would like to take well-informed decisions and is ready to allocate resources for these well-informed decisions to reduce the risk of failure. Whatever the reality, the fact is that working with government is complex.

This chapter is written for researchers who will be working on research projects linked with the policies and practices of government departments. This type of research is often done for the benefit of the government and may be funded by a range of organizations. This chapter explains various dimensions of the government's work, the range of topics with which you may be involved and the appropriate methodologies for dealing with

them. Based on our experience of working with governments, the chapter also explains the likely pitfalls and the lessons learned.

The emphasis on good government and the realization that good policy is the key to development has led to increased attention on understanding the dynamics of researching with the government.

Getting started

The responsibility of governing a state lies with a government. The goal of any well-run government is to maintain and promote the happiness of the society. This is achieved through a system of justice in the broad sense. It may take the form of controls, incentives, accountability and transparency. All these systems are not simple to implement. There are always conflicts of interests and priorities. In practice, a government is a system of departments and political organizations whose main responsibility is for the people and resources of a country. The departments are clustered within different ministries and politicians have the responsibility of leading a ministry. Most of the staff in the ministry are permanent government staff, serving a political leadership. This political leadership may be there just for a few years. The government's political agenda and priorities change but the workings of a government department remain the same. Most of the senior staff in government departments meet the expectations of the political leadership and in many countries senior appointments have a political influence. This is to ensure the commitment to understand and support the political agenda. While previously appointed persons still work with the organizations. There may be conflicting views. As a researcher you must be well prepared to face such complexities.

When working with governments you may be a member of a large research team in a government department, a research assistant in a university or with a private consulting group. Researchers play an important role in the team but they are not usually expected to deal directly with the politicians or senior executives in the government departments. They may be working for the research team leader or senior government officials. One of the senior partners in the research group has been contacted by the government or has been successful on a research programme call and you are selected as one of the team members. The team expects you to have a good knowledge of and an interest in the topic of research. As a team member, it is important to familiarize yourself with the overall context of the research, how the government works and in particular the department with which you are working.

Key points

- Understand the overall context of research within the government
- Familiarize yourself with the structure and working of the department with which you are dealing
- Be prepared to face conflicts and complexities

How governments work

Governments deal with a seemingly infinite number of tasks related to their citizens. Generally, researchers cannot be aware of the full extent and complexity of the government's work. What is often more declared is policy announcement, legislation and its implementation. This is more important for a government's image as citizens pay closer attention to these issues. There is, however, a large web of issues. Important areas, which influence the research but are not clearly visible are policy ideas and ownership, party politics, manifesto commitments, personality clashes, the timing of elections, ministers' priorities, public opinion, political careers, budgets and resources, and operational issues. As a researcher working with the government, you will first need to understand the more visible areas of government working. These are usually what are available in written form. However, a deeper understanding of how things work, the decisions taken, the politics of power, etc., usually comes with spending more time in government departments. Observations and informal discussions with government staff are very helpful in developing an insight into the workings of government and the actual decision-making process. Researchers must not assume that everything is clearly written down, or that whatever is written down is always followed.

On building trust …

Between 1990 and 1994 we worked as research consultants with the municipal government of Karachi, Pakistan, on waste management issues. The project was funded by an international agency with clearly written and agreed terms of reference. The scope of the project was ambitious in our opinion and the deadlines were set. The data and information required for such a project were not available within the municipal offices. Within the resources available we had gathered some data and information, but our greatest wealth of information came from the informal discussions and observations in the municipal offices. By first building trust and then engaging in open discussions we gained useful insight. Observations and understanding of the working of municipal government offices were vital in incorporating different perspectives. The process led to research reports which reasonably informed all the parties and clearly reflected the realities and points of views of all the stakeholders.

You may be dealing with a range of people when working with the government. Some may be directly involved in the research project and others may be influential but not directly involved. In a simple situation, the research could start with a policy question and research activity will generate data, information and evidence to answer the question. The research process and the findings are documented as a report. However, various executive summaries, briefings and notes are produced for different audiences. For research when governments genuinely want to be informed, a good, thorough piece of work is generally appreciated. Governments may consider the research process as a regular feedback of results, an answer to a policy question or a useful piece of work. However, if the findings demand a major shift in the current thinking, they may declare it as a long, boring and inconclusive report. Researchers can be easily perceived as academics who are working in a hypothetical world.

Let us assume that a government department needs some research-based advice which may be centred around a policy question. A policy question can be concerned with advice on a new policy proposal, changes in an existing policy or developing more details of a policy concept. All this needs research. The basic elements of the research process have already been discussed in the introduction of this book. However, all the elements, from the identification of the issue to the research uptake, may not necessarily happen. In some cases, governments commission research without openly declaring their main objectives.

Although researchers inform the policy, they are often not involved in the key policy decision-making. The decision-making process for policy development is often not recorded. Despite a thorough review of secondary information, it is often difficult to fully grasp the context of the policy development.

Although researchers inform the policy, they are often not involved in the key policy decision-making. The decision-making process for policy development is often not recorded. Despite a thorough review of secondary information, it is often difficult to fully grasp the context of the policy development. Researchers' involvement can easily be labelled as 'last-minute' and 'isolated'. Some departments may be quick to reject

89

the findings, stating that researchers do not understand the changing needs of the government.

The government officials who supported the research earlier may get busy in other work. This clearly means that senior staff, decision-makers and not only enthusiastic officials, should be involved right from the beginning. The dialogue must be considered as ongoing and the research process and outcomes must be seen as a flexible process. This will lead to a better policy ownership.

Key points

- Government's responsibility is infinite and its workings are complex
- Need to understand the overall working of the department you are working with
- Decision-makers need to be involved and informed right from the beginning

---

Government priorities and the range of research

Research ranges from a small piece of advice on a certain issue to a long-term programme of research, capacity-building and dissemination. The topics to be researched can change with changing priorities. Researchers are expected to understand and work with these changing priorities. For example, in 2004 the UK government prioritized:

- policy-making with people which is not only restricted to policy design, but also covers policy development, monitoring and feedback
- the promotion of a culture of performance measurement and delivery
- joined-up government, bringing people and their issues closer to the government
- strategic thinking (Duncan, 2004).

This opened a number of important avenues on working closely with people. However, this may change with time or the change of government. Changing priorities can have an impact on the type of research one is expected to do. According to Nutley et al. (2002), research with the government could fall into one of four categories:

1 *Conceptual:* This research leads to changes in knowledge, understanding or attitudes. The findings are a trigger to change and may not be considered as evidence to justify the change.
2 *Instrumental:* This research leads directly to decision-making for policy and practice. It assumes that knowledge already exists.
3 *Mobilization:* This research is similar to conceptual research but with a greater degree of persuasion. It is used as an instrument of persuasion to legitimize action or inaction.
4 *Wider influence:* This type of research leads to larger-scale shifts in thinking. It is entirely up to the government to prioritize a certain type and topic of research.

When research is completed, some government departments are often seen as having a poor capacity to take up the findings. Many researchers see this as a more generic problem. They often identify problems with the exploitation of research in government, commerce, the voluntary sector and the media. There may be a number of reasons for this. The research context may have changed, the research outputs may not be in the right form or there may be a lack of convincing evidence. These may also come about because of poor interface management and communication problems. Some academics who are responsible for carrying out research may also have little capacity to engage with practitioners. Government is a large cluster of many organizations and groups. These groups can be both formal and informal in nature. Researchers may expect communication problems, both within the organization and with external organizations (Jablin and Putnam, 2001).

Who makes the changes ...

Between 1998 and 2000 we examined the actual process of bringing about changes to existing practices. We selected eight changes in the context of urban waste management in Dhaka, Bangladesh. We found that most of the changes had been initiated because of a certain level of demand. The demand often arose as a result of identifying a problem rather than in the search for a solution. Organization and leadership at all levels play a vital part in initiating the demands. City mayors, administrators and sometimes national politicians play an important role in initiating changes. However, in most of the cases all the stakeholders are consulted and taken into trust (Ali and Cotton, 2000).

Key lessons from experience

Researchers do not enter into the context of government research just as individuals. They may be working for a donor, organization or an NGO, a university or as a consultant. The organization they represent has a certain reputation. It is important for researchers to clarify their own position, that of the organization and the objective of the research right from the beginning. If you are working for an NGO or a donor organization, you must confirm whether the research goal is in influencing policy, advocacy or capacity-building. Make sure that the values of the organization you represent do not influence the impartiality of the research.

Researchers are often enthusiastic about their research but they must not expect an equal level of enthusiasm from the government departments. Staff in government departments are often busy with a number of operational tasks. Reaching decisions through research may not be a priority for them. However, some individuals in a department may provide support for research as a matter of interest. In some cases, research may be seen as part of someone's job description. Researchers must use all these potential channels.

In cases where the research is done from a distance, a third party such as a local university or non-government organization can play an important role. Such collaboration is mutually beneficial and can contribute to the capacity-building of the local organization. This also helps in building and maintaining local contacts, to ensure uptake of research and in some cases to save on the cost.

One must not assume that the required data and information are available within the government, even if they are promised in the agreement. Often there is a shortage of reliable data and information. Whatever data are available are often collected for the government's own use and from the government's perspective. The underlying concepts and

91

definitions may differ. This can raise a methodological bias.

In conventional research settings researchers often come from a more powerful position. Consequently, most of the literature on development research is written with the view that the researcher is more powerful than the researched (Scheyvens and Storey, 2003). While working with government, however, the relationship can be different. Gaining access to the researched may be difficult, particularly when the nature of information required is qualitative. Communicating the findings may be challenging. Government ministries may prefer to minimize the risks and before they uptake any findings from research.

For example, participants may want to see how their response is written up and perhaps insist on approving outputs before they are disseminated. Of course this can lead to frustration and delays. Researchers working with government ministries must be mentally prepared to face such challenges.

Finally, secretarial and support staff play an important role for the busy staff in the government. Records and information are maintained to ensure continuity with a change of political leadership. It is very important, therefore, to have a good working relationship with the secretary as he/she is the one who keeps the diaries, makes the appointments, maintains the records and provides the information.

QUESTIONS FOR DISCUSSION

1. When working with government departments or authorities, what preparation will you make as a researcher?
2. Discuss what strategies you will adopt to make the research more relevant to the government departments.
3. What measures can be undertaken to ensure that the research process continues after a change of government or a change of officials in a ministry?
4. Discuss the strengths and weaknesses of some of the data and information collection methods when working with government ministries.

Further reading

Ali, S.M. and Cotton, A.P. (2000) *Process of Change: Field Notes*, Water, Engineering and Development Center (WEDC), Loughborough: Loughborough University.

Holland, J. and Blackburn J. (eds) (1998) *Whose Voice: Participatory Research and Policy Change*, London: Intermediate Technology Publications.

Laws, S., Harper, C. and Marcus, R. (2003) *Research for Development: A Practical Guide*, London: Sage.

Scheyvens, R. and Storey, D. (2003) *Development Fieldwork: A Practical Guide*, London: Sage.

Websites

http://www.gsr.gov.uk/index.asp – A UK Government website providing resources, career information, news, training and the latest methodological developments for government social researchers.

http://www.policyhub.gov.uk/ – Policy Hub is a UK government website developed by the Cabinet Office Government Social Research Unit.

http://www.scottishexecutive.gov.uk/Home – The Scottish Executive's official website.

References

Ali, S.M. and Cotton, A.P. (2000) *Process of Change: Field Notes*, Water, Engineering and Development center (WEDC), Loughborough: Loughborough University.

Duncan, S. (2004) Using social research to shape policy, Government Chief Social Researcher. Presentation to Centre for Research in Social Policy, 17 September, Loughborough University.

Jablin, F.M. and Putnam, L.L. (2001) *The New Handbook of Organizational Communication*, London: Sage.

Nutley, S. et al. (2002) From knowing to doing: a framework for understanding the evidence-into-practice agenda. Research Unit for Research Utilisation, University of St Andrews, UK.

Scheyvens, R. and Storey, D. (2003) *Development Fieldwork: A Practical Guide*, London: Sage.

11

Working with Partners: NGOs and CBOs

Claire Mercer

Researching NGOs   Theory and research questions

Methods, ethics and politics   Advantages of working with NGOs

Problems of working with NGOs   Doing non-NGO research

A practical guide to working with NGOs

Introduction

Across the South, the growth of non-governmental organizations (NGOs) accelerated in the 1980s, propelling them to the forefront of development praxis. According to the World Bank, the number of international NGOs increased from 6,000 in 1990 to 26,000 in 1999 (www.worldbank.org), and 12 per cent of foreign aid to developing countries was channelled through large and small NGOs in 1994. By 1996, the total amount was US $7 billion worldwide (Chege, 1999; World Bank, n.d.).

The significant increase in research and teaching about NGOs and development which followed inspired many students of development (myself included) to investigate non-governmental activity for their own research projects. Much of the interest in non-governmental activity has been driven by disillusionment with the large-scale, top-down development projects so popular with governments and donors during the 1970s. In the early days of NGO research, there was an optimism that NGOs might be the 'magic bullets' for development (Edwards and Hulme, 1995), using their small size and local knowledge to respond positively to the needs of the poorest, who so often remained out of reach of the larger government initiatives. However, the literature on NGOs has since become more diverse and critical. As states everywhere tighten their belts and withdraw from service provision, initial debates about the role of NGOs in service provision has given way to concerns that NGOs are simply becoming surrogate arms of government. More recently, attention has turned to considerations of NGOs' political role in development, and research has focused on NGO contributions to empowering the poorest, building civil society, advocacy work, and creating the conditions for liberal democracy to flourish (see Mercer, 2002).

This chapter aims to help you think about how to do research with NGOs overseas in both conceptual and methodological terms. Most of what follows is aimed at student research projects which focus on NGOs as the object of research. However, it is important to note that, whatever your research question, you may find that local NGOs are active in your field area. Some advice on how NGOs might be useful for non-NGO research is therefore offered. The term 'NGO' covers a whole range of types of organization, such as international NGOs, local community-based organizations (CBOs), religious groups and social movements. This chapter focuses on NGOs and CBOs, two quite distinct types of development organization, which require different research strategies from the student fieldworker. The term 'NGO' refers to organizations which operate on a scale larger than the community or village. Typically, NGOs are international, national or regional in scope. They are staffed by salaried employees and usually have official registration and access to at least one source of funding. CBOs, on the other hand, are likely to operate at a smaller scale, often in one or two villages only. They are usually dependent upon local residents, who receive no remuneration for their efforts in organization or contributing labour, although some CBOs are able to secure external funding for particular projects. In the interests of brevity, I will refer to NGOs throughout this chapter, unless the matter under discussion is particularly relevant to CBOs. The chapter will outline a number of key issues which you need to think about before, during and after your research encounter with an NGO. We start with a consideration of theory, research questions, methods and ethical considerations, before looking at the advantages and disadvantages of working with NGOs in development research. The chapter then offers a practical guide to working with NGOs.

Researching NGOs

Theory and research questions

Research on NGOs and CBOs is wide and varied, and you have several options in designing your study. The first questions you need to ask are:

- Will you be travelling abroad for your fieldwork (see tips below on identifying overseas NGOs for research) or carrying it out in the UK?
- Do you want to focus on a group of NGOs (e.g. education NGOs in Bombay, or the NGO sector in Zambia), one specific NGO (e.g. Oxfam, MKSS in India), or a particular NGO project (e.g. CBO water provision in a Cameroonian village)?
- Do you want to look at (for example) NGO impacts, NGO politics, NGO management and organization, or NGO advocacy campaigns?

I raise these questions at the beginning in order to highlight the point that you will need to be very specific about your research questions. Given the amount of academic literature available on NGOs, simply setting out to 'look at an NGO' will not be sufficient preparation. Think about where you are going, find out about the NGOs there, what they are doing and what the local issues are. The World Wide Web will be a good research resource here (see Chapter 28 on using World Wide Web). Read about the politics, economics and the culture of your field site before you go. Search the literature for other studies on NGOs in the same country or sector, and think about your research questions. What makes your study different? What are you adding to current knowledge about NGOs?

95

You will also need to think about your theoretical approach to your research questions. Although much of the NGO literature falls into this category, it will not be sufficient for an undergraduate or postgraduate dissertation to do a case study of an NGO without linking your empirical analysis to theoretical debates. It is therefore important that you get to grips with current debates in the NGO literature and beyond (see Box 11.1).

Box 11.1 Theorizing research on NGOs

Jonathan Pugh has been working on participatory planning with NGOs in the Caribbean. He suggests that researchers working on NGOs must reflect on their theoretical position, particularly given the faddish nature of academic approaches to understanding NGOs. He advises research students to be very clear, and well read, on the theory that is influencing their outlook before conducting the research. He says, 'even if you think that you are not adopting a theoretical approach, you are. You need to know which discourses are shaping how you look at the NGO you are studying. Further, when you learn more about the NGO that you are researching, have the courage to challenge dominant academic fashions. Don't simply '(apply) them' (Pugh, pers comm., 2004; see also Pugh, 2003, http://planningcaribbean.org.uk/).

Methods

Most studies of NGOs utilize qualitative methodologies, although some quantitative methods can be useful to supplement the qualitative material gathered (see Part III of this book for more on specific quantitative and qualitative methods).

When undertaking research on NGOs the methods you are likely to find most helpful are:

- *interviews* with key informants such as NGO staff and project leaders, donor staff (if the NGO receives donor funding), village or settlement leaders, local leaders from government, business and religious institutions;
- *interviews* and/or *focus group* discussions with project beneficiaries;
- *surveys* in the project location;
- *participatory appraisal* with project beneficiaries;
- *document analysis* of NGO reports and baseline surveys.

You should also try to bear in mind the broader context within which the NGO you are studying is situated (see Box 11.2). Consider whether other NGOs work in the area, and think about the relationships between different NGOs. Think also about the NGOs' relationship with the local state. Finally, consider the 'non-beneficiaries' of project interventions. What do they make of the NGO activity in their locality? In broadening your sources beyond a specific NGO or village, you will not only be triangulating what your informants have told you about the specific project you are investigating, but you will also gain a broader understanding of the social and political implications of the NGO project. A broader perspective will also highlight further areas for research within your project which you yourself had not thought of.

Box 11.2   The politics of NGO research

Emma Mawdsley, Gina Porter and Janet Townsend have carried out two recent research projects with NGOs in Ghana, India and Mexico. An important methodological as well as theoretical consideration for them was the extent to which NGOs are inevitably political and politicized at various scales. When doing research with NGOs, it is important to be sensitive to the fact that, at the local, regional or national level, similar NGOs may be in competition with each other (and sometimes with state agencies) for funds or projects, and very often they are entangled within alliances and/or rivalries based on personalities and institutional histories. NGOs are also 'political' in the sense that the work that they do – from organizing food aid, to promoting participation in governance, to acting as advocates for children's rights – all brings them into a relationship of conflict and/or collaboration with various elements of the government, and with other groups in society. In some countries, NGOs are viewed with deep suspicion (e.g., in Bangladesh and parts of the Middle East), and researchers need to proceed with caution, both in their interests and in the interests of the organizations with which they are working (see Mawdsley et al., 2002).

The ethics and politics of working with NGOs

It is now accepted that good development research should not be an extractive exercise in which the 'value-added' activity takes place at a distance from the researched (see Chapter 3 on ethical practices). Working with NGOs offers clear benefits in terms of providing tangible improvements for both the organization and its beneficiaries. As David Hulme (1994: 252) points out, 'producing an elegant critique of a development intervention is not sufficient'. Rather, 'relevance could be achieved if … researchers explicitly attempt to link knowledge to action by analysing the implications of the knowledge they create for the actors involved in the practice of development'.

If you are epistemologically committed to undertaking action research, for example through the use of participatory methodologies, the benefits arising from your research could be clearly linked to the aims of the NGO you are studying. For example, Mike Kesby and his postgraduate students Fungisai Gwanzura-Ottemoller and Monica Chizororo

at the University of St Andrews used participatory methods to gain insights into the ways in which different groups of people communicated knowledge about sexual health in rural Zimbabwe. They undertook research in collaboration with *Tsungiriria*, a small local HIV/AIDS NGO. Using participatory methodologies, Mike has actively sought to combat the very problems with which both he and the NGO were concerned (see Kesby, 2000a, 2000b). The relationship with the NGO goes further than this though, with Mike and his postgraduate students contributing free consultancies to the NGO, and raising money for them back in Scotland. In return, *Tsungiriria* has helped them gain permissions and legitimacy to do research in a difficult political climate.

In general it is important that you report your findings locally and be willing to account for your conclusions. Jonathan Pugh advises: 'For the most effective test of how much you have learned about an NGO, argue your case with the local people that know it better than anyone else. See if it makes sense to them' (Pugh, pers. comm., 2004). In undertaking

97

my own undergraduate dissertation which evaluated a CBO in Sierra Leone, I wrote a separate report for the CBO which focused on more practical evaluative issues than did the final dissertation itself. This resulted in a rationalization of the CBO's activities. CBOs, which are often smaller and have fewer resources for research and reflection, are particularly likely to welcome such input, especially if your fieldwork is self-funded! Writing the report was also useful for me because I wrote it directly on my return from Sierra Leone, before I started writing the dissertation. This allowed me time to collate the data I had collected and to reflect on what I had learnt before I started writing it up as a piece of academic work. Another option would be to ask the community in which you are working what questions they would most like to see answered through the research process. You could also offer to send copies of photographs, or use your knowledge and contacts to help the NGO in its work. For example, while researching an NGO coalition in Tanzania, I was asked to help the NGOs draft a project proposal to donors, to win funding to monitor the country's Poverty Reduction Strategy Paper. However, the danger here is in promising outcomes which you, as a student, are unlikely to be able to provide. You should be realistic about what benefits (if any) are likely to result from your research. As Simon et al. (2003) experienced during their research in Kumasi in Ghana, communities which have been visited by a string of researchers can understandably suffer 'research fatigue', and be more interested in seeing some 'real' results in their village rather than just another report (see Box 11.3).

Box 11.3   In their words: how research can facilitate communication between NGOs, government and donors

Paul Hodge carried out doctoral research on the relationship between NGOs and donors in Fiji. Reflecting on his role as a researcher within the wider NGO and development community, Paul attempted to find out what the NGO staff he interviewed thought of his research. The final question of his interview schedule was to do with what informants considered to be the role of research, particularly given the recent emphasis on NGO advocacy. It was clear to him that this kind of question was not a typical one that they had been asked, and that NGOs found it refreshing to be asked to reflect on the role of the researcher. On his return from the field, Paul assembled *In your words – anecdotes and reflections from Fiji's NGO communities*, a report based on his interviews which he distributed to key informants in order to stimulate debate and reflexivity among NGOs, donors and others who all deal with similar issues in the course of their work.

Advantages of working with NGOs

There are a number of very good reasons why working with NGOs, even if you are not researching them directly, can be a good idea for student research in development studies.

- **NGOs as a fount of local knowledge**: NGOs are known for being local and responsive to the needs of communities, so take advantage of this in both academic and practical terms. If you can contact NGOs local to your field area before you travel, they may be able to advise on a whole host of logistical issues, such as ease of mobility, where to stay, local costs, necessary equipment, safety issues, etc. They may be able to provide access to communications while you are in the field (e.g. if an office has an email account or a telephone), and they may even have transport, allowing you to hitch a lift to visit projects.

- **NGOs as local field area experts**: Many NGO staff will have been based in an area for some time and may be able to offer local insights into your research questions. They may even advise you that your research questions are irrelevant! (But exercise caution in being influenced too much by NGO staff – see below.) NGO staff will also know what topics are likely to be culturally sensitive in your field area, how to greet and respond to greetings, and what to do when you are offered hospitality. If you don't speak the local language, and you are likely to be in the field a relatively short time, these details are of no small importance if you are to gain the respect of the community in which you are working.
- **NGOs as entry points**: Linking yourself to a local NGO may facilitate community acceptance of you and your work, helping you to gain access to key informants and other information more quickly than would otherwise be possible.
- **NGOs as a source of background information**: Many NGOs have to prepare baseline documents, annual reports, statistics on the local area, project audits, etc. for their donors. If they have a document library, ask to use it.
- **NGOs and local language skills**: If you need an interpreter, local NGOs may have qualified staff who are able to help. They should certainly be able to advise you on local rates of pay for such work (see Chapter 18 on using interpreters).

Problems of working with NGOs

Research collaborations do not, unfortunately, always run smoothly, and you need to be aware of the following common problems which can arise when working with NGOs.

- **NGO access**: With the increasing interest in NGOs as objects of study, and the bursting of the 'NGO magic' bubble, it is becoming more difficult to identify NGOs willing to allow a research student to scrutinize them. In particular, large northern NGOs, which have their own research and audit departments, are very difficult to gain access to. You will have very little joy if you limit your NGO search to a handful of large, UK-based NGOs, asking for permission to study their organization or one of their projects (see below on tips for enrolling an NGO in your research). In part this is also because of time constraints – many NGOs in both the North and the South are extremely busy.
- **NGOs as gatekeepers**: NGOs will want any collaboration to reflect well on them and may try to steer your research in a particular direction. Exercise caution when choosing which project to study and try to stick to your research questions. For example, if you are being encouraged to investigate an NGO's flagship project, consider whether this is appropriate for your own research project.
- **NGOs as research directors**: Be wary of NGO staff who wish to micro-manage your fieldwork on a daily basis. Try to remain independent in your day-to-day activities so that your access to informants is not shaped by the NGO you are studying.
- **NGOs as local political actors**: NGOs may be a fount of local knowledge but do not assume that they are neutral observers of your field area. NGOs and their staff will have long-standing relationships with communities and other local institutions, and specific people within them. Be aware that the community view of the NGO you are connected to will influence how your informants will interpret you, your motives and the questions you are asking (see Box 11.2 above). Moreover, the position of the NGO in local political

99

relationships may affect how they respond to your project and your specific questions.

- **NGO differences**: Research collaborations between practitioners and academics do not always run smoothly, often because 'NGO fieldworkers consider academics to be ignorant of the real world where there is no bookshop, no electricity, no telephones working and frequently no petrol' (Poulton, 1988, in Hulme, 1994: 251). There can be differences of opinion regarding the research questions, methods, location and conclusions, particularly given the quite different outcomes which the different parties expect from the research process.

- **You, the NGO, and the politics of research**: You will no doubt have to grapple with issues of positionality during the course of your research. As a relatively privileged university student you will regularly be faced with the inequities of the contemporary world on a very personalized scale. You should remain alert to the shifting balances of power during your fieldwork (it will not always be one way) and try to remain transparent in your dealings with local NGOs and their beneficiaries.

- **NGO limitations**: Being critical of NGO work can be tricky if the NGO in question has supported your fieldwork. This does not mean you should ignore shortcomings in NGO work, but try to be realistic about what the NGO project is trying to achieve within the limitations of the local environment. Presenting your results to the NGO before you disseminate them more widely will also give both you and the NGO an opportunity to reflect on your findings. For example, as a postgraduate I was given permission, together with Tim Kelsall at the University of Newcastle, to do research in villages in north-west Tanzania where the large international NGO World Vision had well-established community development projects. In return for research permission, World Vision asked us to present our findings to them at head office before we returned home. Although we had some serious

misgivings about the impacts of their 'empowering' approach, the ensuing discussion of the limitations of participatory community development was very useful both for us and for World Vision staff who rarely had the time to scrutinize critically the overall impacts of their daily work (see Kelsall and Mercer, 2003).

Doing non-NGO research

Your research questions may not be directly related to issues about NGOs, but you may nevertheless find them useful sources of information when you are in the field, for the reasons outlined above. NGO staff can be key informants, and CBO leaders can be spokespeople for their community, especially where few other institutions exist in your field area. Data collected by the NGO on, for example, local social, economic and environmental conditions, will of course be useful for a range of research topics. You might use this information to save you collecting it yourself, or you may use it to triangulate your own results or look at changes over time.

NGOs working in specific areas related to your research topic will also be worth contacting. For example, if you are working on questions of access to healthcare, you should find out about local health NGOs and visit them. They will undoubtedly have local knowledge and experience which will be relevant to your study, and they may be interested in the outcomes of your own research. Many of the larger NGOs will have head offices in large or capital cities, so it might be worth making a visit to them if your field site is some distance away.

A practical guide to working with NGOs and CBOs

If you decide to work with an NGO for your project, you will find it a rich and rewarding academic and personal experience. Both you and the NGO will get the most out of your research project if you think about the following pointers:

- **Finding an NGO**: This could be the hardest part of your research. Search using the World Wide Web (although bear in mind that many NGOs and CBOs will not have a web presence), ask your lecturers whether they have any contacts with NGOs, consult charity and voluntary work directories, etc. You will need to start early as it can take time to set up contact with an NGO and you may need to raise funds or apply for travel grants to finance your field trip.
- **Do your homework**: Don't rely on the *Rough Guide to...* when you are on the aeroplane! Be familiar with the relevant NGO and country literature before you start your fieldwork.
- **Get permission**: Unless there are very good reasons for doing so, you should never undertake research without gaining the required permissions first (e.g. from the NGO, local government representatives, stakeholders).
- **Maintain good relations**: Be clear at the outset about the nature of the collaboration between you and the NGO, what each of you is bringing to the collaboration, and what the expected outcomes are (Roper, 2002). Do you understand how the NGO will use your research? Does the NGO understand the potential benefits/limits of your input? Moreover, do the local people with whom you are working understand the benefits and limitations of your research project?
- **Maintain an independent identity**: Although working with an NGO will bring undoubted benefits in terms of access and insight, remember that the potential value of your research lies in the fact that you are an external researcher with no particular local axe to grind. If you become too closely associated with the NGO you are researching, your informants may become less willing to share critical opinions with you, and your status as an impartial observer may be threatened.
- **Share your findings with NGO staff and beneficiaries.**

Conclusion

This chapter has raised many important issues which you need to think about if your collaboration with an NGO is to be rewarding for all parties involved. However, it has only been able to offer a mere introduction to an area which remains to be reflected on in detail in the academic literature. Reading this chapter in conjunction with the rest of this book will be good preparation for producing a robust and ethical research methodology. Overall, though, if you are interested in how development can work in practice, working with an NGO can be an exciting and challenging research experience.

Acknowledgements

The author would like to thank Paul Hodge, Mike Kesby, David Lewis, Emma Mawdsley, Gina Porter, Jonathan Pugh and Janet Townsend for sharing their NGO research experiences, and for commenting on earlier drafts of this chapter.

101

QUESTIONS FOR DISCUSSION

1. How can doing research on NGOs be useful for academic purposes?
2. How can doing research on NGOs be useful for NGOs and development practitioners themselves?

(Continued)

(Continued)

3. What tensions and harmonies can you identify between your responses to questions 1 and 2 above?
4. Realistically, how might your research project maximize benefits for local people?
5. What particular problems, to which the researcher needs to remain alert, might arise when working with NGOs? How might these be overcome?

Further reading

Devereaux, S. and Hoddinott, J. (eds) (1993) *Fieldwork in Developing Countries*, Boulder, CO: Lynne Rienner.

Edwards, M. and Hulme, D. (eds) (1992) *Making a Difference: NGOs and Development in a Changing World*, London: Earthscan.

Edwards, M. and Hulme, D. (eds) (1995) *Non-governmental Organisations – Performance and Accountability: Beyond the Magic Bullet*, London: Earthscan.

Hulme, D. and Edwards, M. (eds) (1997) *NGOs, States and Donors: Too Close for Comfort*, Basingstoke: Macmillan.

Scheyvens, R. and Storey, D. (eds) (2003) *Development Fieldwork: A Practical Guide*, London: Sage.

Also, see the journal *Development in Practice* http://www.developmentinpractice.org/) for regular articles written by both academics and development practitioners, about the role of NGOs in development.

Websites

http://planningcaribbean.org.uk/ – Covers participatory planning in the Caribbean region
http://topics.developmentgateway.org/ngo – The non-governmental section of the development gateway
http://docs.lib.duke.edu/igo/guides/ngo/index.htm – Non-Governmental Organizations research guide
http://www.intrac.org/ – International NGO Training and Research Centre

REFERENCES

Chege, S. (1999) Doners [sic] shift more aid to NGO, http://www.globalpolicy.org/ngos/issues/chege.htm (accessed June 2004).

Edwards, M. and Hulme, D. (eds) (1995) *Non-governmental Organisations – Performance and Accountability: Beyond the Magic Bullet*, London: Earthscan.

Hulme, D. (1994) Social development research and the third sector: NGOs as users and subjects of social inquiry, in D. Booth (ed.), *Rethinking Social Development: Theory, Research and Practice*, Harlow: Longman, pp. 251–75.

Kelsall, T. and Mercer, C. (2003) Empowering the people? World Vision and 'transformatory development' in northern Tanzania, *Review of African Political Economy*, 39 (96): 293–304.

Kesby, M. (2000a) Participatory diagramming as a means to improve communication about sex in rural Zimbabwe: a pilot study, *Social Science and Medicine*, 50: 1723–1741.

Kesby, M. (2000b) Participatory diagramming: deploying qualitative methods through an action research epistemology, *Area*, 32 (4): 423–435.

Mawdsley, E.E., Townsend, J.G., Porter, G. and Oakley, P. (2002) *Knowledge, Power and Development Agendas: NGOs North and South*, Oxford: INTRAC.

Mercer, C. (2002) NGOs, civil society and democratization: a critical review of the literature, *Progress in Development Studies*, 2 (1): 5–22.

Pugh, J. (2003) A consideration of some of the sociological mechanisms shaping the adoption of participatory planning in Barbados, in J. Pugh and R.B. Potter (eds), *Participatory Planning in the Caribbean: Lessons from Practice*, Aldershot: Ashgate.

Roper, L. (2002) Achieving successful academic–practitioner research collaborations, *Development in Practice*, 12 (3–4): 338–345.

Simon, D., McGregor, D.F.M., Nsiah-Gyabaah, K. and Thompson, D.A. (2003) Poverty elimination, North–South research collaboration, and the politics of participatory development, *Development in Practice*, 13 (1): 40–56.

World Bank (n.d.) Defining civil society, http://web.worldbank.org/WBSITE/EXTERNAL/TOPICS/CSO/0,contentMDK:20101499~menuPK:244752~pagePK:220503~piPK:220476~theSitePK:228717,00.html (accessed June 2004).

103

12

Doing Development Research 'at Home'

Tim Unwin

Ethical aspects of doing development research 'at home' • • Practical benefits of researching 'development' 'at home' • • Examples of research on 'development' that can be done 'at home' • • Development policy • • Working with civil society organizations • • Images of 'development' • • Historical constructions of 'development' • • ICT-based research

Introduction

The enthusiasm of undergraduate and post-graduate students for many development studies courses frequently encourages them to think about 'doing' their dissertations on aspects of 'development'. This is particularly so when they have also had the opportunity to parti-cipate in a field course overseas, or have come to learn at first hand about the problems of development and some of the issues that poor people face on a daily basis. However, the costs of travelling overseas and undertaking a sustained period of research in a foreign country can make such students reluctant to embark on this path. This chapter is specifi-cally written for such people, to encourage them to explore the plethora of research that can be done 'at home', and to offer some insights into the challenges that they may encounter in so doing. Doing research 'at home' is no better or worse than doing research overseas. It is simply different, and to do it well one needs to be aware of the relative advan-tages and disadvantages that such work can confer.

Development research 'at home': ethical considerations

For many people who are enticed by the excitement of overseas development research, the thought of doing a dissertation based 'at home' can often be seen as a second-best solution. However, this need not be the case, and there are many highly pertinent issues that can be addressed in both undergraduate and postgraduate dissertations without the need to travel. Indeed, doing development research 'at home' can be equally relevant and ethically sound as undertaking research overseas (for a brief review of ethical considerations in student research see Unwin, 2003). The important issue is to recognize that different types of research on development have their own challenges that need to be identified and explored in advance.

With increased questioning about the nature of development studies over the last decade, following the publication of works such as Arturo Escobar's (1995) *Encountering Development* and the emergence of post-development and postcolonial critiques (Rahnema and Bawtree, 1997), the entire notion of undertaking research in 'another place' and 'on other people' has rightly come into question (Page, 2003). Clare Madge (1997) has written about the ethical difficulties of doing research overseas, and in particular about the argument that the only way of not violating professional ethics in some way is to cease undertaking research altogether. In response, she comments:

> When I returned from The Gambia I had much sympathy with this argument, particularly with specific reference to research in the Third World by people from the First World (and I still do some/much of the time). I thought perhaps the 'solution' was to do research 'at home', studying the society of which I am a part. (Madge, 1997: 120)

This is a common reaction for many sensitive people, who think deeply about the types of research that they do. In the end, she argues that undertaking research 'at home' is also problematic, and that what really matters is the use that is made of the knowledge that is produced. However, by doing research 'at home' it is indeed possible to overcome some of the difficult, and often largely ignored, dilemmas

faced by those doing development research overseas. By 'visiting' or 'working in' a community in a developing country researchers can have an impact far beyond what they might at first think (these issues are explored in more detail in Chapter 3 on ethics). In a short period of overseas research, it is thus almost impossible to understand the complexities of the issues being addressed, and in practice most researchers take out far more from such research trips than they give back to the people in whose communities they have been visitors.

How one addresses such issues depends in large part on the reasons why one chooses to undertake research. For students, this question is in one sense already answered, because an independent dissertation is often a required component of their degrees! However, all researchers have an opportunity to choose *what* they do their research on, and *why* they do it. For many critical theorists (see Habermas, 1974, 1978), the intention is that their research should be used to make the world a better place, and this motive is often central to those undertaking research in the broad field of 'development'. Within this context, it is increasingly being accepted that the problems faced by developing countries have more to do with the policies and practices of people living in the richer countries of the world than they do with the conditions prevailing in the developing world itself. If we are really going to help poor people to make a difference to their lives, it is therefore crucial that we should seek to understand more clearly the reasons for poverty, that we should disseminate our research findings well beyond the confines of traditional academic journals, and that we should actively seek to shape and deliver policies and practices that will indeed make a difference to the world in which we live (Unwin, 1999). For those who accept such an agenda, there is a very clear justification for doing development research 'at home'.

105

Practical benefits of doing research 'at home'

There are not only sound moral grounds for doing development research 'at home', but there are also five clear practical advantages in so doing. First, the taken-for-granted knowledge that the researcher has of *their own society and culture* makes the practice of research very much easier. When there is pressure to complete a piece of research in a limited amount of time, it is very much more efficient to work in a known place, without having to take time to get to know the mundane necessities of where to live or shop for food, let alone the more complex requirements of undertaking the actual research.

Second, working in one's own *language* confers considerable advantages, not only in terms of the time saved in not having to become fluent in a new language, but also in terms of understanding the complex nuances of an interview discussion or textual analysis. The use of interpreters by no means overcomes such problems entirely (see Smith, 1996).

Third, being an '*insider*' confers specific benefits, although it does need to be recognized that there are occasions where 'outsiders' can also contribute valuable new insights into research understanding from their external perspectives. As an insider one can gain privileged access into particular social situations that would remain closed to outsiders, and one can thereby gain sophisticated understandings that an outsider might never be able to achieve.

Fourth, it is often easier for students to undertake research of *practical value* to those with whom they are researching if they do so in their own social and cultural contexts. This is based on the assumption that research should have value over and beyond merely the gaining of a qualification or academic status, but if this is indeed deemed to be desirable, then research done 'at home' can

often contribute more readily to the needs of others because the researcher will already be much more aware of what those needs actually are.

Finally, working at home provides an opportunity to spread the *temporal scale* of research in ways that a single short overseas visit cannot achieve. Not only is it possible 'at home' to return to a place to gain more data, or repeat an experiment, but it is also possible to gain insights into processes operating at different seasons and over longer periods of time.

In making these broad generalizations, it must be stressed that fascinating and important research is clearly also undertaken overseas, as illustrated in the many other chapters of this book. Attention here nevertheless focuses on the positive benefits that can be found in doing research on development at home, for those who have a passion for development but for whatever reason are unable to travel abroad. Moreover, there are increasing numbers of students for whom 'home' is actually overseas, and who will therefore be facing a completely different set of cross-cultural issues as they seek to bring the research practices that they have learnt about to bear on problems 'back home' in their own countries. Given that the majority of chapters in this book address issues associated with doing development research overseas, it is important to stress that there are actually some practical advantages as well as moral differences in doing development research at home.

Topics for doing development research at home

Among the many development issues that students have addressed in their dissertations undertaken at home, there are five areas where this research can be particularly interesting, relevant and rewarding. These include research on development policy, working with civil society or non-governmental organizations (NGOs), interpreting the imagery of development, understanding the historical construction of development, and using the potential of information and communication technologies (ICTs) to contribute to development practices. This is by no means an exhaustive list of the types of topic that can be tackled, but exemplification thereof provides insight into the differing challenges and opportunities offered by various types of development research at home.

Development policy

With the increasingly critical stance taken by many academics towards the practice of 'development' as exemplified in the work of donors and international funding agencies, opportunities arise for students to undertake a wealth of detailed analyses of the activities of particular agencies in specific fields of development practice. Among the most strident recent critiques have been those of the Structural Adjustment Programmes fuelled by the World Bank and the International Monetary Fund (IMF) during the 1990s (see, for example, Mohan et al., 1999). Research on the implications of these programmes for the economic, social and political fortunes of individual countries can readily be undertaken at home through analyses of economic and social data produced by national statistical offices and international agencies such as the IMF (www.imf.org) and the World Bank (www.worldbank.org/data/). Unless they are carefully constrained, such large-scale studies can nevertheless easily degenerate into overly descriptive accounts, and it is often better to focus on more specific aspects of development policy.

In this context donors have recently become very much more transparent about their activities, and the mass of publications and accounts that they are now generating can

provide the basis for a range of policy-related research projects. The key thing in designing such research is to ensure once again that it is not simply descriptive, and that it seeks to interrogate donor policy through particular theoretical lenses. Among the more open and accessible of donors is the UK's Department for International Development (DFID), which now makes a surprisingly comprehensive range of information available in the public domain. By so doing, DFID seeks to help people in the UK gain a more balanced view of development issues, thereby helping to change their practices and thus make it more likely that the Millennium Development Goals (http://www.un.org/millenniumgoals/) may be achieved. Details of DFID's Management Board meetings, for example, are readily accessible through its website (http://www.dfid.gov.uk), and these provide interesting insight into the ways in which the Department seeks to deliver on its Public Service Agreement targets and thereby the Millennium Development Goals. The DFID website's search facility also enables researchers to explore specific aspects of the Department's policies and practices, and it provides access to many internal briefing papers that give a very different perspective on its activities from that which can be obtained from the published literature. Other donors also provide varying amounts of information about their activities, and links to all of the OECD's Development Cooperation Directorate (DAC) members' sites can be found at http://www.oecd.org/linklist/.

Working with civil society organizations

Some undergraduate and postgraduate research projects are done in collaboration with development-oriented civil society organizations (see also Chapter 11 and Laws et al., 2003). These cover a very wide variety of issues, from the piloting of new games about development in schools, to surveys of people's attitudes to specific development agendas, and research on the funding policies and operations of civil society organizations. Very often such research can be done while working on a voluntary basis with an organization, and such experiences can be extremely valuable for subsequent career progression. Nevertheless, it is crucial to recognize that civil society organizations are inundated with requests for such work, and that only the strongest cases will elicit support. It is therefore essential for researchers to do a considerable amount of background research before approaching an organization, and they must be willing to adapt their initial ideas to suit the needs of that organization as the proposal develops. In some circumstances, researchers in higher education institutions may already have developed good collaborative relations with particular civil society organizations. This can facilitate the development of further small-scale collaborative projects that might be suitable for undergraduate or Masters research, and be of mutual benefit to both students and the relevant civil society organizations.

In approaching civil society organizations working in the field of development, it is essential to know as much as possible about them beforehand. The Development Education Association (DEA) provides a good summary of the areas of activity of all of its 220 members, and it is well worth accessing their website (http://www.dea.org.uk/dea/a_to_z_of_members.html) to see which organizations are working on issues in which you are interested. This site also provides links to the websites of all the member organizations and is an excellent source of wider information. Once you have identified a group of organizations in which you are interested, it is then important to think about the ways in which the research you want to do might actually benefit them, and how you can create a win–win situation. Often civil society organizations have a strong interest in helping people, and especially schoolchildren,

to understand the world in which they live so that they can become active global citizens. Research linked to themes such as this can therefore be particularly popular. Having identified a theme, draw up a short outline research proposal of between 500 and 1,000 words, and then send a copy together with a well-crafted covering letter seeing whether they would be interested in letting you work on this with them. Always be open to their suggestions as well because it is often the case that the organization to which you are writing might actually want some research doing on something a little different from that which you had initially intended. Depending on your own interests and competences, this can provide valuable opportunities to do something really worthwhile for them.

Images of development

One topic of particular interest to those from a cultural studies and media background is the way in which 'development' is portrayed visually in magazines, documentaries and posters. All too often, shocking images of poor or sick people are used to grab the headlines and to maximize fundraising by civil society organizations for particular causes. Such issues are discussed in much more detail in Chapter 24, but it is important to recognize that there is no need to travel abroad to gain access to such material. Excellent research projects can be undertaken using materials readily available at home. Visual images of development, both positive and negative, are all around us, and the difficulty is often to decide which actual images one wishes to study. A good starting point is to take one particular theoretical argument and then to try to find images through which this viewpoint can be interrogated. Mirzoeff's (2002) *Visual Culture Reader*, for example, offers a range of key writings covering visual forms such as photography, painting, advertising, fashion, television and digital culture, many of which can act as a catalyst for a detailed and rigorous consideration of the interface between images and development.

Interests in transculturalism and globalization can also provide a fascinating field of enquiry for those exploring the imagery of development in their own societies, be it Southeast Asian influences in the Netherlands Mexican influences in the USA or the role of Islam in contemporary British society. Exciting research can be undertaken at home on subjects as diverse as the effects of globalization on different culinary cultures, on fashion design, and on architecture, all of which have implications for the ways in which we construct and understand the concept of 'development' (see Canclini, 2001). Interviews with international architects can, for example, provide detailed insight into the processes whereby they have helped to shape the processes of urban change in the poorer countries of the world (see Serageldin and El-Sadek, 1982).

Historical constructions of development

Archives across the world are full of documents relating to development processes in the past (see Chapter 25). Among the most accessible of these are accounts by travellers of the places that they visited, and of the processes that they witnessed as European cultures came to dominate the continents of Africa and America. This is not a recent phenomenon, and greater attention, for example to the early sixteenth-century Spanish writings by missionaries such as Fray Toribio de Benavente, known as Motolinía, would emphasize that the processes associated with 'globalization' have very much older roots than is often credited. For those who cannot read foreign languages, many of the better known of these early texts are in translation (see Motolinía, 1950), and increasing amounts of archival material can now be accessed on the World Wide Web (see, for example, British

History Online, http://www.british-history.ac.uk/; the UK's National Archives, http://www.nationalarchives.gov.uk/; or the Multilaterals Project, http://fletcher.tufts.edu/multilaterals.html). Such resources provide much evidence that can be used to examine and assess generalizations made about colonialism and imperialism (Driver, 2001), as well as more recent changes that have occurred through the independence struggles of the mid-twentieth century. Historical dissertations on development issues can readily be undertaken at home, and although under-represented in the array of subjects chosen by those doing development research, they most certainly warrant greater attention.

ICT-based research

A final area that has in recent years opened up a wealth of opportunities for undergraduate and postgraduate research has been the use of new information and communication technologies (ICTs). Not only do these provide online access to data, but they also create a mechanism whereby entirely new kinds of research can be undertaken (see also Chapter 28). At the most basic level, email can enable questionnaire formats to be sent to respondents across the world, but video-conferencing facilities can also permit face-to-face interviews to be undertaken without the researcher having to travel anywhere. This can be very advantageous when a researcher wishes to gain a comparative understanding of development issues, but does not have the time or the funding to undertake journeys across several continents. More innovatively, it is relatively easy to host virtual conferences and discussions, the interactions from which can provide valuable material for a dissertation (for a recent example of successful virtual conferences, see the Commonwealth of Learning's Pan-Commonwealth Forum on Open Learning, http://www.col.org/programmes/conferences/virtual_conferences.

htm). The potential for students to engage in software development as part of their research has also been enhanced through the increased amount of Open Source work fostered across Africa (see, for example, the Free and Open Source Software Foundation for Africa, http://www.fossfa.net).

Conclusions

This chapter has outlined some of the ethical and practical considerations associated with doing development research 'at home' and has provided illustrations of the types of exciting and challenging project that can be undertaken. In the increasingly interconnected world in which we live, the actual place where we do our research is becoming less important. Many of the conclusions drawn in other chapters of this book apply when we do research on development issues based at home, but doing so also provides novel opportunities to shape dialogues and influence people in innovative ways. If we are to make a real difference to the lives of poor people across the world, we may be able to do so much more effectively by starting at home and influencing those nearest to us.

Acknowledgements

I am very grateful to Frances Burns, Rob Potter and Vandana Desai for their helpful comments on earlier drafts of this chapter.

QUESTIONS FOR DISCUSSION

1. *Who is your research going to benefit?* This chapter has implicitly argued for a critical approach to research, that seeks to move it beyond merely self-gratification on behalf of the researcher. In undertaking your dissertation, think hard about who will benefit from it, and what you can do to ensure that the time spent on your research will have wider benefits than simply contributing to your degree!

2. *What data do you have access to 'at home'?* With the availability of increasing amounts of information online, it is increasingly possible to gain access to a wealth of data and other empirical material relating to development issues.

3. *How can you turn working 'at home' into a distinct advantage?* Far too often, doing research 'at home' is seen as a disadvantage for those working on development issues. Instead, this chapter has illustrated the wealth of benefits and opportunities that such research offers. Think about your own circumstances and how you can turn them into positive assets!

Further reading

Laws, S., Harper, C. and Marcus, R. (2003) *Research for Development: A Practical Guide*, London: Sage. A quick reference manual and learning tool for all practitioners, researchers and students doing development work.

Robson, E. and Willis, K. (eds) (1997) *Postgraduate Fieldwork in Developing Areas: A Rough Guide*, 2nd edn, Developing Areas Research Group, Monograph No. 9, London: Royal Geographical Society (with the Institute of British Geographers). This is a good practical guide to undertaking fieldwork in 'developing areas', but it also includes a wealth of sensible material about researching development and is therefore also relevant to those researching 'at home'.

Rogers, A. and Viles, H. (eds) (2003) *The Student's Companion to Geography*, 2nd edn, Oxford: Blackwell. An excellent guide to all aspects of undertaking a Geography degree, including good chapters on 'development', research design, interviewing, ethics and ethnographic research.

Websites

http://www.dea.org.uk – The Development Education Association's website. It includes useful links to all of the Association's members at http://www.dea.org.uk/dea/a_to_z_of_members.html

http://www.dfid.gov.uk – The Department for International Development's website, providing a wealth of information about DFID's work, publications and development education.

http://www.ict4d.org.uk – A portal designed to provide information to, and links about, all aspects of the use of ICT for Development (ICT4D).

http://www.imf.org. – The International Monetary Fund's website. This has useful sections containing information on all the countries of the world where the IMF is active (see http://www.imf.org/external/country/index.htm).

http://www.worldbank.org/data/ – The World Bank's data and statistical website, providing a wealth of 'official' statistical data relating to development.

References

Canclini, N.G. (2001) *Consumers and Citizens: Globalization and Multicultural Conflicts*, Minneapolis: University of Minnesota Press.

Driver, F. (2001) *Geography Militant: Cultures of Exploration and Empire*, Oxford: Blackwell.

Escobar, A. (1995) *Encountering Development: The Making and Unmaking of the Third World*, Princeton, NJ: Princeton University Press.

Habermas, J. (1974) *Theory and Practice*, London: Heinemann.

Habermas, J. (1978) *Knowledge and Human Interests*, London: Heinemann.

Laws, S., Harper, C. and Marcus, R. (2003) *Research for Development: A Practical Guide*, London: Sage.

Madge, C. (1997) Ethics of research in the Third World, in E. Robson and K. Willis (eds), *Postgraduate Fieldwork in Developing Areas: A Rough Guide*, 2nd edn, Developing Areas Research Group. Monograph No. 9, London: Royal Geographical Society (with the Institute of British Geographers), pp. 113–124.

Mirzoeff, N. (ed.) (2002) *The Visual Culture Reader*, 2nd edn, London: Routledge.

Mohan, G., Brown, E., Millward, B. and Zack-Williams, A. (eds) (1999) *Structural Adjustment: Theory, Practice and Impacts*, London: Routledge.

Motolinía, F.T. (1950) *Motolinía's History of the Indians of New Spain*, translated and edited by E.A. Foster, Berkeley, CA: Cortés Society.

Page, B. (2003) Critical geography and the study of development: showers of blessing?, in A. Rogers, and H. Viles, (eds), *The Student's Companion to Geography*, 2nd edn, Oxford: Blackwell, pp. 97–103.

Rahnema, M. and Bawtree, V. (eds) (1997) *The Post-development Reader*, London: Zed Books.

Serageldin, I. and El-Sadek, S. (eds) (1982) *The Arab City: Its Character and Islamic Cultural Heritage*, Riyadh: Arab Urban Development Institute.

Smith, F.M. (1996) Problematising language: limitations and possibilities in 'foreign language' research, *Area*, 28 (2): 160–166.

Unwin, T. (1999) The end of the Enlightenment? Moral philosophy and geographical practice, in J.D. Proctor and D.M. Smith (eds), *Geography and Ethics: Essays in a Moral Terrain*, London: Routledge, pp. 263–274.

Unwin, T. (2003) Geographical ethics: reflections on the moral and ethical issues involved in debate and enquiry, in A. Rogers, and H. Viles (eds), *The Student's Companion to Geography*, 2nd edn, Oxford: Blackwell, pp. 266–271.

Part III

Information and Data Collection Methods

(i) Methods of Social Research and Associated Forms of Analysis

13

Quantitative, Qualitative or Participatory? Which Method, for What and When?

Linda Mayoux

Quantitative, qualitative or participatory research methods? • Different approaches and tools • Which method for what? Relevance, reliability and ethics • Which method when? Integrated research process

Introduction

Research methods are conventionally divided into quantitative, qualitative and participatory research methods, each with differing underlying approaches, tools and techniques.[1] Faced with the glowing claims of proponents and often strident critiques and counter-claims of opponents, one would be forgiven for thinking that they belong to 'different worlds'. Traditional disciplinary divides are, however, becoming increasingly breached. Moreover, new tools and new solutions to the shortcomings of old tools are continually being developed.

This chapter focuses on how the different methods can be integrated into a coherent research process which builds on the relative strengths and weaknesses of each. Underlying the discussion are assumptions about the main criteria for choosing between methods:

- the relevance of the information to the questions being asked and to the context
- the reliability and credibility of the information and analysis
- the ethical considerations in both means and ends of research
- the manageability in relation to skills, resources and time available

The main focus here is on small-scale research projects of the type in which students are likely to be involved. The first section presents the conventional wisdoms about the main lines of division between the different methods in terms of underlying disciplines, goals, questions and specific tools and techniques. The second section then challenges some of the claims and counter-claims of relative strengths and weaknesses in the light of recent innovations. The final section proposes an integrated research process building on participatory methods as a means of linking and focusing qualitative and quantitative methods.

Quantitative, qualitative or participatory research methods: worlds apart?

Quantitative, qualitative and participatory approaches have different disciplinary origins, and have developed distinctive tools (see Table 13.1), and each has developed its critique of the other approaches.[2] In development research, quantitative methods have typically been the main focus, with qualitative and participatory methods often relegated to desirable 'frills'. This is partly because of the overwhelming emphasis in many development agencies on economic growth and the economic dimensions of poverty. In many development agencies, the concern with quantification intensified during the 1990s, with requirements for performance assessment and targets in logical frameworks. Although some development agencies are also concerned with more 'qualitative' social goals, like empowerment and civil society development, there are pressures to quantify impacts to feed into the mainstream assessment process. Pressures for quantification have further intensified to demonstrate progress on the Millennium Development Goals, and the 'scaling up' of impacts and macro-level change.

Quantitative methods, as they are commonly conceived, derive from experimental and statistical methods in natural science. Positivist scientific method is based on the underlying philosophical assumption that reality is composed of unambiguous facts which await discovery by the observer. The main concern is with rigorous objective measurement in order to determine the truth or falsehood of particular predetermined hypotheses. Analysis of these observed facts is deductive and linear to reject or not the null hypothesis. Although

this is somewhat of a caricature even of current practice and knowledge in natural science, these philosophical assumptions underpin claims of the superior rigour of quantitative methods in economics and development research. The main focus is on measuring 'how much is happening to how many people'.

The main tools are large-scale surveys which are analysed using statistical techniques. The quantitative measurable indicators that are relevant to the predetermined hypotheses are identified and combined into questionnaires. These questionnaires are then conducted for a random sample or stratified random sample of individuals, although individuals may be assumed to be representatives of larger units such as households or social groupings. The sample also commonly includes a control group, which is selected to be identical to the main sample apart from those particular variables under investigation. Causality is assessed through a comparison of the incidence of the variables under consideration between the main sample and the control group and/or the degree to which they co-occur.

In large-scale research projects, teams are composed of a number of skilled research designers and analysts who are assisted by teams of local enumerators. Questions can be iterative and repeated over time and samples can be large, enabling sophisticated statistical modelling using advanced techniques. In most student field research, given very limited funds, questions will typically be confined to small samples, therefore enabling only limited statistical analysis. More sophisticated analysis could, however, be conducted on existing data sets.[3]

Qualitative methods have their origins in the humanities: sociology, anthropology, geography and history.[4] Each of these distinctive disciplines has developed its own tools of investigation and methods of analysis. However, they differ from quantitative methods in aiming not primarily at precise measurement of predetermined hypotheses, but at a holistic

Table 13.1   Quantitative, qualitative and participatory: different worlds?

	Quantitative	*Qualitative*	*Participatory*
Underlying disciplines	Natural scientific method and economics	Social science: anthropology, sociology, geography and history	Development activism, systems analysis and anthropology
Development questions	Numerical data: how much are things happening to how many people?	Holistic understanding of complex processes	'Grassroots' views and priorities
Main process and methods	Large-scale surveys based on individual questionnaires	Micro case studies based on informal interviews, participant observation and visual media	Participatory focus groups and workshops Diagram and oral tools Diaries
What: questions and indicators	Hypotheses and measurable indicators determined at the start of the investigation	Open-ended and cumulative formulation of questions and scope	Derived from participatory discussion in relation to local priorities
Who: sampling and representation	Large random or stratified random samples with control group	Small purposive samples Key informants 'Contingent' sampling in chance encounters	Open participation or targeted invitees Careful facilitation of the participatory process to ensure views are heard
Why: causal analysis and attribution	Deductive statistical analysis of 'before and after' and/or comparison of main sample with control group	Inductive causal inference from detailed systematic analysis of patterns of difference and similarity between the various accounts and case studies	Participatory exploration using specific tools
Implementation	Skilled research designers/analysts assisted by local enumerators	Individual 'immersed' and skilled researcher/s	Team of skilled facilitators Local people themselves following training

117

understanding of complex realities and processes where even the questions and hypotheses emerge cumulatively as the investigation progresses. The possibility of 'objectivity' is questioned and instead the aim is to understand differing and often competing 'subjectivities' in terms of very different accounts of 'facts', different meanings and different perceptions.

Qualitative research typically focuses on compiling a selection of micro-level case studies which are investigated using a combination of informal interviews, participant observation and more recently visual media like photography and video. Questions are broad and open-ended, and change and develop over time to fill in a 'jigsaw' of differing accounts of 'reality', unravelling which may be said to be generally 'true' and which are specific and subjective, and why. Different sampling methods are combined depending on the particular dimension of the issue being considered: different purposive sampling techniques, identification of key informants who possess the particular knowledge sought and also 'random encounters' to cross-check information and/or highlight yet more differing perspectives on the problem. Causality and attribution are directly investigated through questioning as well as the qualitative analysis of data. Computer programs may be used to deal systematically with large amounts of data.[5] Qualitative research typically requires the long-term immersion of a skilled researcher in the field who engages in a reflexive process of data collection and analsysis.

Participatory methods have their origins in development activism: non-governmental organizations (NGOs) and social movements.[6] Here the main aim is not so much knowledge *per se*, but social change and empowerment – and this wherever possible as a direct result of the research process itself. In particular, it seeks to investigate and give voice to those groups in society who are most vulnerable and marginalized in development decision-making and implementation. The participatory

process may involve small focus groups, larger participatory workshops or individual diaries and diagrams which are then collated into a plenary discussion. Participation (and hence sampling) may be open or carefully targeted to particular social groups. Larger meetings may be subdivided into what are assumed to be more 'homogeneous groups' or groups with complementary information.

Participatory research typically uses and adapts diagram tools from farmer-led research, systems analysis and also oral and visual tools from anthropology, though many commonly used tools have also been developed by NGOs and participants in the field. The use of diagram and oral tools makes both discussion and analysis accessible to non-literate participants and across language groups. Through sharing their different sources of information, participants themselves may increase their understanding of development issues and the problems they face, and develop solutions, as well as giving more reliable and representative information to researchers. In some cases local people themselves conduct research following an initial design of specific tools and training. Some recent NGO innovations propose doing this on a large scale (Mayoux et al., 2005).

Which method for what? Relevance, reliability and ethics

In recent years, however, these 'different worlds' have begun to merge.[7] There is an increasing awareness of the extreme complexity and political contingency of even definitions of many development problems, notably poverty and empowerment but also health/well-being and literacy/knowledge, and hence also the inevitable complexity of the information needed to find solutions. Interdisciplinary courses in development studies have become more common. Development agencies commonly require multidisciplinary teams. This has led to constructive cross-fertilization of tools and more integrated methodologies to build on the complementarities between different methods.

Traditional disciplinary boundaries are in any case far less rigid than the above account would indicate:

- Quantitative information can be obtained through participatory and/or qualitative methods.[8]
- Qualitative information can be obtained as part of quantitative surveys and/or using participatory methods.
- Participatory diagram tools can be used with individual respondents to get both qualitative and quantitative information, and participatory meetings can be used as a forum for conducting these.[9]

Moreover, new tools and new solutions to shortcomings of old tools are continually being developed.

What is now emerging is a much more nuanced approach. Strengths and weaknesses are not always absolute, but depend very much on how particular methods and tools are used and whether they are used 'well' or 'badly'. Unfortunately also, what may be potential strengths in relation to one context or purpose, may be potential weaknesses in others. A summary of the main potential pros and cons of the different methods is attempted in Table 13.2, although many of these are inevitably contentious. What follows focuses mainly on comparing the 'cons' and the ways in which they might be addressed.

The first key area of debate and contention concerns identification of issues to be investigated and definitions of development problems. On the one hand, the specificity and clarity of the questions and hypotheses that are required for rigorous quantitative research lay it open to challenges of 'measuring the irrelevant' and/or 'trying to measure the immeasurable' (Hulme, 2000). On the other

hand, the very openness and flexibility of qualitative methods create problems of a lack of focus. The participatory solution of relying on local priorities raises the question of 'whose local priorities?' as these are often diverse and open to manipulation by powerful vested interests. Balancing inherent tensions between specificity and flexibility and competing views from the field will inevitably be a difficult task.

The second challenge is translating these broad questions into a workable research frame. In all types of research, considerable thought must be given to the potential effects of precisely which questions are asked, how, from and by whom.[10] Even (or perhaps particularly) in quantitative research, assumptions of 'objectivity' must be continuously questioned.[11] It should not be assumed that 'more information is necessarily better information'. Very long interview schedules may give very inaccurate responses because of both respondent and interviewer fatigue. Very precise questions may not give precise answers because people simply do not know or recall, or they are suspicious of the amount of detail required. Conducting ill-thought-out questionnaires, even for large samples, will not improve the reliability of the information. Any statistical analysis based on these will also be potentially misleading.

In deciding when and how to use quantitative methods, the critical questions will be:

1 For which questions is quantification needed, and with what degree of precision? For which questions is qualitative information more useful or sufficient?
2 For how many people is information required to draw reliable practical conclusions? Which particular people are most important for the analysis or are likely to be able to give reliable information?

In many cases, particularly in small student research projects, high levels of precision will not be either possible or necessary. More in-depth discussions from a smaller number of

119

Table 13.2   Summary pros and cons of different methods

	Quantitative methods		Qualitative methods		Participatory methods	
	Pros	*Cons*	*Pros*	*Cons*	*Pros*	*Cons*
Relevance	Clear focus on specific questions and hypotheses	External and a priori focus may miss relevant questions and issues Not everything can be measured meaningfully	Holistic understanding of complex issues and processes Flexibility and cumulative understanding Captures underlying meanings, the unexpected and sensitive issues	May lack focus Still filtered by subjective external analysis	Based on local perceptions and priorities	May be too context-specific May be over-influenced by power relations
Representation and freedom from bias	Random samples decrease likelihood of bias	In practice the sample actually interviewed is often non-random Choice of control group presumes the relevant variables are already known May under-represent minorities in aggregate conclusions	Captures different local perceptions Purposive sampling enables close focus on cases and issues of interest	Small-scale, open to bias Generalizability of findings are often difficult to prove	Can rapidly collect large amounts of data Captures diversity Careful targeting and collective discussion increases the voice of the most vulnerable	May be over-influenced by power relations Difficult to control who attends Participation in discussion depends on the skill of the facilitator

(Continued)

Table 13.2 (Continued)

	Quantitative methods		Qualitative methods		Participatory methods	
	Pros	Cons	Pros	Cons	Pros	Cons
Reliability of information	Objectivity of measurement	Objectivity may be only apparent Depends on precisely which questions are asked, how and by whom Problems of respondent motivation and falsification	Captures subjectivity In-depth longitudinal investigation decreases the likelihood of falsification	May be over-influenced by the biases of the researcher	Collective discussion enables more reasoned responses and immediate cross-checking of different accounts Diagram captures non-linear complexity	Depends on who participates Depends on the skill and understanding of the facilitator Difficult to sift all the information and record it at the time of the exercise
Credibility of analysis	Objectivity of analysis	Difficult to 'prove' causality Depends very much on the relevance of the questions and hypotheses and the reliability of the information	Cumulative 'jigsaw' Good at uncovering processes and causality	Difficult to 'prove anything' beyond anecdotes May be over-influenced by the biases of the researcher	Collective and immediate analysis of information enables immediate cross-checking of different accounts Diagrams can represent a clear analysis of complex issues	Difficult to aggregate May be over-influenced by power relations and expectations Diagrams may be difficult to interpret It is often the process rather than the diagram product which is key

(Continued)

Table 13.2 (Continued)

	Quantitative methods		Qualitative methods		Participatory methods	
	Pros	*Cons*	*Pros*	*Cons*	*Pros*	*Cons*
Ethics	Collection of 'hard data' to convince policy makers	Direct benefits for respondents are generally not considered	Empathy and understanding	Aim at non-interference	Concerns about empowerment are integral to the process	Empowerment may be assumed rather than actual
		The very questions and ways in which questions are asked has an impact	May give people a chance to discuss things they have never been able to tell anyone before	Even the presence of an investigator has an impact	People learn from each other and reach new understandings	May raise unrealistic expectations
						May make some people more vulnerable

people will get more reliable information. These people may also be able to give a rough estimate of how general their responses are, and these estimates from different people can then be compared to arrive at an approximate figure. More time- and energy-consuming tasks of questioning a larger number of people can then be reserved for those specific questions where it is really needed.

Qualitative and participatory researchers have more often been consciously aware of these issues, and in some cases treated them as a subject of investigation in themselves. Nevertheless even these researchers have often been less than open about the subjectivity of their analysis, and their role in influencing the outcomes of research processes. It is crucial that whatever methods are used, researchers engage in in-depth reflection and acknowledgement of their own biases, and seek ways of countering these which take account of both their privileged 'overview' knowledge and the diversity of local views and perceptions.[12]

All researchers are at least to some extent dependent on the enthusiasm and cooperation of respondents in conducting their research. Ethical issues are therefore practically as well as morally central to the research process. In quantitative and qualitative research, as well as participatory research, considerable thought needs to be given to how questionnaires and qualitative investigation can be designed to benefit respondents: particularly how to facilitate a progression of thinking through issues important to them, sharing information to which the researcher has had access, and the dissemination of the findings back to those who contributed to the research.[13]

Participatory research has commonly claimed the 'empowerment high ground'. However, participatory research may merely extract what everybody already knows for the benefits of the researcher, rather than generating new knowledge for participants or helping

them develop ways forward. Moreover, the very act of organizing group discussions may raise unrealistic expectations. People may be made even more vulnerable if they express their views and problems publicly. Both these factors may lead to unreliable information being obtained as well as undesirable consequences for all concerned. In participatory research, as much as other forms of research, benefits for participants need to be strategically planned rather than assumed (Johnson and Mayoux, 1998). In all types of research, researchers should consider the types of organization, network and support agency which participants might approach in order to take forward issues raised by the research.

Which method when? An integrated research process

There are therefore no easy answers. All research, even that with claims to 'objective truth', is inevitably fraught with complexity and sources of bias and error. Even the subjective biases in analysing competing subjectivities need to be examined. Ethical concerns must always be an integral and planned element in research design rather than assumed outcomes.

Wherever possible, most research will use an integrated methodology. Using complementary methods enables researchers to consolidate strengths, and cross-check and triangulate any information which is central to the particular research questions concerned. An integrated methodology also helps to disseminate information in different ways for different audiences to ensure, as far as possible, beneficial outcomes for the participants. Figure 13.1 gives an outline of a possible research process, the questions which each stage must seek to address and the possible ways in which different methods can be integrated. As can be seen, participatory methods play a central role at all stages from conception,

123

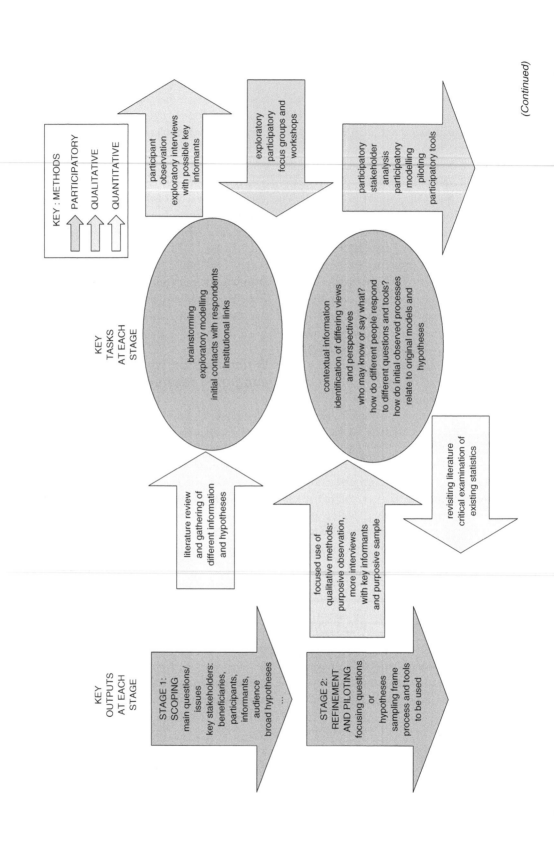

KEY : METHODS

PARTICIPATORY
QUALITATIVE
QUANTITATIVE

KEY TASKS AT EACH STAGE

KEY OUTPUTS AT EACH STAGE

participant observation exploratory interviews with possible key informants

exploratory participatory focus groups and workshops

participatory stakeholder analysis participatory modelling piloting participatory tools

brainstorming exploratory modelling initial contacts with respondents institutional links

contextual information identification of differing views and perspectives who may know or say what? how do different people respond to different questions and tools? how do initial observed processes relate to original models and hypotheses

literature review and gathering of different information and hypotheses

focused use of qualitative methods: purposive observation, more interviews with key informants and purposive sample

revisiting literature critical examination of existing statistics

STAGE 1: SCOPING main questions/ issues key stakeholders: beneficiaries, participants, informants, audience broad hypotheses ...

STAGE 2: REFINEMENT AND PILOTING focusing questions or hypotheses sampling frame process and tools to be used

(Continued)

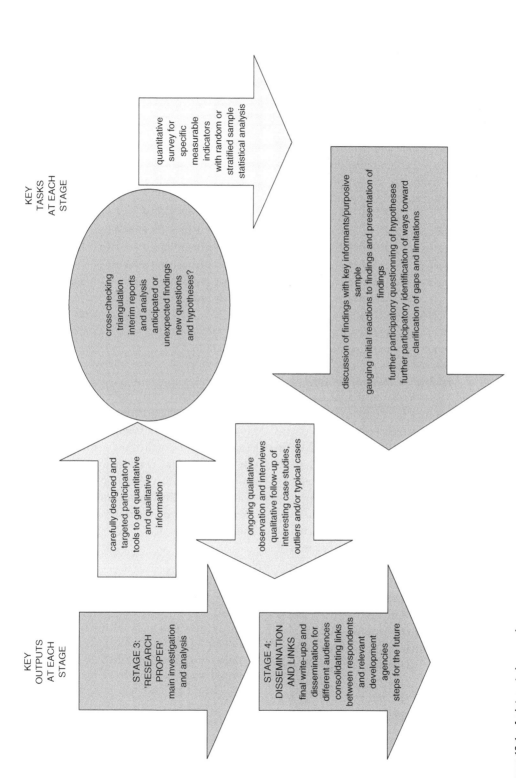

KEY
TASKS
AT EACH
STAGE

quantitative
survey for
specific
measurable
indicators
with random or
stratified sample
statistical analysis

cross-checking
triangulation
interim reports
and analysis
anticipated or
unexpected findings
new questions
and hypotheses?

discussion of findings with key informants/purposive
sample
gauging initial reactions to findings and presentation of
findings
further participatory questionning of hypotheses
further participatory identification of ways forward
clarification of gaps and limitations

carefully designed and
targeted participatory
tools to get quantitative
and qualitative
information

ongoing qualitative
observation and interviews
qualitative follow-up of
interesting case studies,
outliers and/or typical cases

KEY
OUTPUTS
AT EACH
STAGE

STAGE 3:
'RESEARCH
PROPER'
main investigation
and analysis

STAGE 4:
DISSEMINATION
AND LINKS
final write-ups and
dissemination for
different audiences
consolidating links
between respondents
and relevant
development
agencies
steps for the future

Figure 13.1   An integrated research process

through piloting and refinement to the research proper and then finally dissemination.

It is the view of the author that using participatory methods as the 'first port of call' has many advantages in terms of rapidity and reliability of collecting many types of qualitative as well as quantitative information, manageability in terms of time and resources, and also its potential for contributing to the development process. In this the author must confess to be highly influenced by her early work in the late 1970s to late 1980s doing long-term, in-depth qualitative and quantitative fieldwork in India, based on anthropology but also working with economists. Subsequent experience of using and developing participatory methods have shown many ways in which these could have yielded far more reliable information far more quickly. Participatory methods are not necessarily a substitute for other methods, but enable much more cost-effective targeting of everyone's time and energy on those areas of the research for which participatory methods are rather more problematic. They are also generally an essential component of research dissemination to those participating in the research, a stage which is commonly ignored and omitted.

The research process suggested is applicable in many, and probably most, research contexts, both in individual student research and in multidisciplinary research teams. It will nevertheless be important to adapt both process, and particularly specific tools, to the types of question, the context, the skills, understanding and motivation of respondents and the skills and resources available to the researcher. In particular, the relative emphasis on participatory, qualitative and quantitative methods in the main research stage will depend very much on the outcomes of the prior two stages. In some contexts also it may not be advisable to do any participatory research before in-depth qualitative research has overcome sensitivities and/or established networks which could be used as the basis for bringing people together. In some contexts

and for some purposes, quantitative surveys may also be a very useful introduction and pretext for contacting a range of different people. People may be more familiar with the idea of questionnaires, providing a structure which can then be an opportunity for qualitative methods like participant observation and unstructured conversation. This 'random exposure' may also then provide a good basis on which to design a more rigorous participatory process.

The research process suggested is therefore more of a 'rough guide to be adapted or thrown to circumstance' than a rigid prescription. Particular care must be taken when using participatory methods in conflict or highly politically charged environments and/or where the prime intended beneficiaries of the research are very vulnerable. Examples of the latter include, for example, research on child labour, domestic violence and labour relations if it is difficult for victims to meet without the knowledge of those with power over them. At the same time participatory methods can be a very valuable means of helping resolve misunderstandings and conflict, and identify realistic ways forward. Any research on such issues, participatory or otherwise, should also as far as possible liaise with organizations which can follow up on at least serious cases of abuse identified.

Notes

1. In this chapter the term 'approach' is used to refer to underlying philosophies, goals and disciplines, the term 'tools' to the practical and specified 'best practice' ways in which information is obtained and/or analysed, 'techniques' to ways in which tools may be adapted or applied to particular circumstances or challenges, and the term 'method' is used as a generic term encompassing all three.

2. For overviews of claims and counter-claims see Hulme (2000) and Kanbur (2003).

3. For a useful short summary of the issues and pitfalls of statistics in development studies, see Mukherjee and Wuyts (1998). For a more

detailed discussion and introduction to the methods, see Mukherjee et al. (1988). For easily accessible overviews of the strengths and pitfalls of different statistical techniques, see the website for Statsoft: http://www.statsoft.com/textbook/stathome.html. For access to many further resources, see the quantitative methods, statistics and quantitative database sections on the University of Amsterdam's SocioSite: http://www2.fmg.uva.nl/sociosite/topics/research.html

4. For an overview of qualitative methods, see Denzin and Lincoln (1994) and relevant chapters in this volume. For access to many further resources, see the qualitative methods sections on the University of Amsterdam's SocioSite: http://www2.fmg.uva.nl/sociosite/topics/research.html.

5. For detailed discussion and links to trial versions of the different computer-aided qualitative data analysis (CAQDAS) packages, see Lewins and Silver (2004).

6. For a detailed introduction and overview of participatory methods, see Chambers (1994).

7. See, for example, the debates between eminent development researchers at the 2001 'Qual-Quant' workshop held at Cornell University (Kanbur, 2003).

8. For a discussion of quantification and participatory methods, see Mayoux and Chambers (2005).

9. For suggestions on how some recent participatory tools can be used for quantitative and qualitative investigation, see Mayoux (2003a).

10. For a critical overview of research on women's empowerment in micro-finance, see Kabeer (2001). For an overview of issues and questions in relation to different methods, see Mayoux (2002).

11. For a convincing gender critique of inherent biases in quantitative research on poverty, social cost–benefit analysis and population policy, see Kabeer (1994).

12. For a very thoughtful self-questioning combination of quantitative and qualitative research on changing gender relations, see Kabeer (2000).

13. See, for example, Mayoux (2003b) and Chapter 3 on ethics in this volume.

127

QUESTIONS FOR DISCUSSION

Relevance and reliability check

1. What are the questions and issues which the research is designed to address? Whose questions and issues are they? What are the underlying assumptions and biases?
2. For which questions is quantification needed, and with what degree of precision? For which questions is qualitative information more useful or sufficient?
3. For how many people is information required to draw reliable practical conclusions? Which particular people are most important for the analysis or likely to be able to give reliable information? Is information likely to be more reliable in private or in a group discussion?
4. What are the implications of the answers to these questions for the conclusions which can be drawn?

Ethics check

5. Does the research process help build the capacity, skills and learning of those 'researched' and increase their understanding?
6. What are likely to be the practical consequences? Who will use the information generated and how? Are the most disadvantaged and vulnerable participants adequately represented and protected at all stages?

Websites

The Social Science Resource website of the University of Amsterdam has lists of resources and other web links for different types of research method: http://www2.fmg.uva.nl/sociosite/ topics/ research.html

Discussion of quantitative methods, including use of qualitative and participatory methods for quantification, can be found at: www.ssc.reading.ac.uk

The Statsoft website has comprehensive materials on the strengths and weaknesses of different tools for statistical analysis: http://www.statsoft.com/textbook/stathome.html

The Forum for Qualitative Research website brings together resources and debates in English and other European languages: http://www.qualitative-research.net/fqs/fqs-eng.htm

Chronic Poverty Research Centre has links to research methodologies and a toolbox: http://www. devinit.org/CPRC/CPall/www_cprc/www_cprc/default.html

The Monitoring and Evaluation (MandE) website has detailed practical discussions on the use of different qualitative, quantitative and participatory tools in development agencies: http://www. mande.co.uk

Further reading and References

Chambers, R. (1994) The origins and practice of participatory rural appraisal, *World Development*, 22(7): 953–969.

Chataway, J. and Joffe, A. (1998) Communicating results, in A. Thomas, J. Chataway and M. Wuyts (eds), *Finding Out Fast: Investigative Skills for Policy and Development* (pp. 221–236), London: Sage.

Denzin, N.K. and Lincoln, Y.S. (1994) *Handbook of Qualitative Research*, Thousand Oaks: Sage.

Helberg, C. (1995) Pitfalls of data analysis (or how to avoid lies and damned lies). Paper presented to workshop at the Third International Applied Statistics in Industry Conference, Dallas. Available at: http://my.execpc.com?#helberg/pitfalls/

Hulme, D. (2000) Impact assessment methodologies for microfinance: theory, experience and better practice. *World Development*, 28(1): 79–88.

Johnson, H. and Mayoux, L. (1998) Investigation as empowerment: using participatory methods, in A. Thomas, J. Chataway and M. Wuyts (eds), *Finding Out Fast: Investigative Skills for Policy and Development* (pp. 147–172), London: Sage, Open University.

Kabeer, N. (1994) *Reversed Realities: Gender Hierarchies in Development Thought*, London: Verso.

Kabeer, N. (2000) *The Power to Choose: Bangladeshi Women and Labour Market Decisions in London and Dhaka*, London: Verso.

Kabeer, N. (2001) Conflicts over credit: re-evaluating the empowerment potential of loans to women in rural Bangladesh, *World Development*, 29(1): 63–84.

Kanbur, R. (ed.) (2003) Q-squared: qualitative and quantitative methods of poverty appraisal, New Delhi: Permanent Black.

Lewins, A. and Silver, C. (2004) Choosing a CAQDAS (Computer-Aided Qualitative Data Analysis) Package: a working paper. Available at: http://caqdas.soc.surrey.ac.uk/Choosing%20a%20 CAQDAS%20package%20-%20LewinsandSilver.pdf

Mayoux, L. (2001) Whom do we talk to? Issues in sampling, EDIAIS. Available at: http://www.enterprise-impact.org.uk/informationresources/toolbox/sampling.shtml

Mayoux, L. (2002) What do we do with the information? From practical conclusions to influencing change, EDIAIS. Available at: http://www.enterprise-impact.org.uk/informationresources/toolbox/whatdowedo.shtml

Mayoux, L. (2003a) Thinking it through: using diagrams in impact assessment: EDIAIS. Available at: http://www.impact.org.uk/informationresources/toolbox/thinkingitthrough-usingdiagramsinIA.shtml

Mayoux, L. (2003b) Empowering enquiry: a new approach to investigation, EDIAIS. Available at: http://www.enterpriseimpact.org.uk/informationresources/toolbox/empoweringenquiry.shtml

Mayoux, L., Andharia, J., Hardikar, N., Thacker, S. and Dand, S. (2005) Participatory action learning in practice: experience of Anandi, India, *Journal of International Development*, 17: 211–242.

Mayoux, L. and Chambers, R. (2005) Reversing the paradigm: quantification and participatory methods and pro-poor growth, *Journal of International Development*, 17: 271–298.

Mukherjee, C. and Wuyts, M. (1998) Thinking with quantitative data, in A. Thomas, J. Chataway and M. Wuyts (eds), *Finding Out Fast: Investigative Skills for Policy and Development* (pp. 237–260), London: Sage.

Mukherjee, C., White, H. and Wuyts, M. (1988) *Econometrics and Data Analysis for Developing Countries*, London: Routledge.

Thomas, A. (1998) Challenging cases, in A. Thomas, J. Chataway and M. Wuyts (eds), *Finding Out Fast: Investigative Skills for Policy and Development* (pp. 307–332), London: Sage.

Thomas, A., Chataway, J. and Wuyts, M. (1998) *Finding Out Fast: Investigative Skills for Policy and Development*, London: Sage and The Open University.

14

Field Surveys and Inventories

David Barker

An introduction to field mapping • An introduction to field inventories • Urban surveys in small market towns • Farm plot maps and land degradation indices • Hazard maps and damage assessment

This chapter focuses on the use of field surveys and inventories in development research. It shows just how versatile such data are in the study of development-oriented topics. First of all, basic ideas and concepts are reviewed, before looking at examples drawn from three important research contexts, namely, the urban milieu and small market towns, farming and land management, and the impact of natural disasters.

Basic issues in completing field surveys and inventories

Field mapping

A field survey often involves field mapping – the process of compiling a map while working in the field. Data collection is *in situ*, and the data are depicted in map form. The format may be a sketch map of land use, or a map of relevant features in the human and/or physical landscape (buildings, infrastructure, erosion features, water sources, etc.). A field map illustrates layout and key aspects of the spatial organization of the phenomena you are studying. The final version of your field map is completed later, at a desk, often using computer software, but is not necessarily drawn to scale. Remember to retain your original fieldwork maps as these might form part of the overall assessment of your research project.

Field mapping techniques require patience and attention to detail rather than highly developed cartographic skills. The process is time-consuming and physically arduous in a hot, tropical climate. Good eyesight and a pair of binoculars facilitate field observation, but knowing what to look for and recognizing what you see are critical skills. Thorough planning and preparation are prerequisites for fieldwork in an unfamiliar country, and you need to be thoroughly conversant with any relevant literature, including any technical manuals available. The added-value of field mapping is that during the mapping process you assimilate contextual information, often without realizing it. Thus, the field context provides exposure to your study area, its people, its environment and ecology, and in doing so fosters an appreciation of the subtle interrelationships between social, economic, cultural, topographical, environmental, ecological or geological phenomena.

Field inventories

Field inventories are used extensively in geography and other field-based disciplines such as forestry, ecology, resource management and social anthropology. A field inventory is a checklist of items or phenomena you are likely to encounter in the field. The technique enables you to record presence or absence, and/or other properties and attributes of specific items you observe in the field. The items may be human features of the landscape (houses, shops, roads) or physical features (hillsides, landslides, beaches). Field inventories are pre-designed in the same way a questionnaire is prepared before the data are collected. They are designed for easy use in the field. Generally, an inventory is tailored to the specific needs of a project. Help is sometimes available through previous field studies, published field guides or specialized technical websites. These sources can provide basic templates for data recording, which can be modified to suit your own research. Booking sheets and other data recording sheets are also included in this category of data collection techniques since they also involve the field recording of quantitative and qualitative information based on field observations.

The simple design of a field inventory ensures data recording under field conditions is a straightforward and unambiguous process. Data recording sheets often have the physical appearance of a table or matrix. Observed information can be recorded as presence or absence data, or items may be counted and tallied on the data sheet. Some field methods require subjective assessments of field observations, such as assigning a score or a rank on a rating scale between two extremes, for example, when assessing housing quality or damage to a building after a flood event.

Field equipment

Simple equipment is often needed for field surveys. A field notebook is normally essential and a sketch pad useful. Field notebooks are the prerogative of physical geographers but are invaluable in development research and human geography too. A pocket-sized, field notebook also can serve as a personal diary when conducting research in a foreign country. A sketch pad is useful because of its larger page size. Binoculars are helpful for observing inaccessible places, and a digital camera is virtually obligatory for recording visual detail and context. More specialized equipment may be needed in some types of field research. A measuring tape, a couple of ranging poles, a compass and a clinometer are important for accurate measurements of the size, shape and slope angles of small geographical areas such as a farm plot or a house plot. A hand-held GPS provides precise latitude and longitude coordinates. Where accurately-scaled field maps are required, more rigorous methods of land surveying are employed. Certain types of research may require soil sampling kits or water quality sampling equipment.

Research design and complementary data collection methods

Field surveys and inventories in developmental research are invariably used in conjunction with other data collection methods, especially questionnaire surveys, in-depth interviews,

131

focus groups and ethnographic techniques. Field methods are multifaceted in the same way that the research itself is often multidisciplinary and, in your research, you may be required to integrate socio-economic data with environmental and ecological data. Research design usually forges logical connections between complementary data collection methods. For example, in developing countries it is frequently necessary to create and improvise a sampling frame prior to data collection in order to conduct a proper random sample because no suitable, published sampling frame is available. A farmers' register or a business directory may be hopelessly out of date or a potential sampling frame may be frustratingly incomplete. In such cases, field survey methods can be used to compile and create an up-to-date base map. Thus, by field mapping you can update a published map of a town's commercial buildings. For example, you can add the position and location of shops not shown on the published map, perhaps because they were built after the map was published. Similarly, in a rapidly growing squatter community, recently erected homes can be identified, mapped and superimposed on to an earlier map of the area, once access is gained to the community. The new base maps you have updated (or created) through field mapping can be utilized at the next stage of your research, as your physical sampling frame. In effect, all the buildings or houses on your base map become your sampling units.

Small market towns and the urban milieu

Small market towns are key spatial nodes for rural–urban interaction between agricultural regions and primate cities (Potter and Unwin, 1989). Rural service centres provide commercial, retailing and service activities for their hinterlands and have large periodic markets.

They are transport centres and house regional offices for government, education, health and social services, NGOs and rural development projects. Small market towns in developing countries, more so than their counterparts in the industrialized world, are often literally physically bursting at their geographical seams in terms of spatial layout. Congested, bustling with economic activity, especially on market days, they are a nexus where facets of globalization (fast food establishments, the offices of cell phone companies, etc.) are located in the main street alongside traditional informal sector activities like hawking and vending (see Figure 14.1). Affluence and poverty conspicuously co-exist in apparent symbiosis. As a researcher in a foreign country, such small towns afford an opportunity to experience the dynamism of development in a microcosm – a place where town meets country and tradition embraces modernity.

Urban field surveys

In the postcolonial period, small market towns grew rapidly and haphazardly, without any formal town planning to regulate the pattern of physical development. Nevertheless, urban fabric has a distinctive spatial layout, reflecting the convergence of local and global economic, social and cultural forces in the development process, and creating a distinctive urban morphology. Architecture styles and building façades are likely to be a mixture of traditional and vernacular with the trappings of modernity. Occasionally bordering on the bizarre and obscure, urban morphology reflects the character-defining symbols of urban complexity in an idiosyncratic landscape of development.

A useful starting point is a land use survey of the main business district. You may be familiar with the techniques of urban land use mapping, and in development research the field methods are similar, though need

Figure 14.1   In this Jamaican market town, informal sector vendors sell their wares on the high street (in front of the premises of a local fast food chain, and a multinational cell phone company

133

fine-tuning to the local cultural context. The first step, common to all fieldwork, is the field reconnaissance. Field reconnaissance familiarizes you and/or your group with the spatial extent of your study area, helps form an impression of its vitality, and suggests potential problems you may encounter later. However, in this case, the reconnaissance needs to be used to map street pattern and general layout of the town since there is unlikely to be a published street map or shopping centre plan

available. Indeed, your urban field survey may be the first of its kind, and no other maps may be available for reference. Field notebooks and sketch pads are essential in the reconnaissance, and note carefully the location of individual shopping plazas requiring detailed attention, and potential problem locations.

You will also need to develop a classification of land use/business establishments. Its categories may differ from those in your home country. You will need to record information on informal sector activities as well as the formal sector, so operational definitions are important considerations. Many shops in developing countries sell a bewildering array of goods (including food) and are all-purpose 'general stores' or 'variety stores'. Commercial buildings may have multiple functions, some of which may not be obvious from the store front; for example, informal sector activities may be located obscurely in the same building. Informal sector enterprises may be located directly in front of a formal business establishment at the roadside (see Figure 14.1) – the relationship between the two might be complementary or in conflict. Where time permits, the classification of business types is best finalized after the field reconnaissance and before the main land use survey, for maximum exposure to the range of commercial activities present in the town. The process of formulating operational definitions in the classification is itself a useful exercise, and is most effectively done in group discussions, preferably in consultation with local students.

Field mapping for an urban survey involves recording the categories of business establishment directly on your sketch of the street pattern, resulting in a land use map. Symbols used to record categories should be simple and flexible enough to accommodate places where multiple commercial functions exist (e.g. buildings with more than one storey). A simple lettering system or colour code can differentiate banks, bars, variety stores, hairdressers, lotto outlets, gas stations, and so on. A land use sketch map is not drawn to scale but pacing out shop fronts (one pace = one metre) allows a scaling factor to be introduced into the mapping process. Remember to record any informal sector activity outside the store front (but note whether it is a mobile operation – it may not be there next time you pass the store front).

Another dimension to the urban survey is to collect data about the business establishments themselves. This will be much easier for formal sector enterprises. A data sheet is designed as a matrix, with rows corresponding to each establishment, and columns recording attributes such as size category, building style and material, building age, number of storeys, family business/chain store, number of employees, estimated floor space, etc. Some of this information may involve interviewing employers and employees.

Photographs are important in urban surveys. Good photographs provide an accurate visual record of cultural variations in architectural styles and other features of urban morphology (see Figure 14.1). They can also depict innovative local sign-writing, humour (sometimes inadvertent) and improvisation. Photographs add an extra dimension to your research reports provided the material is used sparingly and creatively, and are useful in class media presentations and for creating posters. On a cautionary note, photography needs to be done sensitively and unobtrusively, and may meet with a hostile reaction from local people if it is intrusive or undertaken without the consent of those being photographed.

There are a range of other urban-type surveys that exist that also may prove useful for your research; for example, assessments of urban environmental quality or architectural form. Virtually any aspect of the urban environment can be assessed once appropriate and relevant dimensions and rating scales are derived.

Bus stations

Bus stations are locations that offer both opportunities and challenges in urban surveys. If you are undertaking field research in a developing country for the first time, remember that the local transport system actually works, even if it appears totally chaotic. There is almost certainly an underlying spatial order or logic in the apparent confusion and bustle. Don't be put off by the congestion and proliferation of informal sector business people milling around the bus station, even trying to sell their wares and services on the buses themselves.

Field maps of the spatial organization of a bus station are useful, information about destinations, counts of bus movements, and estimates of passenger capacity or volumes all provide information on the town's function as a transport node. Bus stations are good locations to collect data on informal sector activities. These might range from fresh food and cooked food vending (both mobile and fixed-location vendors), drinks vendors, hustlers soliciting passengers, vending of craft items, religious paraphernalia, begging, to all manner of services like shoe-shine, local guides, music and entertainment. Bus stations are not easy places to conduct interviews, neither with transport operators nor origin and destination surveys of passengers. However, certain types of information can be gleaned unobtrusively, through intelligent observations and simple data recording. For example, an interesting field exercise is to identify as many different types of informal sector activity as you can. Record the information on an inventory, together with other basic attributes – gender, age group, type of merchandise, degree of mobility, visible equipment, type of service, presumed legality/illegality, etc. You can observe and record useful information even without recourse to an interview.

Produce markets

Produce markets also provide interesting data collection opportunities. Again, the bustle of the market makes interviewing vendors and customers difficult, and successful interviews require time and creative patience. But other simple methods of recording data abound. Local markets have an internal spatial organization despite their congested appearance – separate areas for fruit and vegetables, meat, perhaps fish, and dry goods. Sketch maps can be prepared to show a market's geographical layout. Vendors can be classified and enumerated, and customers

counted. The daily and weekly rhythms can be discerned by staggering the timing of field visits. Third World produce markets act as central places for the sale of fresh food to the hinterland population. But increasingly, produce markets also retail a staggering array of dry goods that reflect the flotsam and jetsam of our globalized world of manufacturing – cheap plastic buckets from China, cooking utensils from Brazil, plastic flip-flop shoes from Thailand and designer trainers from Taiwan. How on earth did all these items get into a rural market in East Africa or a Caribbean island?

Sometimes a produce market is upgraded or relocated by local planners to improve health and sanitation or relieve traffic congestion. A field survey of the market can illuminate the impacts of local planning decisions. A common problem is that the planners' views of a good market location may not coincide with vendors' views of where they would like to be located in relation to their potential customers. In the Caribbean, for example, market vendors often congregate where they can intercept potential customers before they enter the main covered market area (see Figure 14.1). In the absence of regulations, local produce and dry goods markets spill on to nearby pavements and roads outside their designated areas, causing traffic congestion and crowded confusion.

Farming, food production and land management

The principal research tool for collecting primary data on farming systems in developing countries is the farm survey. Questionnaire interviews and participant observation with farmers, however, can be usefully complemented by field mapping and field inventories. Below, we highlight two topics in agricultural research where field mapping and data recording sheets play a more pivotal role in research design.

135

Tropical home gardens

Tropical home gardens are the small areas around people's homes that provide food for the household and are characterized by the presence of food-bearing trees. Home gardens are ubiquitous throughout the tropics (Landauer and Brazil, 1990) and are known by a variety of names, including kitchen gardens and multi-storey tropical gardens. They are vital to household food security and are recognized as a distinctive type of farming since they are farmed more intensively than other types of farm plot. Chickens, goats and pigs are often present and closely integrated into the food production system. The literature emphasizes the multi-functionality of home gardens because the plants, bushes and trees have many additional uses – medicines, teas, beverages, tonics, timber, furniture, roofing material (Hills, 1988). Kitchen garden studies can complement a farm survey, or themselves be the focus in a study of household food security, self-reliance, and the role of traditional indigenous knowledge in rural livelihoods.

A field survey of a home garden begins by creating a sketch map of the plot, and should be done with an adult member of the household. A walk around the perimeter can establish a spatial framework for the map – the boundary, size and shape of the plot. The map should depict land use and include building structures (house, outside toilet or pit latrine, outside cooking facility, chicken coop, pig pen, etc.) and the location of all major food and shade trees. The spatial organization of other crop areas (beds of cabbage, peppers, maize and lettuce, etc.) are sketched as zones, and symbols are used to depict mapped items using an appropriate key (Figure 14.2). The land use map should include other features such as paths, drains and irrigation trenches, ponds, terraces and boundary fences.

The second stage involves a census or survey of all the useful plants, bushes and trees in the kitchen garden. A field inventory is used to record the presence or absence and/or to count the number of each species present. Your route through the plot needs to be systematic (you do not want to miss things or double-count). The farmer should be intimately involved to help with field identification of unfamiliar plants and to explain how leaves, bark, fruit, seeds, flowers are used – you will be surprised at the number of plants used for medicines, beverages, folk remedies and other household items. A fairly quick method is to walk strategic transects through the plot. For a more accurate work, a comprehensive plant census may be needed, dividing the plot into quadrants using a measuring tape or rope, and identifying, counting and recording each plant that occurs in each quadrat.

Land degradation

Farm surveys may require information to be collected on soil erosion problems and on soil conservation methods. Such data can be obtained by a combination of asking questions and recording field observations. Alternatively, your research may focus specifically on the physical environment and land management practices, so detailed data on the geographical extent and severity of soil erosion may be required, at the scale of the farm and wider rural community, or for an individual hillside and a broader drainage basin. You will need field equipment like a tape measure and ranging poles, instruments for measuring slope angles and compass bearings, and perhaps a GPS for accurate locations, a soil auger or soil sampling equipment, or even equipment for measuring and monitoring soil loss.

A thorough grounding in the relevant literature is an essential preparatory step to field map work. In this case, you will need to read about tropical farming systems and tropical geomorphology and land management. Field recognition of landforms and other physical features associated with erosion and mass wasting processes are critical skills. For example, there are many visible signs of tropical soil erosion and land degradation, including rills and

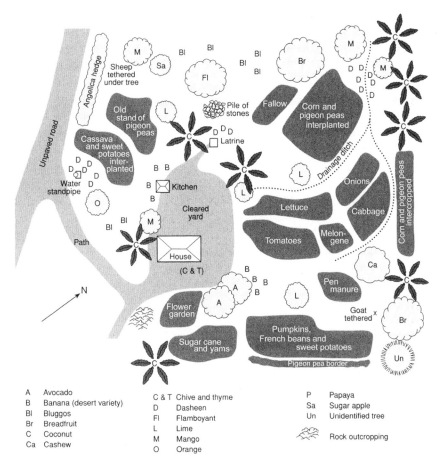

A   Avocado
B   Banana (desert variety)
Bl   Bluggos
Br   Breadfruit
C   Coconut
Ca   Cashew

C & T   Chive and thyme
D   Dasheen
Fl   Flamboyant
L   Lime
M   Mango
O   Orange

P   Papaya
Sa   Sugar apple
Un   Unidentified tree

Rock outcropping

Figure 14.2   Plan of a kitchen garden
Source: adapted from Brierley (1985: Figure 3.12). Reproduced with permission

gullies, tree root exposure and waterfall loss, rock exposure, and pedestals. An excellent field guide (Stocking and Murnaghan, 2001) includes sample field booking forms for measuring and recording different erosion indicators. Field maps of the spatial extent and severity of soil erosion and associated landforms can be produced at a variety of scales (plots, hillsides, etc.). These maps can also include land management features such as soil conservation measures. Such field maps can be supported by annotated field sketches and photographs.

A simple method for assessing land degradation at the level of the farm plot has been devised and used in Jamaica (McGregor et al., 1998). The technique combines field survey and data recording sheets to quantify the problem of land degradation and focuses on five physical indicators of land degradation: soils, topography, vegetation, land management and erosion factors. For each individual farm plot, a land degradation index is compiled as a basis for comparing different cropping systems and land uses, in contrasting topographical and geological settings in your study area.

The first step in compiling an index is to prepare a sketch map of the farm plot. It should depict plot boundary, location of crops, and any site-specific indicators of land degradation and soil conservation. Collaboration with the farmer is essential, especially in the early stages of the work. Remember that in developing countries most small farms have not been properly surveyed, and farmers may not have a legal land title. Field boundaries are not normally clearly demarcated with fence posts and hedgerows, as in Europe, so the farmer's help is needed to pin-point the perimeter of the farm plot. You will need to devise a spatial scheme of transects across the farm plot, and sites are sampled at regular intervals along each transect.

Table 14.1 illustrates the format of the basic data recording sheet (McGregor et al., 1998). Field data are recorded at each sample site along each transect. A value is assigned to each item using a nominal ranked scale. The numbers on the scale reflect a mixture of objective and subjective assessments. The values are determined by reference to conversion tables and operational definitions. For example, measured slope angles are allocated into one of five categories, ranked from gentle to steeper slopes (Table 14.1). At a later stage, in the office, an average for each inventory item is calculated, and these values are aggregated into the land degradation index for that farm plot. The basic method can be extended by including additional items on the recording sheet, such as information on plot history (length of the fallow period, time elapsed since fire was last used to burn vegetation, etc.).

Natural hazards and disaster impacts

Natural disasters increasingly affect the lives of people in developing countries (Smith, 1996). The Asian tsunami disaster on Boxing Day 2004 highlighted their tragic significance and the globalization of relief and reconstruction efforts following major natural disasters. Smith (1996) has argued that the trend is for an increase in the number and magnitude of natural disasters. The causes of natural disasters

are complex; most have geological and/or meteorological trigger mechanisms (earthquakes, torrential rains and strong winds) but deeper, underlying causal factors derive from bad land management practices, inappropriate residential locations, or an absence of effective planning controls on building development. People living in developing countries are most vulnerable, and certain locations such as coastal areas are more vulnerable than others (see Figure 14.3). Poverty often forces poor people to live in hazardous, marginalized locations such as landslide-prone hillsides or flood-prone valleys, gullies and flood plains. Squatter communities tend to appear on land no one else wants and their residents are often unaware of the risks involved in living in vulnerable locations. Nor do they have the resources to invest in mitigation measures.

Development research may focus on the perception of hazards by local people and institutions, or on the effectiveness of different phases of the disaster cycle – response, recovery, prevention, mitigation and preparedness (Potter et al., 2004: 148). Disaster-related projects tend to combine socio-economic data with environmental data, and employ a range of data collection methods to buttress standard interview surveys. Field surveys, field mapping and inventories are useful in this type of development research when the focus is on local impacts of disasters at the community level. Impacts might relate to infrastructure, homes and residential areas, or disruptions to industry, commerce, agriculture and tourism. Mapping and inventories can be used in a variety of different ways.

Hazard maps (e.g. landslide hazard maps and flood plain hazard maps) are prepared by using a combination of field mapping and secondary data from topographic and geological maps, and meteorological and hydrological data. Ideally, they are prepared before a disaster occurs. Hazard maps identify vulnerable populations and communities at risk from particular hazards. On the other hand, field mapping is useful in the aftermath of a

Table 14.1   Elements used in a data recording sheet to compile a land degradation index

Soil factors	Topographical factors	Vegetation factors	Management factors	Erosion factors
Soil texture 1–3	Slope angle 1–5	Canopy cover 1–5	Land use quality 1–5	Sheet erosion 1–5
Consistency Plasticity 1–3	Over-steepening or undercutting of slope 1–5	Bare soil exposed 1–5	Tillage methods 1–2	Evidence of overland flow 1–4
Pulverescence % non-coalesced 1–5	Slope length 1–5	Litter cover 1–5	Manure 1–2	Tree root exposure 1–5
Stoniness 1–5	Slope shortening 1–5	Litter distribution 1–5	Conservation techniques 1–3	Erosion pedestals 1–5
Stone size 1–5		Roots in soil 1–5	Efficiency of conservation 1–5	Lag gravels 1–5
Surface crusting 1–2		Root size 1–5	Upkeep/maintenance 1–5	Colluvial deposits 1–4
Depth of A horizon 1–5		Distribution of roots 1–5	Cultivation intensity 1–5	
Humus content 1–5		General vegetation 1–5	General crop health 1–3	
Moisture content 1–3		Vegetation quality 1–5	Weed occurrence 1–5	
pH 1–5			Evidence of recent weeding 1–2	
Evidence of fire clearance 1–5				

Notes:

1. *Each item on the recording sheet is assessed along a nominal rating scale. Numbers on the recording sheet indicate the number of categories on the scale, ranked from low to high values. These numerical values are used to weight each item in the calculation of the land degradation index.*
2. *Example of assignment of slope angle at each sampled site to a ranked weighting value*
   $0–15° = 1$; $16–20° = 2$; $21–25° = 3$; $26–30° = 4$; $>30° = 5$

Source: McGregor, et al. (1998)

139

Figure 14.3   This Jamaican middle-class house was built on a vulnerable beach front location and was severely damaged by storm surge after Hurricane Ivan in 2004

disaster too, for example, to identify the spatial extent of a flash flood or disruptions to transport caused by severe landslides. Thus, field observations like the height of water mark on a wall can indicate the maximum depth of flood waters. In the case of landslides, field maps can be compiled to depict the incidence of landslides along a road network. This technique is often used in combination with a landslide field inventory, to record information on the characteristics of each landslide in a given area (see, for example, Maharaj, 1995).

Inventories and other types of data recording sheet are useful in disaster impact studies where data is required about the site-specific damage to infrastructure (roads, water supply, electric supply, telephones, etc.). Field inventories can be used to record damage to road surfaces, blocked roads, blocked drains, broken water pipes, fallen or damaged utility poles, or damage to cables of various types (Table 14.2). Alternatively, an inventory of damage to people's homes in the aftermath of a flood or hurricane can be part of a more general questionnaire survey of affected households.

A typical damage assessment form for a building requires basic information on its age, construction techniques and material used in the construction of walls and roofing. Property damage can be itemized, the nature of the damage recorded and even replacement values estimated. Damage can be recorded as presence or absence data on a checklist, or magnitude can be assessed using criteria such minor/major damage or more complex categories. Whenever subjective assessments of building quality and damage magnitude are needed, clear and unambiguous operational definitions for each damage category must be devised prior to data collection. A thorough briefing or specific training regarding what to expect in the field, how to interpret field observations, and how to record the information is also a prerequisite to fieldwork. Local expertise is a useful input to training sessions. Disaster agencies in developing countries often use local students like you for damage assessment surveys, so recording and

Table 14. 2 Field observation sheet for inventory of infrastructure damage in a community following a natural disaster

Event.................

Assessor...............

Date assessed...........

Area..................

LOCATION	SUB-LOCATION	Physical conditions									Functional condition					NOTES
		Fallen trees	Fallen poles	Fallen lines	Broken bridge	Landslides	Broken railway	Broken sewer	Broken water lines	Broken gas lines	Other – specify	Road passage	Electricity	Telephone	Sanitation	Water	Boxes marked with ticks or crosses to indicate yes/no information. Blank boxes indicate information not determined or not available
																	Comments
TOTAL																	

Source: adapted from Office of US Foreign Disaster Assistance (n.d.)

assessments techniques can be readily and quickly grasped.

Acknowledgements

The author wishes to thank the ODPEM (Office of Disaster Preparedness and Emergency Management), Government of Jamaica, for making available for consultation numerous data recording sheets used by their field staff. Doctoral candidate Steve Bailey (Department of Geography and Geology, University of the West Indies) is thanked for his insights based on extensive field experience in the use of land degradation index.

QUESTIONS FOR DISCUSSION

1. Read an article on the informal sector in a developing country of your choice. Make a list of all informal sector activities you are likely to encounter in the main street of a small town in that country. Design a field inventory to record items of information about each of these informal sector activities, within a logical classificatory framework.
2. Discuss the problems you may encounter in arriving at operational definitions for three types of informal sector activity: a food vendor, a service provider, a mobile operator. What types of data do you think it is feasible to record in a brief encounter of ten minutes with each type of informal sector business?
3. Make a list of all the non-food products that you might find in a tropical home garden in a developing country of your choice. Discuss which of these items are most likely to represent a financial saving to the household and say how and why. How could you try to estimate the monetary values of these financial savings?
4. A rural community has been dislocated by a hurricane strike. You are undertaking field research in the community two weeks after the disaster. List and discuss the various types of damage to (a) houses (b) infrastructure (c) agriculture, that you might observe, identify and record during your fieldwork.
5. You are studying the impact of a flood event in a community. Discuss how best to combine questionnaire interviews and field assessments of flood damage in your data collection methodology.

Further reading

Landauer, K. and Brazil, M. (ed.) (1990) *Tropical Home Gardens*, Tokyo: United Nations Press.

Potter, R.B., Barker, D., Conway, D. and Klak, T. (2004) *The Contemporary Caribbean*, Harlow: Pearson/Prentice Hall.

Stocking, M.A. and Murnaghan, N. (2001) *Handbook for the Field Assessment of Land Degradation*, London: Earthscan.

References

Brierley, J.S. (1985) West Indian kitchen gardens: a historical perspective with current insights from Grenada, *Food and Nutrition Bulletin*, 7 (3): 52–60.

Hills, T.L. (1988) The Caribbean food forest: 'ecological artistry or random chaos?', in J.S. Brierley and H. Rubenstein (eds), *Small Farming and Peasant Resources in the Caribbean*, Geographical Studies No. 10, pp. 1–28. Manitoba: Department of Geography, University of Manitoba.

Landauer, K. and Brazil, M. (eds) (1990) *Tropical Home Gardens*, Tokyo: United Nations Press.

Maharaj, R.J. (1995) Evaluating landslide hazard for land use planning: upper St Andrew, Jamaica, in D. Barker and D. McGregor (eds), *Environment and Development in the Caribbean: Geographical Perspectives*, Kingston, Jamaica: UWI Press, pp. 170–186.

McGregor, D.F.M., McCoubrey, A. and Stidwell, R. (1998) Development of an index of land degradation, *Caribbean Geography*, 9 (2): 136–147.

Office of US Foreign Disaster Assistance (OFDA) (n.d.) *Field Reference Guide: Initial Damage Assessment*, Washington, DC: OFDA.

Potter, R.B., Barker, D., Conway, D. and Klak, T. (2004) *The Contemporary Caribbean*, Harlow: Pearson/Prentice Hall.

Potter, R.B.P. and Unwin, T. (eds) (1989) *The Geography of Rural–Urban Interaction*, London: Routledge.

Smith, K. (1996) *Environmental Hazards: Assessing Risk and Reducing Disaster*, 2nd edn, London: Routledge.

Stocking, M.A. and Murnaghan, N. (2001) *Handbook for the Field Assessment of Land Degradation*, London: Earthscan.

15

Interviewing

Katie Willis

Types of interview · · Why do interviews?
· · Recruiting interviewees · · Where and when
to interview · · Asking questions · · Recording · · Accuracy

Introduction

Many forms of development research include an interview of some kind. For some researchers, interviews are the main channel of information-gathering, while for others, interviews are used as a starting point or background to support other forms of data collection. In this chapter, I will outline some of the main types of interview and what issues you should consider before embarking on interviews.

Types of interview

While the concept of an 'interview' often implies something rather formal, in reality 'interviews' can range from a rather unstructured conversational style to a much more rigid question-and-answer format. There is no one right way to conduct interviews. Rather, as with all research, you need to think about the research topic, the person you are interviewing and the context. For example, interviewing a government official about water provision in a shanty town is different from interviewing shanty-town residents about their access to clean water.

Interview types are often divided into 'structured', 'semi-structured' and 'unstructured', although the differences are sometimes difficult to distinguish. 'Structured' interviews follow a pre-set list of questions which are often standardized across interviewees. 'Semi-structured' interviews follow a form of interview schedule with suggested themes, but there is scope for the interviewees to develop their responses. Finally, 'unstructured' interviews provide the interviewees with the opportunity to take the discussion in whichever direction they choose. Such interviews are often more 'conversational' in that they are not directed by the interviewer and may cover topics which are completely unexpected.

The choice of interview style depends largely on the nature of the research (see below). Structured interviews may be appropriate if you want to standardize across interviewees, or are short of time, but they provide no scope for allowing unforeseen topics or interpretations to be introduced. They are therefore similar to some forms of questionnaire (see Chapter 17 on questionnaires). Unstructured interviews may be an excellent way of finding out about key issues within a community when developing a

research question, but if you have limited time and need information to address a particular research question, this method may not be appropriate. Because of these factors, semi-structured interviews are usually the most popular. By doing this, you can ensure that the areas you think are important are covered, but you also provide the interviewees with opportunities to bring up their own ideas and thoughts (see Box 15.1).

Box 15.1 Interview schedule

This was part of a study of women's paid and unpaid work in Oaxaca City, Mexico, looking at similarities and differences between socio-economic groups and the importance of social networks within women's working lives. All women interviewed had already completed a household questionnaire, including basic data about household membership, employment patterns, social networks, domestic chores and community organizations. Interviews were conducted in women's homes and took from 30 minutes to 2 hours.

1   Introduction to the research, confidentiality, taping, etc.
2   General conversation about household, house, neighbourhood.
3   Paid work – choice of employment, how job was secured, opinion of work, future plans, difficulties. If not in paid work at moment discuss paid work in the past, reasons for not being in paid work, future plans.
4   Domestic tasks – types of activity, time taken, help provided, opinions on domestic work.
5   Community activities – community organizations, church, work-based groups: reasons for involvement/non-involvement; nature of involvement.
6   Socializing – meetings with friends/family; *compadrazgo* (fictive kin); neighbours; feelings of belonging/isolation.
7   Other questions?

Source: adapted from Willis (2000)

145

Of course, the context of the interview and the preferences of the interviewees should also be considered. If you are using an interpreter (see Chapter 18 on the use of interpreters), unstructured interviews are more challenging (Devereux and Hoddinott, 1992). Having an interview schedule can help save time because interpreters get to know the basic patterns of interviews and how to express particular ideas, so you do not repeatedly have to explain. For some

interviewees, particularly so-called 'elite' interviewees such as government officials, company managers or local chiefs, the degree of formality which a structured or semi-structured interview can provide may be viewed more positively and encourage involvement. Elizabeth Francis worked on the impact of labour migration in Kisumu District, western Kenya. She explains her choice of semi-structured interviews was partly a response to local expectations:

I had initially hoped to collect a great deal of this sort of information [beliefs, attitudes and strategies] informally, but I found that one consequence of people's understanding that I was a 'student' who was 'studying' their way of life was that they expected me to carry out formal interviews. Out of courtesy, people tended to stop what they were doing when I arrived at their homes and sit expectantly, waiting for me to start questioning them. (Francis, 1992: 92–3)

She chose to adopt a life-history approach which encouraged respondents to discuss their life stories and changes they had observed within a more structured interview framework.

Why do interviews?

Interviews are a commonly used method in development research because of the range of information that can be obtained. When selecting the type of interview, the questions and the interview arrangements, you should think carefully about why you think an interview is an appropriate method for your particular research questions.

Interviews are an excellent way of gaining 'factual' information, such as details of NGO policies and government initiatives. However, you should make sure that you cannot obtain this information from other sources. Many organizations and governments now make information available on the internet (see Chapter 28 on using the World Wide Web) or in paper form. If this is the case, do not expect someone to give up their time to provide you with factual information available elsewhere. In such situations, it may be more useful to arrange an interview to find out more about the ways in which particular policies were devised, or how different groups have responded to certain initiatives. By preparing well in advance by reading all the available material, you should be able to get more out of the interview. Interviews may, therefore, be an opportunity to examine processes, motivations and reasons for successes or failures.

These qualitative dimensions are a key reason why interviews are a very popular methodology. While questionnaire surveys can provide you with data on employment, agricultural yield, migration patterns and household structure, for example, surveys are limited in the degree to which they can provide explanations for patterns or consider attitudes and opinions. Elizabeth Francis (see above) collected basic information from all her informants, such as education level, landholding patterns, crop production and children's activities, and how these had changed over time. All this information could have, in theory, been collected through a questionnaire survey. However, 'it was also important to try to get behind the bare outlines of reported behaviour to the underlying beliefs, strategies and constraints which had shaped that behaviour' (Francis, 1992: 92). Using the interviews allowed her to do this because she could tailor the questions to the particular individual, but she also found that this approach allowed her to develop greater rapport with interviewees, and understand the processes of change in detail (see also Box 15.2).

Box 15.2   Water management techniques in Tunisia

Jennifer Hill and Wendy Woodland used semi-structured interviews in their work on the sustainability of water use in agriculture in Southern Tunisia to supplement their physical geography data collection in the region. They interviewed 24 farmers to find out

(Continued)

(Continued)

about their agricultural techniques, but also to examine why they chose particular methods and how these had changed over time. The interview format was ideal for finding out about farmers' motivations and also to investigate their understanding of water management techniques. By using interviews, Hill and Woodland were able to find out the details of rainwater harvesting, such as the use of earth and stone bunds on hillsides, and how these practices were decided upon and organized. The importance of indigenous knowledge in relation to the local environment was revealed in these interviews. Farmers were also able to highlight potential problems, including the impact of out-migration on the maintenance of rainwater harvesting systems.

Source: adapted from Hill and Woodland (2003)

Recruiting interviewees

When deciding who to interview, you need to think carefully about what kind of sample your research questions require. If you want to find out about a particular organization, such as an NGO, the NGO president or chair may not be the most appropriate person to deal with. In a large organization they may be removed from the day-to-day activities in which you are interested. In addition, you may have problems accessing key individuals because of their busy schedules. When designing your research make sure that the success is not reliant on talking to certain people as this is a decidedly risky strategy.

If you are using interviews to find out about people's attitudes and perceptions, you need to consider the population from which you will be selecting interviewees. This may be a geographically limited group, such as the residents of a village or urban district, but it may also be a group defined by activities, such as city-centre informal traders or participants in an NGO project. While the aim of interviews is not to gain statistically significant results, you do need to make sure that you have targeted a diverse range of people who might have different opinions or perceptions based on their own experiences and context.

If you are combining your interviews with a questionnaire survey of some sort, you may use this route to recruit interviewees. For example, the questionnaire results may show certain patterns such as differences by age group or ethnicity. If this is the case, you can then select interviewees from each category. Alternatively, at the end of the questionnaire you can ask people to indicate whether they would be willing to be interviewed. If you followed this route you would need to consider whether self-selecting interviewees were all from a similar group.

In many research situations there are 'gatekeepers' whose permission is needed to access the research site. This may be a village elder, an NGO president, school headteacher or a community leader. Given their position, you may want to follow their advice as to the recruitment of interviewees. However, the use of gatekeepers in this way is problematic. They will guide you, not always intentionally, towards particular individuals, so leaving out certain sections of the group or community (Valentine, 1997). In addition, interviewees may feel forced to cooperate with you if you are introduced in this way. For ethical reasons, you should always try to ensure that individuals can refuse to participate in the research. Finally, being closely associated with the

147

gatekeeper may result in interviewees answering your questions in particular ways, depending on their views of the gatekeeper involved, so biasing the findings in a certain direction (see the section below on accuracy).

The 'snowballing' technique is often used to recruit interviewees. This is when one contact suggests other possible interviewees who in turn suggest others, so the list of potential interviewees get longer and longer. This can be the only way to find out about potential interviewees when there is no clearly bounded group, such as village residents, or records of group members, as with organizations. When using snowballing it is advisable to try to start with as many contacts as possible to maximize the diversity of the interviewees, rather than following one person's network. In addition, you should keep reflecting on the nature of your interviewees and try to get greater diversity if and when it is possible or appropriate. For example, if you are studying informal traders and all your interviewees to date have been young women and men, then you might want to ask specifically if any of your interviewees know any older men or women who might be interested in talking to you.

Where and when to interview

While in many cases you will not have a choice about where to conduct the interview, you need to think very carefully about how the location may affect the material gathered, the dynamics of the interview and also the way in which you present yourself to your potential interviewees. When choosing the location you clearly want to make sure that it is somewhere the interviewee will feel comfortable, such as in their own home. Conducting interviews in this environment may provide important insights into your research. For example, it may give you a chance to see living conditions and also, potentially, dynamics within the household.

However, there are other dimensions to interviews within the home. For example, the interviewee may be distracted by the presence of other household members. When conducting interviews with women in low-income settlements in Oaxaca City, Mexico, I found that interviews were often interrupted by children wanting attention from their mothers, or husbands wanting to know what was going on. In addition, loud music, television or chatter from other household members made it impossible to tape-record the conversations. Despite these issues, I was happy to continue interviewing in these environments. Women were clearly happier talking to me 'at home' rather than in a more public or supposedly 'neutral' environment, while I found the opportunity to see inside women's homes very important to inform my understandings of women's lives in the settlements.

You should also be aware of how the interview location can be interpreted by the interviewees or others in the community. When conducting 'elite interviews' it is often a good idea to carry out the interviews in the workplace. By dressing appropriately, you can present yourself as a 'serious researcher' who is not out of place within that environment. The interviewee is then more likely to take you seriously and answer your questions appropriately.

While you want to make sure that your interviewee is comfortable with the location, make sure that you do not put yourself in potentially dangerous situations or agree to locations where your motives could be misconstrued. Sarah Howard (1997), in her research into indigenous land rights on the Atlantic Coast, Nicaragua, warns against assuming that arranging interviews in 'informal' settings such as bars will be interpreted in the same way by your interviewee as yourself. This is particularly the case for women researchers wanting to interview men. Gender also plays a part in interviews within the domestic realm. Male researchers should be wary of trying to arrange interviews with women at home as this may be frowned upon and could have unwanted repercussions on the researcher and/or the female interviewee.

The timing of interviews can be very important. There may be some key individuals to whom you want to speak as part of your research. While it may be reassuring to interview them at the start of the research, in some cases it may be better to wait until you are more familiar with the research material and can, perhaps, use your interview with them to discuss some of your findings or initial conclusions. If you are able to arrange such meetings at both the beginning and the end of the fieldwork, then this would be an ideal solution, but in many cases it is impossible to do this and you just have to fit around people's schedules. If you are working in a particular community, it may be a good idea to spend time getting to know the area and the people before launching into more formal interviews. This will make people feel more comfortable with you and may also help you frame your interview schedule in a more appropriate way.

Asking questions

Interviews vary considerably and you will find that some people are easier to talk to about particular topics than others. However, if you think about the ways in which questions can be asked, you can help set your interviewee at ease and also gain the kind of information required for your research. Before starting the questions, make sure that the interviewee knows what the research is about and they have been assured of confidentiality and the tape recorder (if used) has been switched on. You should also establish how long the interviewee has for the interview and stick to that time.

Remember that an interview is not an interrogation and you should try to be as unthreatening as possible in your questioning. Even if you have a pre-set list of questions, try

not to fire them at the interviewee. Give them a chance to develop their ideas and also to ask for clarification if necessary. In the first few interviews you may feel nervous and rely greatly on your interview schedule, but as you become familiar with the material, you should be able to relax further and really engage with the process. Even if you are nervous, make sure that you listen to the responses. This may alert you to a new area of discussion and will also stop you asking a question to which the interviewee has already provided the answer.

Do not launch into complicated and sensitive questions at the start of the interview. Instead, open the interview with some uncomplicated, more factual questions. For example, in the Oaxaca City study (see Box 15.1) I opened by asking women about their houses and how long they had lived in the neighbourhood. When framing your questions, try to make them as open-ended as possible. This prevents very short answers and gives the respondent the chance to develop his/her own ideas on the topic. When dealing with sensitive topics be prepared to move on to another issue if the interviewee is clearly very uncomfortable with the direction of the interview. Finally, at the end of the interview, you should provide the interviewee with an opportunity to ask you questions (McKay, 2002).

Recording

How to record interviews is highly context-specific, depending on a range of factors, such as interviewee preference, logistics and language ability, as well as the nature of your research. Possible forms of recording are using a tape/mini-disc recorder, taking notes throughout the interview or writing up notes after the interview.

Direct recording has a number of benefits. It allows you to concentrate completely on the interview without having to worry about taking notes or remembering points to write up later. This can be particularly important if you are conducting interviews in a language in which you are not completely confident. Having a recording of the interview allows you the opportunity to check the meaning of words and phrases that you may have missed during the interview itself. Direct recording is also very important if your research is examining forms of discourse. By having the actual words and forms of expression, you will be able to have much greater source material for this form of analysis. However, some interviewees feel rather inhibited by the presence of a recorder, or may be reluctant to provide sensitive information if they feel it could be traced back to them. In addition, very noisy environments mean that recording is often difficult or impossible. Finally, it must be stressed that transcribing taped interviews is very time-consuming and this should be factored into any research of this sort.

Taking notes during the interview may be an appropriate compromise, but it requires great skill to be able to note down the appropriate material, while also paying attention to the interviewee and thinking about your next question. Your interviewee may also be influenced by your note-taking, in that he/she will be able to see when you are taking notes furiously and interpret this as being what you are most interested in. Taking notes is often easier when you are using a translator because you are able to write up when they are asking the next question, but it is important that you still appear to be engaged with what is going on. By taking notes throughout the interview you can also jot down observations about interviewee behaviour or the surroundings which may help to contextualize your analysis later.

Writing up notes after the interview is a strategy that relies on a very good memory, but also time and space to record the notes as soon as possible after the interview. I have adopted this approach in my research in Mexico and found that scribbling down notes while sitting at the bus stop meant I was able

to cover the main topics discussed. I would then review the notes at the end of the day and write them up so they were legible and would add any additional material as appropriate. Where I have tape-recorded interviews, I have often added my own comments on coming out of the interview in terms of the location, non-verbal communication during the interview, or comments made once the tape recorder was switched off. This was a particularly effective strategy in China, where I often went from interview to interview in taxis. I would sit in the back of the taxi dictating into the tape recorder.

Accuracy

Issues around the accuracy of interview material frequently cause researchers concern. These concerns revolve around the two main issues of representativeness and accuracy. While these are debates in all forms of research, they are often applied to qualitative research more frequently. When using a small selection of interviewees to discuss wider trends in a group or community, researchers need to consider how representative their interviewees are of this wider group (see above). If there are obvious biases, then these should be identified in the writing up of the research.

In terms of accuracy there are a number of debates about interview material. There are issues of whether interviewees are telling 'the truth' or whether they are telling the interviewer what they think is the 'right answer' (in relation to what they think the interviewer wants to hear or what they think will present them in the best light). For example, in research on NGO effectiveness, interviewees may dwell on the positive outcomes of NGO projects if they feel the interviewer is closely allied with that organization. Your positionality and the way it will be interpreted by interviewees must always be considered (Skelton, 2001).

Another aspect of accuracy relates to household interviews. Interviewers should not assume that all household members know about the activities of the other members. Garry Christensen (1992) conducted research on livestock and credit in Burkina Faso. Because of local norms about male status in these matters, most of his formal interviews were conducted with male household heads. However, through living in the community for some time, Christensen began to realize that there was a whole network of transfers and transactions involving women and adult siblings, of which male household heads were either unaware or decided not to mention in the interview. Finally, research which involves participants describing events and activities in the past may be less accurate because of recall problems.

When considering the accuracy of interview material, it is important to realize that in most situations there is no one correct response. Rather, all answers are partial and reflect the context in which they are given. Thus, it is important to be reflexive and consider the ways in which the material that interviewees give you will be framed by the research process itself. In terms of assessing factual information, within the interview you may be able to ask for clarification when there are contradictions. In addition, the use of multiple methods may be helpful. For example, you may be able to supplement interview material with observations and questionnaires. Again, if there are discrepancies in the information, then you can discuss these sensitively with appropriate individuals.

Conclusions

Interviews can be a very valuable source of information for development research. In this chapter I have discussed some of the different forms of interview and some of the issues you need to be aware of when designing and organizing your interviews. Because of the interpersonal nature of interviewing it can be a very rewarding research method, allowing insights into individuals' lives which go beyond observations and questionnaires surveys.

QUESTIONS FOR DISCUSSION

1. Discuss the differences between unstructured, semi-structured and structured interviews and when each form is most appropriate.
2. How does a researcher's positionality affect the interview process?
3. What factors should be considered when deciding on an interview location?
4. How can interviewee recruitment strategies affect the research process?
5. What factors should be taken into account when assessing the accuracy of interview material?

Further reading

Devereux, S. and Hoddinott, J. (eds) (1992) *Fieldwork in Developing Countries*, London: Harvester Wheatsheaf.

Skelton, T. (2001) Cross-cultural research: issues of power, positionality and 'race', in M. Limb and C. Dwyer (eds), *Qualitative Methodologies for Geographers*, London: Arnold, pp. 87–100.

References

Christensen, G. (1992) Sensitive information: collecting data on livestock and informal credit, in S. Devereux and J. Hoddinott (eds), *Fieldwork in Developing Countries*, London: Harvester Wheatsheaf, pp. 124–137.

Devereux, S. and Hoddinott, J (1992) Issues in data collection, in S. Devereux and J. Hoddinott (eds), *Fieldwork in Developing Countries*, London: Harvester Wheatsheaf, pp. 25–40.

Francis, E. (1992) Qualitative research: collecting life histories, in S. Devereux and J. Hoddinott (eds), *Fieldwork in Developing Countries*, London: Harvester Wheatsheaf, pp. 86–101.

Hill, J. and Woodland, W. (2003) Contrasting water management techniques in Tunisia: towards sustainable agricultural use, *The Geographical Journal*, 169 (4): 342–357.

Howard, S. (1997) Methodological issues in overseas fieldwork: experiences from Nicaragua's Northern Atlantic Coast, in E. Robson and K. Willis (eds), *Postgraduate Fieldwork in Developing Areas: A Rough Guide*, 2nd edition, Developing Areas Research Group, Monograph No. 9, London: Royal Geographical Society and the Institute of British Geographers, pp. 19–37.

McKay, D. (2002) Negotiating positionings: exchanging life stories in research interviews, in P. Moss (ed.), *Feminist Geography in Practice*, Oxford: Blackwell, pp. 187–199.

Skelton, T. (2001) Cross-cultural research: issues of power, positionality and 'race', in M. Limb and C. Dwyer (eds), *Qualitative Methodologies for Geographers*, London: Arnold, pp. 87–100.

Valentine, G. (1997) Tell me about…: using interviews as a research methodology, in R. Flowerdew and D. Martin (eds), *Methods in Human Geography*, Harlow: Longman, pp. 110–126.

Willis, K. (2000) No es fácil, pero es posible: the maintenance of middle-class women-headed households in Mexico, *European Review of Latin American and Caribbean Studies*, 69: 29–45.

16

Focus Groups

Sally Lloyd-Evans

• • Definitions of focus group methodology in the context of development-related
research • • The strengths and limitations of using focus groups • • Focus groups
as a tool for understanding collective action in the field • • 'Doing' focus groups as
part of a multi-method development project • • The logistics of using focus groups
in 'doing development' – how to plan, recruit and conduct focus
groups • • Basic checklists for using focus groups

Introduction: understanding group ways of 'doing development'

Qualitative research encompasses a family of approaches, methods and techniques for understanding and documenting attitudes, behaviours and the 'meanings of people's worlds' (Brockington and Sullivan, 2003: 57; see also Bloor et al., 2001). A prime research tool of this family of approaches is the 'focus group' and it has a well-established history of application in the field of development, particularly in seeking to understand community dynamics and viewpoints (Laws et al., 2003; Morgan, 1997). Focus groups, also referred to as 'group depth discussions', are group-based interviews typically lasting from 1½ to 3 hours and are conducted with around six to

eight participants. The person or researcher who convenes the group interview is often called the *moderator*, and his/her role is to *facilitate* interaction between members of the group rather than control the discussion. Focus groups can be used as a stand-alone technique but they are most commonly employed as part of a multi-method approach to field research.

The use of the focus group as a methodology is most commonly associated with commercial market research, but has also been widely used in the social sciences since the 1960s (Bloor et al., 2001; Greenbaum, 1998; Krueger and Casey, 2000). In a development context, there has been a universal move towards more participatory research techniques that attempt to redress issues of unequal power, positionality and Eurocentricity that can occur while undertaking field research in the 'South' (Holland and Blackburn, 1998; Mikkelsen, 1995), and focus groups have become one of the main processes for engendering public participation and facilitating the use of non-verbal techniques. In the context of development research, they can offer a more effective and rapid way of engaging with community groups than other methods can.

So, when is it appropriate to use focus groups in development research and how are they implemented? This chapter explores the strengths and weaknesses of using focus groups in the field. First, it offers a brief critique of the method and its application in academic research before providing a basic guide to the logistics of organizing and moderating focus groups in the field. Second, the chapter explores the focus group as a valuable tool for development-related research by drawing on some interesting fieldwork examples.

154

Focus groups as a methodology: understanding collective social action and community voices

Focus groups have always been portrayed as a means of generating information on public perceptions and viewpoints. As an ancillary method to other qualitative and ethnographic techniques, focus groups offer an excellent tool for exploring *group* behaviours, interactions and norms, and they are now widely used as part of a multi-method approach to development field research. According to Bloor et al. (2001: 90), 'focus groups have become part of a mixed economy of social research, one component in multi-method strategies, where multiple methods are themselves an emblem of methodological rigour'.

Focus groups can be used for a wide range of qualitative research aims and objectives, but they are commonly used to ascertain information on *collective* views of social

issues, such as a community's perceptions of HIV risk or young people's perceptions of crime and violence, to explore *group contradictions* and uncertainties, or to assess the relative success of a particular strategy or project. In a multicultural or development context, they can provide data on the meanings that lie behind group assessments and perceptions, or on group processes that underline particular behaviours or viewpoints. Why does a community doubt the success of a public sector initiative? Why are young people not voting in the local election? Why are mothers sceptical about a vaccination programme? In summary, focus groups provide a good environment for understanding *collective social action* and accessing group beliefs, understandings, behaviours and attitudes that might be overlooked in in-depth interviews.

Individual human behaviour is influenced by collective behaviour and thought, and the focus group can be as important as the in-depth interview in understanding the importance of codes of behaviour and 'ways of doing' in relation to a wide range of political, social and economic activities. They are an excellent tool for highlighting the uncertainties, tensions and contradictions that must be played out before 'collective decisions' are reached, and as such they have many advantages in the participatory development process. As Giddens (1991) poignantly argues, understanding the extent to which individual and group identities and motives are influenced by different factors and other social groups is of fundamental importance in social science. In my own research on young informal sector workers in the Caribbean, group discussions highlighted the power of peer pressure and collective views on youth identities that shaped young people's ideas about work and the labour market.

Focus groups also provide an occasion for people to engage in what Bloor et al. (2001) call 'retrospective introspection', that is to explore taken-for-granted assumptions in

Table 16.1 Strengths and limitations of using focus groups in field research

Strengths	Limitations
Groups generate excellent data on group views, beliefs and reasons for collective action	Groups evoke misguided notions of a collective or community consensus
Groups can be participatory and empowering as participants find strength in numbers and feel in control of the research process	Groups can be subject to peer pressure and dominated by powerful 'voices' – controversial views can be silenced
Groups are good for discussing sensitive topics among people whose lives are influenced by the same issue	Groups are not good for understanding individual motivations
They can lead to collective action as a result of people sharing their experiences	Recruitment can be difficult, time-consuming and unsuccessful
They form a good platform for using PRA/PLA techniques such as rankings, mapping and other visual methodologies	Moderation/facilitation is a skilled technique and requires practice
They can generate rich and abundant data	Data can be difficult to analyse
They are accessible to people who have difficulties with literacy, such as children	

Source: adapted from Laws et al. (2003)

155

everyday lives. It is not uncommon for group participants to speak of how they have never reflected on why they act in a particular way or maintain a daily routine. Thus, the data produced by focus groups are distinct from those produced by other types of qualitative technique, but they also have their limitations, as highlighted in Table 16.1.

First, focus groups are an inappropriate methodology for exploring individual motivations or behaviours, and researchers often make the mistake of forming assumptions about individuals' lives from the stories they tell during group discussions. Second, as focus group research is often intended to be participatory and benefit the 'group', it runs the risk of evoking a misguided notion of a 'homogeneous community' or 'group consensus'. It is important to remember that the material collated in focus groups is a reflection of the views of the group at that given space and time. Groups can fail to show tensions and contradictions between participants, particularly when dominant or more powerful voices overshadow controversial views. Likewise, it is equally dangerous to hope that focus groups will provide the authentic 'voice of the people' as the group environment can actively shape and alter group understandings *in situ*.

There have been some philosophical debates over the methodological approach of the focus group (Hammersley, 1995). A commonly asked question is the extent to which the focus group can be seen as either a 'feminist' or 'participatory' method and placed alongside other more popular ethnographic techniques (Oakley, 1981). Focus groups can be used to explore feminist research topics but they are not always a feminist method, as this will depend on how the researcher facilitates or 'moderates' the group discussion

(Wilkinson, 1999). Feminist methodologies are distinctive due to their participatory and reflexive approaches, and a feminist researcher will endeavour to facilitate a group discussion within the boundaries of this approach.

Third, although focus groups can be excellent for researching sensitive topics, problems can arise if the topic is politically volatile or controversial. It is not uncommon for local communities, or powerful individuals, to explicate a different research agenda from that of the external researchers or 'experts'. I have worked on projects in the UK where community leaders have attempted to regulate the research process to serve their own political interests, and focus groups can easily fuel community tensions and even promote unrest and outrage. Finally, as the next section will discuss, focus groups can easily be biased through their recruitment, moderation and analysis.

Incorporating focus groups into a development project

As previously discussed, focus groups are best used as an adjunct to a range of qualitative field research methods. In circumstances where in-depth ethnographic work is likely to be difficult (and unfeasible), due to time restrictions or safety in the field, then focus groups will provide the researcher with some insight into community relations and identities, and some understanding of group feelings about a particular topic. However, it is important to understand that as atypical, controversial or extreme opinions are less likely to be explored in a group situation, focus groups are best used alongside other qualitative methods, such as individual, in-depth interviews or participant observation (Krueger, 1998). Focus groups are commonly introduced at three different phases of a research

project, but there are no set rules for their application.

First, they can play an invaluable role in gaining background information on a research topic or provide an overview for more in-depth ethnographic research. They are frequently used in *pre-pilot studies* to explore issues that require further examination or to gain background data on a particular issue. The stories and anecdotes that invariably come from group discussions can provide rich material for devising questions for in-depth interviews or for defining research objectives. They can also be used to explore *differences in the use of language and vernacular terms* that social groups feel most comfortable with. When conducting research with teenagers, for example, is it appropriate to use slang or will it offend anyone? These questions are also adequately explored in pilot studies for in-depth interviews, but the focus group can sometimes offer a more accessible method when time in the field is limited.

Second, as focus groups encourage a *'reflexive capability'* (Bloor et al., 2001), they are often employed to qualify or explore issues in depth that have been raised elsewhere in the research process, maybe in a more structured survey. They are an excellent tool for gauging public attitudes to events, campaigns, policies and social issues, such as evaluating public attitudes to the use of mobile phones in public spaces (see Conradson, 2005).

Third, focus groups are often used to engender co-public participation as part of Participatory Rural Appraisal (PRA) or Participatory Learning and Action (PLA), and are commonly used to facilitate public and community participation in development projects (Mosse, 1994). They offer an effective tool in communicating research agendas and findings with communities in order to encourage groups to take ownership of the research agenda. The focus group is often the starting point for the use of PRA methods, but it is important to note that focus groups are not always participatory as they can be facilitated in a non-reflexive and controlled manner that regards group participants as passive objects.

Ideally, groups would be held at the beginning, middle and end of a research project. In the early phase of a study, focus groups can be used to inform and include communities working with the research. Group discussions may centre on key topics or generate contextual data such as stories, rumours or historical references, all of which might be explored later on in the research. For example, a project exploring community violence and social capital would benefit from a number of early focus groups to understand how different community or social groups perceive crime and identify what are the issues most important to them.

Once research objectives have been defined, the next stage is to plan, recruit and moderate the groups. The following section explores the logistics and difficulties of focus group research by drawing on an example of a Save the Children project which explored perceptions of infant immunization in Somalia (La Fond, 1992).

Logistics and realities of using focus groups for 'doing development'

Planning a focus group in the 'field'

Good research is about good design and it is important to set aside sufficient time for the selection, recruitment and organization of the groups. This process can be a lengthy and complicated experience. In order to illustrate the process of focus group research, I have chosen to draw upon an example where focus groups were successfully employed by Save the Children Fund and the Somalian Ministry of Health to assess the acceptability of

immunization in Somalia (La Fond, 1992). The research project, which aimed to identify the factors influencing the acceptance of immunization, was undertaken in 12 weeks and consisted of focus groups, key informant interviews and observations. In the Somalian context, the team recognized that immunization was a complex and politically sensitive issue which required an appropriate methodology. Due to political pressures, officials were often suspicious of traditional surveys, especially when they involved foreign researchers.

Group composition

Focus groups are not determined through a random sampling technique, so there are a number of basic issues that the researcher needs to consider when recruiting participants. As group interaction is the main advantage of the focus group method, the researcher must carefully consider the social composition of the group. For example, would it be better to convene groups of a similar age, ethnicity or gender? Groups can be convened on a wide range of social criteria, such as age, gender, religion, ethnicity, occupation, a shared interest, lifestage or geography. Is the research aimed at understanding a wide range of viewpoints or is it hoping for some group consensus on a particular issue? Here, issues of power and social status must also be considered if you want to encourage participants to speak freely. I have convened mixed gender groups of teenagers only to find that some male members of the group intimidated female participants. Diversity might encourage spirited debate, but it can also lead to conflict and contradiction. Conducting a focus group with participants from rival political groups, for example, will probably fail to produce any meaningful discussion and may even result in confrontational behaviour.

In Somalia, the research team needed to design the social structure of the groups and

157

recruit participants from the communities. In order to assess whether life-stage and experience impacted upon women's decision-making processes, five categories of focus group participants were selected. Mothers were divided into three age groups that reflected their level of experience of parenting and life-stage. The team felt it beneficial to group together young mothers (aged 15–30), mothers aged 31-45 and a third group of 'grandmothers' or women who served as powerful health advisers on child health issues (La Fond, 1992: 3). These divisions ensured that women were comfortable among their peer groups in terms of their levels of experience and would feel able to contribute feely to the discussions. If the groups had consisted of a mixed age range, younger women might have felt less able to contribute value to the discussion. Such methodological considerations are paramount to the success of focus group research. In this project, focus groups were also held with a mixed group of mothers and child health staff and a group of traditional birthing attendants. The quantity of groups undertaken depends on the objectives of study but it is usual to undertake a number of groups.

Recruitment and incentives

There are no set rules for the recruitment of focus groups as there are many contradictory processes that shape the social dynamics of group interactions. Focus groups can consist of strangers or of pre-existing social groups based on family or kinship ties, or social or community networks such as churches or cooperatives. The use of pre-existing groups will be advantageous if the research is exploring a sensitive topic, or if a particular characteristic is the basis of membership of a group, such as a disability or medical condition like HIV (Laws et al., 2003). Young people are more likely to turn up to a focus group if they are in the company of friends, but peer pressure is more likely to shape the dynamics of such a group. Pre-existing groups can also be problematic, particularly in community situations where participants may not want neighbours to 'know their business'. For example, I recently moderated a heterogeneous group of men and women from different ethnic backgrounds about their views on the representation of diversity in the media. One of the most outspoken respondents was a Pakistani Muslim woman who later told me that she would not have felt it appropriate to discuss some issues if the group had consisted of other members of her local community, for fear that her stories would have been seen as 'inappropriate' and may also become 'common knowledge'.

Similar contradictions arise when using local or 'indigenous' moderators or interpreters. When researchers are new to a field location, coming from a different social and cultural background, then they might lack the skills to interpret important interactions between the groups. The use of local moderators can be invaluable if they are trusted by the community and may greatly help facilitate recruitment, but they can equally provide a barrier to free-flowing and honest discussion.

In participatory research, where there is usually a community focus, participants are often recruited from local networks, clinics, markets, cooperatives or existing social groups. Another effective strategy can be recruitment through an intermediary, such as a community leader or teacher, but the researcher must ensure than research ethics and guidelines are adhered to. Focus groups can be time-consuming to organize and there will always be occasions where participants will not show up.

The use of incentives in research is under much current debate within academic and policy circles. It is increasingly recognized that researchers should value their participants' inclusion in a research project by offering an incentive or gift of some kind, particularly in lower-income communities whereby people's time is limited by income-earning activities. In the UK, it is common for respondents to be given book tokens or vouchers as a token of appreciation. In a development context, views on the appropriateness of incentives are varied, particularly in circumstances where incentives are likely to cause problems when recruiting only a small number of participants and where resources are limited (see Kindon and Cupples, 2003). Who do you leave out? It might be more appropriate to offer some food and beverage at the discussion, photographs of participants' children or assistance with an errand or task (see Robson, 1997). This is a matter for personal consideration in the field, and everyone's experiences will be different.

Consideration must also be given to where and when the groups will be held. Familiar, but neutral, quiet meeting places such as community centres are usually a good place to convene groups. Alternatively, many groups are held in an individual's home but care has to be taken as not to exclude participants if there are internal community politics at play. Similar consideration should also be given to the timing of the focus group so as not to place respondents in a time-stressed situation. In Somalia, the 2-3-hour discussions with the mothers took place during the afternoons, over flasks of hot tea.

Conducting focus groups

It is standard practice for researchers to devise a discussion guide for moderating the group. This can be as structured or informal, as desired, but it is always a good idea to think about key questions and issues to be raised in the discussion. In the immunization project, the moderator wanted to explore a number of issues with the mothers, including their knowledge of, and attitudes to, immunization, their perceptions of common diseases and their prevention, sources of advice on health matters and their attitudes towards health service providers. In some instances, stimulus material such as display boards, images or music can be used to provoke discussion. Focus groups can also provide a good environment for more innovative participatory techniques during the session and it is often a useful idea to encourage participants to put their ideas on paper, draw images or maps, devise flow charts, respond to images, take their own photographs with disposable cameras, or use ranking exercises (Kesby et al., 2005). Visual exercises provide a focus for talking about issues and they also play a useful role in encouraging quieter members of the group to take part in the research.

There are no set procedures for moderating focus groups but there are a few basic principles that will help facilitate a successful group discussion. The moderator should start by introducing him/herself and briefly outlining the purpose of her/his research. Focus groups are often taped to assist in the analysis of the data and this should also be mentioned at the start of the group. There will be occasions where tape-recording is not permitted, or is unsuitable, or where language is a barrier, and then the researcher may choose to employ a note-taker or use an interpreter. It is then good practice for the moderator to remind the group of the basic 'rules' regarding confidentiality and anonymity of the topics or stories raised during the discussion. It is often helpful to remind participants that they should feel free to be able to debate, disagree and critique, and that there is no right or wrong way of thinking.

Participants should be asked to introduce themselves to the group. It is usual for the introductory discussion to evolve around a familiar background issue in order to make the group feel at ease. It is usual to start with 'how' questions that allow all members to make a contribution before moving on to more sensitive or difficult 'why' questions when more confident and empowered. Ethical considerations in focus groups are similar to those presented in other research methods, such as the in-depth interview. Groups are perceived to be a conducive environment in which to discuss a sensitive issue, such as violence, on the premise that people feel more relaxed and communicative among friends. The ethical issue here is not whether the group encourages frank discussion but whether such a discussion in an open forum is in the interests of the participants or whether individuals feel intimidated or uncomfortable with the topic.

A good moderator is one who facilitates discussion among the respondents but who does not dominate or lead the group. The moderator should keep an eye on the group, try to involve members and make sure that any 'group consensus' is valid for all participants. At the end, it is useful to summarize what participants have said and make sure that your interpretation of the discussion is correct. Participants should be asked if they have any further questions, and thanked.

Analysing focus group data

In comparison to other methods, focus groups can be particularly difficult to analyse. Analysis of data should draw on established qualitative methods, but researchers must be aware that focus group data are unique because the group, and not the individual, is the unit of analysis (see Laws et al. (2003) and Conradson (2005) for good discussions of analysing qualitative field data). First, the researcher needs to transcribe any taped data from the group. Transcription is extremely time-consuming and the number of 'voices' on a tape make this a complex process. An effort should be made to transcribe all the recorded data as this will highlight any contradictions or agreements between group members. Second, speech should be transcribed as it was spoken, complete with any grammatical errors or hesitations, and other types of verbal communication, such as laughter or tone of voice, should be noted. An attempt should be made to identify the different voices on the tape and this will be easier if some handwritten notes were made during the group. The researcher should then identify themes or issues that arose from the discussion and locate material in the transcripts which relate to the themes or 'codes', which can be considered in depth.

Conclusions

Focus groups provide a good method for accessing group viewpoints and perceptions, highlighting differences between participants. They are also useful in demonstrating that there is rarely such a thing as a single 'community viewpoint' which can be universally applied in public policy. The latter is particularly important in 'doing development' research as it highlights the ambiguities of decision-making processes and community politics. They are particularly useful for exploring the importance of social networks, peer pressure and community politics, but they can be difficult to analyse. Recruitment can also be problematic. Although the insights into community experiences offered by focus groups can never be as intuitive as those developed through in-depth ethnographic fieldwork, they remain a valuable tool as part of a multi-method strategy. For the researcher who is new to conducting field research, Box 16.1 provides a basic set of guidelines for the planning and moderation of focus groups. Ultimately, one of the greatest challenges for the focus group researcher is to find ways of incorporating focus group methods into truly participatory research and development.

Box 16.1   A quick guide to focus groups

Location – find a suitable neutral location with which the group will feel comfortable

Difference and diversity – social composition is of paramount importance

Quantity of groups – a single focus group will rarely be sufficient to provide a valid representation of people's points of views.

Ethics – similar to other methods but remind participants about their obligations regarding the confidentiality of the stories raised

Researcher's approach – make people feel at ease with an informal and pleasant approach – this is not a test

Participants – encourage everyone to participate and give them equal chances to speak

Peer pressure – try to stop dominant members of the groups from pressurizing others to agree with their viewpoint

Data – remember that the data collected relates to the group and not individuals – don't attempt to start pulling out individual stories as you may get it wrong

Analysis – transcriptions of the discussions is time-consuming, so plan your time accordingly

Dissemination – an end-of-project group is a good way to give feedback of the findings to your participants and thank them for giving you their time

Source: adapted from Laws et al. (2003)

QUESTIONS FOR DISCUSSION

1. Examine why focus groups are more appropriate for studying group viewpoints rather than individual perceptions.
2. Compare and contrast the roles of the focus group moderator and the in-depth interviewer.
3. Explain the different ways in which focus groups might be used as a supplementary method in a research project exploring public attitudes to HIV/AIDS.
4. You have just arrived in an unfamiliar overseas field location and are planning to use focus groups for your research. Critically discuss the advantages and disadvantages of employing a local researcher to recruit and moderate the groups.
5. Examine how focus groups might be used to engender co-public participation in a community-based development project.

Further reading

Bloor, M., Frankland, J., Thomas, M. and Robson, K. (2001) *Focus Groups in Research*, London: Sage.

Krueger, R. (1998) *Focus Groups: A Practical Guide for Applied Research*, London: Sage.

Laws, S, Harper, C. and Marcus, R. (2003) *Research for Development*, London: Sage.

Morgan, D.L. (1997) *Focus Groups as Qualitative Research*, London: Sage.

References

Bloor, M., Frankland, J., Thomas, M. and Robson, K. (2001) *Focus Groups in Research*, London: Sage.

Brockington, D. and Sullivan, S. (2003) Qualitative research, in R. Scheyvens and D. Storey (eds), *Development Fieldwork: A Practical Guide*, London: Sage, pp. 57–72.

Conradson, D. (2005) Focus groups, in R. Flowerdew and D. Martin (eds), *Methods in Human Geography: A Guide for Students Doing a Research Project*, Harlow: Pearson, Chapter 8.

Giddens, A. (1991) *Modernity and Self-Identity: Self and Society in the Late Modern Age*, Cambridge: Polity Press.

Greenbaum, T. (1998) *The Handbook for Focus Group Research*, London: Sage.

Hammersley, M. (1995) *The Politics of Social Research*, London: Sage.

Holland, J. and Blackburn, J. (eds) (1998) *Whose Voice? Participatory Research and Policy Change*, London: Intermediate Technology Publications.

Kesby, M., Kindon, S. and Pain, R. (2005) Participatory approaches and diagramming techniques, in R. Flowerdew and D. Martin (eds), *Methods in Human Geography: A Guide for Students Doing a Research Project*, Harlow: Pearson, pp. 144–165.

Kindon, S. and Cupples, J. (2003) Anything to declare? The politics and practicalities of leaving the field, in R. Scheyvens and D. Storey (eds), *Development Fieldwork: A Practical Guide*, London: Sage, pp.197–215.

Krueger, R. (1998) *Focus Groups: A Practical Guide for Applied Research*, London: Sage.

Krueger, R.A. and Casey, M. (2000) *Focus Groups: A Practical Guide for Applied Research*, London: Sage.

La Fond, A.K. (1992) Qualitative methods for assessing the acceptability of immunisation in Somalia, *Rapid Rural Appraisal (RRA) Notes* 16, pp. 22–26 (available at: www.planotes.org).

Laws, S., Harper, C. and Marcus, R. (2003) *Research for Development*, London: Sage.

Mikkelsen, B. (1995) *Methods for Development Work and Research*, London: Sage.

Morgan, D.L. (1997) *Focus Groups as Qualitative Research*, London: Sage.

Mosse, D. (1994) Authority, gender and knowledge: theoretical reflections in the practice of participatory rural appraisal, *Development and Change*, 25: 497–526.

Oakley, A. (1981) Interviewing women: a contradiction in terms, in H. Roberts (ed.), *Doing Feminist Research*, London: Routledge, pp. 30–61.

Robson, E. (1997) From teacher to taxi-driver: reflections on research roles in developing areas, in E. Robson and K. Willis (eds), *Postgraduate Fieldwork in Developing Areas: A Rough Guide*, 2nd edn, Developing Areas Research Group, Monograph No. 9, London: Royal Geographical Society and the Institute of British Geographers.

Wilkinson, C. (1999) How useful are focus groups in feminist research?, in R. Barbour and J. Kitzinger (eds), *Developing Focus Group Research: Politics, Theory and Practice*, London: Sage, pp. 64–78.

17

Your Questions Answered? Conducting Questionnaire Surveys

David Simon

● ● Conducting questionnaire surveys is rewarding if carefully planned and
executed ● ● There are three principal types of questionnaire, which differ in terms
of the extent to which the responses sought are to be restricted or open-ended
● ● It is important to know what you want to find out, from whom and why, at the
outset, so that the questionnaire can be designed accordingly ● ● Your knowledge of
the population to be sampled, and hence choice of sampling strategy, is as important
to the task of obtaining a representative set of responses as the actual questionnaire
itself ● ● Different types of questionnaire, or of questions on a single questionnaire,
lend themselves to different forms of analysis ● ● As with other fieldwork techniques,
ethical issues need to be considered in advance, during and after implementation

Introduction

One of the oldest and most widely used social
research methods, including in development
research, is the undertaking of surveys by means
of questionnaires. If used appropriately, the
different formats of questionnaire represent
potentially invaluable tools for ascertaining a
wide range of factual information and subjective views and perceptions from a representative
sample of a particular population. A key reason
for the diversity of situations in which they
can be undertaken is that questionnaire
design is flexible, permitting variable degrees

of flexibility of response, according to circumstances. It is therefore important to know as
much as possible about the group of people
being studied and to be clear about what it is
that you wish to explore, so that an appropriate
questionnaire can be designed and tested.

Nevertheless, these are only the first steps.
Successful questionnaire surveys also rely on
the subsequent stages of obtaining a representative sample of the population concerned,
administering the questionnaire (either in
person, using assistants or relying on self-
completion by respondents), collecting the
completed proformas and undertaking careful

analysis of their contents. The analytical techniques used will also depend on the circumstances but could be qualitative, quantitative or a combination of both. Each of these stages will be explored below in successive sections.

Although more recent methodological innovations, such as focus group discussions and participatory appraisals, have become increasingly popular, these are often used in combination with questionnaire surveys. Most commonly, such surveys provide baseline information on the basis of which a sub-sample is then selected for more detailed research using face-to-face interviews or focus group discussions (see Chapters 15 and 16).

The use of questionnaires in development and other cross-cultural research contexts forces us to consider several issues of difference, diversity, linguistic ability, the literal and figurative intercultural 'translatability' of terms and concepts, and research ethics. This applies as much to research in one's own country as to the more conventional Northern practice of undertaking most development-related fieldwork abroad in the global South.

What exactly is a questionnaire? A simple definition is a device or tool for collecting information to describe, compare, understand and/or explain knowledge, attitudes, behaviour and/or socio-demographic characteristics of a particular population (target group).

General considerations

In order to decide on the most appropriate research methods and tools, it is important to be clear about:

- the objectives of the project, i.e. what it is that you want to learn or understand;
- which population(s) you intend to study, what period of time is available and what sample size (in both percentage terms and absolute number) is necessary to achieve the desired level of representativeness.

This information, in turn, will provide you with the basis to decide on the scale of your research operation and the approximate likely resource costs. It is essential to ensure that you have the necessary resources (including field assistants and/or interpreters where appropriate) to undertake the intended work effectively.

Another key issue is to consider the relevant ethical factors (Scheyvens and Storey, 2003). Although these might differ to some extent according to the particular research tool (questionnaire type) chosen, the most basic issues are likely to centre on:

- confidentiality of personal information provided by respondents;
- possible unintended uses to which even broad or summary findings might be put by others and which might disadvantage the respondents in relation, say, to government officialdom or possible discrimination; and
- the need to avoid embarrassing, or contravening the cultural and social norms of, respondents during interviews or while completing the questionnaires.

Certainly, if an undertaking regarding confidentiality is given – and this is often essential to win prospective respondents' confidence in relation to personal or potentially sensitive information – then it must be adhered to. The words 'strictly confidential' or equivalent should appear on top of each copy of the questionnaire. When writing up your research findings, these points should also be mentioned explicitly as part of the methodology.

Whichever questionnaire format you choose for your survey (see below), ensure that you introduce yourself and explain your project's purpose and its questionnaire methodology briefly at the beginning of an interview, or write a clear introduction at the top of (or on a covering sheet to) a self-completion questionnaire. This will help respondents to understand the context and will provide important information enabling them to answer you most helpfully. Equally importantly, it should help to put them at ease and to establish your credentials and those of any assistants you may have.

Use of assistants and interpreters

For small projects or surveys, it is often advisable to undertake all interviews personally, in order to ensure familiarity with the whole sample, to maximize the consistency of approach to interpretation and recording of information, and to be able to deal with any problems or unexpected reactions as they occur. If a large or complex project dictates the use of one or more research assistants, great care should be exercised in their selection, in order to obtain someone with appropriate skills (including local language capability, literacy and probably enough formal education to understand the issues and ideas central to your work) and experience (Devereaux and Hoddinot, 1992; Smith, 1996; Scheyvens and Storey, 2003).

A face-to-face interview with potential assistants is recommended, followed by an appropriate level of training and explanation to ensure that the assistant(s) you have selected are fully appraised of the intended tasks and are clear about the aims, objectives, individual questions to ask, methods to use, methods of recording information and extent to which preliminary analysis could be undertaken during the actual survey. Formal or informal training may be necessary. Your assistant should not be left to guess such information; it is your responsibility to provide it and any required training. Otherwise, effective work is unlikely.

If working in a cross-cultural situation, especially if there are linguistic barriers and/or clear customs in terms of intergenerational or gendered interviewing norms, careful choice of assistants/interpreters can greatly facilitate the research; conversely, an inappropriate choice can foreclose many avenues of enquiry or, in extreme cases, even jeopardize

your ability to complete the survey. For instance, men are generally not permitted to interview (or run focus group discussions with) observant Muslim women, especially in their homes. A male researcher would therefore need to have a female assistant or colleague in order to undertake such work.

There may also be difficult choices between local or non-local assistants. A local person may know or be acquainted with many of the interviewees. This may have the very positive value of facilitating access to, and cooperation by, interviewees – a classic gatekeeper situation. Conversely, however, the assistant may introduce biases on that account by gravitating towards friends and relatives or respondents whom s/he perceives as likely to give 'better' responses. Furthermore, especially if the topics to be discussed are sensitive, such as sexual behaviour, attitudes towards HIV-positive people, household dynamics in terms of divisions of income and income-related decisions, or religious and moral beliefs (Renzetti and Lee, 1993), then respondents may be reluctant to speak freely to someone they know. Finally, use of a local assistant, especially in diverse or fractured social situations, might identify the researcher too clearly with the assistant's group or faction, thereby introducing biases in terms of how other community members might respond. Under such circumstances, a non-local interlocutor may be more useful. If the scale of research warrants it, a mixture of local and non-local assistants, or local assistants from different constituencies, could be used (see Chapter 18; Devereux and Hoddinot, 1992; Scheyvens and Storey, 2003).

Questionnaire design

Types of questionnaire

The first design step is deciding which type of questionnaire to use. The three principal categories are:

165

1 **Structured** – in which short, specific answers in prescribed format (such as ticking the relevant box, circling one alternative, or inserting one or two words into a box) are sought.

2 **Semi-structured** – which combine some structured questions to obtain basic information with others that permit more flexible answers to convey ideas or perceptions in an open-ended manner.

3 **Unstructured** – where there is little if any prescribed format and the interviewee is encouraged to speak or write freely and subjectively in an entirely open-ended manner, perhaps even leading the direction taken by the interview. Such questionnaires may be little more than checklists of topics to be covered and use of a tape recorder may be advisable, if interviewees agree (see Chapter 15).

Naturally, these formats are most appropriate to different circumstances. A structured questionnaire is best suited to the collection of basic, uncontentious information, for instance through face-to-face interviewing of passers-by in the street or by means of self-completion questionnaires sent by post or left at a prominent place like a doctor's waiting room, hotel reception desk or popular tourist attraction. The questionnaire must therefore be short, quick to complete (ideally less than 5 minutes for self-completion or 2–3 minutes by interview, especially in the street) and entirely unambiguous. In cross-cultural and other development situations, great care is therefore necessary in the design stage.

Semi-structured questionnaires are probably the most widely used, since their mixed format makes them suitable in a diverse range of situations. Examples would be attitudinal and/or behavioural surveys; research into preferences for infrastructural or service improvements; understanding how visitors perceive and value tourist attractions and suggestions for improvement; or explorations of differences

between people's stated preferences and those revealed through their behaviour. In view of the more open-ended and subjective content of at least part of the questionnaire, face-to-face interviewing is normally recommended.

A golden rule in designing semi-structured questionnaires is to commence with the most basic and uncontentious – usually factual – information using structured questions. If a long series of questions is necessary, it might be helpful to divide the questionnaire into sections. The more contentious, controversial or subjective questions should come towards the end. This has two major advantages. First, it enables you to record the essential data so that, in the unusual case that an interviewee runs out of time or takes offence at later questions and terminates the interview prematurely, you still have some usable data. Second, it represents a good way to maximize the value of interviews by putting the respondent at ease and building some rapport while covering the contextual information, and then gradually moving on to explore ideas, opinions, perceptions and the like in a more expansive manner, using the open-ended questions. Ensure that sufficient blank space is left after each such question to allow fuller responses to be noted down. It is also helpful to print the questionnaire on one side of the paper only, so that more blank space is available on the back.

Semi-structured questionnaire interviews can be of variable duration but most commonly 45–60 minutes. Do allow somewhat longer in your interview timetable in case of delays or overruns, especially if the interviewee becomes animated and discussion blossoms. You should certainly not design a questionnaire that requires more than an hour to complete in an interview.

Unstructured questionnaires are best suited to ethnographic or anthropological-type interviewing, where extended, in-depth discussion is required, as in the exploration of life histories, philosophical and moral beliefs, politically fractured situations or traumatic and difficult experiences. Samples are often small and there may be no requirement to ensure that the sample is statistically representative. The checklists may be quick and easy to compile. Nevertheless, considerable interviewing skill and experience are needed in order to detect and interpret hidden meanings and to encourage and stimulate the interviewee to elaborate on issues that may be painful, emotional or otherwise difficult. Empathy is vital. Brusqueness or even careless, insensitive comments and questions can easily 'turn off' the interviewee and lead to premature termination of the discussion (see Chapter 15; Renzetti and Lee, 1993). These issues are important in any unstructured interviewing situation, but acquire additional significance in cross-cultural and/or intergenerational research of the types commonly undertaken in development research, not least on account of the often sharp power/knowledge/wealth differentials between many interviewees and their interviewers, and the possible biases and intimidatory effects that can result (Bulmer and Warwick, 1993: 206–9). Successful unstructured interviews may last anything up to two hours or occasionally longer. It is therefore important to plan accordingly and to ensure that interviewees are agreeable beforehand.

Compiling your questionnaire

The same considerations apply when devising a questionnaire for use in a development context (see for example De Vaus, 2002), except that the cross-cultural, intergenerational, gendered and power/knowledge differentials already mentioned imply that even greater care and attention are required in order to avoid ambiguities, misinterpretations, boredom/frustration and possible offence. The value of an appropriate introduction was dealt with earlier. Examples of specific questionnaire applications are given in Bulmer and Warwick

(1993). The following general guidelines will facilitate your design task (see also Mikkelsen, 1995; Thomas et al., 1998):

1 Be clear about your purpose and the main issues of interest. Focus on them and avoid the temptation to explore many side issues.
2 Ask one thing at a time and in simple terms; avoid multi-part questions.
3 Bear in mind what broad social and economic characteristics your respondents are likely to have. Avoid asking questions to which many respondents will be unable to relate or about which they are unlikely to have views.
4 Use the simplest possible words and phrases, avoiding technical or political jargon, slang (unless directly relevant) and ambiguous terms, for example 'gay', which will be interpreted as 'happy' or 'jolly' by many older people but as 'homosexual' by younger ones.
5 Avoid confusion through, for instance, posing questions with negative or double-negative grammatical constructions.
6 Ensure that you do not bias the response(s) by seeming to imply that you are expecting either a negative or positive response; it is important to phrase the questions neutrally. This applies both to the wording of the question and to the permissible categories and numbers of responses in a structured questionnaire and/or closed question.
7 Similarly, think carefully whether it is best to ask particular questions in the form of statements, direct questions or indirect questions, as this can influence the response rate and accuracy of answers provided. Choose the form that is least ambiguous or contentious, especially in relation to sensitive topics. In many cultures, disagreements or negative answers are traditionally avoided. Affirmative answers are strongly preferred. The phrasing of questions assumes even more importance in terms of such perceptions

167

by respondents. This cultural trait is sometimes interpreted by outsiders as simply telling interviewers what the respondents think they want to hear, a phenomenon that can occur anywhere but the likelihood of which is certainly increased by the potential differences in power, knowledge and/or wealth between interviewer and interviewee (see above).

8   Consequently, consider carefully and take advice from your field assistant or people experienced in local social research regarding any possible cultural biases in terms of responses to different types of question or response format. As already discussed, the most basic distinction is between closed and open questions. In the former, the range of answers and their format are predetermined; in the latter, they are not. Closed questions can be organized in different ways, including a numerical scale (e.g. tick or circle the appropriate answer); a rating scale (strength of agreement or disagreement with a particular statement); a semantic scale (the respondent's subjective view or response); checklists (e.g. tick or underline one or more relevant items from a list); a preference ranking (e.g. stating the order – either ascending or descending – of preference from a list); or attitudinal choice (selecting the most appropriate responses from a list). These have the advantage of avoiding the cultural problem over overt agreement or disagreement. Cultural interpretations should also be considered in terms of whether the number 1 represents the best/highest or worst/lowest rank in a ranking scale.

9   Be precise regarding the time period or geographical area covered by a question. For instance, if asking about shopping behaviour, you will get very different answers according to whether you are asking about daily, weekly, fortnightly or monthly patterns, or where people buy convenience food, their main weekly supplies or durable goods.

10 Take care to avoid overlap between, or double-counting across, categories of possible response. For instance, with age cohorts, use 0–4, 5–9, 10–14, etc. and not 0–5, 5–10, 10–15, etc.; with time periods, use 1980–89, 1990–99, etc., not 1980–90, 1990–2000, etc.; also avoid ambiguities such as whether 1990 constituted the end of the 1980s or start of the 1990s.

11 Ensure that you use units of measurement with which respondents are familiar. Two sets of examples will suffice, relating to time and area respectively. Many cultures and religions use different calendars from the Western/Christian one. The Jewish, Buddhist and Islamic calendars, for instance, are based on the lunar cycle while others follow solar patterns. Although civil servants and elites may be able to relate to the Christian calendar (especially in this age of computerization), many ordinary people will not. The Buddhist calendar is 543 years ahead of the Christian one, so 2004 was 2547 in Thailand. Nevertheless, as a result of the pervasive impact of Portuguese, Dutch and British colonial rule, Sri Lankans generally use the Christian calendar, despite their country being predominantly Buddhist. In a different sense, illiterate, semi-literate or (semi-) nomadic people very often have a more immediate, informal method of marking the passage of time. This usually relates to some major event and it is helpful to base one's research questions in relation to these. In remoter parts of Kenya and Ghana, for instance, I have used a devastating drought, a terrible flood, completion of the first trunk road through an area, and a political rebellion as such markers. In terms of land area, the unit used in Thailand is the *rai*, 1,600 of which equal one hectare. Conversely, both Sri Lanka and Nigeria officially use the metric system but many ordinary people, particularly older generations and those in rural areas, still tend to use acres

rather than square metres as a reflection of the British imperial system with which they grew up. Earlier indigenous units are no longer used.

Pilot testing

As with any questionnaire, it is important to 'road test' the prototype before commencing the full survey, as this often throws up unanticipated problems or interpretational difficulties that should be ironed out. Particularly if you draft the questionnaire before reaching your field area, local reconnaissance and discussions with key informants and your research assistant may suggest modifications (including the insertion of local terms in the vernacular language, units of measurement, etc.). However, a small pilot survey should still be undertaken. In practice, the first few cases of the survey could be treated as a pilot, especially if you are able to revisit those respondents afterwards to ask any new or significantly amended questions. Sometimes it is advisable to translate your questionnaire into the local vernacular, especially if that would facilitate the work of your assistant(s) and/or respondents. Under such circumstances it is important to pilot the translated version as well as, or perhaps instead of, the original. After all, certain terms and concepts do not translate literally, while perfectly innocent terms in one language may have little meaning or give rise to ambiguity, misunderstanding, amusement or offence in translation.

Sampling strategy

The final important step before undertaking the survey is to determine what percentage of the total population you need to or can afford to sample, and how to select that representative group. There are many possible strategies, with detailed guides provided by

De Vaus (2002) and several chapters in Bulmer and Warwick (1993). Here I point only to some particular considerations with respect to sampling in the context of the complex conditions in many development contexts.

For large, relatively homogeneous but geographically concentrated populations, straightforward strategies like *random* or *systematic* (e.g. every fifth house or tenth pedestrian) sampling are often adequate to capture a representative sample. Sometimes these may be combined into *systematic random sampling*, where the starting point is chosen randomly but subsequently the sampling interval is systematic.

However, complexity and diversity are common characteristics, especially in urban areas and those where major population shifts and displacements have occurred. Hence it becomes necessary to adopt a sampling technique that enables one to capture not just an appropriate sampling fraction, but a reasonably representative sample of each category of the population concerned, however these categories may be defined (e.g. in terms of ethnicity, religion, class, home language, income group, housing type, residential area or political affiliation). This may be very important where attributes such as voting patterns, dietary habits, disease patterns or life expectancy appear to vary significantly by population category.

Stratified sampling is the most common and straightforward strategy under such conditions. This involves identifying the relevant population categories (strata) and the approximate proportion that each comprises of the total population, and then taking an appropriate random or systematic sample within each. Usually this would mean that the absolute size of the sub-samples is proportional to the size of each stratum in the overall population.

For particularly complex and diverse populations, *multi-stage clustering* may prove ideal. Despite being more complicated to undertake, it is effective and cost/time efficient.

169

As the name implies, this involves three or four successive stages of sampling. Generally, there is a trade-off between the number of initial clusters and the number of people/households to interview in each. To give the widest spread of the population, a larger number of initial clusters should be selected and a smaller number of interviews conducted in each successive scale of unit. An urban example would be city wards, districts or substantial shanty settlements (stage 1), unit committee areas or street blocks (stage 2), then individual streets (stage 3) and dwellings (stage 4). In a rural context, a watershed or valley might be divided up into altitudinal or agro-ecological zones (stage 1), then individual villages and their farmland (stage 2), distinct areas or subdivisions within each village (stage 3) and dwellings (stage 4). At each stage, random, structured or systematic random sampling of households or particular individuals per household may be used, according to prevailing circumstances.

Conclusion

Questionnaire surveys represent an important and flexible research tool in diverse development contexts. As anywhere, care is required to avoid some obvious but also many less obvious pitfalls that arise in the context of cross-cultural and development research, where differences of language, custom and practice, wealth, power and knowledge can represent formidable barriers to effective data collection and research.

QUESTIONS FOR DISCUSSION

1. Explain why cross-cultural and development situations represent particular challenges for questionnaire survey design and implementation.
2. Discuss the various factors to consider in relation to using research assistants and translators in questionnaire surveys.
3. What are the principal limitations of structured questionnaires in development research?
4. 'It is important to match the sampling strategy to the task at hand'. Discuss in respect of a specific questionnaire survey you are familiar with or are planning.

Further reading

Laws, S. with Harper, C. and Marcus, R. (2003) *Research for Development*, London: Sage.

Peil, M. (1982) *Social Science Research Methods: An African Handbook*, London: Hodder and Stoughton.

Whitehead, T.L. and Conaway, M.E. (eds) (1986) *Self, Sex and Gender in Cross-cultural Fieldwork*, Urbana and Chicago: University of Illinois Press.

References

Bulmer, M. and Warwick, D. (eds) (1993) *Social Research in Developing Countries,* London: UCL Press.

De Vaus, D.A. (2002) *Surveys in Social Research*, 5th edn, London: Routledge.

Devereux, S. and Hoddinot, J. (eds) (1992) *Fieldwork in Developing Countries*, Boulder, CO: Lynne Rienner.

Mikkelsen, B. (1995) *Methods for Development Work and Research: A Guide for Practitioners,* London: Sage.

Renzetti, C.M. and Lee, R.M. (eds) (1993) *Researching Sensitive Topics*, Newbury Park, CA: Sage.

Scheyvens, R. and Storey, D. (eds) (2003) *Development Fieldwork: A Practical Guide,* London: Sage.

Smith, F. (1996) Problematising language: limitations and possibilities in 'foreign language' research, *Area,* 28(2): 160–166.

Thomas, A., Chataway, J. and Wuyts, M. (eds) (1998) *Finding Out Fast: Investigative Skills for Policy and Development*, London: Sage.

18

Lost in Translation? The Use of Interpreters in Fieldwork

Janet Bujra

Research into other cultures involves a process of translation through from data collection to analysis and dissemination ●● Social researchers should aim for a working knowledge of the local language ●● There are situations where this is impractical or impossible (e.g. short-term research or settings with multiple languages) ●● Local assistants can double up as translators and ethnographic informants ●● Translators make their own judgements about how and what they translate – the terms on which this is done need to be negotiated ●● Choosing a translator requires attention to the social dynamics between researcher, interpreter and respondents

All research culminates in multiple modes of translation as the researcher not only has to make sense of the social group or phenomenon under study but then to communicate this understanding by reframing it conceptually and analytically for an academic audience. Translation is more than a technical exercise; it is also a social relationship involving power, status and the imperfect mediation of cultures. Drawing on my own experience and that of fellow researchers, I discuss here the challenges and opportunities of using translators in the field, explaining why they are needed, how best they can be employed and what features characterize a good translator.

There is a limited literature on using interpreters in social research methods texts; conversely, writing by academic translators is both suggestive and revealing.

The need for translators

I have been fortunate in rarely needing to use translators in the field. I learnt a language, Swahili, during my first fieldwork in northern Kenya, which served (with dialect shifts) for most of my later research in other parts of Kenya and Tanzania. But in 1995, when I was working in Lushoto district in northeastern

Tanzania, I realized that while most people spoke Swahili fluently, elderly women were far more comfortable in the local vernacular of Kisambaa. I remember vividly my discomfort when I met with several women to talk about a local institution called *kidembwa* (of which more below) and they switched to Kisambaa. Suddenly I found myself unable to hear or to communicate. It was like being struck deaf and dumb. Although there are Swahili loan words in Kisambaa and the gestures and laughter enabled me to get the gist of the conversation, the limitations left me supremely frustrated. I had to rely on the hesitant translation efforts of a bilingual young woman who was one of my local assistants, efforts which she employed so sparingly that the rich flow of words was reduced to a desert. Later we were joined by a woman who had married into the community from another ethnic group, but had learnt to speak Kisambaa fluently. Probably with more empathy on this account than my assistant, she began to explain to me in Swahili what was being said. However, I knew that this woman was not wholly trusted by the Sambaa women and I suspected that it was her opinions as much as fidelity to their words that was transmitted to me. In this encounter I lost most of the control which a researcher would normally have to guide the agenda of debate. I found myself side-lined and alien, reduced to the situation I faced as an apprentice researcher when my initial knowledge of Swahili was based on standard dictionaries bearing little resemblance to the ancient dialect of the area in which I conducted my first fieldwork.

Although full knowledge of a community requires a facility in the local language, and researchers should aim at the gold standard of achieving appropriate language skills, there are circumstances which legitimately require translation assistance. The early phase of learning a language is like inhabiting a twilight zone where knowledge is still hazy and it is essential to have local assistants who, even if they cannot translate the local vernacular into English, might at least offer an extended gloss which facilititates a better grasp of meaning. Researchers do not always work in monoglot communities either – national or urban settings are often ones where many languages would be required to surf all social situations. In Nairobi I worked in an impoverished urban neighbourhood where Swahili was the local lingua franca. It also played an integrative role in a situation of great ethnic diversity and was the first language of its core Muslim community of urban Africans. Swahili sufficed for most interactions here, though it was of less use in communicating with recent immigrants. Most of the residents of this neighbourhood could speak their own vernaculars and often those of others too, switching language codes as the social situation demanded. The assistant of a traditional healer could speak his own native Lusoga, as well as Luganda (in which he had been educated), Swahili and some Arabic (a language with some supernatural power in this context). He had acquired some facility in Kikikuyu, Kikamba and Kigusii as well, the better to serve his customers. To follow, as people negotiated complex language shifts, would have required more skill than most researchers could muster. Obviously it was vital in this situation to have some local assistance in identifying the languages used and in translating at points where the lingua franca was inadequate to the task.[1]

There are settings which require even more complex translation assistance. A colleague was involved in team research in Namibia, a country with eight or nine major languages, some mutually unintelligible, and no lingua franca. The study demanded interpreters, and sometimes a chain of translators was required to elicit information. Clearly, the finished work could lay no claim to represent the original speakers and their speech in all its

173

nuanced wisdom, but the process was adequate to collect comparative material of a factual kind. Another colleague, engaged in development work on social conflict, brought together Tamil and Sinhala speakers in the same workshops. Translators were vital to initiating dialogue, and their translations had to include both the researchers (who spoke only English) and the two other language communities.

Researchers sometimes rely on the global reach of English to mediate their research. If the research topic is appropriately restricted, say to the operations of high-level government personnel and the formal issues and relationships of office, English might be adequate. A good proportion of English-speakers might also be found among NGO staff. But a study of NGOs (even international NGOs) would be impoverished if interactions between staff and local people could not be understood – the outcome would be a one-sided and potentially biased view of the operations of the organization, seen only through the eyes of donors and officials. Extending beyond this would demand interpreters from client categories. In general, English-speakers are likely to be a socially distinctive stratum of the educated, wealthy or powerful and more likely to be men than women.

Most researchers will *work towards* being their own translators, where local people (preferably those from the group or community under study[2]) are the best guides to understanding both speech and action. A local interpreter is far more than a translator of language. They can and often do become 'informant[s] in an ethnographic sense' (Bragason, n.d.). They can become intermediaries who will open doors; they can also help to unravel why people behave as they do, who is related to whom or why the next village is different. Such assistance may be crucial where researchers are operating in dangerous or sensitive areas and need to be aware of key terms (and slang equivalents) for 'friends' and 'enemies' and for other imminent threats to their

safety (Sluka, 1990: 114). Naming groups can be a hazardous exercise, as anyone who has worked on issues of race or ethnicity will be aware. Using a label which is unacceptable to respondents can blight research and one needs to be initiated into this terminology by those who are already in the know. Working on domestic servants in Tanzania, I soon discovered the power politics of naming. Employers used terms like 'boy' for grown men while the standard Swahili translation *mtumishi* was also unacceptable as it implied one who was 'used'. *Msaidizi* ('helper') was a form acceptable to all. Meanwhile, in the academic literature, a politically correct formulation, 'domestic worker', was in vogue (Bujra, 2000a: 3).[3]

Heavy reliance on single sources of information is not to be recommended, nor to have a single person represent your purpose to others. The problem with dependence on local translators is that one can be restricted and trapped within their perspective on their own society. It is not until one begins to speak the language and enlarge the canvas of relationships that one can decipher how social location or political position might affect a translator's interpretations.

The implications of researching through a third party

While a legitimate need for translators and interpreters is encountered in all types of development research, the implications of conducting research through a third party are rarely discussed. These can be divided into practical issues, 'technical' matters and the negotiation of social relations.

Practical issues

In practical terms the need for a translator can be satisfied only within budgetary limits. A highly skilled interpreter, proficient in at least two languages, is expensive and may exceed the resources of many researchers. Costs would be augmented where there is no locally available person. Alternatively, local people (who, after all, would be most likely to have the particular language knowledge) could be trained, or learn through experience. When other researchers or development agencies are operating in an area, there may be competition to secure such people and labour would generally go to the highest bidder. Operating effectively may require more than one translator, as in multiple language settings, but also because the job is very tiring and interpreters need breaks. When interactions using an interpreter are taped and another translator independently transcribes and translates the text to check its validity, this also adds to costs, without undoing any inadequacies in the original encounter.

Time is also a factor. Translating interactions into another language and back again doubles the time spent on an interview. In workshops or focus groups such a tortuous process can completely stifle debate. As my colleague said of an attempt to run a workshop whose English-speaking facilitators were aiming to initiate discussion between Sinhala and Tamil speakers, 'people lost the rhythm'. A fall-back position was adopted, to have separate English–Sinhala and English–Tamil workshops and to bring participants together once they had a better grasp of the issues in debate. The time expended was no less, but debate flourished.

Technical problems

Professional interpreters write more perceptively than social analysts about the technical problems entailed in translation and about the dilemmas faced in the search for effective communication and fidelity to sources.[4] We need to consider their accounts as they can help to explain some of our frustration in having to rely on inadequate translations, enable us to think more critically about our

own practice as translators and also help to identify training issues in employing interpreters. One colleague identified a general problem – explaining the rationale for research to people who have never encountered a researcher before and are understandably apprehensive and suspicious. Her translator was the woman of the household in which she lived during fieldwork and by whom she was introduced to local people. Because the introduction was not translated back into English, my colleague was left in the dark about how she was being presented to others. It also raised the problem of how this woman herself understood the purpose of the research. Later they agreed on a form of words, but this first required my colleague to have more linguistic facility.

Professional translators themselves struggle with how to do the job. Is a literal translation better than a colloquial one? 'Better' could be read as 'more accurate and true to the original' or it might be understood as 'facilitating communication'. Peterson (2004) worked for a translating company in Japan. He often had to translate technical manuals which manufacturers sent to customers and where literal adherence to the original Japanese text was demanded (which perhaps explains why so many of us cannot make sense of the instruction booklets for videos or computers!). Is a word-by-word definition the most legitimate, or do the words make sense only in the context of the whole speech? To what extent should the translator creatively improve upon clumsy or awkward speech or sanitize the grammar? How to deal with rhetoric or irony[5]? Or politically ambiguous pronouncements?

By now the alarm bells may be ringing for us as social researchers, if we had understood the translator to be merely the transmitter of what others say. We may not have seen them as actively participant intermediaries making judgements which may transform the message received. Temple (1997: 615-16)

175

describes a case where the same words in Polish could be taken as an endorsement of a sociobiological perception of women's positionality, or as an indication of the politics of defining what women can do. Her Polish translator had taken the former interpretation, though she concurred that either was correct; the researcher, as a feminist, insisted on the latter. Another example comes from my own recent research with Asian young men who rioted in Bradford in 2001. Interviews were transcribed by someone who largely ignored the dialect of broad Yorkshire in which many of these men spoke – and which said something very significant about their local roots and social identity. 'It were…' was rendered as 'it was'; 'me mum' became 'my mum'; and 't'street' was transformed into 'the street'. Fortunately, I had been there and heard the accents or I might have missed all this. I was then able to adjust the transcriptions, excellent in every other respect. The transcriber had acted on her own initiative, translating Yorkshire dialect into standard English, but losing sociological data in the process.

Translators are not simple ciphers without political or social views of their own. They may find it hard not to betray this in their translations, presenting one side's position with more conviction and elaboration than the other, or even contradicting the accounts that are given in order to present their own opinions. More generally, it is common for the translators to 'filter out' what they consider unimportant, even though this might be precisely what the researcher needs and wishes to know.

Ideas and concepts from one language cannot always be translated into another. The term *kidembwa* in Lushoto was not only a Kisambaa, rather than a Swahili, word, but it had no Swahili (or English) equivalent. At first I took it to be the name of an organization, as it clearly referred to women acting collectively. But when I looked for this association I found no corporate entity, no leader, no hierarchical organization, no headquarters – only small, scattered clusters of older women (and not always the same women) coming together in response to the need to collect money for particular purposes or to celebrate events like weddings (Bujra 2000b). Eventually I defined *kidembwa* as a network, or an institution which materialized only in action. This understanding was achieved by multiple acts of observation and discussion, and after a lot of trial and error. I am in good company here – the founder of participant observation, Bronislaw Malinowski, was faced with a similar puzzle when he tried to understand the term *kula* among the Trobriand islanders and gradually uncovered the chain of social relations of ceremonial exchange and auxiliary interactions which it denoted (Malinowski, 1922). This exploration and delineation of indigenous concepts is more the job of the social analyst than the professional translator. This is clear from Bragason's gloss on an untranslatable Thai concept *nam djai*. He demands that 'the interpreter must explain the meaning in detail to the researcher, for example with a reference to real-life situations and by using metaphors, and the best that can be hoped to come out of this is some form of equivalent meaning' (Bragason, n.d.). But as he points out, the more distinctive two cultures are, the less likely they are to use languages with perfect equivalence between concepts.

Negotiating relationships

Aside from the technical difficulties of translation which may impede the researcher's grasp of unfamiliar social settings, the relationship between translator and researcher may need careful negotiation. It is generally not a relationship of equals since it is the researcher who pays, although this may not be true for non-professional local interpreters who genuinely double up as friends and acquaintances. Whether the exchange is one of money or friendship, the researcher is bound to relinquish some control over the process of extracting data when this is done through a third party who thereby gains considerable leverage. Translators are probably most useful in an interview situation which is formal and time-limited and where some preparation may be done. They are probably least useful in parti-cipant observation where the researcher aims for informality and to become a player in the social game. In whatever case, consideration has to be given to the three-way dynamics between the researcher's goals, the translator's capacity and interests and the view which is taken of both by the research subjects (dynam-ics described by Rudvin (2000: 2) as 'a delicate and difficult, at times painful, collaboration'). A colleague's work in Sudan on gender issues illustrates the point. It was difficult enough to find an interpreter and it was clear that a man would not be appropriate for this topic.[6] The young woman chosen came from the area, but not from the district under study. Because she was young she was not taken seriously – indeed, informants found her translated ques-tions improper and lacking in appropriate respect for elders.

Sometimes the power relations are com-plex. When researching armed groups or interviewing important political figures, inter-preters are often in a problematic position, where the translation of sensitive or challen-ging questions or responses can put them in danger or difficulty. A thought-provoking analysis of one such encounter shows that even professional translators may fear to trans-late words intended as weapons. Baker's account (1997) is of an interview between Trevor McDonald of ITV and Saddam Hussein, in the period leading up to the first Gulf war. The translators were provided by the Iraqi state. On occasions they appeared anxious and under pressure, in case fault was found with their interpretations by Saddam (who might have exacted vengeance). They stuck to literal renderings of his rhetorical style, which obliterated heavy sarcasm and lost

fluency by incorporating many synonyms to absolve themselves of responsibility for mis-representation. Baker describes Saddam as a 'very persuasive speaker and a skilled orator' in Arabic; the translation made him appear 'incoherent and paranoid' (1997: 124) – an unintended consequence of strategies devised by translators to protect themselves, but one which could not have helped the cause of world peace or mutual understanding.

Choosing an interpreter

Let me conclude with some suggestions as to what to look for in a translator and how to maximize their usefulness. Social researchers will find interpreters who speak the local lan-guage as their first tongue and have a first-hand knowledge of the area under study more useful than those whose English is perfect. At best, such people can be both translator and ethnographic informant. Clearly, other quali-ties are also essential – a basic competence, which would include skill both in listening and in offering full accounts of what is said, but also the capacity to be self-effacing and to 'put their own ego aside' so that they do not inhibit informants. People who are socially aware and interested in other people's views are better than those who have rigid attitudes which they might impose on the data. The researcher may need the translator to be pre-sent on all occasions of data collection, so they need to work well together. Ultimately, there has to be trust on both sides, which can only be built up over a period. It is good practice to tape-record formal interviews (if this is feasible in the setting and acceptable to inter-viewees) so as to be able to verify the accu-racy of the translations from other sources (Birbili, 2000: 4).

Considerable time is needed for debriefing after fieldwork sessions so that the translator can expand on what was said at the time, or explain difficult concepts at more length. There

177

needs to be space to discuss the significance of non-verbal communication – the body language of demeanour, gesture, laughter – and the meaning of silences.

The experience of not being able to communicate is an alienating one and the use of translators and interpreters is not an adequate substitute for learning to speak oneself. But at some stages and in some kinds of research there is no alternative to employing the linguistic skills of others and this can have unexpected bonuses as the translator becomes a partner in the struggle to achieve a mediation of cultures. There is no perfect mediation and we need all the help we can get.

Acknowledgements

I am indebted to colleagues in the Department of Peace Studies at the University of Bradford who shared their experience of using interpreters, especially Dr Donna Pankhurst and Dr Nick Lewer.

Notes

1. Since my initial study here was a sociolinguistic one, these language shifts were of central interest (Bujra, 1974).
2. Social matching in language and ethnicity, but also in features like class, gender, religion, age or occupation would facilitate access to insider views.
3. Sutton (1997), a professional translator, describes how he inadvertently sparked a minor international incident when an American television news channel took up his translation of a text on a traditional Spanish fiesta for an in-flight magazine. The actors in the fiesta were described as *judios* in the Spanish text, but literally translated into 'Jews' this was taken to be an anti-semitic reference by Jewish airline travellers, who then made an official protest.
4. See, for example, Simms (1997), Hatim and Mason (1997) and Wadensjo (1998), or the on-line *Translation Journal*. Rudvin (School of Modern Languages for Interpreters and Translators, Bologna, Italy) indicates the extent to which Translation/Interpreting Theory is sociologically aware, with its 'shift away from a positivist, essentialist as well as linguistically-based approach to a more holistic and relativist methodology taking into account … political inclinations and motivations, cultural difference, power relations and hierarchies … contributing to the formation of "meaning"' (Rudvin, 2000: 2).
5. Hatim and Mason (1997) insist that styles of argumentation vary across cultures. This presents problems for the translator and may inhibit cross-cultural communication. They also suggest that 'persuasive strategies' in Arabic contrast with those in English and that the two languages present irony in distinctive ways.
6. Researchers often emphasis the value of having both male and female interpreters to cover gender-sensitive areas. Interpreting women's (or men's!) words raises other issues of mediation between actors' speech and analytical interpretations (see the thought-provoking accounts in Gluck and Patai, 1991).

178

QUESTIONS FOR DISCUSSION

1. In what circumstances might it be least appropriate to use an interpreter?
2. Which is more important – a technically superb translation or an imperfect but insider interpretation?
3. How can silences be 'translated' and what is their social significance?
4. How can the potential prejudices of an interpreter be handled?
5. What does it mean to say that perfect equivalence can never be found between the languages of different cultures?

Further reading

Birbili, M. (2000) Translating from one language to another, *Social Research Update*, 31, University of Surrey, Guildford.

Temple, B. and Young, A. (2004) Qualitative research and translation dilemmas, *Qualitative Research*, 4 (2):161–78.

Wadensjo, C. (1998) *Interpreting as Interaction*, London: Longman.

References

Baker, M. (1997) Non-cognitive constraints and interpreter strategies in political interviews, in K. Simms (ed.), *Translating Sensitive Texts: Linguistic Aspects*, Amsterdam and Atlanta, GA: Rodopi, pp. 111–129.

Birbili, M. (2000) Translating from one language to another, *Social Research Update*, 31, Guildford: University of Surrey, pp.1–7.

Bragason, E. (n.d.) Interviewing through interpreters, Psychology Institute, Aarhus University, Aarhus Available online at: http://www.psy.au.dk/ckm/newsletter/nb23/23-egil.htm

Bujra, J. (1974) Pumwani: language usage in an urban Muslim community, in W.H. Whiteley (ed.), *Language in Kenya*, Nairobi: Oxford University Press, pp. 217–252.

Bujra, J. (2000a) *Serving Class: Masculinity and the Feminisation of Domestic Service in Tanzania*, Edinburgh: Edinburgh University Press.

Bujra, J. (2000b) Target practice: gender and generational struggles in AIDS prevention work in Lushoto, in C. Baylies, and J. Bujra, *AIDS, Sexuality and Gender in Africa: Collective Strategies and Struggles in Tanzania and Zambia,* London: Routledge.

Gluck, S. and Patai, D. (1991) *Women's Words: the Feminist Practice of Oral History*, New York: Routledge.

Hatim, B. and Mason, I. (1997) *The Translator as Communicator*, London: Routledge.

Malinowski, B. (1922) *Argonauts of the Western Pacific*, London: Routledge.

Peterson, D. (2004) Source language vs target language bias, *Translation Journal*, 8 (3).

Rudvin, M. (2000) Community interpreting in the area of mental health: psycho-social implications of interpreting strategies, Conference paper for the Issues in Interpreting Research Conference, Manchester.

Simms, K. (ed.) (1997) *Translating Sensitive Tests: Linguistic Aspects*, Amsterdam and Atlanta, GA: Rodopi.

Sluka, J.A. (1990) Participant observation in violent social contexts, *Human Organisation*, 49 (2): 114–126.

Sutton, P. (1997) A translator's dilemma, in K. Simms (ed.), *Translating Sensitive Texts: Linguistic Aspects*, Amsterdam and Atlanta, GA: Rodopi, pp. 67–75.

Temple, B. (1997) Watch your tongue: issues in translation and cross-cultural research, *Sociology*, 31 (3): 607–618.

Translation Journal, online at http://accurapid.com/journal/29bias.htm

Wadensjo, C. (1998) *Interpreting as Interaction*, London: Longman.

179

19

Ethnography and Participant Observation

Jan Kees van Donge

- - What is ethnography? - - Ethnography and development studies
- - Ethnography and the development practitioner - - The distinctive
contribution of ethnographic methods

What is ethnography?

Ethnographic research methods attempt to study social life as it unfolds in the practices of day-to-day life. These methods avoid as much as possible artificial research situations. Artificiality is obvious in some instances, particularly in the highly controlled experimental method, but it is found also in other methods. For example, the interview situation in surveys using highly controlled questions is a social construction. In participatory rural appraisal (PRA), meetings are set up specifically to ask questions that people may never ask spontaneously. From the ethnographic point of view, the ideal is not to be noticed as an observer and to be accepted as a normal member of social life, as this results in minimal disturbance. Such participant observation is, however, an ideal that is rarely reached in practice. Artificial research situations, to a certain degree, usually enter the social field that

is being studied. The word 'ethnography' emerged in the period of European expansion to denote the observation of exotic peoples. It is thus in its origin closely associated with the confrontation of different cultures. The latter makes it especially relevant for development studies as a confrontation between cultures is inherent in development work.

Ethnography and development studies

There is widespread scepticism about the suitability of ethnographic methods in the field of development. Research for development management has often to give answers to support urgent decision-making. Ethnography, on the other hand, often requires a large investment in time. First, one must gain the confidence of the people to be studied so that one can be near to them and therefore able to carry out the research. Second, it often involves the need to at least get acquainted with another language. If one masters the language, one must ideally be at home in specific group languages. Third, systematic observation of behaviour takes time. An image is gradually built up of what is happening in a particular social setting on the basis of continued observation.[1] As research proceeds and one gathers more and more data, the question arises as to when data change into insights. The moment of wider understanding usually occurs when one gets repetitive results, but it is difficult to say when exactly that happens. Boredom is often a threat to the researcher when stories become repetitive, but that is usually the sign of understanding. In ethnographic research it is therefore difficult to see how far one has progressed, and this is obviously difficult to reconcile with the need for deadlines. Ethnographic research methods were therefore a major butt of attack in Robert Chambers's call for more relevant development research: he argued that 'quick and dirty' research methods were needed if findings were to be related to practical action (Chambers, 1974, 1983).

Nevertheless, development organizations these days increasingly commission ethnographic-style research. A major reason for this is dissatisfaction with the PRA methods. Indeed, these can make development organizations quickly acquainted with a community, but the answers they give often lack depth. The same answers emerge in many different situations; for example, wealth ranking will usually result in distinguishing a few rich households, a large number in the middle and an underclass of extremely poor. This is compounded by an increasing awareness that dominant interests often overshadow others in participatory meetings. The relevance of observation, the hallmark of ethnographic methods, to check and deepen these images through watching people and situations, taking notice of casual conversation and the divergent opinions of individuals therefore becomes apparent.

A second major reason for development organizations favouring ethnographic-style research is the growing awareness of the unexpected effects resulting from development interventions. The open-minded observation employed by ethnographic methods, more than other methods, can focus attention outside the field of expected outcomes. This can be illustrated with an example (see Box 19.1).

181

Box 19.1 Unexpected outcomes and ethnographic methods

Family Life Training Centres were established in Central Kenya where mothers of malnourished children could regain strength and learn about methods of nutrition. An evaluation found that these did not perceptibly change knowledge or patterns of nutrition, nor did they have any long-term impact on the growth of children. It found, however, that many women attending these nutrition centres were poor and in the process of divorce. Land in Central Kenya is in the hands of men and therefore divorce provokes for women a crisis in livelihood in this peasant society. A stay in a nutrition centre was a way to reorganize their lives. The centres had thus no effect on malnutrition, but their establishment had important effects as shelter for women in a vulnerable situation. (Summarized from Hoorweg and Niemeijer, 1981)

This finding was actually revealed through a survey, but it illustrates the need to have an open mind in planned intervention. If one simply compares intended output with outcomes, then one must come to the conclusion that the Family Life Training Centres are a failure. However, such a position overlooks important, unintentional effects of the intervention, which in this case can be valued positively. Free-ranging observation outside the bureaucratic, programmed culture of terms of reference, etc., is particularly valuable for this.

The work of Norman Long (2001) is particularly significant in this respect. He sees development interventions as taking place in an interface of cultures where there is a continuous adaptation, struggle and meshing of cultural elements and social practices. The language that talks in terms of target populations and that expects a linear process from intervention to outcomes is wanting. The intervening actors are not steering society as a machine but are only some actors among the many in the ongoing struggles to create social practices. Long's perspective on planned intervention clarifies a wide spectrum of policy interventions. Such interaction at the interface can, for example, be seen in election observation. Observers will stress neutrality: adherence to international standards often based on human rights. However, their presence and findings play a significant role in the ongoing local political process. Interaction between a local political culture and the political culture of outsiders is essential to understand what is going on. There is thus a growing awareness that confrontation between cultures is inherent in development practice.

While development practitioners may thus increasingly appreciate the value of ethnographic assessments, they still have need of short-notice information relevant to management. To fulfil this need, researchers, especially social anthropologists, increasingly provide ethnographically inspired reports at short notice. This is possible because the stress on the long-term commitment in ethnographic methods appears to have been too simplistic. First, some societies are much more open than others, and this allows the researcher to enter relatively quickly into the culture. Second, if ethnographers have done an elaborate study before, then they can often work much faster on subsequent occasions. This is especially the case if the previous study was in the society in question or a closely related one. Third, ethnographic methods are difficult to codify, but training in anthropology gives people a penetrating attitude towards looking at social practices that is often referred to as the 'anthropological eye'.

Ethnography and the development practitioner

The anthropological eye refers to an ability to observe oneself and the social environment. The usefulness of this ability is not necessarily restricted to researchers but can be very beneficial to practitioners as well. They can be participant observers in their own situation. Researchers in development are often not sufficiently aware that the principal may direct attention to the target population, whereas participant observation in a development project including the principal may be more productive. The probable reason for this obliviousness to their own social context is the demythologizing, sometimes even subversive, character of exercising the anthropological eye: if it is used in an all-embracing manner, discrepancies between what people (including practitioners as well as the target population) say and how they act become apparent. A beautiful example of this comes from the work of David Mosse on participatory rural appraisal methods based on his own participation in these exercises:

> While from the point of view of the 'outsider' development workers an organized PRA is an informal event, in social terms the PRA is often highly formal and public: PRAs are

182

group or collective activities; they involve important and influential outsiders (even foreigners); they take place in public spaces (schools, temples, etc.); they involve the community representing itself to outsiders; and information is discussed publicly, recorded and preserved for use in planning. Such activities are far from informal, everyday life. It seems highly probable that this social formality imposes a selectivity on the kind of information which is presented and recorded in PRAs. (Mosse, 1994: 508)

A training in ethnographic methods makes journal-keeping – generally an ordinary part of development work – a more productive exercise. Ethnographic research requires extensive journal-keeping to keep track of all the observations. These notes usually seem random in the beginning and not leading anywhere. However, insights into social practices often suddenly emerge from these notes. For example, I had difficulty collecting meaningful statements from people while doing research in the Uluguru Mountains in Tanzania. People talked a lot but said very little. I interpreted this as a failure on my part to penetrate that society. However, another interpretation emerged while I was repeatedly writing about those remarks without social meaning. It was an essential trait of that society to avoid commitment in conversation, as they did not trust each other: people were gregarious (e.g. they came together in large numbers around Catholic churches on Sunday and on market days), but they were extremely private as regards emotions and opinions.

An anthropological eye – and ear – entails the ability to build insights on interpretations of everyday life and this enriches working with research assistants who are insiders in the societies being studied. While working in a ranching area in Namibia, we found ourselves in a situation where doubt arose about the number of cattle kept on a particular farm. We heard from a neighbour that there were far more animals on the farm than stated by the farmer in question. It also transpired then that the informant was a close friend of the research assistant's mother. She was a Tswana whereas the neighbour overstocking the farm was Herero. Implicit in the remarks made was a confrontation of cultures showing distrust between the two groups.

The distinctive contribution of ethnographic methods

While ethnographic research may essentially entail an attitude rather than a set of codified methods, nevertheless, there are a number of definite elements to be found in ethnographic work.

First, ethnographers depend primarily on observation. An ethnographic approach adopts a distrust of society as it is presented to us. On entering a community, one is presented with a particular interpretation of the social reality. A confrontation of these ideas with observations makes this explicit. For example, in an attempt to find the ultra-poor in Dedza district in Malawi, observing housing, clothes, etc. could identify only these. Agricultural extension workers considered them as failures and thus not interesting. Chiefs wanted to introduce relatives in the first place as benefits were expected from contacts with outsiders. On the other hand, observation is an important tool to correct preconceived ideas of researchers. For example, small livestock is often overlooked in African rural studies, and casual observation may show the importance of goats, sheep, etc.

Second, ethnographic research implies an open approach. It avoids as much as possible framing a research situation beforehand, for example through formulating particular, detailed questions. Ethnographers often use checklists to fall back on when asking questions or observing, but these should be continuously adapted in the light of information gained. The purpose of interaction

183

with informants is to elicit responses rather than get answers to particular questions. The fundamental awareness in ethnographic research is that one has to learn gradually the language that allows one to ask sensible questions as one penetrates deeper into that society. During my research in the Uluguru Mountains in Tanzania I was regularly confronted with the remark 'he has water' (*ana maji*) or the reverse. The meaning of this statement became clear only when I discovered how important access to a small perennial stream was for irrigating vegetable plots in the dry season. Whatever one hears in open or loosely structured conversation should always be checked against observation. If one works with research assistants, it is often fruitful for each to write up independently what each has seen and heard and then confront each other with differences. In this way, interpretation is built up as well.

Third, ethnographic research uses the case study method. It studies particular situations in depth and makes no claims to be statistically representative. It is wrong, however, to conclude that case studies have no wider significance. Indeed, if a case study is merely an apt illustration of a particular point made, then its importance is marginal. However, a good case study involves systematic analysis in depth.

This can be done in two ways. First, it is possible to collect a large number of instances that are then classified to see particular patterns emerging. For example, in a study of land conflicts, I collected cases from regular court sessions. These were then categorized as relating to sale of land, border disputes, inheritance, etc. It transpired that an appreciation of inheritance and the social construction of a past was crucial to understanding the number and virulence of these conflicts. Second, it is possible to study a particular situation intensively so that a very detailed analysis emerges. This process has been dubbed by the anthropologist Geertz (1993) as 'thick description'. This methodology is particularly associated with the Manchester School in social anthropology. Gluckmann (1961: 5) gave the following concise definition: 'The anthropological case study is a method that seeks to illuminate principles of social organisation by examining in detail a single social event, or case'. It is also referred to as the analysis of social drama or the extended case study method (Van Velsen, 1967). Intensive analysis of social situations leads to the emergence of a particular social structure and/or culture. This then allows us to perceive similar or contrasting patterns in other situations (see Box 19.2 for an example).

Box 19.2   Anthropological case study as a method of ethnographic research

Porter et al. studied the Australian-sponsored Magharini project in Western Kenya. After a few years it appeared that this project was based on wrong assumptions. Nevertheless, there were strong pressures to continue. The authors provide an elaborate analysis of the use of surveys and cost–benefit analysis in these struggles. Cost–benefit analysis is based on the assumption that we know future costs and benefits reasonably well. Its value is limited in situations where that is not the case. Nevertheless, actors in this case clung to the arguments in the form of cost–benefits. Porter et al. then analyse it as a ritual to cope with insecurity. Proper reading of this case leads to the asking of sceptical questions in any situation where cost–benefit analysis is used. (Summarized from Porter et al., 1991)

Fourth, ethnographic methods try to understand society from the inside. The essential question to be asked is: How would I feel if I were in the situation of the people studied? Ethnographic research is often closely related to symbolic interactionism. It tries to understand through language the lifeworld of people – their interpretation of the world – that structures social practices (Berger and Luckman, 1966). For example, in Africa urban migrants often continue to cultivate strong links with the rural areas from which they or their relatives originate. This structures in turn investment behaviour, as shown in the following example from Buhera in Zimbabwe:

> Even after a lifetime of urban employment and urban family life, people want to be buried in their rural homestead. Thus we can also understand a migrant worker's effort to establish a rural homestead (*musha*) at some stage in his urban career. Although he may stay with wife and children in town and has no economic need to supplement urban income with agricultural production, a 'traditional' round cooking hut has to be constructed. It is possible, therefore, to see homesteads that are occupied by family members, or absent migrant workers who leave their fields uncultivated or hire people to work the land for them. Building a homestead on a plot of some few acres is an expression of a migrant worker's membership of the rural community and, subsequently, of the naturalness of being buried there. (Andersson, 2001: 106)

Such an interpretation of cultures is, of course, most relevant for development interventions. In the case of Buhera district, it meant, for example, that the interest in rural links was not synonymous with an interest in agriculture. With regard to any intervention in agriculture, it must be borne in mind that urban migration is the dominant and most prestigious way to make a living, despite

appearances to the contrary, as shown in the building of houses.

Development interventions usually assume a logic of intention or cause and effect. Such a logic may not make sense in particular cultural configurations. This is a field where ethnographic assessments can be a particularly potent means of analysis. This is also an area where methods can be developed that give relatively fast results. For example, one can translate project documents into local languages and read these to key informants to hear reactions. Another way in which the logic of development interventions can be confronted with local cultures is through developing a set of statements that refer to the logic of the intervention. These should be balanced, with an equal number of statements supporting or opposing the intervention. The idea that there is a correct answer should be avoided; the statements are primarily meant to elicit responses. For example:

185

> The targeted input provision (TIP) programme in Malawi distributes free inputs – fertiliser and seeds – to poor households. Underlying this programme is the belief that people value growing their own food rather than buying it and that this is especially the case for poor people. We asked respondents to react to fifteen statements relating to this, and their responses showed a clear and consistent cultural pattern.

> In response to the statement: 'Not growing one's own food is a reason for shame', people typically gave responses such as the following:

> 'It is shameful when you do not have your own food because whenever you go looking around for maize to buy, people perceive you as a beggar who is totally desperate and stranded for food. This is unlike when you have your own food whenever you have need of it.'

'Not growing one's own food results in a loss of trust in rural areas because the reliable source of livelihood is farming.'

In response to the statement: 'People who do not grow their own food are not necessarily poor', we had comments such as:

'This is not true because, in a village set up, most of the people that are poor are also those who do not grow their own food.'

'Someone who has food is in control of the money because those who have nice clothes do not have then to exchange their clothes into food. In fact, for someone to put on trousers means his belly is full. Without food, the trousers will fall down. (Summarized from Van Donge et al., 2001: 20–21)

Ethnographic methods can thus be an inspiration to develop new ways of obtaining relevant cultural insights, clarifying what is happening around development interventions. However, it is difficult to give a toolbox to that end. First, it depends upon something that can be cultivated but not learnt: empathy with people who live totally different lives from ourselves. Second, ethnographic methods often involve a cultivation and development of observation, an essential activity in everyday life. The best way to develop an aptitude for ethnographic research is therefore to read ethnographic studies that stimulate emulation. Above all, one should beware of one's own cultural dispositions. Often, a particular rationality is imputed to actors where there may be none, or where there may be one functioning in quite different values systems. For many people, it is tempting to see behaviour as resulting from conscious choice guided by what is perceived as immediate economic self-interest. Such a culturally determined assumption in behaviour is common in North America and Western Europe, but ethnography is needed precisely to set this culture in its relative place.

Summary

Ethnographic methods study the daily flow of social life.

- Ethnographic methods used to be considered unsuitable for development research as they were time-consuming and not immediately policy relevant
- There is a growing re-appreciation of ethnographic methods in development because of: (a) the realization of the limitations of PRA methods; (b) an awareness of the unexpected effects of development intervention; and (c) the emerging view of development as a cultural encounter
- Development practitioners can benefit from training in ethnographic methods as it enriches the understanding of the situations in which they find themselves
- Good ethnography is dependent on standard techniques only to a limited degree, but it requires a sensibility to culture, an appreciation of the value of observation and intuitive empathy. These elements are sometimes referred to as the 'anthropological eye', which is difficult to define
- Nevertheless, there are concrete elements that distinguish ethnography as a method: (a) a reliance on observation; (b) an open approach in questioning; (c) a reliance on the case study method; and (d) an understanding of behaviour from inside a society instead of imposing a logic of cause and effect on social situations

Note

1. Ethnographic methods are closely related to the idea of grounded theory: one starts research with as few pre-conceived ideas as possible but general concepts are formulated as they emerge from the observations (Strauss and Corbin, 1990).

Further reading

The best way to understand the special contribution of ethnography to development studies is reading exemplary work. The following article is an ethnographic account of a development intervention in the field of health: Yamba, Bawa (1997) Cosmologies in turmoil: witchfinding and Aids in Chiawa, Zambia, *Africa*, 67(2): 200–223.

The work of David Mosse is especially influential in the promotion of ethnographic methods in development studies: Mosse, David (2004) Is good policy unimplementable? Reflections on the ethnography of aid policy and practice, *Development and Change*, 35(4): 639–673.

187

The following book does not contain consistent ethnographic work, but it gives a superb insight based on close ethnographic observation in the search for certainty in development interventions: Porter, Doug, Allen, Bryant and Thompson, Gaye (1991) *Development in Practice: Paved with Good Intentions*, London: Routledge, Chapter VI 'Institutions for managing uncertainty'.

The link between ethnographic methods and a general theoretical orientation stressing an actor-oriented approach can be found in: Long, Norman (2001) *Development Sociology: Actor-Oriented Perspectives*, London: Routledge.

References

Andersson, Jens A. (2001) Re-interpreting the rural–urban connection: migration practices and socio-cultural dispositions of Buhera workers in Harare, *Africa*, 71 (1): 82–112.

Berger, Peter L. and Luckman, Thomas (1966) *The Social Construction of Reality: A Treatise in the Sociology of Knowledge*, Garden City, NY: Doubleday.

Chambers, Robert (1974) *Managing Rural Development: Ideas and Experience from East Africa*, Uppsala: Scandinavian Institute of African Studies.

Chambers, Robert (1983) *Rural Development: Putting the Last First*, London: Longman.

Geertz, Clifford (1993) *The Interpretation of Cultures*, London: Fontana.

Gluckman, Max (1961) Ethnographic data in British social anthropology, *The Sociological Review*, 9 (5): 5–17.

Hoorweg, Jan and Niemeijer, Rudo (1981) *The Effects of Malnutrition Rehabilitation at Three Family Life Training Centres in Central Province, Kenya,* Leiden: African Studies Centre.

Long, Norman (2001) *Development Sociology: Actor-Oriented Perspectives,* London: Routledge.

Mosse, David (1994) Authority, gender and knowledge: Theoretical reflections on the practice of participatory rural appraisal, *Development and Change,* 23 (3): 497–527.

Porter, Doug, Allen, Bryan and Thompson, Gaye (1991) *Development in Practice: Paved with Good Intentions,* London: Routledge.

Strauss, Abselm and Corbin, Juliet (1990) *Basics of Qualitative Research: Grounded Theory, Procedures and Techniques,* Newbury Park, CA: Sage.

Van Donge, Jan Kees, Chivwaile, Mackenzie, Kasapila, William, Kapondamgaga, Prince, Mgemezulu, Overtoun and Sengore, Noel (2001) *A Qualitative Study of Markets and Livelihood Security in Rural Malawi,* Module 2.2 of the evaluation of the TIP 2000–2001 Targeted Inputs Programme, Lilongwe: DFID Malawi and Ministry of Agriculture and Irrigation Malawi.

Van Velsen, Jaap (1967) The extended case study method and situational analysis, in A.L. Epstein (ed.), *The Craft of Social Anthropology,* London: Tavistock.

20

Participatory Methods and Approaches: Tackling the Two Tyrannies

Harriot Beazley and Judith Ennew

· · Tyranny of the quantitative · · Participatory research · · Tyranny of participation · ·
· · A rights-based alternative · ·

Introduction

Development research entails a confrontation between the powerful and the powerless, a relationship fraught with possibilities of misunderstanding and exploitation. This is because the research focus is always a vulnerable, powerless group, compared to which researchers and development agencies are especially powerful. This chapter examines so-called 'participatory methods' for collecting data, and aims to provide a practical guide to research action. We do this by clarifying certain misconceptions, which we call the 'two tyrannies', referring to the original Greek meaning of 'power seized without legitimate cause' to describe two dominant, but not necessarily scientifically valid, tendencies in development research.

The first of these tyrannies is the common misconception that there is an unmistakable distinction between 'quantitative methods' and 'qualitative methods', combined with the fallacy that the former consist solely of questionnaires and are in some way more 'scientific' and superior. This tyranny is as common among academic social scientists as it is among the general public; it acts as a barrier to collecting and analysing data that may be a means of reducing inequalities of power.

In describing the second tyranny we follow Cooke and Kothari (2001), who see participation as a 'new tyranny', in the name of which vulnerable people are coerced into activities and decisions for which they are unprepared, which almost always overburden them in the name of (limited and largely spurious) 'empowerment'. Translated into research, this tyranny becomes a series of techniques that encourage people to express their experiences and views, but which rarely 'empower' them. In addition, the variety of similar systems and accompanying acronyms often confuse new researchers who sometimes see them as competing, rather than overlapping, approaches. The similarities are clear, however, in the repetition of 'participatory' in the full names attached to the acronyms:

PRA Participatory Rural Appraisal
RRA Rapid Rural Appraisal
PR Participatory Research
PLA Participatory Learning for Action
PAR Participatory Action Research
PARC Participatory Action Research with Children

In this chapter we warn that participatory approaches often consist only of techniques for data collection, rather than research, and that there must be proper procedures for data gathering and analysis. We provide a human rights framework through which these highly useful techniques can be assessed and from which the elements needed for scientific research can be extracted. Using examples from our research and development experience, we show that it is possible to collect and analyse scientific data with the various participatory approaches, *provided* that the research is implemented in a systematic, ethical and replicable way.

Tyranny of the quantitative

Central to our line of reasoning is a distinction between theory, methodology and method. The methodology, or philosophical basis, of social science research determines the type of method (technique) used. Methodology is itself derived from theory, which establishes how human beings are viewed. These theories provide the basis for research approaches to the human being(s) about whom – or with whom – information is being gathered. The difference between the two prepositions ('about' and 'with') is vital. How human beings are viewed – as objects in or subjects of their lives – determines the overall research approach, or methodology, which, in its turn, determines the techniques or methods used in the research process.

Social science researchers, particularly those involved in policy-related work, have long suffered from an inferiority complex with respect to natural or physical sciences, so that they construct a notion of scientific processes that endeavour to treat human beings as if they are similar to the inanimate objects of the physical sciences. This approach (which is typical of census work, household and labour surveys and epidemiological research), tends to count, order, and make decisions about human populations, often within the context of government. In this approach to social science, both theory and methodology assume that human beings have no agency – as if they can neither think nor act. This combination of a scientific insecurity and the necessity to plan on the basis of statistics has resulted in what we call the 'tyranny of the quantitative'.

The most scientific approach?

The tyranny of the quantitative privileges numerical information by assuming that only one method – the questionnaire or survey – can provide facts good enough for planning policies and programmes. Yet no research method is superior to any other. More than one method should always be used in order to cross-check results and compare data from different methods and social groups. Questionnaires are poor methods of research if they are used on their own, at the beginning of research, or with children or other vulnerable groups at any time.

It is our contention that the tyranny of the quantitative is based on a misconceived division between numerical and descriptive information. Yet, in essence, all research data are both qualitative (words and images) or quantitative (numbers and statistics), and both are mutually supporting and equally important. This is because descriptions are the *basis* of numbers, which means that qualitative/descriptive data must be collected first, so that unambiguous categories can be established for counting. It is impossible to collect quantitative data without first having definitions of what the numbers mean.

The tyranny of the quantitative rests on a misconstruction of scientific method as somehow exemplified by 'hard' sciences such as physics. But social research is not like 'hard' sciences, such as physics, because people have minds and lives of their own. This is one of the reasons why it cannot always produce exact, convenient samples, especially on sensitive topics. People can decide whether or not to take part in research, or to tell the 'truth' about their lives, and they may be difficult to include in research if their activities make them very mobile or cause them to hide because of guilt, fear or the illegality of what they do. It follows, therefore, that social research must include the research population as participants at all levels of research, including compliance by researchers with the ethical principle that research participation must be voluntary.

Participatory research

In the social sciences opposition to the tyranny of the quantitative has led to a tradition of descriptive research methods, culminating in the ethnomethodology approach, which explores the meanings people construct and use in their everyday live (see, for example, Garfinkel, 1967). In the context of development, this approach is associated with an ideological position that insists on the involvement of local people in the decision-making processes that affect their lives (Chambers, 1994, 1997). The result is an widely espoused development orthodoxy – based on pragmatic and humanitarian considerations – with its own language, including terms such as 'stakeholders', 'ownership' of 'problems/solutions', 'empowerment' and 'full participation' (Cornwall, 2003). Related to this is the increased

recognition that participation is not simply a humanitarian consideration but also a human right. According to the 1948 United Nations Universal Declaration of Human Rights, and all subsequent international legal instruments,[1] participation means that people must be involved in decision-making and the management of their own lives.

The emphasis of participatory research is on generating knowledge from the perspective of those being researched, rather than from the perspective of the researcher. The methodology recognizes that the concepts used by government, medical and other professionals to understand and interpret problems in a community are often different from the realities and perceptions of the communities they try to reach. This approach helps identify and respond to the local cultural, historical, socio-economic, geographical and political factors that influence the behaviour and practices of a community.

The main principle of the approach is that the people whose lives are being studied should be involved in defining the research questions and taking an active part in both collecting and analysing the data. This begins a process in which the research findings are used to facilitate a community's design and implementation of programmes.

The example of PRA

Probably the most influential and popular participatory research approach is based on methods developed over two decades ago by Robert Chambers and his associates at the Institute of Development Studies (IDS), University of Sussex, known as Participatory Rural Appraisal (PRA). PRA techniques are primarily visual, designed for use with illiterate rural communities, although they are now increasingly being used in urban communities. They are frequently labelled 'qualitative' and are called 'participatory methods', but both of these terms are misnomers. First, as discussed, it is difficult to designate any research techniques as qualitative or quantitative because describing and counting are fundamentally interdependent components of research. Second, no method is inherently 'participatory'. It depends how a method is used. If community members design and use a questionnaire to research a problem of their choosing, this is a participatory process. 'Participatory methods' are not participatory if a researcher chooses both research questions and research technique (e.g. a visual method), takes the data collected away to a distant university and analyses them with no further discussion with the research subjects.

PRA has had considerable success in gathering information on the lives and views of people who lack power and whose opinions are seldom sought. It is based on the proposition that people construct social meanings and that every individual, regardless of education and status, is capable of research, analysis and planning. This philosophical principle leads to the ideological assertions that in practice:

- people should be active agents in their own lives;
- research should respect research participants' own words, ideas and understandings;
- researchers and research participants are equal;
- research methods should be flexible, exploratory and inventive;
- both researchers and research participants should enjoy the research.

The most significant principles of participatory research have to do with the behaviour and attitudes of researchers, including being self-critically aware, not rushing, and helping participants to express themselves in their own way and to formulate their own analyses (Chambers, 1994). The researcher's role is to act as a facilitator, to establish trust, listen, learn and, as far as possible, 'hand over the stick', or control, to participants (Chambers, 1994). As a result, all the people and organizations that will be affected by the information collected are fully involved in the research process. The collective name of these people and organizations is 'stakeholders' because they have a stake (interest) in research and its outcome. For example, stakeholders in research on infant mortality include women, men, communities (parents, grandparents, children and young people), midwives, traditional birth attendants, village heads, health workers, doctors, government agencies, donors, intergovernmental organizations (such as UNICEF, UNESCO and WHO), non-governmental organizations and the media. Participatory research, therefore, is about 'giving everyone who has a stake a voice and a choice' (Cornwall, 2003: 1325).

The strength of using participatory approaches is that researchers are able to gain access to people and bring their problems to public notice. It is unlikely that satisfactory assessments of vulnerable groups could be made using any other approach. This kind of research takes more time, and costs more money, than household surveys or questionnaires but is cost-effective in the long run because the results are more relevant and lead to more successful interventions. It also often generates more precise information, and helps to gain insights into how communities 'think'.

For example, participatory research was carried out in a village in Lombok for an AusAID-funded maternal health project. A government-trained midwife (from Java) was asked to 'map' where all the pregnant women and newborn infants were in her village, which she completed confidently. The research team later asked the women in the village to draw their own map. When the two maps were compared it was found that the midwife did not know of all the infants and pregnant women, because not all of them had presented themselves to her. Through the use of participatory techniques a variety of reasons were provided for not going to the Javanese midwife, including cultural differences, preference for the traditional birth attendant, lack of transport, and fear of the Indonesian biomedical approach to pregnancy and birth (including the practice of compulsory episiotomies).

Methods used in participatory research

As mentioned, many methods used in participatory research are visual, and for this reason are an ideal means of communication for illiterate and less articulate people, such as children. The techniques are also very useful when a topic is hard to talk about, such as corporal punishment, bodily functions (e.g. sexual and reproductive health) or sexual abuse.

Table 20.1 provides a summary of some of the methods successfully developed by practitioners of participatory approaches, and describes issues they have been used to explore. These are simple techniques, requiring little in the way of equipment or preparation, and have been well described in many manuals and discussion papers. One danger of listing 'participatory methods' in this way is that the originally creative approach of Robert Chambers can become, through inadequate training, a narrow set of orthodox techniques from which no deviation is permitted.

Tyranny of participation

Despite the success of PRA and associated approaches in involving community members as research participants, the practice has not been problem-free. Often only vulnerable groups in a community are asked to participate, so that participation takes place only at the lowest social levels or with the most excluded groups. Without the participation of powerful groups, it is unlikely that the results can be used to develop practical policies to transform the lives of the poor and powerless.

Thus, the downside of participation – the reason for our agreement with Cooke and Kothari (2001) that it is a 'tyranny' – refers primarily to its use as a development strategy as a whole, through which 'participatory research' effectively furthers structures of oppression. In Peru, for example, the evaluation of an intervention in child-rearing practices targeted to women's community organizations showed that women themselves complained of being 'overburdened'. In this example, the use of female volunteers to provide community child care succeeded in displacing state obligations as well as violating the rights of the women, because, as volunteers, they have no rights as workers. The system also discriminated against them by perpetuating their 'traditional' female role, while simultaneously depriving them of a proper education.

Further, the concept of 'empowerment' within participatory research remains largely undebated (Bell, 2004; Guijt, 2003). Calls for a more critical understanding of 'empowerment' include the observation that participatory approaches have focused on adult gender relations and have failed to explore the process of empowerment for children and young people. Ideally, empowerment through participation should be about stimulating social transformations that enable all socially excluded groups to make the decisions affecting their own lives (Parpart, 2002).

Andrea Cornwall (2003) has also tackled these concerns, particularly the issue of the importance and complexity of women's involvement and engagement in participation. Other problems which have been raised but not necessarily solved are stakeholder 'burnout' and the inappropriate raising of community expectations (Guijt, 2003). Over time, participants themselves have sometimes become disillusioned as the techniques have been used extensively, without bringing about any of the promised improvements in their lives.

193

Table 20.1   Summary of the use of some widely used 'participatory methods'

Method	Process	Issues explored
Social mapping	Participants in a group draw a visual map of the houses, important institutions (village head, doctors, midwives, hospitals) and places people congregate – shops, mosque, church, river, etc. – transport hubs, in the community	Importance of institutions in the community Where health services are, including traditional midwives Where children, single, pregnant women, old people live, etc. Where and how people spend their time Location and availability of transport
Resource mapping	Participants draw a visual map of where they go to get the important resources in their community	Where water pumps, wells, rivers are Wetland resources (Mekong Delta) Where wood, fish, grass, thatch for roofs is collected Location of gardens, crops, animals
Mobility mapping	Participants individually draw a visual map of where they go every day/week/month/in the past year, etc.	Mobility of men, women and children in rural and urban areas. Where they go to work, school, look for resources, for leisure and entertainment, for health seeking practices, to hang out/sleep (street children)
Body mapping	Participants individually or in a group draw the outline of a body and mark places on it when asked specific questions	To ascertain maternal health issues Issues of sexual abuse; where young people have been touched/abused Corporal punishment; where children have been hit
Social network diagrams	Participants are individually asked to answer questions that allow a facilitator to draw a map of the social networks participants are engaged in	Questions asked of street children included who do you go to when you are lonely? When you are hungry? When you are scared? When you have a secret? When you need some money? When you are tired? When you have money and want to have fun, etc.?

(Continued)

Table 20.1   (Continued)

Method	Process	Issues explored
Matrix ranking and scoring	Participants in a group list items during a guided brainstorming session, and then rank them in importance and frequency	Severity and frequency of disease Types of food eaten in a community Health seeking preferences
Seasonal and social calendars	Participants in a group draw events that happen during different seasons of the year	Wet, dry seasons; cycles of migration; cycles of religious events; work patterns; when people are rich, when poor; when people are sick
Time transects	Participants individually draw how they spend their time on a time-line or in a pie chart that is divided into 24 hours	How people spend their time Time as a factor related to seeking services Time for being involved in work activities Time spent looking for food/resources
Causal flow analysis	Participants in a group draw a diagram of what causes certain problems or situations	Community perceptions of causes of infant and maternal mortality Reasons for going on the street (street children) Reasons for migrating for work
Focus group discussions	Participants discuss a topic in a group, facilitated by a researcher with a record taken by a note taker	Identification of community priorities Good for establishing questions for a questionnaire

195

Another frustration often cited is how to analyse 'participatory' data with adequate rigour to provide a reliable basis for programme design and monitoring. This is due to the unsystematic approach sometimes taken during data collection, resulting in messy or inconclusive data, which is then written up into generalized statements in reports (Guijt, 2003). The research cannot be compared over time or between different places, and interventions are based on impressions rather than scientific analysis. Consequently, participatory research is usually associated with descriptive rather than numerical data, and the results are often discounted as being unscientific. The tyranny of participation, therefore, has what might be called a negative link with the tyranny of the quantitative.[2]

A rights-based alternative

There is, however, a way to approach development research that is not only participatory but also challenges both tyrannies. Such an approach establishes participation as a human right, and leads to systematic scientific research that results in 'quantitative' data backed up by 'qualitative' understanding of what the data mean. The key human rights principles involved are non-discrimination, self-determination and participation. The difference between the participatory approach and the rights-based approach in development research is not just one of degree or perception. The two are not mutually exclusive – the methods adopted may be the same – but they do entail considerable differences in research design.

The process required for systematic scientific data collection and analysis grew from pilot capacity-building in several countries, sponsored by Save the Children Sweden and UK (Boyden and Ennew, 1997). This showed that it is possible to use participatory research techniques in a systematic research process to provide both descriptive and numerical results, as the basis for programme planning and monitoring as well as for comparative studies (Ennew and Plateau, 2004).

As in all participatory approaches, the research questions are determined by stakeholders, in this case the entire range of interested bodies, rather than simply the research subjects at community level. The scientific basis of the process is a research protocol – or instruction booklet – used by all researchers throughout data collection. The protocol should be drafted and designed by the research team. Properly and systematically used, a research protocol can result in large-scale data collection of robust information, which can be analysed using computer programs to produce reliable statistics (Ennew and Plateau, 2004).

The order of methods

An essential principle in this approach is that research methods can be ordered in their use

(Table 20.2). Although this may appear rigid, researchers have found that it provides freedom and security later, when they analyse the data. The first period of data collection is exploratory, examining the research questions and how people talk about the research topic. Questionnaires are not appropriate for the first phase, but may be designed for the second phase of data collection in order to check the data collected during the first phase by other methods. Further, researchers must keep research diaries, and observations must be recorded throughout data collection (Ennew and Plateau, 2004).

Rights-based research also entails adhering to an ethical strategy, which is written into the protocol. One basic ethical principle is that research participants provide information voluntarily, and have the right to refuse to answer questions as well as to withdraw from research at any time. Further, researchers are responsible for ensuring that participants are not harmed by taking part in the research or by the way results are disseminated. This includes issues of respect, confidentiality, privacy and anonymity.

Analysis

Properly collected data are already half-way to being analysed. There are existing techniques for analysis of 'qualitative' data, but the first requirement for all of these is that the data must be collected by all researchers in the same way, using the same methods set out in a jointly designed protocol (Ennew and Plateau, 2004).

Conclusion

This chapter has focused the discussion on participatory approaches in a practical guide to research action. Much criticism has been levelled at the notion of participatory approaches and methods in development, and

Table 20.2   Research methods and when to use them

Method	When/why/how it should be used
Research diary	Every day, for planning and reviewing day-to-day research activities
Observation	Unstructured observation should take place every day at all times, wherever they are. It can also take place at specific times/places (such as bus terminals) Structured observation takes place after patterns have been noted and need to be checked
Drawings and other visual methods	Can be used at any time to break the ice and give material for comment in interviews and focus group discussions; to examine ideas with people (especially children) who are shy or find it difficult to speak; for particularly sensitive subjects; for mapping areas, rapid censuses, ranking and decision-making
Recall	Can be used at any time after initial observation. Use diaries, time-lines, recall sheets. Recall is used to gather information on past events or experiences
Ranking	Can be used at any time after initial observation. Ranking methods are used to find out about people's preferences and priorities
Focus group discussions	Use early in fieldwork to check opinions, language, ideas Should be limited to a relatively small number as they are difficult to record, transcribe and analyse
Drama and role play	Use when researchers have a good relationship with participants; to explore sensitive issues
Written methods	Can be used at any time with literate people and especially good for school-aged children. Diaries and recall schedules can be written or filled in by participants. Essays can be used to explore issues about which not much is known. Written methods also include life histories, written checklists and rankings, sentence completion and self-completed questionnaires
Interviews	For information about individuals. Interviews are usually used later in the research process, when appropriate questions have been identified. Interviews can include sentence completion. Life histories/oral testimony can be collected from people who cannot (or do not want to) write. Interviews can be structured, semi-structured or highly structured (questionnaires). Questionnaires should not be designed until the final period of fieldwork.

Source: Ennew and Plateau (2004: Table 18, pp. 97–98). Reprinted with kind permission of International Save the Children Alliance, Southeast, East Asia and Pacific Region (Bangkok). An electronic version of the book is available at http://www.scswedenscap.org

the concepts cover a diverse set of principles and practices. Ultimately, these are academic criticisms about 'empowerment' and also reflections on the position of the researcher. They have little to do with the practical consequences of muddles in models of participation, which researchers on the ground in real development projects have to deal with on a daily basis.

Development research has been limited because of the two opposed, but related, tyrannies of 'quantitative superiority' and 'participation'. This chapter has shown that both tyrannies rest on misunderstandings about scientific processes. We have proposed a new approach, which uses numbers and description, as well as systematic participatory processes. We recommend that development researchers and practitioners recognize that qualitative and quantitative approaches are in fact interrelated in both data collection and data analysis, and that participatory research must be based on human rights principles, rather than on humanitarian ideology. It is also important to realize that research cannot be truly participatory – or effective in advocacy or development programming – unless stakeholders at all levels are involved.

Notes

1. Particularly the 1966 Covenants on Civil and Political Rights and Economic, Social and Cultural Rights, but also in more specific treaties such as those applying to Development, Race, Women and Children.
2. Although there is no scope in this chapter for a full discussion of the difficulties practitioners have encountered with PRA, ongoing debates have been well summarized by, for example, Cornwall and Pratt (2003).

198

QUESTIONS FOR DISCUSSION

1. Why are participatory approaches so critical to development research?
2. What is problematic with the term 'participatory methods'?
3. Should participatory research serve the needs of the researcher or the subject?
4. What is the difference between a humanitarian approach and a rights-based approach to participatory research?
5. Who are the 'stakeholders' in participatory research?

Websites

PLA Notes (International Institute of Environment and Development, London), via their website: http://www.iied.org/sarl/pla_notes/about.html

Participation Resource Centre of the Institute of Development Studies, University of Sussex: http://www.ids.ac.uk/ids/particip/information

Further reading

Boyden, J. and Ennew, J. (eds) (1997) *Children in Focus: A Manual for Participatory Research with Children,* Stockholm: Save the Children Sweden.

Chambers, R. (1997) *Whose Reality Counts? Putting the First Last,* London: ITDG Publishing.

Cornwall, A. and Pratt, G. (eds) (2003) *Pathways to Participation: Reflections on PRA*, London: ITDG Publishing.

Ennew, J. and Plateau, D.P. (2004) *How to Research the Physical and Emotional Punishment of Children*, Bangkok: Save the Children.

Pretty, J.N., Guijt, I., Thompson, J. and Scoones, I. (1995) *A Trainer's Guide for Participatory Learning and Action*, London: International Institute of Environment and Development.

References

Bell, S. (2004) *Does Participatory Development Encourage Processes of 'Empowerment'?*, CEDAR Research Paper, no. 4, Department of Geography, Royal Holloway, University of London.

Boyden, J. and Ennew, J. (eds) (1997) *Children in Focus: A Manual for Participatory Research with Children*, Stockholm: Save the Children Sweden.

Chambers, R. (1994) The origins and practice of participatory rural appraisal, *World Development Report*, 22(7): 953–969.

Chambers, R. (1997) *Whose Reality Counts? Putting the First Last*, London: ITDG Publishing.

Cooke, B. and Kothari, U. (eds) (2001) *Participation: The New Tyranny?* London: Zed Books.

Cornwall, A. (2003) Whose voices, whose choices? reflections on gender and participatory development', *World Development*, 31(8): 1325–1342.

Cornwall, A. and Pratt, G. (eds) (2003) *Pathways to Participation: Reflections on PRA*, London: ITDG Publishing.

Ennew, J. and Plateau, D.P. (2004) *How to Research the Physical and Emotional Punishment of Children*, Bangkok: Save the Children.

Garfinkel, H. (1967) *Studies in Ethnomethodology*, Englewood Cliffs, NJ: Prentice Hall.

Guijt, I. (2003) Intrigued and frustrated, enthusiastic and critical: reflections on PRA, in A. Cornwall, and G. Pratt (eds), *Pathways to Participation: Reflections on PRA*, London: ITDG Publishing.

Parpart, J.L. (2002) Gender and empowerment: new thoughts, new approaches, in V. Desai and R. Potter (eds), *The Companion to Development Studies*, London: Arnold, pp. 338–342.

21

Diaries and Case Studies

JoAnn McGregor

The importance of case study research involving a portfolio of methods   Solicited diaries as an interactive, potentially empowering research tool   Pros and cons of commissioning diaries   Practical and ethical considerations   Examples of the use of solicited diaries in development research   Audio, video and photographic diaries

Introduction

In development research, some of the information required may be politically sensitive, highly personal, mundane or, for other reasons, may not be easy to access using conventional methods, such as formal interviews and questionnaires. Furthermore, it may involve issues that people are not happy to discuss in public fora, such as focus groups or workshops convened for participatory action research. This chapter looks at the potential utility of solicited diaries as a means of accessing such information, and considers contexts where the method has been used in development research. It discusses the advantages and potential drawbacks of solicited diaries as a research tool, emphasizing the importance of using them alongside a range of other research methods, particularly as part of in-depth case studies. The themes addressed here overlap with other chapters in this book that explore interactive or participatory methods,

which are designed to give more control over the research process to the informant. In some contexts, such methods may also have the potential to be empowering or therapeutic for the participants. As solicited diaries may involve the recording and discussion of personal issues, it is important to think through the ethical issues involved in their use in any particular context.

Why do a case study?

The character of development interventions – and the availability of funding for them – are often driven by broad trends and fashions among international donors and policy-makers. But it is crucial that projects are shaped so as to be sensitive to particular historical, political and cultural contexts. In-depth research, taking the form of a case study, can play an important role in planning and carrying out a development project, particularly in designing interventions that are tailored to suit the local context. A case study may be undertaken as background research to assess the need and feasibility for a particular type of intervention; it may constitute part of an ongoing process of information gathering, or be part of a process of evaluation. Ideally, case study research would not be a one-off activity, but should continue alongside intervention, as a means of ensuring ongoing feedback from the supposed beneficiaries of the development project, and helping to ensure its continued relevance.

An in-depth case study requires the use of a wide range of research methods: it may combine qualitative and quantitative techniques, focus groups and other interactive or participatory methods detailed in this book. The mix of methods enables the different techniques and their results to be compared against each other, allowing judgements to be made as to which method (or combination of methods) is the most appropriate for any particular purpose. Solicited diaries should be used as one of a portfolio of methods in the context of in-depth case study research. Although this research method is often overlooked, it has long been used by anthropologists undertaking ethnographic fieldwork, who have found commissioning diaries can be a useful means of deepening cultural insight into the places they study (Caplan, 1992, 1997). There is also a tradition of using diaries and other forms of personal narrative in feminist research (Stanley, 1995; Swindells, 1995). Moreover, it has found recent advocates among sociologists of health, as a means of gaining insight into daily bodily practices, perceptions and attitudes (Elliott, 1997) and in AIDS research (Coxon, 1988, 2002).

The advantages and drawbacks of solicited diaries

The use of solicited diaries may take different forms. Sometimes the diaries are open and unstructured (to varying degrees), and the diarists are asked to record whatever they feel is relevant. In other contexts, diarists have been asked to record or log specific, tightly defined activities. Solicited diaries are usually combined with preliminary interviews or focus groups to introduce the idea of the diary and its purpose, as well as follow-up interviews to discuss the completed diary. The benefits of solicited diaries as a research tool have generally been seen as the following:

- Soliciting diaries is an interactive method, in which the writer has more control over participation in the research process than in an interview. The diary-keeper has time to reflect on what he/she wishes to record (or not record), and how to present the experience or activity to the commissioner.
- Diary-writing can be empowering or therapeutic for the writers, enabling them to think through the issues they record. In some contexts, if the content of the diary is open, the process of writing can tap into people's creativity, and allows for personal expression.
- The process of soliciting diaries can help build relationships of trust between researcher and researched, and can make the research a more enjoyable and fruitful activity for all.
- In an extractive sense, the completed diaries provide the researcher with a record of daily activity and reflection, which can give insight into sensitive, politicized, stigmatized or mundane and hidden issues. The written diaries may be revealing of concerns people may not be prepared to voice in a formal interview or group context. They may also be revealing about matters the writer considers unremarkable, and hence give insight into the unspoken, taken-for-granted assumptions that shape everyday life and action. In open diaries, where the writer rather than the researcher selects what is recorded, the diaries can highlight the

201

importance of issues the researcher had not thought relevant, and in general can enhance the researcher's depth of cultural, political and social understanding. In structured diaries, the entries may be used quantitatively or qualitatively, and may overcome problems of recall in retrospective interview.

The drawbacks of using solicited diaries have been outlined as follows:

- The writing of a diary may be considered time-consuming and laborious, making it difficult to find willing diary-keepers or undermining the quality of information they contain.
- Diary-keeping requires literacy, which limits the number of potential writers in some contexts, and undermines the potential for a 'representative' sample of diary-keepers.
- The diary-keeper may deploy considerable self-censorship. Some informants may feel writing something down is potentially incriminating or for other reasons may not report particular experiences or reflections.
- The writer may not understand what the researcher wants, and may not keep a regular or daily record.
- The contents of solicited diaries can be subjective and idiosyncratic. This means the information they contain needs to be assessed with care, particularly if it is to be generalized.

How to commission diaries

If the decision has been made to solicit diaries from informants as part of a broader research process, there are various practical and ethical issues that need to be considered. These will vary according to any particular context, for example, whether the diaries are open or structured, whether the research results are to be used for qualitative or quantitative insights

(or both). The period over which diaries are kept may also vary. In all contexts, however, the researcher needs to consider who to commission diaries from, and why particular writers may be able to provide insight into the research topic. It is important that prospective diary-writers are willing participants, that they understand (and are happy with) the broader aims of the research and the uses to which it will be put, and comprehend what kind of information should be written in the diary.

A second question to address relates to payment. Should the writers be paid and, if so, how much? This issue should be resolved on the basis of dialogue with community leaders and key informants, and discussion among the research team. If the decision is made to remunerate participants, levels of payment should also be agreed with the prospective diary-keepers themselves. Most researchers who have used this method in developing world contexts have paid informants or offered a gift for the finished diary, in recognition of the amount of time and effort required, in understanding of some participants' struggles to make ends meet, and perhaps to allow the diary-writer to forgo other work in order to complete the diary.

A third set of considerations relate to issues of anonymity, authorship and other ethical considerations. Once again, these topics need to be debated among the research team, with key informants and the diary-keepers themselves. Diary-keepers should be offered anonymity and confidentiality in all circumstances. However, in some contexts, individual writers may have responded to the opportunity for creative personal expression, and may want recognition as authors. The researcher must reflect closely on whether the diaries raise issues that might incriminate or stigmatize the author or others. If the writers are encouraged through the research to record traumatic experiences, illegal activity or other highly sensitive issues, it is important that the research team has thought through how to respond. Are counselling, medical or other relevant professional services and back-up to be provided to the participants either through the development project or through referral to appropriate institutions (and if so, have these other bodies been consulted and involved)? Is the research team able to provide ongoing opportunities for the informants to meet either with others or with the research team, to discuss potential courses of action?

While solicited diaries have often been used in situations where there are already well-developed relations of trust between the researcher, the diary-writer and the broader community, in some circumstances, the exercise of soliciting diaries may help to build such relations of trust. All general, practical considerations involved in soliciting diaries will need to be refined to fit any particular context.

Applications of solicited diaries in development research

This section reflects on some examples of how solicited diaries have been used in development research, focusing on three particular areas: (1) projects requiring information relating to bodily health practices and attitudes; (2) research in the aftermath of war, conflict and violence; and (3) research with marginalized social groups.

Bodily health practices and attitudes

Solicited diaries have been found to be particularly beneficial in health research, in investigations of bodily practices and attitudes (Elliott, 1997). They have proved particularly valuable in AIDS research, which has now assumed a prominent place in many developing-world contexts. In HIV/AIDS research, collecting data relating to sexual attitudes and practices through formal surveys and questionnaires has often been found to be unreliable and has produced data of dubious quality. The use of sexual diaries as a research tool alongside interviews now has a standard place in AIDS research in Western contexts. The approach was pioneered in relation to gay men's sexual behaviour, for example, through Project Sigma, but has now been extended to research on other groups. Project Sigma asked gay men to keep a daily diary for a month, with writers being commissioned through appeals for volunteers or from past respondents. Researchers found that the information in the diaries was in many ways more reliable and more valid than that derived from interviews, and that it was more specific and detailed (Coxon, 1988, 2002; Project Sigma, n.d.). In an African context, some researchers have also used solicited diaries in AIDS research, for example, highlighting the differences in the ways in which young people presented themselves and their attitudes towards sexuality and harassment, when asked to discuss these issues in mixed-sex focus groups and in personal solicited diaries (Pattman and Chege, 2003).

203

Aftermath of war, conflict and violence

Researchers have also reported the benefits of using commissioned diaries in projects with communities that have suffered war and conflict, such as refugees and survivors of violence. For example, Meth (2003) used solicited diaries as part of an investigation into women's experiences of violent crime in Durban in South Africa. Women were asked to keep diaries for a month, to record their everyday experiences and fear of violence, for which they were paid. The diaries were commissioned after focus group discussions and were followed up by interviews. Some women recorded experiences (e.g. of rape and child abuse) that they were not prepared to talk about in group meetings, or wrote about historical experiences and their lingering effects in addition to keeping a record of incidents during the month. Some diarists found the process of writing therapeutic, as it had helped them to think through their own experiences, and in some instances they raised matters they had not spoken of before, which they felt made them more able to cope. Meth argues that solicited diaries provided a better space for raising traumatic personal issues than a focus group, and provided valuable research material. She had planned to use the solicited diaries purely in an extractive sense, to generate data, but suggests that the exercise was 'supportive for some women or at least provided them with a space to reveal particular stories' (Meth, 2003: 203). Given the traumatic nature of some women's experience, there were emotional costs in addition to the sense of relief, the long-term effects of which were difficult to judge.

Marginalized social groups

Solicited diaries may also be a valuable tool in working with marginalized social groups engaged in illegal activities. For example, I commissioned diaries from fishermen on Lake Kariba in Zimbabwe, whose daily livelihoods involved poaching fish from state-protected waterways and other illegal economic activity, as a means of investigating conflicts over the resources of the lake, which pitted marginalized fishing communities against state authorities upholding conservationist and other regulations. The fishermen were paid to keep diaries for two periods of one week, in different seasons: they were asked to make a record of their daily experiences as fishermen, and to report on significant events and gossip in the fishing camps. The completed diaries were followed up with individual interviews and group discussion. Although the information in the diaries was partial and had to be assessed with

care, as the fishermen employed considerable self-censorship regarding what they wrote about, the exercise proved valuable in many ways. The diaries provided a means of building a relationship with a marginalized and stigmatized social group, allowed the diary-keepers to chose the topics they were happy to discuss, revealed insights into the daily physical risks their livelihoods entailed, and raised important issues that the research had not planned to address, such as conflicts with 'problem' wildlife, particularly crocodiles, and the significant under-reporting of death from crocodile attack (McGregor, 2004).

Non-written diaries – audio, video and photo diaries

So far, this chapter has discussed the pros and cons and potential applications of soliciting written diaries. However, there has been much interest recently in the use of audio and visual technologies in research to document the everyday from the perspective of the community or individual being studied. Regarding audio-diaries, researchers have given informants cassette recorders to make an oral rather than written record. Such technologies have been advocated for situations where literacy is a constraint on written diaries. Visual technologies have received more discussion in the literature. Some researchers have experimented with soliciting video diaries from selected informants or have encouraged the making of one-off videos by members of a community. Others have encouraged the compilation of photographic records; for example, by giving disposable cameras to members of the community or social group being researched, and inviting them to make a record of their life or what they think is interesting. The latter approach has usually aimed to provide insights into everyday activities and to give insight into the photographers' world, but the photographs do not constitute a daily record of activity and reflection in the same way as written, audio or video diaries.

Researchers have advocated visual methods as interactive and potentially empowering, and have reported situations in which people responded with imagination and creativity. Informants who might have found writing a diary a tedious chore may respond enthusiastically to these visual technologies. Although use of a video requires considerable technical training and expensive equipment, the use of disposable cameras does not. The latter has been used in particular in the context of research with children. Examples of the use of disposable cameras in development research include work with street children in Kampala, Uganda (Young

and Barrett, 2001), research on Jamaican schoolchildren's differential perceptions of their environment (Dodman, 2003), and studies of homeless and mobility impaired children (Aitkin and Wingate, 1993). Contexts in which community members have been trained to use video cameras and commissioned to make their own videos are discussed in Johansson (1999) and Kindon (2003), and visual methods more generally are elaborated in Pink (2001).

In short, the recent interest in solicited diaries, whether written or visual, and the benefits researchers have found in using them, suggest that this method should be given full consideration in the planning of in-depth case study research for development.

QUESTIONS FOR DISCUSSION

1. What range of methods might be appropriate in a case study?
2. In what sorts of context might solicited diaries be an appropriate tool?
3. How can the research process become interactive rather than simply extractive?
4. How can an interactive research process, including solicited diary-keeping, best inform policy-making and development interventions?
5. In a particular context with which you are familiar, what are the ethical issues raised first by commissioning diaries and then by using informants' written texts or visual creations?
6. If you encourage a diary-keeper to record a traumatic experience, highly personal information or illegal activity, how will you respond to the author and the information?
7. How might paying informants (such as diary-keepers) influence the relationship between researcher and researched, and the character of the material collected?

205

Further reading

Caplan, P. (1992) Spirits and sex: a Swahili informant and his diary, in J. Okeley and H. Callaway (eds), *Anthropology and Autobiography,* London: Routledge.

Coxon, N.H. (2002) Diaries and sexual behaviour: the use of sexual diaries as method and substance in researching gay men's response to HIV/AIDS, in M. Boulton (ed.), *Challenge and Innovation: Methodological Advances in Social Research on Aids*, London: Taylor and Francis, Chapter 8.

Elliott, H. (1997) The use of diaries in sociological research on health experiences, *Sociological Research Online*, 2 (2). see: http://www.socresonline.org.uk/socresonline/2/2/7.html

Meth, P. (2003) Entries and omissions: using solicited diaries in geographical research, *Area*, 35 (4): 195–205.

Stanley, L. (1995) *The Auto/Biographical I,* London: Manchester University Press.

Swindells, J. (ed.) (1995) *The Uses of Autobiography,* London: Taylor and Francis.

References

Aitkin, S. and Wingate, J. (1993) A preliminary study of the self-directed photography of middle-class, homeless and mobility-impaired children, *Professional Geographer,* 45: 65–72.

Caplan, P. (1992) Spirits and sex: a Swahili informant and his diary, in J. Okeley and H. Callaway (eds), *Anthropology and Autobiography,* London: Routledge.

Caplan, P. (1997) *Africa Voice, African Life: Personal Narratives from a Swahili Village*, London: Routledge.

Coxon, N.H. (1988) Something sensational…: the sexual diary as tool for mapping detailed sexual behaviour, *Sociological Review*, 36 (2): 353–367.

Coxon, N.H. (2002) Diaries and sexual behaviour: the use of sexual diaries as method and substance in researching gay men's response to HIV/AIDS, in M. Boulton (ed.), *Challenge and Innovation: Methodological Advances in Social Research on Aids*, London: Taylor and Francis, Chapter 8.

Dodman, D. (2003) Shooting in the city: an autobiographic exploration of the urban environment in Kingston, Jamaica *Area*, 35 (3): 293–305.

Elliott, H. (1997) The use of diaries in sociological research on health experiences, *Sociological Research Online*, 2 (2). see: http://www.socresonline.org.uk/socresonline/2/2/7.html

Johansson, L. (1999) Participatory video and PRA: acknowledging the politics of empowerment, *Forests, Trees and People Newsletter*, 40/41: 21–23.

Kindon, S. (2003) Participatory video in geography research: a feminist practice of looking?, *Area,* 35 (2): 142–153.

McGregor, J. (2004) Crocodile crimes: people versus wildlife and the politics of postcolonial conservation on Lake Kariba, *Geoforum,* 36 (3): 353–369.

Meth, P. (2003) Entries and omissions: using solicited diaries in geographical research, *Area*, 35 (4): 195–205.

Pattman, R. and Chege, F. (2003) Dear diary, I saw an angel, she looked like heaven on earth: sex talk and sex education, *African Journal of AIDS Research*, 2 (2): 103–112.

Pink, S. (2001) More visualising, more methodologies: on video, reflexivity and qualitative research, *The Sociological Review*, 49: 586–599.

Project Sigma (n.d.) Information about sexual diaries, http://www.sigmadiaries.com (accessed 26 August 2004).

Stanley, L. (1995) *The Auto/Biographical I,* London: Manchester University Press.

Swindells, J. (ed.) (1995) *The Uses of Autobiography,* London: Taylor and Francis.

Young, L. and Barrett, H. (2001) Adapting visual methods: action research with Kampala street children, *Area*, 33: 141–162.

Part III

Information and Data Collection Methods

(ii) Using Existing Knowledge and Records

22

Literature Reviews and Bibliographic Searches

Paula Meth and Glyn Williams

When you're looking through the literature, what are you searching for? Where and how do you find appropriate sources? How do you analyse the literature once you have found it? How should the literature review be written up? How does the literature review link up with the rest of your project?

Introduction: why a good literature review matters

For many students embarking on development research, the literature review may at first sight seem to be 'the dull bit' and quite a daunting task. Early on in the research process, it seems to get in the way of more pressing practical issues (booking your flight to Honduras, learning which venomous snakes you're likely to come across in Kenya, etc.), and later on sifting through other people's research may seem far less important than writing up your own findings. Although this is understandable, the literature review is far more central to the whole research process than many students initially think. If we look at what makes a good literature review, we can see that it both provides some

critical elements of your dissertation, and tests a number of key areas. If you can write a good review, you will have demonstrated a range of skills and competencies:

- You are a 'well read' student: you've got a good grounding in the relevant literature.
- You've got analytical skills: you can identify key themes and offer constructive criticism of existing work.
- You can link 'library' (secondary sources) and 'field-based' work: you can demonstrate that your knowledge of the literature has informed your research questions, practice and analysis.
- You can communicate your ideas: you can outline and synthesize other people's work effectively, and provide your own clear commentary on their arguments and research questions.

In most universities, these skills and competencies will feed directly through to the grade your research project will receive. This probably gives you an immediate incentive to get the literature review right (!), but beyond this, writing a good review is an important part of stating your credentials as a researcher. These are all also issues of quite subtle judgement, which can make them difficult for students to grasp what they might actually mean in practice. In this chapter, we therefore ground our discussion in our own recent work: Paula's research on women's strategies for dealing with violence in informal settlements in Durban, South Africa, and Glyn's work on participatory development in rural eastern India. Take a look at the five questions at the start of this chapter. We now address these in turn.

When you're looking through the literature, what are you searching for?

Before you plunge headlong into the library, ask yourself this important question. The answer may seem obvious. If your research topic is 'Who benefits from government participatory development programmes in rural West Bengal?' you need to find material relevant to that. But relevant in what ways? Material on rural West Bengal will be important, so too will literature on participatory development more generally. Also useful is literature on how other people have researched similar topics. So looking for information on your *case study area*, your *research themes* and your *methodology and theoretical approach* are all important generic areas that any good literature review should cover. But given that you have got to demonstrate 'a good grounding' in the relevant literature, how do you know whether you've read widely enough, or in sufficient depth? One

idea is to produce a 'literature map' that lays out the themes of your research: as you read individual articles or chapters, include these on the map and trace your own progress with your review. We've produced one here (Figure 22.1) based around Paula's work, her central research concern being 'An analysis of violence in informal settlements in Durban'.

This is how the map works. At the centre is the research topic and around that are a series of 'sectors', each being a different theme relating to it. So, for Paula's work, these include themes of *gendered power relations, institutional failure, strategies to manage violence, causes of violence* and (because she wants to spend her time using solicited diaries with women in Durban) *qualitative methods*. The choice of sectors may not be obvious at first, and will evolve as your research progresses (as you read more, new themes will emerge, and old ones disappear!), but it is important in helping you to identify themes. Your search should then move you 'outwards' along each sector (so you are looking for the underlying links to wider theoretical debates), and also inwards (so that you look for links to specific case studies).

To take the *gendered power relations* theme as an example, the literature closest in towards the centre of the diagram may be on experiences of domestic violence in Durban and other South African cities. The literature at the outer edge will address broader issues of how we *think* about questions of gender and power, by examining theoretical literature on masculinity. This may well be 'distant' from Durban in terms of the areas studied, but relevant in that it is thematically linked, and investigates relevant theoretical debates.[1] It may well take you out towards the boundaries of academic disciplines – in this case from 'mainstream' development studies to social geography – but with the support and guidance of your supervisor, this can be a useful exercise.

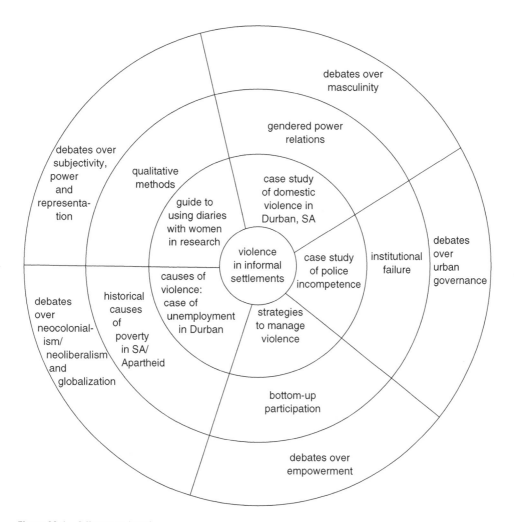

debates over
masculinity

gendered power
relations

debates over
subjectivity,
power
and
representa-
tion

qualitative
methods

guide to
using diaries
with women
in research

case study
of domestic
violence in
Durban, SA

violence
in informal
settlements

case study
of police
incompetence

institutional
failure

debates
over
urban
governance

causes of
violence:
case of
unemployment
in Durban

historical
causes
of
poverty
in SA/
Apartheid

debates
over
neocolonial-
ism/
neoliberalism
and
globalization

strategies
to manage
violence

bottom-up
participation

debates over
empowerment

Figure 22.1   A literature 'map'

A good literature review, then, will be looking for a collection of sources that fill out this map in some detail. Clearly defining themes for each sector is important, otherwise your search won't be sufficiently focused. But it's equally important to get a balance between the context-specific materials (knowing about your case-study area) and the thematic/ theoretical literature (knowing about key debates and approaches to your theme).

Where and how do you find appropriate sources?

Now you know what you're looking for from the literature, where do you actually get hold of your sources? Rather than trying to provide you with a list of key journals or websites, it's more useful here to think about what you actually *do* when you are looking for literature. Table 22.1 lists a range of searching strategies (which is far

Table 22.1   Searching strategies

Searching strategy	How you do it	Things to think about
Electronic library catalogues	Use title, key word and author searches to maximize the potential of the catalogue	Lets you know what is actually available on site (thus saving frustration later!) but most won't find chapters within books, or articles within journals
Electronic bibliographic databases e.g. IBSS via BIDS; ASSIA; and GEOBASE (see your library website)	Choose key words, author or title to describe your research, and then use the site's own search engine	Will be up to date but requires careful selection of key words.[2] Many won't find book chapters! Many of the citations are often book reviews – also a useful source
Back issues of relevant journals[3]	Trawl through recent back issues – manually or electronically. Some journals have annual index inserts that list a whole year's collection (saving you a lot of time)	Time-consuming (so skim-read abstracts) but gives an overview of current debates. As well as articles, many journals have editorial commentaries and book reviews
Key authors' websites	Enter author's name (and academic institution) into Google to find their personal site, then look for lists of publications	Provides detailed insight to an individual author's work (and research group[4]) – and will include all forms of publication (books, papers, etc.)
Bibliographies of existing sources	Make active use of bibliographies while reading – note relevant case studies, areas of debates, key authors, etc.	Will provide references only to *earlier* work, so may need updating through other methods
Websites of development agencies (World Bank, DfID, UNDP, etc.). See also Mawdsley in this volume	Find key institutions' websites on Google or via links pages, e.g. that of the Developing Areas Research Group (http://www.gg.rhul.ac.uk/DARG/)	Ease of access *within* websites can be variable, but can reveal material (up-to-date data, reports and analysis) not yet in the academic domain

from exhaustive). Each of these has its own advantages and disadvantages, but all are much more effective when used *in combination*.

For example, Box 22.1 shows how a search on Glyn's topic, 'participatory development in India', might proceed.

Box 22.1 Undertaking a literature search

A paper your lecturer recommended cites a journal article by Giles Mohan on participation. So, you note it down and use Google to find him on the Web. His publications
list (http://dpp.open.ac.uk/publications.htm#gmohan) includes a book chapter in an
edited collection, *Participation: the New Tyranny*? This didn't show up in an earlier
search on BIDS, but typing keywords from the title back into BIDS provides you with a
couple of reviews of the book in development journals. The book looks spot on, so you
get it out of the library, and flick through the bibliography which generates a range of
possible leads, including a really important-looking journal you'd not previously been
aware of, *Development in Practice*. You find this and photocopy a paper by Sarah White
(noting this as a name to chase up on the Web later), but you're worried that so far you
have not found much that is India-specific. So, you change tack, and try a simple
Google search: 'India NGOs Participation'. Among others, this throws up a web portal,
Serve India Forum (http://www.serveindiaforum.net/links.html), where two websites run
by the World Bank (http://www.worldbank.org/participation) and the British Council
(www.indev.org) catch your eye. These are recognized organizations and the sites
provide a range of reports and other useful information.

Searching is an iterative process and the
strategies above need to be used flexibly and
with imagination. If you do this, there should
be no problem in generating what quickly
becomes a *massive* reading list (but be warned
that this can also very quickly become overwhelming). It should also make the process of
collecting sources active – shuttling between
websites, catalogues, library shelves,[5] and
photocopiers – rather than plodding through
a book from cover to cover. A key tip here is
to keep a full list of references as you come
across them (including, most importantly,
date, page numbers, place of publication and
publishing details). Struggling to find details
about various references on the morning of
your hand-in date causes unnecessary anxiety!

So much for the mechanics of searching,
but hiding within this question is another
more subtle one – what makes a source *appropriate*? Sometimes students' dissertations get
low marks for 'overuse of the web', or 'using
out-dated sources'. To avoid this, it is important to return to the question of what you are

searching for. Start by thinking carefully about
the limitations of the sources themselves – just
because it's in print (or on the Web) doesn't
mean it's perfect for your needs. As Table 22.2
shows, thinking carefully about the quality of
each source is important.

Going back to our literature map, most of
your web-based materials may be filling in the
case-study specific detail near the centre,
whereas the academic journals will tend to
dominate the theoretical debates towards the
edges. Although we cannot give an absolute
number of journal articles and other materials
you should have found and read, it is important that each of your 'sectors' is well
developed with reference to the *academic* literature. If a key theme is covered only by web
materials, think carefully about why, and discuss
this with your supervisor and/or get searching
again. Often the reason for an apparent lack of
academic sources is that you haven't thought
widely enough about which broader field of
literature your topic is located within.
Students often say that 'there is absolutely

Table 22.2 Evaluating the appropriateness of different sources

Key attributes	Web-based sources	Academic textbooks	Academic journal articles
Reliability/ authenticity of information	Very varied! The institution hosting the website may provide some guarantee, but very careful judgement is required	'Quality controlled' – have been reviewed by other academics (but you can and should think critically about content!)	Excellent – have been through a thorough refereeing process (but you can and should think critically about content!)
Linkages to theoretical debates	Varied – but most will *not* be written from an academic standpoint	Varied depending on the author, some are more explicit than others. Most make useful references to related literature	Good – linkages to wider theoretical debates generally explicit (and referenced)
Breadth of coverage	Generally good – you will be likely to find *something* on your study area and research question	Usually excellent in providing an overview of issues, historical backgrounds and generalized cover	Weaker – there may well be no coverage of your study area/precise themes
Coverage of current events	Good – but make sure you check websites for details of when they were last updated	Often the most out of date (depending on date of publication)	Usually worse than websites, but generally more up to date than academic books. Check carefully for dates of fieldwork/data collection

nothing academic written on my topic': generally, there *is*, it is just written on related research themes or theoretical debates rather than their particular case study! So, be prepared to think laterally.

How do you analyse the literature once you have found it?

Analysing the literature you have found is a gradual process and needs patience. Knowing what to focus on in your sources (i.e. knowing what you are going to analyse) depends entirely on what you are trying to argue in your dissertation. So, at this stage remind yourself of what your original research questions were: remember that after you have carried out any primary or secondary research, both your main research questions and thus the focus of

your literature review may have changed. This is not a bad thing! Just remember to check that the key debates you have focused on actually relate to your new questions.

Analysis itself is about reading the literature *selectively* but also about reading it *critically*. Reading critically is often a major worry for students, as they think that to read critically means to 'criticize', that is to say something negative about a particular reading. This is not true! Evaluations can be very positive. Reading critically simply means that you are expected to evaluate and interpret what you are reading rather than simply accepting it as 'the truth'. To achieve this you need to read material with some 'critical' questions in mind. We have outlined some possible questions you might ask, but this is not an exhaustive list (see Hart, 1998: Chapter 3 for further advice on classifying and reading research).

1. What is the key focus and argument of the document?
2. What particular audience was it written for (and has this affected its argument)?
3. What conceptual framework does it use (neoliberal, anti-development, feminist, etc.) and how has this shaped the author's argument?
4. What methods has the author used and are they appropriate?
5. Has the author provided evidence to back up the claims made?
6. What issues has the author overlooked, for example gender differences, an historical perspective, questions of politics and culture, etc.?

Once you have read a number of different sources – and thought about them – the next step is to bring these together under different themes. The best way to choose the themes you want to use is to go back to your original literature map on which these appear as different slices or segments. Treat each little theme as a mini-essay in itself and aim to discuss each using the sources you have found. In Paula's work *gendered power relations* is a key theme on her literature map that has generated a lot of reading material: discussion of this may include sources on masculinity, domestic violence and power relations between men and women. This needs to be drawn together through a critical review that shows its relevance to the Durban case study. The key point here is that your literature review should be structured thematically (not around individual articles) and be linked back to your central research question. This takes us on to the specifics of writing a literature review.

How should the literature review be written up?

Writing up a literature review is *NOT* about summarizing and describing the points made by each author you have read. Instead, your review should be a coherent argument where you interpret (i.e. analyse) the arguments of others. You have an important role in synthesizing different people's work on a particular theme and by doing this, you are 'adding value' to this work by presenting it in a new light (for help on developing your own arguments, see Holloway and Valentine, 2001). Writing a good review is therefore quite a specific skill. You need to demonstrate your familiarity with work in your field of study, but without regurgitating a list of point-by-point summaries of individual authors' articles or chapters. Turning to research papers published in your field can give you an idea of the style and content of a good review, as Box 22.2 indicates.

215

Box 22.2   Learning from published papers

Take an article in any development studies or other journal that is relevant to your research topic, and skim-read it for its structure. Many papers take the general form 'literature review, presentation of original fieldwork, conclusions'. Two of our recent papers that fit this format contain literature reviews on participation (Williams et al., 2003) and the home and violence (Meth, 2003). These are likely to provide a good model for your own review, and will also be useful in demonstrating how to make the links between the literature you are reading and the field materials you eventually collect (see below). Focus on the literature review. Note the following:

(Continued)

(Continued)

- In what ways is other literature discussed? (Referencing and citation style, level of detail)
- What is the balance between quotations/summaries of other work and the author's own words? (The latter should dominate – in your own review too)
- How does the review identify key debates and develop its own argument? (Your literature review map should help you in developing yours)

To show you how these writing tips work in practice, Box 22.3 presents two examples of literature reviews – one bad and one good – based around themes in Glyn's research. These are of course only excerpts, but they show that your writing style and structuring are very important. Student A had found some good sources, and read

---

Box 22.3   Good and bad literature reviews

Student A

A lot has been written on participation, which is an important theme in development. Robert Chambers (1997) has said that participation should help 'to put the first last' within development. This means that participation should include the views of the poorest within development programmes, and not just those of 'experts'. This review addresses a number of different authors' work on participation.

> This introduction is a bit dull, and more importantly, there's no indication of the themes that will be addressed, or how the review is structured

David Mosse (2000) writes about a rural development project in eastern India. In this project (the Western Indian Rainfed Farming Project), an NGO aimed to use participatory methods to include the views of the community within the running and management of this project. Mosse says that this did not fully work, as the project coordinators already had their own ideas about the goods and services they would provide villagers with.

> This (and the other references) are really good papers, but these are *described* without critical commentary

Another example of participatory development in India is described by Jenkins and Goetz (1999). They discuss the role of the MKSS, which fights for the right to information about government programmes in Rajasthan. Here the NGO works by publicizing the accounts of government development programmes, and holding public meetings where the actions of government officials can be criticized.

> Here and elsewhere there is no linkage between individual paragraphs. The result is a list of papers rather than a critical review

Heller (2001) discusses the involvement of people in local government planning in Kerala...

(Continued)

(Continued)

> A link forward to the student's fieldwork that will follow – good practice

Student B

Although seen as an essential part of 'good' development practice by its promoters, participation has recently come in for much academic criticism. This review addresses three elements of this criticism that are particularly relevant to this dissertation's West Bengal case study: misunderstandings around the engagement of 'communities', the problems of PRA methods, and biases introduced by donor agencies.

> Subheadings – each dealing with a separate theme – can help you to structure your review

> Short but good introduction – shows that the student is structuring this review around his own themes

Engagement of Communities

Various authors have noted that careful attention needs to be paid to existing power-differences at the micro-level when engaging 'communities' in participatory development (Nelson and Wright, 1995; Guijt and Shah, 1998; Cleaver, 2001). Participation does not usually take place within a closed, homogeneous local space (Mohan and Stokke, 2000), and if these power differences are ignored, they can undermine attempts to 'put the first last' (Chambers, 1997). Gender is an important component of these power differences[1], and gender roles can lead to the silencing of women in participatory events (Guijt and Shah, 1998; Mosse 1994), and the misrepresentation of community needs.

> Use footnotes like this one to link to more generic literature, or make other points that are related, but not central, to your main argument

> Clear indication that the student has read a range of supporting material – you don't always need to discuss all of this in detail

[1]For a wider discussion of the evolution of approaches to gender within development studies, see Peet and Hartwick (1999, Chapter 4).

217

and understood them too, but his write-up let him down by not demonstrating the skills of critically reviewing work or structuring the review clearly. Bringing in your own analysis and commentary on what you have read will ensure you get credit for all this effort!

How does the literature review link up with the rest of your project?

Ideally, your literature review should not be a stand-alone essay tacked on to the beginning of your project. Rather, the thinking within it

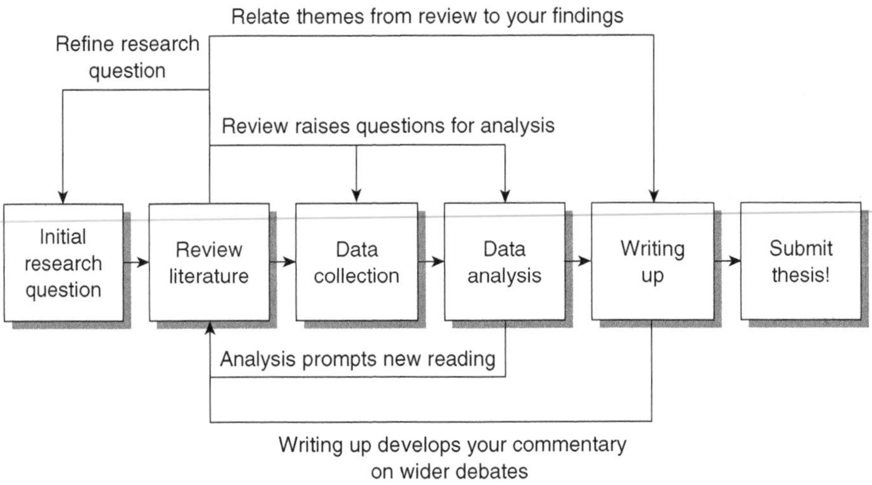

Figure 22.2   Linking up your literature review

should be taken up throughout your dissertation. Figure 22.2 shows some of the stages all research projects go through, and there should be strong links between all of these and your literature review.

The 'good' review example in Box 22.3 gives one example of how these links can be made – you link 'forward' from the literature review to the particular research questions, which you then address in the main part of the project. This is one important way in which your literature review can be made to work for you: you use the review to identify gaps in the literature, or interesting questions or approaches that you then address/put into practice through your own fieldwork or other data collection.

Importantly, the links here don't just go 'forward' from the literature to your questions and data collection, but 'backward' too: your data collection can suggest new avenues of enquiry, which should themselves be linked back to the literature (perhaps involving more reading). One way of dealing with these multiple links is to return to the map of the literature review and to annotate this further with themes and ideas emerging from your data analysis (Figure 22.3).

Here, Paula's literature map has evolved *after* her fieldwork in Durban. The theme of

'spirituality and culture' has been added to the sector on strategies to manage violence. This late addition occurred because the use of witchdoctors, who 'solve' crimes by using their powers to determine who the criminals are, emerged as an issue during focus group interviews. Perhaps unsurprisingly, this theme was not even thought of before carrying out empirical research, so no reading was done on it! But because it emerged as an issue that she wants to use in her research, Paula has to go back and find relevant literature to support any discussion she wants to make. Keeping and updating your literature map like this throughout the writing-up process should make sure that your literature review and data analysis are well connected throughout.

As with the literature review itself, it is important to *demonstrate* the linkages you are making through your writing style. For example, in your data analysis chapters you can make explicit links back to the literature you have already reviewed. In Glyn's work, this might be a statement like: 'In contrast to Mosse's (1999) work in Rajasthan, 81 per cent of villagers in the study area felt that they were free to participate in village meetings…'. Even more importantly, your *conclusions* should link directly back to your

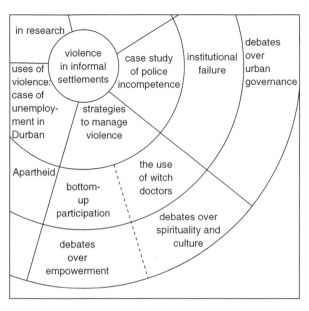

Figure 22.3   Revising your literature map

literature review. It is vital that you do this so that you can demonstrate that your own research project has identified issues that are relevant to wider academic debate within this area of study. This can make the difference between a good and an excellent project. Rather than being just a study of a few villagers in West Bengal, or a handful of township dwellers in Durban, you are showing that your study has something interesting or challenging to say about definitions of participatory development, or ideas of gender and violence. By being *informed by* and *linking to* a wider literature, you are showing all the key skills of a good researcher with which we began the chapter.

So, hopefully we've given you some insights here. And made it clear that spending time in the library is just as important for your research project as getting that aeroplane ticket booked …

Notes

1.   Paula's review included looking at work on violence in North American/European cities

as this raised important theoretical points. Generally, there shouldn't be a 'Third World'/ 'First World' divide in your reading, but when you are using ideas developed in other contexts, think through how they might apply (or not!) in your own field area.

2.   For example, entering the keyword 'violence' will yield different literature, as when using the keyword 'crime'. Be patient and try a range of combinations and synonyms.

3.   'Relevant to what?' is a key question here. These could be 'core' development journals (e.g. *Third World Quarterly*), region-specific journals (e.g. *Modern Asian Studies*, etc.) or those conceptually linked to a particular sub-discipline/theme (e.g. *Gender, Place and Culture*). Discussion with your supervisor should help here.

4.   Research groups sometimes have useful web pages and electronic publications, for example, on participation see the IDS participation group's home page (http://www.ids.ac.uk/ids/particip/index.html)

5.   Important tip: Don't be limited by your own institution's resources here! Visits to specialist collections (e.g. the School of Oriental and African Studies library in London) or neighbouring universities can vastly improve your access, as can inter-library loans. Ask your librarian about these.

219

QUESTIONS FOR DISCUSSION

In this chapter, we raised five questions to guide you through researching and writing a review. Once you have drafted your own review, return to these questions, and evaluate your performance:

1. Were you searching for the right things when you conducted your literature search?
2. Did you find appropriate materials (in terms of the quality and range of sources)?
3. How analytical were you in your use of this literature (have you 'added value')?
4. Is the style of your literature review correct (did you avoid descriptive lists)?
5. Is your literature review linked to the rest of your research project?

Further reading

Hart, C. (1998) *Doing a Literature Review*, London: Sage.

Hay, I. (1995) 'Writing a review', *Journal of Geography in Higher Education,* 19: 357–363.

Holloway, S. and Valentine, G. (2001) Making an argument: writing up human geography projects, *Journal of Geography in Higher Education*, 25(1): 127–132.

Rudestam, K.E. and Newton, R.R. (1992) *Surviving Your Dissertation: A Comprehensive Guide to Content and Process*, London: Sage (Chapter 4 in particular).

Websites

Serve India Forum: http://www.serveindiaforum.net/links.html

The World Bank: http://www.worldbank.org/participation

The British Council: www.indev.org

The Institute of Development Studies (Sussex University) Participation Group: http://www.ids.ac.uk/ids/particip/index.html

The Developing Areas Research Group of the Royal Geographical Society/Institute of British Geographers: http://www.gg.rhul.ac.uk/DARG

References

Hart, C. (1998) *Doing a Literature Review*, London: Sage.

Holloway, S. and Valentine, G. (2001) Making an argument: writing up human geography projects, *Journal of Geography in Higher Education*, 25(1): 127–132.

Mawdsley, E. (2006) Using the World Wide Web for development research, in V. Desai and R. Potter (eds), *Doing Development Research*, London: Sage.

Meth, P. (2003) Rethinking the 'domus' in domestic violence: homelessness, space and domestic violence in South Africa, *Geoforum*, 34(3): 317–327.

Rudestam, K.E. and Newton, R.R. (1992) *Surviving Your Dissertation: A Comprehensive Guide to Content and Process*, London: Sage.

Williams, G., Veron, R., Corbridge, S. and Srivastava, M. (2003) Participation, poverty and power: poor people's engagement with India's Employment Assurance Scheme, *Development and Change*, 34(1): 163–192.

23

Using Indigenous Local Knowledge and Literature

Cathy McIlwaine

The types of indigenous local knowledge and literature commonly available
Accessing indigenous local knowledge and literature ● The importance of using
indigenous local knowledge and literature ● Limitations of using indigenous
local knowledge and literature

Introduction

Consultation of local and indigenous literature, and engagement with local knowledge more generally, is integral to conducting research in the Global South. While this may sound like stating the obvious, it is surprising how often local circumstances and information generated by local people have been ignored when carrying out development-oriented research. Yet, using indigenous knowledge and information is practically, ethically and theoretically important. Practically, it is essential to listen to the voices of those linked with a research project, whether it is the participants themselves or local people's views on them or a given situation. This relates more broadly with the spirit of ethical participation of research subjects in any project, encouraging real and responsible engagement with the issues under investigation. It is also theoretically important from the perspective of recent postcolonial and

post-development discourses that have criticized the ways in which traditional knowledge has sometimes been seen as irrelevant or an obstacle to development in favour of Western knowledge as superior (Briggs and Sharp, 2004). Most fundamentally, using local knowledge and literature can open up the life-worlds of those involved in research and, in turn, produce high-quality findings that challenge the so-called scientific views of 'Western experts'.

This chapter considers the entire realm of indigenous and local knowledge and how it is accessed in ways that may be academic or non-academic in nature. The term 'indigenous' is used broadly to denote people from the country, region or locality in question from a local perspective. This is in contrast to the narrower focus on a particular ethnic group that has a long history of settlement in an area and a particular language and culture, such as indigenous Indian groups including the Mayans, Aztecs and Incas in Latin America or the

Adivasis tribal communities in India. The core argument outlined here is that local knowledge and literature must be acknowledged or consulted as a basic first step for conducting research in any development context. While gathering primary local knowledge may be an integral part of the methodology of a research project, consulting and accessing the local literature is also a crucial aspect of the process.

What is indigenous local knowledge and literature?

Knowledge generated by the people involved in a research project or linked with it in some way can take a variety of forms. Local knowledge can be verbal, such as that encompassed in particular customs, traditions, myths, ways of life and ways of thinking. This is knowledge that is created by local people and shared within particular communities, capturing both the voices and values of local people (Sillitoe, 1998). These are also views that are not always included in dominant discourses. Such knowledge has to be directly accessed through the research process and methodology itself (see below). Invariably, unless discussion or performance is presented verbatim from an interview or situation, this type of knowledge is interpreted in some way by whoever records it.

The ways in which such knowledge is presented constitutes the other types of local literature that are available. One of the main types is literature generated by local researchers producing knowledge within and about their own environs. Until recently, much research on development has been generated by researchers working in institutions in the North and certainly outside the region on which the information is based. This is primarily because it is expensive to create. Although this is often still the case, local researchers are increasingly closing the so-called 'knowledge gap' as they conduct their own research. Most developing countries now have several research organizations and/or universities that conduct research on local issues using their own staff. These may be state-owned or private institutions (as in universities) or NGOs who operate as think-tanks and who often obtain their resources from international donors. Indeed, international donors are increasingly recognizing the importance of locally produced research, and many funding organizations will fund work by Northern researchers only if it involves collaboration with local researchers as well as the production of locally relevant outputs. Outputs can be publications produced in local languages, such as research reports, books or journal articles, or other materials, such as pamphlets, briefing papers, sourcebooks or manuals (see Box 23.1 on two research organizations in Guatemala). Most of these will be published by local publishers, and in the case of journals in particular, many universities run their own periodicals. For instance, the University of Costa Rica (the main state university) runs a journal called the *Revista de Ciencias Sociales* (Journal of Social Sciences) that produces up-to-date, high-quality research on the Central American region as a whole.

223

Box 23.1   Local research organizations: Asociación para el Avance de las Ciencias Sociales en Guatemala (Association for the Advancement of the Social Sciences in Guatemala – AVANCSO) and Centro de Investigaciones Económicas Nacionales (Centre for National Economic Research – CIEN), Guatemala

AVANCSO is a research centre for the social sciences established in 1986 in Guatemala. Its aim is to produce socially relevant research that is useful for the popular sectors

(Continued)

(Continued)

(social organizations involved in designing public policy) with a particular focus on conducting high-quality fieldwork.

AVANCSO has been well known for producing research with a national impact, especially their pioneering work on population displacement linked with the country's armed conflict, together with the phenomenon of return migrants. In general, it works in four main areas, focusing on peasants, socio-urban issues, local history and social imagining. It has a radical tradition in terms of its analysis of the state and is well known for being outspoken. At the end of the 1980s, one of its anthropologists and founders, Myrna Mack, was killed because of her research on the armed conflict.

AVANCSO produces a series of publications that can be accessed both nationally and internationally (in Spanish). These include essays by guest writers, monographs on research and a series on current debates.

CIEN is also a research centre established in 1982. While CIEN works on social issues, it is best known for its research on the economy, having become one of the main sources of economic analysis in Guatemala, with considerable influence on the government and with close links with multilateral and bilateral international organizations. As well as conducting research projects, CIEN also provide technical assistance to the business sector.

CIEN produces a wide series of publications, all of which are available on the internet (in Spanish). These include documents on assistance for businesses, reports on economic and legislative analysis, a bulletin called *Carta Económica* comprising briefings on key issues for the country, and a technical report for congress on issues such as budgets.

Both organizations are funded from a range of national and international donors. Both are also non-governmental organizations, although CIEN has much closer links with the state than AVANCSO.

Sources: http://www.avancso.org.gt; http://www.cien.org.gt

224

The production of local research is not specifically confined to organizations and/or universities. There may also be groups of researchers working in different types of institution who are joined either formally or informally through the topic on which they specialize. In Colombia, for example, local experts on the topic of violence are known as *violentólogos* or violentologists. Based mainly in the country's universities and research centres, these people conduct invaluable local work on the issue, much of which is published in books and local journals (see Moser and McIlwaine, 2004 for examples).

Another important source of locally produced knowledge are project-oriented local NGOs who produce so-called 'grey material' that can be useful for researchers. These may be project-design, evaluation or technical documents that contain important background information on a given issue. For instance, an NGO that works on local development issues in El Salvador called FUNDAMUNI (*Fundación de Apoyo a Municipios de El Salvador* – Foundation for the Support of Municipalities of El Salvador) regularly produces descriptive documents about their projects in terms of their design and implementation. These provide important insights into how local government functions, and especially how issues of participation have been incorporated into decision-making processes (see McIlwaine, 1998). NGOs also produce literature that is used for lobbying purposes. In Botswana, a women's NGO, Emang Basadi Women's Association, published *The Women's Manifesto* in 1994 which outlines a series of issues and demands on the status of women. This provides one of the most comprehensive outlines of the situation of women in the country as well as acting as a core document in encouraging and gaining important strides in the goal of gender equality (McIlwaine and Datta, 2004).

Governments also provide an extremely rich source of local literature for researchers. These may be background or project documents, policy papers or specifically designed mechanisms for sharing local information and knowledge. In relation to the latter, the Philippine government's National Economic and Development Authority (NEDA), which is responsible for economic planning, not only publishes its plans both electronically and on paper (such as the Medium-Term Philippine Development Plan 2004–2010), but it has recently set up a Children's Knowledge Center (KC). This provides online access to a range of databases, fact sheets and articles on children as well as providing a resource centre that acts as a National Database Depository for all information about young people in the country (see www.neda.gov.ph and www.philchild info.neda.gov.ph). More generally, government policy documents can also provide crucial information and summaries of up-to-date research on a topic. Again in Botswana, the government has produced a comprehensive National Youth Policy that provides one of the few analyses of young people available in the country (see McIlwaine and Datta, 2004).

While this section has highlighted the diversity of different types of knowledge and literature available, it should also be noted that until relatively recently there has been a tendency to overlook local analyses of issues and

conditions. When local knowledge has been deemed important, the focus has often been on technical information in relation to agriculture and the environment such as soil management, medicinal plants and so on. A classic example of this is the World Bank's *World Development Report on Knowledge for Development* (1988) and their associated framework for action. These adopt a technocratic approach, focusing on very specific knowledge rather than wider knowledge systems (see Briggs and Sharp, 2004 for a discussion). Although this approach is still prevalent in some circles, the need to adopt a much wider perspective has increasingly been recognized.

Accessing indigenous local knowledge and literature

Local knowledge and literature can be accessed in a range of ways. Gathering first-hand local knowledge will probably be the core element of any research project. While the range of strategies and methodologies that can be employed to gather such information are discussed elsewhere in this volume, it is also worth pointing out that drawing on local knowledge has become an important focus of methodological concern in recent years. This has partly reflected the shift towards the need for more participatory development strategies, especially in recent debates on poverty which have emphasized listening to the 'voices of the poor' (see World Bank, 2001). Methodologically, this has been achieved through using various types of participatory appraisal techniques, including Participatory Rural Appraisal (PRA), Participatory Urban Appraisal (PUA) and Participatory Action Research (PAR) among others (see Chapter 19). Pioneered by people such as Robert Chambers (1994), a core tenet of this approach has been to valorize the local knowledge of the marginalized and to find practical ways in which this can be shared in non-exploitative ways. Although these approaches have been widely criticized,

225

Figure 23.1   Drawing of groups associated with violence in Cali, Colombia (drawn by a 9-year-old boy).
Pandillas = gangs; ladrones = thieves; ELN = a guerrilla group (adapted from
Moser and McIlwaine, 2004)

invariably on the grounds of their limited ability to be truly participatory or representative (see Kapoor, 2002), they have been significant in acknowledging that research subjects themselves must be fully engaged in the research process, and that their views and analyses are important. The outputs from this type of methodology are usually drawings or diagrams made by people themselves, although, as noted above, it is inevitable that some level of analysis on the part of the researcher also permeates the process (see Figure 23.1).

While this type of approach makes it possible to capture indigenous knowledge as part of empirical data collection in a relatively short period of time, some would argue that an ethnographic approach where research is conducted over longer time-frames is the only way to really learn about local customs and practices. In some cases, such information may be represented through life-histories of people, case studies or diaries, often using transcripts derived from in-depth interviews.

Accessing secondary local knowledge and literature is more straightforward. On the one hand, it can involve primary data collection through conducting interviews with researchers and employees from NGOs, universities and so on. As well as eliciting views on particular issues, part of these interviews can also involve collecting relevant material published by organizations or individuals (often, such materials are available only through direct contact with the individuals who have written the work). In addition, many universities and research organizations have libraries, archives or resource collections that can be used by the public or by appointment. Another good way of accessing local literature is through visiting local bookshops. Depending on the country in question, many bookshops, especially those situated within or near universities, are a good place to locate books, journals, leaflets and government documents. Finally, important secondary information can increasingly be accessed from the internet (see Box 23.1 on CIEN).

Why should local indigenous knowledge and literature be used?

The importance of using local knowledge and/or literature can be practical, theoretical and ethical. On a practical level, using it serves to enhance the quality of information gathered and to provide a much more complete research project or case study. While the generation of primary local knowledge will be integral in opening up the life-worlds of those who form the focus of the research, it is also important to complement this with the types of secondary information outlined above. Only then can a truly rounded picture of the

topic under consideration be provided. Not only can useful primary data be collected, but the analytical work of local researchers can also be taken into account, providing different perspectives and ensuring against any potential ethnocentrism (see below). This can act as a form of triangulation of views from different sources.

Failure to include the views of local people and researchers can lead to widespread ethnocentrism. A classic example here is how women in the South have been treated until relatively recently. Until the cutting critiques of people such as Chandra Mohanty in the late 1980s, women in the South were portrayed in a grossly stereotypical fashion. According to Mohanty (1991), research conducted primarily by women from the North assumed, first, that all women in the South were the same, and, second, that they were uniformly poor, ignorant, victimized, bound to their families and sexually constrained. This was in direct contrast to women from the North who represented themselves as educated, modern and in control. While such views were rooted in ignorance, it could also be argued that if the views of these women had been carefully taken into account, and if the views and writings of female researchers from the South had been listened to, then such representations would never have appeared in the first place.

This provides an important lesson in the sense that it must always be remembered that those who are being researched are the ultimate experts on an issue, and that local researchers will invariably be much more in tune with the realities of life in a given context. The external researcher will always be an outsider, even though there are ways in which this status can be negotiated and the quality of the information gathered sustained. Accessing and using indigenous knowledge and literature is one such way of guarding against ethnocentrism and misrepresentations.

The need to consult local knowledge and its related literature also has theoretical significance. As noted in the introduction, recent work within postcolonial and post-development debates have centred around the need to valorize indigenous knowledge as a way of challenging the hegemony of the Western researcher and so-called 'expert' together with the primacy of Western conceptual ideas. While debates rage as to whether and how it is ever possible to let local people 'speak' on an equal footing with Western researchers (Kapoor, 2004; also McIlwaine and Datta, 2003; Radcliffe, 1994 on gender), the principle has been firmly established. Yet, it is also important not just to listen to the voices and read the words of local people, but also to acknowledge indigenous conceptual frameworks and 'ways of knowing' which may be at odds with Western construction of knowledge (Kapoor, 2004).

This has also fed through to the policy arena. As part of the participation debates discussed in relation to participatory methodologies, the need to consult and include research subjects and/or project beneficiaries at the local level is now viewed as integral to project success. For policy-related researchers, such a perspective is also necessary if social change and/or empowerment are to be engendered (Mohan and Stokke, 2000: 252). The extent to which this type of viewpoint has fed into mainstream policy debates is evidenced by the publication of the recent UNDP *Human Development Report* (2004), which focuses on cultural liberty and diversity. Among other things, it argues for the need to include the marginalized of the world, many of whom are members of religious or ethnic minorities, into mainstream political decision-making. Although the focus is on multiculturalism and cultural identities, the need to challenge a Westernized and homogenized view of the world, and to value local variations in cultures and ethnicities, is a central dimension of the report and of relevance in the current context.

The ethical dimensions are also a major consideration when assessing the importance of using local knowledge and literature. Closely linked with the theoretical dimensions, it can be argued that it is the responsibility of researchers to try to uncover the most genuine form of local knowledge possible, usually only facilitated through involving local people in the process. From the point of view of local literature, outside researchers have a moral responsibility to be as beneficent as possible in terms of highlighting the findings of local researchers who may not have access to the dissemination channels available to Western researchers (see Smith, 2002 on the role of beneficence in development). It is also increasingly deemed important to involve local researchers in the research process (see above), and to give them full access to data gathered as well as equal authorship of any published research arising from the project (Briggs and Sharp, 2004).

The limitations of using local indigenous knowledge and literature

While there are obvious advantages in using local indigenous knowledge and literature, a number of drawbacks must also be recognized. From a practical perspective, the quality of local literature can be highly variable. Besides some academic journals based in universities in the South, most published research does not go through a review process, meaning that anything can be published. Also, while there is a moral responsibility for researchers to use and cite local literature, this will often not be accessible for others to consult. This will be exacerbated if the work is written in a non-European language (and even if it's not written in English). In terms of knowledge generation, all local research cannot be assumed to be superior to that generated by outsiders; local researchers are just as susceptible to flaws in data gathering as anyone, and in some cases may be more so because of their proximity to the issues. As a result, they may be unable to view issues objectively and/or without letting local allegiances or perceptions come into play. This type of issue arose in fieldwork I conducted in Guatemala with some local researchers in 1999 while working in a high-conflict, violent, low-income settlement in Guatemala City. While we worked with well-trained and experienced researchers, several of them were too scared to conduct the fieldwork in the ways that had been agreed (i.e. house to house) because they felt afraid, first, as women because of the gendered abuse they perceived they would receive and, second, because of their perceptions that the settlement was full of gangs, thieves and delinquents. In contrast, I and two other external researchers were not affected by such perceptions.

From a more theoretical viewpoint, and in relation to using local knowledge in particular, there is a danger of romanticizing the local (see Kapoor, 2004). Related to this, there is also a tendency to treat the local as harmonious, when in reality there are likely to be widespread conflicts among local groups over technical knowledge or the construction of events, for instance (Mohan and Stokke, 2000). These conflicts may revolve around gender differences, ethnicity, age or sexuality, depending on who the research subjects are. In turn, it should not always be assumed that Western knowledge is tainted, and that indigenous knowledge is free from being essentialized (Kapoor, 2004).

In conclusion, the importance of consulting local indigenous knowledge either through first-hand data collection or local literature is paramount for any research project. Although there may be limitations associated with this, these are far outweighed by the advantages. Indeed, it is safe to say that a research project that ignores local knowledge and literature will be fundamentally flawed.

QUESTIONS FOR DISCUSSION

1. In considering a given setting, outline the main types of local knowledge and literature available and assess the merits of each type.
2. Which types of such knowledge or literature are the easiest and most difficult to access?
3. Why is it practically important to use local knowledge and literature in a research project?
4. What are the theoretical and ethical reasons for including it?
5. Outline the types of danger and problems inherent in using local knowledge and literature.

Further reading

Briggs, J. and Sharp, J. (2004) Indigenous knowledges and development: a postcolonial caution, *Third World Quarterly*, 25:4, 661–676. On local knowledge from a postcolonial perspective.

Mohan, G. and Stokke, K. (2000) Participatory development and empowerment: the dangers of localism, *Third World Quarterly*, 21:2, 247–268. On thinking about the importance of the local level.

Websites

http://www.indigenouspeople.net – Indigenous People's Literature which is a non-profit educational resource to showcase the views, ideas, music, images and writings of indigenous people throughout the world.

http://www.kivu.com – KIVU Nature Inc. (Knowledge, Imagery, Vision and Understanding) is an organization providing consulting services to those involved in sustainable project management with a focus on natural and cultural resources.

References

Briggs, J. and Sharp, J. (2004) Indigenous knowledges and development: a postcolonial caution, *Third World Quarterly*, 25:4, 661–676.

Chambers, R. (1994) The origins and practice of Participatory Rural Appraisal, *World Development* 22:7, 953–969.

Kapoor, I. (2002) The devil's in the theory: a critical assessment of Robert Chambers' work on participatory development, *Third World Quarterly*, 23:1, 101–117.

Kapoor, I. (2004) Hyper-self-reflexive development? Spivak on representing the Third World 'Other', *Third World Quarterly*, 25:4, 627–647.

McIlwaine, C. (1998) Contesting civil society: reflections from El Salvador, *Third World Quarterly*, 19:4, 651–672.

McIlwaine, C. and Datta, K. (2003) From feminising to engendering development, *Gender, Place and Culture*, 10:4, 345–358.

McIlwaine, C. and Datta, K. (2004) 'Endangered youth?': Youth, gender and sexualities in urban Botswana, *Gender, Place and Culture*, 11:4, 483–511.

Mohan, G. and Stokke, K. (2000) Participatory development and empowerment: the dangers of localism, *Third World Quarterly*, 21:2, 247–268.

Mohanty, C.T. (1991) Under Western eyes: feminist scholarship and colonial discourses, in C. Mohanty, A. Russo and L. Torres (eds), *Third World Women and the Politics of Feminism*, Bloomington: Indiana University Press, pp. 51–80.

Moser, C. and McIlwaine, C. (2004) *Encounters with Violence in Latin America: Urban Poor Perceptions from Colombia and Guatemala*, London: Routledge.

Radcliffe, S. (1994) (Representing) post-colonial women: authority, difference and feminisms, *Area*, 26:1, 25–32.

Sillitoe, P. (1998) What know natives? Local knowledge in development, *Social Anthropology*, 6:2, 203–220.

Smith, D.M.S. (2002) Responsibility to distant others, in V. Desai and R.B. Potter (eds), *The Companion to Development Studies*, London: Arnold, pp. 131–139.

UNDP (2004) *Human Development Report, 2004*, New York and Oxford: Oxford University Press.

World Bank (1998) *World Development Report on Knowledge for Development*, Oxford and New York: Oxford University Press.

World Bank (2001) *World Development Report*, Oxford and New York: Oxford University Press.

24

Using Images, Films and Photography

Cheryl McEwan

Photography and field research · Using film and video
Crafts-based images in community development

Introduction

Most development researchers are by now familiar with the idea of development as a discourse. Most are well versed in the importance of interrogating words and pictures within development discourses and their material effects. In this chapter, I am less concerned with deconstructing images and representations as partial, often simplified and distorted, but rather, I want to explore how images are used in processes of development. I want to demonstrate that there is a wealth of graphical material related to 'doing' development – including photography, video and other images – that begs consideration, and to encourage researchers to contemplate the possibilities that these methods might open up.

Photography and field research

In contemporary development, photographs are used in a variety of different ways.

Photo-essays have been used by NGOs to record successes in community development. One example of this is the photo-essay on the Philippines Homeless People's Federation (VMSDFI, 2001), which describes its success in bringing together low-income community organizations that have formed housing savings groups. The photo-essay records the strong emphasis on community-managed savings schemes, on community-to-community exchanges (so that members can learn from each other's experiences and formulate solutions for particular problems) and on the importance of negotiating with governments with clear, carefully costed proposals that demonstrate what communities can do for themselves. This is one example of how visual images such as photographs can be used, either in and of themselves or alongside text, to present specific arguments.

In contrast to the photo-essay, most researchers confine themselves to the odd illustrative photograph that is often assumed to be a factual record of the field. As Cook and Crang

(1995) argue, photographic theory has suggested that this is not the case and that photographs are not transparent media for recording or presenting facts. Rather, they are taken purposively and displayed in contexts that can dramatically alter their meaning. It is worth remembering, then, that while photographs can be used to make ethnographic or political arguments, they also construct meaning. Contemporary visual ethnography uses photography not so much to claim 'this is what is', but to create a dialogue around the competing and complementary meanings of images (Harper, 2003). Use of photography, particularly in ethnography, has shifted from an emphasis on documentary studies to research that addresses the polysemic quality of images – their multiple meanings and interpretations. According to Cook and Crang (1995: 69):

> photographs can often provide more insights into the social milieu of actors than into the 'reality' they supposedly capture, and as a means for studying the culture of groups they can also provide not only a useful research avenue but may already be part of the very culture you seek to study.

With this in mind, Espelund et al. (2003) use photography deliberately to unsettle stereotypical images of contemporary Africa, shifting the focus from stories that tell of war, hunger and crisis to more positive representations. Photographs are used alongside journalistic accounts to tell alternative stories about parts of Africa that have hit the headlines, focusing on hopeful stories of ordinary people (more often than not women) who have made a positive difference in their communities and whose abilities to survive are more impressive than the achievements made by people in more privileged parts of the world. The photographs tell alternative stories of women reverting to traditional farming during severe droughts in Malawi and not just surviving but creating a business out of cassava

production; they tell of people in different countries putting their lives on the line to make peace with murderers, of a woman's success in the corporate world of male-dominated Morocco and of shack owners in South Africa selling the township experience to tourists. Their potency is in telling a more hope-filled story about Africa and human development there.

These examples demonstrate the potential for photography as a research technique, which might include photo-essays and photo-diaries and documentaries. In addition, researchers have also begun to use participant auto-photography, where participants are encouraged to take pictures of their environments or activities in order to cast light on how they understand and interpret their world. New technologies such as disposable cameras make this a relatively cheap and simple-to-use technology in developing countries, while digital cameras make recording visual images easier for the researcher. As discussed subsequently, these methods have the potential to create new relationships between researchers and researched.

Using film and video

Like photography, video is not a neutral medium, 'having distinct class overtones in terms of ownership' and being 'redolent with ideologies about technology' (Cook and Crang, 1995: 70). However, it can be used in the same way as auto-photography, allowing participants to produce video diaries and their own filmic representations of their world, as well as the skills to critique other people's representations. There is a long tradition of using participatory video in community development practice, particularly in developing countries. Its application usually involves:

> a scriptless video process, directed by a group of grassroots people, moving forward in

iterative cycles of shooting-reviewing. This process aims at creating video narratives that communicate what those who participate in the process really want to communicate, in a way they think is appropriate. (Johansson et al., 1999: 35, cited in Kindon, 2003: 143)

Participatory video is perceived to be an effective way of reaching and including the most powerless people, traditionally lacking agency in community development, as a means of increasing equitable outcomes (Kindon, 2003). It is often used in processes of public consultation and mobilization, policy dialogue and to communicate the outcomes of participatory development processes within and between communities or to funding agencies (see Box 24.1).

Box 24.1 The Masithembane Housing Association Video, Khayelitsha, Western Cape

The Masithembane Housing Association is located in Khayelitsha, one of South Africa's largest townships, and is one of the most impoverished in the Western Cape. It was established in Site B, an area dominated by informal settlements. Masithembane is a grassroots organization founded by women; it uses the People's Housing Process as a framework based on the assumption that people and communities can deliver better and more cost-effective housing than the government. The women of Masithembane worked with a national NGO (People's Housing Partnership Trust), a local NGO (Development Action Group) and an experienced developer in the area (Marnol) and organized to build 220 houses in under a year. This first phase was highly successful and Masithembane is now proceeding with further developments to house more families currently living in shacks. A written evaluation has been completed of the Masithembane project and a video has been produced by the women and the People's Housing Partnership Trust to document its remarkable success and the stories of families involved. The video was screened for the first time at the community hall in Khayelitsha on 25 March 2001 and copies were handed over to the community.

The video serves two purposes. First, it shares the achievements of Masithembane and the knowledge and experience gained through the People's Housing Process with other communities in South Africa. The aim is to inspire poor people in other areas to build their own homes, to share knowledge on how to form partnerships with provincial governments, NGOs and local developers, and to mobilize and employ in local grassroots development many of the existing skills in poor communities that often remain untapped. Second, it records the agency of women who have been most marginalized by poverty and gender relations in homes, communities and society at large. It demonstrates to the other community members and NGO and local government agents that poor women can have agency in decision-making and development, and have considerable abilities given the opportunities to lead local development projects. It also serves to underline the nature of the women's achievements and, in seeing themselves on film

(Continued)

233

(Continued)

as role models for other communities, enhances their sense of self-esteem. For women who have long been oppressed by colonial power relations, apartheid racisms and persistent unequal gender relations, this sense of self-esteem is essential in providing the foundation for further human and community development.

Participatory video is regarded as an effective tool for participatory research (Frost and Jones, 1998). By producing, watching and discussing the video with local people, the researcher can more quickly comprehend their complex perceptions and discourses. This is also a dialogic process that allows communities to analyse their own realities critically and, like auto-photography, has the potential to create a more equitable relationship between the researcher and research participants (Kindon, 2003).

Participatory video often helps research participants to become 'so familiar with the technology of image production that they become image makers themselves' (Banks, 2001: 122). One example of this is the work of Eric Michaels, who facilitated Australian Aborigines' use of video in ways that enabled him to: 'understand differences between Aboriginal and European uses of visual representation and information but also one that empowered his informants to respond in a global media context in which they might be seen as marginal or "invisible"' (Pink, 2001: 593).

Sara Kindon (2003) has also used participatory video successfully with a group of Maori people from the North Island of Aotearoa New Zealand, exploring relationships between place, identity and 'social cohesion' in communities in the Rangitikei district. In this work she built deeper relations of trust with the community members she worked with and destabilized the usual researcher/researched relationship in a more equitable, participatory research process. This, Kindon argues, allowed other transformations to occur.

In this case, participatory video facilitated the sharing of technical and 'local' knowledges between the research team and participants. Using video to record the research process of negotiations and decision-making, as well as the production of locally-embedded audio-visual texts, enabled an ongoing or iterative reflection upon the knowledges produced. They thus provided important visual information that, when combined with field notes and interview transcripts, have the potential to create new knowledges and critiques. Since the project was participatory from the beginning, many problems of access and confidentiality that often limit the research process were circumvented, with community members able to set the terms of the research process through negotiation at the beginning of the project. Moreover, there was a transformation of the research process with many of the ideas for the use of video coming from community members rather than the researchers. Many of the community participants also indicated the transformative potential of participatory video at the personal level by expressing their feelings of empowerment, agency and self-worth (Kindon, 2003).

There is, of course, a caveat in the use of video – it is time-consuming and relies on building trust with participants. Researchers, therefore, have to be aware of the commitment required when contemplating using participatory video and the importance of maintaining ongoing research relationships once the 'fieldwork' has finished (Kindon, 2003). Video is also comparatively expensive. However, as equipment costs have fallen it is becoming more accessible. Aboriginal and Inuit communities, for example, are using video in trying to move from being images in the culture of hegemonic groups to producing their own images of themselves. As Cook and Crang (1995) argue, approaching these sorts of groups allows the researcher to gain access to various processes whereby numerous communities are seeking to redefine themselves in the modern world.

Crafts-based images in community development

A less obvious use of visual images in development research might include analysing crafts-based images such as memory cloths (see Box 24.2). These are of interest to development researchers for a number of reasons, not least because there is a rich social history context for crafts and diverse material cultures and these traditional skills are becoming part of an economic enterprise for poor people. As with other forms of craft (for example, see Morrow and Vokwana (2001) on Xhosa male clay modelling in the Western Cape), women's memory cloths are 'beguiling objects' – designed to appeal as art but simultaneously encapsulating the history of a poor community – that can cast light on both historical processes and current social, cultural and economic contexts.

Box 24.2 Memory cloths and community development: KwaZulu-Natal's *Amazwi Abesifazane*

The *Amazwi Abesifazane* memory cloths programme is part of community rehabilitation programmes in South Africa, which are aimed at promoting the healing and recovery of individuals and communities that have been affected by human rights violations. It is a unique project to provide black South African women from rural and urban areas with a vehicle to articulate traumatic experiences of the apartheid era, and to preserve and promote their creativity and memories. Women from urban and rural areas of KwaZulu-Natal who had experienced the trauma of the apartheid era were asked to create a pictorial and verbal record of their experiences. The project was initially set up through women's organizations, including the Self-Employed Women's Union (SEWU) and the National Women's Coalition, who facilitated workshops. Painful memories are transformed into creativity by embroidery, appliqué and beadwork, drawing on indigenous arts and crafts, as well as Euro-American traditional sources, such as samplers and quilts (see Figure 24.1).

Amazwi Abesifazane is part of Create Africa South, a non-profit, non-governmental organization established in 2000 to promote and develop creativity in South Africa, particularly within historically disadvantaged communities. The President is sculptor Andries Botha, and Mazisi Kunene, one of Africa's senior poets, is Vice President. A trust fund has been established under the auspices of Create Africa South, but administered and contributed to by the participating women. This was launched at an exhibition of memory cloths held at Durban Art Gallery in June and July 2001, where as many cloths as possible were exhibited in an educational environment. The educational focus is on the process of memory retrieval, loss, women's issues (especially gender violence), the role of catharsis in healing a nation, and the role of women in communities.

(Continued)

235

(Continued)

Figure 24.1 An example of a memory cloth: No. 41 by Ntombi Agnes Mbatha. The accompanying text reads 'In 1992 my husband and I were going into town. Our son of 20 asked us to buy him some shoes. We bought him the shoes, but when we returned home our son was not there and then we heard he had been gunned down. We were so sad ...'

236

The 2010 project goal of the trust fund is to acquire 5,000 stories and cloths and to create a permanent exhibition and educational programme in an appropriate facility in KwaZulu-Natal (see http://www.cas.org.za), forming a collective memory of life in South Africa up to the present day. Each cloth is an original work, to which is attached a profile of the artist and her story, written in her first language as well as English. The national archive is organized around themes, including AIDS, home life, work, domestic violence, rape, alcohol abuse, discrimination, forced removals and police brutality under apartheid, faction fighting, murder, polygamy, witchcraft, floods and fire. Although the vast majority of cloths relate memories of dispossession, loss, trauma, violence and death, several also record happier memories about everyday rural and community life. While being aimed primarily at memory retrieval, the project is dedicated to all aspects of social development, improving the lives of women by encouraging peer support, nurturing dialogue within communities and developing women's self-employment industry that creates products to market internationally.

In the case of *Amazwi Abesifazane*, the use of beads is particularly significant because in South Africa (and especially in Ndebele and Zulu cultures) they are not merely for adornment but play a part in cultural rites (courtship, marriage, homage to ancestors) and modes of communication (status symbols, love letters). The inclusion of beadwork within a formal archive is part of a growing recognition of the place of ancient traditions and customs within contemporary nationhood. Sewing is also significant since, in many cultures and historical contexts, it has been used to communicate when, for various political and sociological reasons, oral disclosure has not been possible.

These images demonstrate how culture and economy might be brought together in a broadened notion of development. In the case of *Amazwi Abesifazane*, for example, once the national archive is completed, the intention is to create a computer-based record of the original cloths and testimonies and to sell the entire archive. The proceeds of the sale will form the first major donation to the trust fund. Each memory cloth sold commercially through a networking system will also contribute to the trust. The purpose of the trust is to promote similar self-empowerment projects, within communities and especially for individual mothers experiencing difficulty in educating their children, enabling women to develop their own creative, economic initiatives that will lead to personal autonomy.

Crafts-based images also have the potential to link developmental issues to issues of social justice. For example, in South Africa memory is being connected through the *Amazwi* cloths to notions of social justice in order to be truly transformative. In developmental terms, decisions for societal transformation cannot ignore the gendered experience of conflict and violence and these images provide a valuable means of memorializing the past in order to prevent further repression and discrimination. Projects like *Amazwi Abesifazane* offer new perspectives on locally based initiatives concerning empowerment and social justice, drawing on the centrality of culture to development and proposing an alternative to neo-liberal development with an emphasis on community rehabilitation.

We might think of these images as part of counter-discourses to dominant development discourses that seek to erase or 'sanitize' the polarizing effects of neo-liberalism and the devastation of diseases like HIV/AIDS. For example, Simon Lewis (2000) argues that contemporary representations of South Africa

and the apartheid past are very often sanitized (primarily by the business community) for international consumption, with a renewed confidence in the significance of sport, expenditure of money and organized leisure, the recycling of old images of wild animals and exotic landscapes, and the transforming of unacceptable racial exclusivity into acceptable class exclusivity. In contrast, cultural workers such as policy-makers, historians, teachers, writers and artists see the local processes of re-making and re-presenting South Africa as 'ongoing projects of considerable urgency, complexity, and precariousness, projects in which the often uncomfortable de-sanitizing of apartheid era stories and images plays a key role' (Lewis, 2000: 47). The gap between 'entre-preneurial empire-builders' and 'community-minded nation-builders' has widened since the ending of apartheid in 1994. As Lewis attests, while historians and artists have been labouring to create a 'new' South Africa that can come to terms with its violent past and the suppressions and misrepresentations of that past, 'South African business has tended to want to take 1994 as a marker of an end of history or an end of politics' (Lewis, 2000: 47). Crafts-based images are important, therefore, in preserving the memories of the people who experienced the 'minutiae of social and community life under apartheid'.

Crafts-based images are also of significance to broader issues of gender and development. They give voice to marginalized women in the development process and restore their historical agency to the creation of national identities. In emphasizing catharsis, economic empowerment and social transformation, they can play a significant role in societal transformation at both local and national levels, particular around notions of women's empowerment and emancipation. For example, the reconstruction of post-apartheid South Africa and the development of a viable democracy requires acknowledgement of the central role that women play in consolidating the building of nation, homes and communities

237

and of the gendered constraints and inequalities that still shape their lives. Memory cloths are a powerful way of acknowledging the agency of ordinary women and recounting lived experiences of daily struggle both in the past and in the present. Their radical potential lies in the fact that they can be used to counter the erasure of poor people's historical agency. For black women, the simple act of publicly telling a story in their own language has provided, and continues to provide, a sense of symbolic liberation. Crafts-based images are, therefore, rich in potential for development research.

Conclusion

No vision is natural or objective and there is no interpretation of social action through visual images that can claim to be definitive. All uses of visual images rest on specific ways of seeing and our experience of the world is always mediated. Our way of seeing is always shaped by a broader social and cultural milieu (which might include constructs like photography, film, industry, advertising, aesthetics, religion, tourism and education). In other words, all images are mediated to some extent and are only ever partial ways of organizing worlds. Despite this, the use of images, films and photography is potentially extremely useful to development researchers, especially given calls for a more culturally informed approach to development and the urgency to move away from purely economistic analyses (Prabhu, 2003). This is particularly

significant for gender and development and studies of/with people most marginalized within their own societies.

Images, film and photography provide a means by which to understand the lives and agency of women and poor people in all their complexity. Such an understanding opens up possibilities for reading development that can take into account multiple spaces, especially those inhabited and generated by women and other marginalized groups, and unconventional types of action, with a new understanding of 'production'. This raises the possibility of a more complete, nuanced understanding of women and poor people in the context of development, which engages their creative resistances to various hegemonic forces. As Appadurai (2004) argues, there is a need to strengthen the capacity of the poor to exercise 'voice' – treating voice as a cultural capacity – because it is not just simply a means of inculcating democratic norms but of engaging in social, political and economic issues that work best in their cultural worlds.

In this chapter, I have demonstrated how visual images provide ways in which these voices might be activated and understood in potentially radical and empowering ways. I have also outlined some ways in which visual imagery might be used in development research. Ideally, more than one method would be used to triangulate the information generated, but the development researcher might consider all of these approaches in adapting to the contingent realities of 'fieldwork'.

QUESTIONS FOR DISCUSSION

1. Mediated vision: consider your taken-for-granted images of developing world contexts and where these come from.
2. What other kinds of visual images might be used in development research?

(Continued)

(Continued)

3. Consider the logistical issues involved in using video, photography and other images/image-based methods.
4. How might visual methodologies connect to broader issues of human, social and economic development?
5. Can you think of examples where participatory video or auto-photography has been used in developed world contexts?

Further reading

Banks, M. (2001) *Visual Methods in Social Research*, London: Sage.

Kindon, S. (2003) Participatory video in geographical research: a feminist practice of looking?, *Area*, 35, 2: 142–153.

Pink, S. (2001) *Doing Visual Ethnography,* London: Sage.

Rose, G. (2001) *Visual Methodologies: An Introduction to the Interpretation of Visual Materials*, London: Sage.

Website

239

http://www.cas.org.za (Create Africa South and *Amazwi Abesifazane* archive)

References

Appadurai, A. (2004) The capacity to aspire: culture and the terms of recognition, in V. Rao and M. Walton (eds), *Culture and Public Action*, Stanford, CA: Stanford University Press.

Banks, M. (2001) *Visual Methods in Social Research*, London: Sage.

Cook, I. and Crang, M. (1995) *Doing Ethnographies*, Norwich: Environmental Publications.

Espelund, G., Strudsholm, J. and Miller, E. (2003) *Reality Bites: An African Decade*, Cape Town: Double Storey.

Frost, N. and Jones, C. (1998) Video for recording and training in participatory development, *Development in Practice*, 8: 90–94.

Harper, D. (2003) Framing photographical ethnography: a case study, *Ethnography*, 4, 2: 241–266.

Kindon, S. (2003) Participatory video in geographical research: a feminist practice of looking?, *Area*, 35, 2: 142–153.

Lewis, S. (2000) Sanitising South Africa, *Soundings*, 16: 46.

Morrow, S. and Vokwana, N. (2001) 'Shaping in dull, dead earth their dreams of riches and beauty': clay modelling at e-Hala and Hogsback in the Eastern Cape, South Africa, *Journal of Southern African Studies*, 27, 1: 137–161.

Pink, S. (2001) More visualizing, more methodologies: on video, reflexivity and qualitative research, *The Sociological Review*, 49: 586–599.

Prabhu, A. (2003) Mariama Bâ's *So Long a Letter*: women, culture and development from a franco phone/postcolonial perspective, in K.-K. Bhavnani, J. Foran and P. Kurian (eds), *Feminist Futures: Re-imagining Women, Culture and Development*, London: Zed, pp. 239–255.

VMSDFI (2001) Meet the Philippines Homeless People's Federation, *Environment and Urbanization*, 13, 2: 73–84.

25

Using Archives

Michael Jennings

What is an archive? What can archives tell the researcher? What questions should the archive be asked by the researcher? How does one use the archive? What are the challenges and ethical dilemmas of using the archive?

Introduction

The archive is mostly thought of as the natural territory of the historian: dusty documents in old files, closed to public access for years. What use, one might ask, can the archive have for the type of research that is focused on the present or dedicated to informing future policy debates? There is an understandable tendency in undertaking development research to stress the human element. However, archive sources are an important, and all too often neglected, source of useful information about development processes and practice, the evolution of and shifts in policy formulation, debates amongst development practitioners and analysts, and so on. Archives can provide what a reliance on contemporary-focused documents and other participatory research methods can sometimes leave out: the long-term context of a particular programme or policy.

Development projects are not single events, untouched by past experiences or uninfluenced by previous successes and failures. In order to place the research into a wider context, the researcher needs to be aware of the *longue durée* nature of development. It has a past as well as a future, and it is a past that cannot be ignored if the research is to speak to a wider audience and not simply be a narrow snapshot of a fixed moment in time.

Increasingly within the development sector, the importance of fully understanding the historical context of interventions and broader policy has been recognized. In the past, explanations for why Africa has remained poverty-stricken (indeed, has become more so) over the past four decades have remained polarized between those who blame the colonial legacy and those who target the fecklessness of the post-independence African governments. To some extent, both camps have based their arguments on polemical diatribes, on the perceived strength of the logic of their positions, rather than on actual evidence and facts. In recent years, a more nuanced narrative of African poverty has emerged that has considered its historical roots, as well as the shifts and turns in policy at national and international levels that have served to mitigate, or worsen, poverty.

The Africa Commission Report, published by the British government in March 2005, deliberately looked at the history of development and development policy in Africa to help find the way forward. The report examined the impact of international trade policy over the past 50 years in leaving African economies more vulnerable; the record of broken promises by the rich world despite a half-century of rhetoric about vanquishing poverty; the legacy of geography and climate on African societies; and its history of colonial oppression and subsequent failures of governance following independence. In other words, African poverty, according to the Africa Commission's report, is inextricably rooted in its history, and the history of international policy towards that region (Africa Commission, 2005: 21–29). Policies which are designed to meet the needs of today and tomorrow reflect the events of yesterday. The analysis of the failure of past policies (such as Structural Adjustment, the easy provision of credit to developing nations in the 1960s and early 1970s, the failures of central planning, etc.) inform perceptions of how policy should be constructed anew, but only if the lessons of the past have been learnt and learnt well.

The need to properly understand the past is important not just for a full comprehension of the causes of poverty, or the turns and shifts in development policy. One of the failures noted by many researchers in development organizations is that of a lack of institutional learning (Van Brabant, 2001). Organizations, in focusing on the future, spend little time reviewing past programmes, projects, successes and failures. In other words, institutions from the smallest non-governmental organization to the largest international organization frequently display a marked absence of organizational memory: they have forgotten

their past, and thus cannot learn anything from it. The demands of institutional learning – that organizations involved in development understand what it is they are doing, why they are doing it, and what they and others have done in the past – is regarded as one of the key requirements for a more efficient, more effective development sector. As Ian Smillie (1995: 241) notes:

> Knowledge, combined with heart and commitment, has always been a key to development, and moving away from *ad hoc* charitable amateurism towards lasting, longer-term solutions, and the policies needed to sustain them, will require politically aware, focused, specialised organisations that can learn, that can remember and share what they learn, and that are prepared to build on what they remember.

If the key to change is knowledge, then that knowledge must be as all-encompassing as possible, reflecting not only the present, but the past from which the present was formed.

The archive is indispensable in this, whether it be a national record, as housed in institutions such as the British National Archives (formerly known as the Public Record Office), a store of files and papers that document the work of an individual non-governmental organization (NGO), or collections of letters that speak to the experience of someone living or working in the area in which the research is based. But what is an 'archive', and how can it be used to draw out the essential information that is necessary to the research process? This chapter will examine how archives can contribute to development research, why they may be important, if not vital, to that exercise, and some of the potential challenges that archive research presents.

What is an archive?

The *Oxford English Dictionary* (1989) defines an archive as 'a place in which public records or other important historic documents are kept', or an 'historical record or document so preserved'. The key word is 'historic'. Archives are essentially records of the past. The archive refers to a collection of documents relating to a particular organization which are no longer in active use. Depending on the nature of the archive, they may consist of personal letters, internal memoranda, minutes of meetings, policy documents, drafts and final versions of statements, speeches, and comments on individual documents within a file or collection. Archives might contain photographs, film, video, even objects, all linked to the organization from which the records have been collected.

The archive, then, is a collection of papers and written records from a specific organization or individual that are officially 'closed' and no longer in use. So, for example, a record of minutes from quarterly meetings locked in the office filing cabinet would not be considered an archive. However, at the end of the administrative cycle during which regular access to those minutes by all the attendees and responsible staff is necessary, those minutes might be placed in a file along with other minutes from previous years. They are no longer required on a day-to-day basis, and are kept as a record of decisions taken in the past. They have been archived.

What can archives say?

Given the historical nature of archives, development researchers might question their use in policy-focused and contemporary research, especially when some archives (particularly archives of national governments) may restrict access for up to 30 years after the file has been closed. However, many people working on development issues are increasingly discovering that archives are proving an invaluable, and sometimes essential, source of information and knowledge.

Current policies, individual projects and programmes do not operate in a temporal vacuum. Policies and development narratives have emerged over time, in response to past failures, new fads and fashions, and changing needs and interest groups. Knowledge of the historical antecedents of current development practice are vital to understanding why things are done the way they are today, and how they might be done in the future. The archive can offer vital information on such processes to the development studies researcher.

For example, one researcher working on the refugee crisis in western Tanzania during the mid-1990s used the Tanzanian National Archives to examine what had occurred during previous large-scale influxes of refugees in the 1960s and 1970s. Tanzanian refugee policy had been developed in response to successive waves of people fleeing violence and terror, and hence this past was critical in understanding the present. Another research project looking at the role of NGOs in development and humanitarian aid examined Oxfam-UK programmes in Tanzania in the 1960s and 1970s. Through analysis of the archived files of projects funded and supported by Oxfam, the project was able to detect patterns that emerged over the long term, shifts in those patterns, and hence judge to what degree the NGO met its aims of impacting upon poverty and social deprivation in that country. The archives allowed for a comparison of over 100 different projects over a long period and thus provided a level of analysis that would not have been possible by studying a few current or recently ended projects.

A project designed to offer a critique of definitions of development that regard it purely as a benign force, along the lines of Chambers's 'good change' definition (Chambers, 1997: xiv) also made extensive use of archival material. The project sought to examine how development has often been used as a peg upon which to hang a series of political (sometimes relatively benign, often less so) policies and actions. In order to demonstrate this, the archival research looked at drafts of various development plans, internal memoranda

243

to government and administrative officials, reports by planners, implementers and other officials, and other key documents to show how political imperatives and interests, not the desire to improve living standards *per se*, lay at the heart of much development planning and policy. Again, only a long-term perspective, and the ability to see internal government documents, allowed such analysis to be made. The research, put simply, could not have been undertaken without the archive.

Of course, some might argue that their research project, looking at a single project or programme today, does not need such a perspective. However, archives can give insights as to why that project was proposed, problems found in implementation as well as the raw, unpolished evaluation data that is later refined for production of the more publicly available reports. Archives show the divisions between different members of an organization before a decision, to which all members publicly subscribe, is reached. In other words, while 'grey literature' may be more easily available, it can often represent the public face of an organization, a project or a policy. The archive reaches into the innermost sanctums where dissent, debate and discussion exist. The archive allows the private voice to emerge from behind the public face.

How do I interpret the archive?

The material kept in archives is considered by researchers to be less a document of record than an indication of the worldview of the author or institution that has produced it. The organizational and individual assumptions and interests shape the way that facts have been presented, and lead to some groups being marginalized and rendered invisible (e.g. the role of women, gay and disabled communities, etc.). Archival documents *may* contain facts, but those facts have been filtered through the author and the organization of which the writer is a member. The researcher may then ask what the purpose of the archive is, and whether anything can be gathered from the archive. The answer is yes. However, it requires the active engagement of the researcher with the archive. The researcher is not, and cannot be, a passive observer of a document.

All archival documents need to be interpreted through three essential questions: *How* did the document come into being (is it a commissioned report, an internal memo, a letter from one individual to another)? *When* was it prepared (is it a contemporary account or produced later after an event)? And, most importantly, *why* was the document produced (to lobby for a particular policy, to push the claims of an interest group, to justify a past success or failure)? Archival research is, then, part of the interpretivist tradition, and where quantitative data from an archive is used (e.g. from surveys or other statistical data) these considerations must be borne in mind.

How do I use the archive?

The organization of archives

The most difficult task facing the archival researcher is to decide which file, or collections of files, is relevant to the particular research project. In smaller collections, such as those of NGOs, this task might be easier. But for archives of larger organizations, deciding which departments or groups might have had an input relevant to the research can be a challenge. The researcher needs to have an historical understanding of shifts in the administrative structure in order to identify which collections might be relevant. For example, the current Department for International Development will store its documents as a ministry in itself. However, it used to be known as the Overseas Development Administration (part of the Foreign Office). Further back, funding for colonial development projects were largely run from the Colonial

Office, with inputs from other departments. Finance, trade and foreign affairs ministries might also contain information on development, even if their primary focus is not on such issues.

While the archive might seem a frighteningly complex and fractured place on first visit, subsequent trips and use serve to simplify the process. The key to effective use of the archive is understanding how the collection has been organized. Although there are many different ways of organizing a collection, there are some standard features common to most. An archive collection will generally consist of documents produced by or pertaining to an individual organization or institution. The map that guides you through the collection and allows you to identify the files you require is the hand-list (which is increasingly a web-based catalogue allowing you to use key words to search for documents). The hand-list will generally be organized departmentally, regionally, chronologically and/or thematically, depending on the nature of the individual archive collection. They tend to give the title of the individual file (e.g. a file relating to a specific policy or issue), the origin of the file (from which department the papers have come, or which field office), and the location of the file (a code which guides the archivists to the exact location of your file in the storage area).

A degree of lateral thinking is required in looking for files. For example, information relating to health policy in a country might be found in Health Department files. However, it might also be found in files relating to the implementing agency (e.g. a faith-based organization such as a local mission, a non-governmental organization or local community group).

Below are three examples of different archival collections, and how they have been organized. While this is not an exhaustive account of the ways in which collections are collated, it should give some guide as to how archives are organized.

National records I: the National Archives, UK

The National Archives in Kew, London, formerly known as the Public Record Office, houses the British government papers. Archives are organized into departmental groups, and then into subject and period. Most records relating to British overseas interests and policy will be kept in the Foreign Office and Colonial Office papers. Thus researchers working on Africa would go first to the Foreign Office hand-list (or Colonial Office for papers relating to the colonial period). The collection is divided into specific files which might relate to a particular section within the Department, or to a specific policy issue. Relevant files might also be kept in other Departmental collections, depending on whether that particular Ministry had a role to play in the issue under consideration. Materials relating to British NGOs and charities will be in the files relating to the Charity Commissioners, as well as appearing in other departmental collections (such as, again, the Foreign Office).

Under British law, most official papers are closed for 30 years. As a researcher in 2005, the most recent documents that would be on open access would date from 1975. Any file that ended in 1977 would remain closed until 2007. Other national archives allow for many government papers to be made available to the public immediately. Each archive will show the access rules for its collection.

The Freedom of Information Act, which came into force in January 2005, will change some of these access rules. Individuals can request certain documents and information on particular issues from the relevant public bodies (although such requests will not always be met). However, the rule that most official documents (regardless of whether requests for viewing were denied at the time of their production) will be on open access after 30 years remains the case.

National archives II: 'Nyaraka Za Taifa' ('National Archives'), Dar es Salaam, Tanzania

The national archives of Tanzania follow a similar pattern: papers relating to a particular ministry or government department are kept together. However, the colonial era and postcolonial administrative policies have led to more complex arrangements in the cataloguing of documents. Collections relating to the period of German colonial administration (from the 1880s to 1917) are kept as a separate collection. The British colonial records (1918–1961) are divided into Secretariat files (the administrative equivalent of 'the Ministry'), and regional files containing reports and documents relating to regional administration. In the independent period, the Tanzanian government instituted a policy of 'decentralization', establishing local Ministerial offices in each region in the country. Ministerial documents from this period are thus catalogued as both ministerial and regional files. However, changes in the regional structure between colonial and postcolonial periods mean that some 'regional' files belong to regions that no longer officially exist, and some colonial-period files are filed under the current regional structure.

A researcher seeking to look at archives related to, say, development interventions in southern Tanzania over the course of the twentieth century would thus need to consult the hand-lists of secretariat and ministerial files, as well as those for the Southern Province (the colonial administrative unit) as well as those for the current regions of Lindi and Mtwara (among others). If the parameters of the research project go back far enough, the researcher might also need to look at German-period archives. Information on health-related projects in Tanzania would be found in files from the Health Secretariat and Ministry, as well as in the regional file collection.

National archives III: The National Archives of India

The National Archives of India again follow a broadly similar pattern (as, indeed, do most national collections). Unlike the British or Tanzanian archives, it contains more than just public records, and divides its collection into four distinct categories: public records (i.e. official papers); 'oriental records'; manuscripts; and private papers. The material stretches over a much longer period than that for many African countries, containing papers related to the later Mughal period, those from the East India Company and British-rule eras, and collections documenting the post-independence government. Papers are kept closed for 25 years, and those stored under the Official Secrets Act for significantly longer.

Records relating to the colonial government of India are divided into 'A' Proceedings and 'B' Proceedings. The former includes much material that is duplicated in the British National Archives (the former colonial power in India). The 'B' Proceedings consist of material that is found only in India. The collection is catalogued according to the government department from which the material originated. There are also individual state archives which contain the collection from the provincial government (divided into departmental collections). There are also district-level archives, although the collection can be patchy.[1]

In order to access the archives, foreign nationals are required to hold a letter of introduction from their sponsoring institution as well as from their embassy or consulate, and the permission of the Head of Archives. Requiring official permission is not unusual for national collections. In Tanzania, for example, researchers require a research permit (which they must pay several hundred dollars for) as well as a contact in a Tanzanian university.

Organizational archives: the non-governmental organization

Over the past decade or so, NGOs have opened up their documents to researchers, granting different levels of access, with different rules regarding how those documents can be used in published and unpublished research. Such collections may be housed in libraries of other institutions (e.g. the Christian Aid archive is based in the archive collection of the School of Oriental and African Studies) or kept by themselves (as is the case with the collection of papers relating to the British NGO Oxfam).

Although each individual agency will catalogue its collection in line with its own organizational structure, many follow a general pattern of dividing their collections, first, according to country or region, and then into individual project/programme or local partners. There will normally be a heading or several headings under which central administration, committees and related documents are stored. NGO archives will also typically contain copies of leaflets, fact sheets and other publicity material produced in the past, which can be extremely useful in comparing the public and private face of a programme of agency as a whole.

Most NGOs restrict access to files for programmes and projects that are still current. Additionally, many organizations will insist on researchers agreeing to submit any work based on the archive collection for comments prior to publication or dissemination. This causes some researchers problems, fearing that organizations are seeking to stifle comments that might be critical of the institution. However, this is largely not the case. NGOs, who rely on their reputations in order to raise funds and maintain a public profile, have a right to ensure that research does not misrepresent or misinterpret documents. For the most part, any comments will be useful to the

research project in giving an additional level of analysis and criticism, and few reputable agencies would attempt to prevent criticism, provided that criticism is based on solid and decent analysis.

Referencing the archive

As with all referencing, the key is to ensure that other researchers will be able to identify the precise location of a cited document. References should also give an indication of who the author of a particular document is, the date it was written, and where possible to whom the document was addressed.

For example, a report on malaria in the British army in Salonika during the First World War, kept in a file in the National Archives in London. The reference should include the location of the archive, the title of the report, and the page number on which the precise quote or information used can be found, and file reference number. The reference would thus look like this:

> *Report on the Incidence of Malaria in the Salonika Army in 1916*, p. 7. Public Record Office (PRO)[2] WO32/5112.

On the first use, the location of the archive would be spelt out in full, with the abbreviation in brackets which would be used thereafter. Hence the following reference – *Medical Research Committee to Col. Webb, re malaria at Salonika, 9 January 1917*. PRO WO/32/5112 – tells the reader that the document cited is correspondence from the Medical Research Committee (the author), to Colonel Webb (the recipient), written on 9 January 1917. The letter is in file WO/32/5112 (the reference one would write on the file request slip) and is located in the Public Record Office.

Let's look at some other examples.

The first time a document from an individual archive is referenced:

Community Development Department Division, Mbeya region, Annual Report 1963, pp. 3 & 7. Tanzanian National Archive (TNA) 465 D3/18.

Oxfam Field Director (FD) to Africa Desk, 23 January 1979. Oxfam Archives (OxA) Tan 64.

On subsequent occasions:

Mbeya Regional Development Committee minutes, 27 July 1965, p. 2. TNA 471 C5/44/2.

Oxfam FD, Grant Application Summary Form, 9 November 1976. OxA Tan 86c.

In each case, by ordering up the specific file and looking through it, the original document can be found by anyone wishing to check the document for themselves.

Potential challenges

The initial challenge is to identify where an archive might be based. While for national papers this is relatively simple, some organizational collections and those of individuals are sometimes harder to locate. Internet searches have made the task easier, and for a specific organization it is always possible to contact them directly and ask where their archives are housed and enquire as to their access policy.

Once in the archive, the challenge becomes one of identifying how that particular catalogue system works. The descriptions above indicate the main types of ordering documents, but in large collections it may take some time to find out all the headings and sub-divisions. It is important to understand the nature of the organization in order to work out how that collection has been catalogued. Most archive collections will have assistants who are able to help you find what you are looking for.

In developing countries archive collections tend to receive much less funding, and thus are frequently in a much poorer condition. This is especially the case in many sub-Saharan African countries. Lost or missing files can be a major problem (in a 10-month period of working in the Tanzanian archives, just under half the requested files proved to be missing), as can documents damaged through insects and climate and which are at a point of near disintegration. There is little that one can do about lost files other than exercise patience. It is deeply frustrating, especially as it always seems to be the most interesting-sounding file that is missing, but such are the challenges of undertaking archival research.

Ethics and good practice

The archive carries with it some ethical implications peculiar to the medium itself. The most important consideration is that of preserving the archive for future use. While the fragility of old documents will be obvious, the more modern collections of papers, reports, etc. that the development studies researcher will be using also require careful handling if they are to survive to become old documents themselves.

Documents should never be removed from the file, the building or the collection. This might sound obvious, but some researchers have been known to take one of multiple copies of documents from a file. Inevitably, if everyone did this, the copies would dwindle over time to one, which increases the risks of it being lost forever should damage occur, or an even less principled researcher decide to remove the last one. While it may be tempting to remove a document temporarily to make a copy, especially where time pressures are high and archive staff are slow, this should not be done. Removing a document, even temporarily, increases the likelihood of it being damaged or lost. Only archive staff should remove individual documents for photocopying, and researchers should build the time lag between initial request and final receipt into their research timetable.

Frequent photocopying damages documents, and where possible the researcher should transcribe the text by hand or on a laptop. However, there will be many occasions when there is no alternative to having a document photocopied. Digital cameras offer a less harmful alternative, and many archives allow the use of such technology. Some institutions forbid this, especially archives based in developing countries who use the fees from photocopying as a vital source of funds to maintain their often cash-starved collections. Arrangements can sometimes be made with the archivist whereby the researcher pays the same photocopying fee.

On some rare occasions, researchers in the archives of developing countries have been asked for 'facilitation' payments to speed up requests, finding lost files, etc. It should go without saying that researchers should not participate. It is more often the case that researchers themselves enquire about whether a particular payment would speed things up. This is both insulting to the archive staff and makes life more difficult for other researchers.

Conclusion

Archival research is an often neglected part of much social science research, especially that of development studies. However, it is neglected at a cost. It offers an access to material and information that cannot be found elsewhere. It is indispensable in providing a context into which data and knowledge gathered from other sources can be placed. It can show the evolution of policies and programmes. It can help break down the image of the organization as monolithic entity and reveal the divisions and contested notions that lie at the heart of institutions working in development. It can, ultimately, break down the public face and reveal the private heart. Archival research is often deeply frustrating: that missing file, the long wait, plodding through what can seem like an endless row of hand-lists of obscure titles and reference numbers. But despite these niggles, it is an immensely rewarding means of research, and one which can speak to development studies in a very real and meaningful manner.

Notes

1. Thanks to Mark Harrison, Director of the Wellcome Unit for the History of Medicine, Oxford, for advice on the Indian archives.
2. Traditionally, researchers have used the designation 'PRO' when referencing documents from the British National Archives. However, given the recent name change, 'NA' (for National Archives), or 'UK NA' might become common usage. Researchers are free to adopt such a designation if they wish, provided they make it clear in the very first usage that this is their referencing system.

249

QUESTIONS FOR DISCUSSION

1. What can archival research offer the development studies researcher?
2. What are the challenges of using archival research?
3. How important is the history of development in development studies research?
4. What type of information and data can be obtained from an archive that cannot be found through other research methods?

Further reading

Chambers, R. (1997) *Whose Reality Counts? Putting the First Last,* London: Intermediate Technology Publications.

Finnegan, R. (1996) Using documents, in R. Sapsford and V. Jupp (eds), *Data Collection and Analysis*, London: Sage, pp. 138–151.

May, T. (1993) *Social Research: Issues, Methods and Process,* Buckingham: Open University Press, Chapter 8.

Tosh, J. (1991) *The Pursuit of History: Aims, Methods and New Directions in the Study of Modern History,* London: Longman.

Websites

http://www.nationalarchives.gov.uk (British National Archives)

http://www.archives.gov.us (US national papers)

http://archiveshub.ac.uk (guide to UK-based collections)

http://www.informationcommissioner.gov.uk (the UK government officer in charge of freedom of information and access to official papers less than 30 years old)

References

Africa Commission (2005) *Our Common Interest: Report of the Commission for Africa*, London: Commission for Africa.

Chambers, R. (1997) *Whose Reality Counts? Putting the First Last*, London: Intermediate Technology Publications.

Oxford English Dictionary (1989) 2nd edn, Oxford: Oxford University Press. Available at: http://dictionary.oed.com/

Smillie, I. (1995) *The Alms Bazaar: Altruism under Fire. Non-profit Organisations and International Development*, London: Intermediate Technology Publications.

Van Brabant, K. (2001) Organisational and institutional learning in the humanitarian sector, in O. Barrow and M. Jennings (eds), *The Charitable Impulse: Non-governmental Organisations in North East and East Africa*, Oxford: James Currey.

26

Remote Sensing, GIS and Ground Truthing

Dennis Conway and Shanon Donnelly

Geographic Information Systems and geographic information science – GIS
Remote sensing data: passive and active sensor platforms and imagery
Imagery date processing: georegistration, atmospheric correction and topographic
normalization   Analysis and integration of remote sensing/GIS data   Monitoring,
mapping, classifying and analysing when doing development research

GIS: Geographic Information Systems and geographic information science

The emergence of GIS as both a disciplinary practice and a socially embedded technology represents an important change in the way in which the geographical is being conceptualized, represented, and materialized in the built environment.

As both a system of information processing and for the creation and manipulation of spatial images, and as a technology which is diffusing rapidly through the apparatuses of the state and the organs of business, GIS requires a critical theory reflecting sustained interrogation of the ways in which the use of technology and its products reconfigure broader patterns of cultural, economic, or political relations, and how, in so doing, they contribute to

the emergence of new geographies. (Pickles, 1995: 25)

Now derived from many private-sector airborne and satellite-based sensors and employed in a host of scientific activities, remote sensing (and its progeny, geographic information systems, or GIS) has a clear military pedigree. Aerial photography was first accomplished from tethered gas balloons in the mid-nineteenth century in order to survey battlefield positions, but came into wider use with the availability of aeroplanes in the early twentieth century. Beginning in the First World War, aerial photography achieved prominence as a primary source of military intelligence. The use of aerial photography steadily increased through the 1970s, with the high information demands of the Second World War, and, later, the Cold War. Thereafter, the development of orbital platforms increased the potential uses of remote sensing, but the time needed to retrieve and develop film and the spectral limitations of photographic sensors restricted their usefulness.

Satellite imagery has now replaced aerial photography in many applications, partly because it addresses the shortcomings of photographic technology and partly because of the suite of (non-military) orbiting sensors. These new platforms are a major source of consistent, continuous data for atmospheric, oceanographic and land use studies at a variety of spatial and temporal scales. The physical and biological scientific communities, and most recently the social and land sciences communities interested in global environmental change, have made extensive use of satellite image data for mapping, monitoring and inventories (Turner et al., 1994). The conversion of analog electrical signals to digital information now allows the collection of satellite remote sensing via telemetry in near real time. The growing demand for remote sensing data for scientific and commercial uses has increased the number of both governmental and private platforms. Decision support systems, management information systems, land use/land cover change monitoring and analysis, and geographical information science also use remote sensing data, in addition to more primary forms – going beyond 'ground truthing' of the imagery, to incorporate indigenous knowledge systems, participatory, interactive practices and local GIS mapping and monitoring into their institutional frameworks (ICIMOD, 2004: Tabor and Hutchinson, 1994).

We need, however, to heed Pickles concern (quoted above) that our monitoring and mapping of the geographies of sustainable development, global environmental change, and of natural resource inventories always need to be critically evaluated in terms of its societal and democratic responsibilities. Remote sensing or GIS for whom? This is the question that should always be a cautionary

qualification when evaluating or advocating applications of this socially embedded technology to people's (and their built environment's) development prospects.

Beyond this concern for social accountability, utilizing remote sensing and GIS approaches to doing development research must match the methodological sophistication of these computer-assisted technologies with social and environmental science agendas in the development field. Accordingly, this chapter introduces readers to the obstacles and opportunities, promise and prospects of remote sensing and GIS. First, these related fields of analysis and monitoring of the earth's surface are detailed. Then, 'doing development' is addressed.

Remote sensing data: passive and active sensors and imagery

The types of data gathered via remote sensing can be grouped into several broad categories according to the portion of the electromagnetic spectrum recorded by the sensor. Another useful distinction that can be made is passive versus active sensors. Passive sensors are those that capture wavelengths that are either reflected solar radiation or emitted thermal radiation. Aerial photography, both colour and black and white, records wavelengths of reflected solar radiation visible to the human eye. In addition to these visible wavelengths, multi-spectral sensors record wavelengths outside the visible range, including ultraviolet and infrared wavelengths. The specific portions and combinations of the electromagnetic spectrum, called spectral bands, that are captured by a sensor are chosen because of their usefulness in delineating specific types of feature, such as vegetation or atmospheric moisture. While multispectral sensors often have five to ten spectral bands, more recent hyperspectral sensors may record hundreds of spectral bands. In contrast to passive sensors, active

Table 26.1   A comparison of the resolutions of a range of orbital sensors

Sensor	Spatial resolution (m)	Temporal resolution (days)	Spectral resolution	Radiometric resolution (bits)
AVHRR	1100	0.5	5 bands	10
Landsat MSS	79	18	4 bands	6
Landsat TM	28.5	16	7 bands	8
Landsat ETM+	15	16	Panchromatic	8
SPOT HRV	20	Variable	4 bands	8
SPOT	10	Variable	Panchromatic	8
IKONOS	4	1.5 to 2.9	4 bands	8 or 11
IKONOS	1	1.5 to 2.9	Panchromatic	8 or 11
Quickbird	2.5	1 to 4	4 bands	8 or 16
Quickbird	0.61	1 to 4	Panchromatic	8 or 16
MODIS	250/500/1000	1 to 2	2/5/29 bands	12
Hyperion	30	16	220 bands	12

sensors record reflected wavelengths that are emitted by the sensor. Types of radiation used by active sensors include microwave (radar) and focused light (laser).

The potential utility of any remote sensing data is largely dictated by the *resolution* of the data. For this discussion, resolution is defined as the smallest homogeneous unit distinguishable in the data. The most common example is spatial resolution, but temporal, spectral and radiometric resolution issues are also of considerable importance in remote sensing. In digital remote sensing data, spatial resolution is synonymous with the size of one pixel. For example, the Landsat Thematic Mapper (TM) has a spatial resolution of 30 metres by 30 metres. Temporal resolution refers to the minimum time between data collection for a sensor. The satellite carrying the TM sensor acquires data for any given location on the globe every sixteen days and so this can be considered the temporal resolution of the sensor. Spectral resolution refers to the ability of a sensor to discriminate between different electromagnetic wavelengths. The Landsat TM sensor is said to have higher spectral resolution because it collects reflectance values in seven different bands while the Landsat Multi-Spectral

Scanner (MSS) collects reflectance values in only four bands. The term panchromatic is used to describe a single, wide spectral band that covers part of the visible spectrum, similar to a black and white photograph. The radiometric resolution of a sensor describes the precision with which the recorded reflectance values are quantified. The range of values that a sensor can measure is broken up into a number of divisions measured in bits or powers of two. For example, a sensor with 8-bit radiometric resolution can distinguish 256 (2^8) different reflectance values for a given band while a sensor with 12-bit radiometric resolution can distinguish 4096 (2^{12}) different values. The spatial, temporal, spectral and radiometric resolutions of a range of orbital sensors are shown in Table 26.1.

The availability and cost of remote sensing data varies greatly. Once a study period and location are chosen, the process of finding available remote sensing depends on the sensor. Often initially obtained by governmental programmes, archived aerial photography may be available through local governmental offices or private vendors. The available dates of aerial survey, quality of reproduction and cost also vary substantially. The cost and

253

availability of satellite remote sensing data is more standardized. Many governmental and commercial image databases exist on the internet and allow relatively quick searches of available data. While purchasing remote sensing data can be quite expensive, the data from some sensors may be legally shared without cost and archives of free images for download do exist. Several websites useful in locating data are listed at the end of the chapter.

Processing remote sensing data: georegistration, atmospheric correction and topographic normalization

The successful use of remote sensing requires that the data provides meaningful information about a phenomenon of interest. Image classification is the process of translating the reflectance values collected by the sensor to the conceptual classes of interest to the user. In concept, this process is one of classifying different combinations of reflectance values recorded in the different spectral bands of the sensor into different land cover types. In practice, however, there are several preprocessing steps that may be necessary to ensure the highest possible classification accuracy. While the necessary preprocessing steps vary by sensor and conditions specific to the study location, three tasks that are often necessary are *georegistration, atmospheric correction* and *topographic normalization*.

Spatially referencing a remote sensing data set can be accomplished by either image-to-image or image-to-map registration. While image-to-image registration is useful for change detection and is more easily accomplished, image-to-map registration is usually necessary as it allows integration with other spatially referenced data sets. Image-to-map registration is composed of two separate processes. First, the spatial location of pixels must be calculated and, second, the pixel value

must be calculated. The process of spatially registering a remote sensing data set is accomplished by assigning ground coordinates, called ground control points (GCPs), taken from a known source (e.g. topographic maps or with GPS) to identifiable features in the data set such as road intersections or buildings. Beyond the obvious rule that more GCPs are better, the distribution and accuracy of points must also be taken into consideration. Fewer GCPs that are spatially dispersed and accurate may provide as accurate a registration as a higher number of less dispersed or less accurate points. The presence of features suitable for use as GCPs may be an important consideration in determining the optimum geographic extent of a data set. The collection of sufficient GCPs can require substantial effort and so needs to be incorporated into field data collection protocols. The root mean square (RMS) error is a standard measure of spatial accuracy calculated by image processing software.

Once the pixel locations have been spatially transformed to the desired coordinate system, the pixel values must be resampled. Several resampling methods exist that balance the creation of positional error with estimates of how much the data values are altered. Nearest-neighbour resampling simply uses the value of the nearest pixel. While the overall distribution of data values is relatively unaffected, linear features such as roads or streams are more likely to have a broken appearance with this method. The bilinear interpolation and cubic convolution resampling methods use a spatially weighted average of pixels in a defined neighbourhood to determine the new pixel value. These methods reduce the positional distortion of linear features but the smoothing process can change the distribution of pixel values. Because georegistration necessarily alters the data, the order in which preprocessing and classification steps are undertaken can lead to differences in the final classification.

Because remote sensing data of the earth's surface must be collected through the atmosphere, variation in atmospheric conditions affects the apparent reflectance values collected by passive sensors. While numerous methods of atmospheric correction exist, Lu et al. (2002) group the calibration methods useful for Landsat TM data in the Amazon into physically based, image-based and relative methods. Even though the satellite carrying the Landsat sensors acquires imagery in the morning, local weather conditions, such as clouds, can limit the usefulness of any given data set. Tropical mountainous areas may be completely cloud free only very infrequently, reducing the set of usable data time points.

Inconsistent solar illumination due to variation in slope and aspect affects the reflectance values collected by passive sensors. Using band ratios can in some cases alleviate differences in reflectance values caused by topographic variation, but often auxiliary data sources, such as a digital elevation model (DEM) and sun angle at the time of image acquisition, are necessary. A variety of mathematical transformations are available for topographic normalization in which the reflectance differences caused by topographic variation are objectively standardized. In a study comparing the use of Landsat TM data in mountainous terrain in the tropics, successful topographic normalization required a non-Lambertian model where surface reflectance is not assumed to be equal from all viewing angles (Colby and Keating, 1998).

Image classification is the process of translating combinations of reflectance values into land cover types. Two broad categories of classification methods can be described. First, *unsupervised classification* methods employ one of a variety of clustering methods to find numerical patterns in the data. Parameters of the clustering algorithm, such as the minimum and maximum number of clusters, can be supplied by the analyst. The simplest and most common clustering methods employ one of several possible distance measures to group pixels based on the set of reflectance values derived from the spectral bands of the sensor. Texture, or the spatial pattern of values, may also be incorporated into unsupervised methods as an additional clustering consideration. Once a clustering of the data has been achieved, the clusters must then be interpreted to land cover types using other information such as field visits or aerial photography.

Supervised classification methods begin from a known set of land cover classes that have been identified in the field. The data collected in the process of ground truthing, called *training samples*, are used to construct the classes in several ways. *Parallel-piped classification* methods use the range of reflectance values in the training data to delineate areas in the data space that define discrete classes. A major disadvantage of this method is that data falling outside these areas must be classed as 'unknown'. *Minimum distance classification* methods allocate all of the pixels in a data set to clusters defined by the mean value of the training data sets. In addition to simple Euclidean distance, many other measures of distance have been defined for use in this type of classifier. While this method has the advantage of classifying all pixels, classes may overlap, decreasing classification accuracy. *Maximum likelihood classification* methods employ not only the mean value of training data but also the sample variance to better predict into which class pixels should be grouped.

While unsupervised and supervised classification methods are in some ways distinct, they are often used in conjunction in an iterative process of classification and field data collection to achieve a more accurate end product. Hybrid classification algorithms, such as the ISODATA classifier, employ user-defined cluster centres initially but iteratively search for cluster centres that decrease the distance of data values from the cluster centre. As improved but increasingly complex

255

classification methods are developed, user expertise must be taken into consideration when selecting a method (Lu et al., 2002).

The specific protocols used for ground truthing must be designed according to the desired land cover classes, the resolution of the sensor, and the precision of the georegistration. Many land cover classification systems exist, but tailoring the classification to the specific research objectives is important for both conceptual clarity and efficiency of field data collection. The spatial and spectral capabilities of the sensor must be taken into consideration when designing field data collection protocols, so that sample plots capture distinguishable areas and land cover types that will be useful for interpretation and analysis.

After a classification has been produced, the accuracy can be assessed by using a subset of the training data that was not used in the classification process. By comparing the land cover class assigned to a pixel from the classification and its known class from fieldwork over the entire set of testing data, measures of classification accuracy can be calculated. Classification accuracy is often reported in an error matrix where a row and a column exist for each possible land cover class. By convention, the columns usually represent the reference data derived from the field and rows represent the product of the classification. The usefulness of this type of error matrix is that specific class confusions can be easily recognized and addressed. Several common single measures of classification accuracy include the overall accuracy, a kappa statistic, and producer's and user's accuracy.

Analysis and integration of remote sensing data

Visual image interpretation is often the first step in analysing remote sensing data of any kind. Because the visual interpretation of aerial photography has been going on for more than a century, methods for identifying features are well described using commonly cited elements such as shape, size, pattern, shadow, tone, texture, and site (Slama, 1980). Beyond identification of objects in the image, measuring properties of those objects, such as height, length, area, perimeter and relative spatial relationships, requires further quantitative methods.

The analysis of remote sensing data from a single time point can be very informative, but understanding change over time is often of greater importance. Research on change detection methods is an active field. Jensen (1996) identifies several considerations for choosing a change detection method, including whether either time point needs to be classified, whether analysis will be qualitative or quantitative, and if specific 'to–from' change types are needed.

Remote sensing data are important sources of information about the condition of the surface of the earth. Understanding the processes that shape this condition, however, often requires the synthesis of many types of information. Geographic information systems (GIS) provide a powerful set of tools for incorporating different types of spatial data into a single database where relationships can be analysed. GIS facilitates analysis of spatial relationships, such as proximity and coincidence, as well as more traditional database queries on the attributes of digital spatial data.

While remote sensing and GIS provide the tools for analysing spatial relationships, incorporating any data into a spatial database requires that the data be spatially referenced. Some types of information, such as the location of a community well or a major road, are easily located and integrated with other spatial data sets. Locating (and spatial referencing) other types of data whose locations are not clearly defined, such as village boundaries, or whose patterns change frequently, such as the movements of livestock, may be beyond the method's scope. As discussed earlier, flows and movements, indeterminate functional areas of information dissemination, communication fields, transitional conditions, and many rapidly changing patterns and flows, are spatial features of people's life-worlds, even their development experience, that are beyond the capabilities of GIS and remote sensing measurement technology. There still remain scale and scope limitations to the use of these sensing technologies, that limit their application in the fields of development studies and global environmental change, despite the growth in their technological sophistication.

What remote sensing and GIS monitor and map, classify and analyse when doing development research

Satellite data acquisition is 'from afar', but 'ground-truthing' establishes the validity of signature associations, allowing classification and categorization rules to be formally sanctioned and verified. What then might be the development indicators – spectral signatures, spatial patterns, locational indices, and the like – that satellite imaging and derived GIS surfaces recognize, identify and map? To what uses can remote sensing imagery, GIS methods and their analytical rigour be put, which will enhance, improve or increase understanding of the patterns and processes of global environmental change, people's development and the sustainable development of our 'life-worlds'?

- If development signifies human-induced changes, which bring quality of life improvements to people and places, their 'spaces' and immediate geographies, then infrastructural improvements, landscape developments, settlement consolidation, farm enhancements, housing and neighbourhood environmental improvements, road development and surfacing, and so on would appear to qualify as quantifiable

signatures and indicators (Liverman et al., 1998).

- If human-induced change occurs 'in the name of development' or as a consequence of development initiatives promulgated by outside agencies (e.g. the hydro-power schemes of the World Bank or the Inter-American Bank, or some of the 'programmes of action' by Britain's Department for International Development, USAID, or Canada's International Development Agency) where the results are destructive rather than constructive, then remote sensing might also monitor these disastrous effects.

- If human-induced change occurs as a consequence of NGO activities or grass-roots communal endeavours, where the achievements of the small-scale development projects can be observed in terms of tangible biophysical outcomes, then remote sensing and GIS monitoring and mapping has utility.

- If human-induced change in regional and local land cover, forest cover, vegetative cover, crop diversity, or more complex patterns of anthropogenic-cum-biophysical changes come about because of global structural realignments, corporate penetrations and depredations, civil conflicts, and unruly, destructive warring, then these modifications of the earth's surface are 'developments' that need careful monitoring (Falconer and Foresman, 2002). Satellite data acquisition and analysis might very well be appropriate global monitoring systems for such wider-scale impacts and environmental changes at the continental level (National Research Council, 2002).

- If, however, development signifies societal changes in human mobility, where people's movement patterns are not at all reflected in biophysical alterations of the fixed environments of their homeland, or their temporary destinations, then remote sensing is unlikely to be of any direct use. Similarly, transportation flows,

257

communication flows and information flows might move along physical spaces, but satellite sensing and data collection is not conducted at the required temporal rate to provide useful estimates of these transfers. These spatial assessment technologies are at their best monitoring and evaluating spatial changes of landscapes, land covers, built environments, urban infrastructural change, suburban sprawl, peripheral expansion, infilling and the like. Patterns of movement, flows of people, capital, ideas, knowledge and other non-physical transfers, complex patterns of interaction, among other processes, cannot be easily captured, or estimated, using remote sensing.

- If, on the other hand, migration has developmental and environmental consequences, and environmental changes need estimating, then remote sensing and GIS depictions of the changing spatio-temporal rural and urban landscapes (see Figure 26.1), land, forest and agrarian covers add immeasurably to a 'mixed method' approach of this empirical scenario (Moran et al., 1994).

- If the mapping of spatial distributions, or the monitoring of spatial environmental change in GIS is technologically feasible, and the local IT environments and infrastructure are sufficient to support computer-assisted spatial decision support systems, then 'development activity' and 'interactive-project development' is feasible (Batty and Densham, 1996). Indeed, Yapa (1991) argues persuasively that GIS tools can be an 'appropriate intermediate technology' in helping bring about regional development via the introduction of creative programmes to help local communities use cartographically rich, local information systems when undertaking their participatory decision-making.

- Remote sensing imagery, GIS multi-layer sets of land cover, and GIS cartographic depictions of biophysical landscapes and the urban built environment can provide maps of the regions, territories and spatial

'systems of interest', which then serve as useful contextual frameworks for empirical investigations at more micro-scales (Falconer and Foresman, 2002). Patterns of deforestation or reforestation, patterns of urban sprawl, of suburban encroachment of wetlands, and of pioneer settlement of forest reserves can be mapped (see Figure 26.1), while the behaviours of the people involved – supply-side agents, as well as those involved more directly – are better investigated utilizing primary survey/interview methods.

- If development does not modify the biophysical or built environment in any tangible change of spatial form, landscape, land cover and does not have a physical manifestation which can be sensed and monitored by the array of satellite technologies currently in use, then remote sensing mapping is not an appropriate data-gathering method.

GIS systems of land cover information can, of course, be generated without recourse to satellite, air-borne or other remote sensing data, and they might very well help our examination of development consequences at the meso- or regional scale, if a relatively static situation is the case. This kind of spatial analysis – using census data, for example – is commonly relatively time dependent, and the best that could be hoped would be 'comparative statistics' efforts in which change between spatial distributions is inferentially, rather than directly, examined. Satellite data adds a temporality that is extremely valuable, unless cloud cover or other interruptions of image generation prevent regular enumeration and imaging. Image generation, with acceptable degrees of low-cloud coverage, is not always possible in some tropical regions, such as the Caribbean, or Central America's Panama peninsula (Conway et al., 2004).

Methodological and technological sophistication has prospered in both fields. Therefore, remote sensing and GIS and applied research

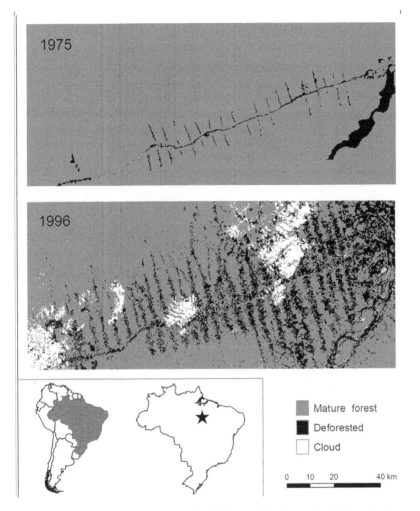

Figure 26.1   Pattern of development near Altamira, Brazil: image of the Amazonian 'fishbone' pattern (1975–96)

Source: Anthropological Center for Training and Research on Global Environmental Change, Indiana University, Bloomington, IN 47405

259

seeking answers to questions about environmental change, environmental hazard impacts, landscape and land cover changes have benefited considerably from these developments (Jensen, 2000: Turner et al., 1994). Development studies, as a specific domain, have not been an academic arena where remote sensing and GIS have found fertile avenues to pursue, however. The mapping and cartographic potential of these spatial technologies is considerable (Hall, 1993), but, to date, the contributions have been relatively modest. Exceptions, of course, can be found in the interdisciplinary research domain of 'human dimensions of global environmental change' (e.g. see Liverman et al., 1998; McCracken et al., 2002).

QUESTIONS FOR DISCUSSION

1. Assess the importance of the *scale* of the 'system of interest' or of the investigative context before pursuing the use of remote sensing imagery in development research.
2. Imagery availability in a usable and appropriate time–space sequence of coverage and its spatial resolution are especially important operational considerations when designing remote sensing and GIS frameworks for development research. Discuss.
3. What might be the significant 'signatures' to depict modernization and infrastructure developments in changing rural and forested environments as opposed to urban landscapes, urban built-up areas and peripheral environments?
4. How much 'ground-truthing' confirmation of remotely sensed imagery should be undertaken to examine the social and biophysical processes behind the spatial patterns the imagery and GIS maps provide?
5. How can the collection of necessary 'ground truthing' information for processing and analysis of remotely sensed imagery be incorporated into more traditional, social and biophysical fieldwork protocols?

Further reading

Jensen, J. (2000). *Remote Sensing of the Environment: An Earth Resource Perspective*, Upper Saddle River, NJ: Prentice Hall.

Liverman, D., Moran, E.F., Rindfuss, R.R. and Stern, P.C. (1998) *People and Pixels: Linking Remote Sensing and Social Science*, Washington, DC: National Academy Press.

Maguire, D.J., Goodchild, M.F. and Rhind, D. W. (1991) *Geographical Information Systems*, New York and London: John Wiley and Longman Scientific and Technical.

Moran, E.F., Brondízio, E., Mausel, P. and Wu, Y. (1994) Integrating Amazonian vegetation, land use and satellite data, *Bioscience*, 44(5): 329–338.

Websites

University of Maryland Global Land Cover Facility: http://glcf.umiacs.umd.edu/data/
United States Geological Survey EROS Data Center: http://edc.usgs.gov/
Center for the Study of Institutions, Population and Environmental Change (CIPEC): www.cipec.org
Center for International Earth Science Information Network (CIESIN): www.ciesin.org
Carolina Population Center: www.cpc.unc.edu

References

Batty, M. and Densham, P. (1996) *Decision Support, GIS and Urban Planning*. Working Paper, Centre for Advanced Spatial Analysis, University College, London. Available at: http://www.geog.ucl.ac.uk/~pdensham/SDSS/s_t_paper.html

Colby, J. and Keating, P. (1998) Land cover classification using Landsat TM imagery in the tropical highlands: the influence of anisotropic reflectance, *International Journal of Remote Sensing*, 19(8): 1479–1500.

Conway, D., Boucek, B. and Lorah, P. (2004) Environmental protection mechanisms in small island developing states and policy implications derived from scale issues: some Eastern Caribbean examples, in E.F. Moran and M. Batistella (eds), *Environmental Monitoring in Latin America*, São Paulo, Brazil: SENAC.

Falconer, A. and Foresman, J. (2002) *A System for Survival: GIS and Sustainable Development*, Redlands, CA: ESRI Press.

Hall, S.S. (1993) *Mapping the Next Millenium: How Computer-driven Cartography is Revolutionizing the Face of Science*, New York: Vintage Books.

ICIMOD (2004) Strengthening of training capabilities for GIS applications in integrated development in the Hindu-Kush-Himalayan region, Kathmandu, Nepal: International Centre for Integrated Mountain Development-Geoinformatics. http://www.icimod.org/focus/gis/gis_cap.html

Jensen, J. (1996) *Introductory Digital Image Processing: A Remote Sensing Perspective*, Upper Saddle River, NJ: Prentice Hall.

Jensen, J. (2000) *Remote Sensing of the Environment: An Earth Resource Perspective*, Upper Saddle River, NJ: Prentice Hall.

Liverman, D., Moran, E.F., Rindfuss, R.R. and Stern, P.C. (1998) *People and Pixels*: Linking Remote Sensing and Social Science, Washington, DC: National Academy Press.

Lu, D., Mausel, P., Brondízio, E. and Moran, E.F. (2002) Assessment of atmospheric correction methods for Landsat TM data applicable to Amazon Basin LBA research, *International Journal of Remote Sensing*, 23(13): 2651–2671.

McCracken, S., Boucek, B. and Moran, E.F. (2002) Deforestation trajectories in a frontier region of the Brazilian Amazon, in S. Walsh and K. Crews-Meyer (eds), *Linking People, Place, and Policy: A GIScience Approach*, Amsterdam, Kluwer Publishers, pp. 215–234.

Moran, E.F., Brondízio, E., Mausal, P. and Wu, Y. (1994) Integrating Amazonian Vegetation, Land use and satellite data, *Bioscience*, 44(5): 329–338.

Moran, E.F., Brondízio, E. and McCracken, S. (2002) Trajectories of land use: soils, succession, and crop choice, in C. Wood and R. Porro (eds), *Deforestation and Land Use in the Amazon*, Gainesville: University of Florida Press, pp. 193–217.

National Research Council (2002) *Down to Earth: Geographic Information for Sustainable Development in Africa*, Washington, DC: The National Academies Press.

Pickles, J. (1995) Representations in an electronic age: geography, GIS and democracy, in J. Pickles (ed.), *Ground Truth: The Social Implications of Geographical Information Systems*, New York and London: Guilford Press, pp. 1–30.

Slama, C. (1980) *Manual of Photogrammetry*, 4th edn, Falls Church, VA: American Society of Photogrammetry and Remote Sensing.

Tabor, J.A. and Hutchinson, C.F. (1994) Using indigenous knowledge, remote sensing and GIS for sustainable development, *Indigenous Knowledge and Development Monitor*, 2(1). Available at: http://www.nuffic.nl/ikdm/2-1/articles/tabor.html

Turner, B.L. II, Meyer, W.B. and Skole, D.L. (1994) Global land use/land cover change: toward an integrated program of study, *Ambio*, 23: 91–95.

Yapa, L.S. (1991) Is GIS appropriate technology?, *International Journal of Geographical Information Systems*, 5(1): 41–58.

261

27

The Importance of Census and Other Secondary Data in Development Studies

Allan M. Findlay

Why census and other secondary data are important in development studies
The changing context of census taking and analysis • • Problems in working
with census material in developing countries • • The strengths and
weaknesses of different secondary data sources • • Using secondary
data to highlight some key concerns about global population issues

Introduction

National census statistics and other secondary data sources are vital to evaluating development progress and making comparisons over time and between countries. These secondary data sources are also useful to development studies researchers wishing to provide a context for their own in-depth field studies and have been used by some to make wider generalizations from the results of small-scale questionnaire surveys and focused interview research. Secondary data (defined as information that has been collected by someone else) can also be useful in making an initial exploration of potential relationships in the development arena that can later be examined in more detail through primary fieldwork. Most importantly, census and other secondary data

can be used as essential evidence to test ideas in development studies, yet regrettably they are too often overlooked by researchers eager to base their understanding of the world only on their own primary data. This is a pity since national statistical data based on censuses, government surveys and registration systems, while in some ways problematic, provide the opportunity to tell a powerful story about important aspects of economic, social and demographic change in developing countries. It is the purpose of this chapter to explore the relevance of using such data in development-oriented studies.

Researchers in development studies should treat with great suspicion countries that have neither published census reports, nor other sources of reliable secondary data. Lack of reliable statistical information is not only an obstacle to the researcher seeking to evaluate development trajectories and the impacts of economic and social policies on a country's most important resource, its human population, but it also opens the door to politicians making un-testable assertions about the validity and success of their policies. Census information, whether it be about population characteristics, agriculture or other forms of production, service activities, consumption patterns or trade exchanges, should be an essential starting point for most evidence-based research concerned with past and future policy-making. This is so since census material and other official statistics provide a benchmark for what government and state organizations recognize (through their own data collecting systems) to be the state of affairs pertaining to the populations and economic systems over which they exercise power.

This chapter commences by considering the changing contexts in which census statistics are being gathered at the national and international scales. It then turns to investigating the nature of different data sources and the problems of using such material, before investigating a few key development trends evident in the statistics that underpin the Human Development Index.

New times, new data

Never before has technology made it so easy to collect and analyse census data. The penetration of modern transport networks to most of the world's inaccessible regions has reduced the need for population estimates to be made by aerial surveys of the kind that produced the Yemen census of 1975, for example. The vast majority of countries in Latin America, Africa and Asia have conducted detailed population censuses since 2000. It is not just the quantity of information that has grown but also the quality. Improvements in literacy have led to more accurate and meaningful responses to census questions and to other demographic

surveys. At the same time, advanced computing has made possible more rapid preparation of population counts and other statistical information in the wake of national censuses, while for researchers on the advanced side of the digital divide, the advent of the internet has given unprecedented access to census material from a wide range of countries (see list of websites at the end of the chapter).

The cost of collecting, collating and analysing census statistics has, however, been a severe challenge for many of the world's poorer countries. This has usually meant long delays in the release of more detailed cross-tabulations of census results, thereby reducing the value of censuses both to researchers and policy-makers. This is a huge frustration to all development-oriented researchers and especially to those concerned with current social and economic trends who often feel that census data are hopelessly dated by the time they are finally published. It is important to recognize, however, that it is not just developing countries that face delays in releasing census data. In the UK more than three years after the 2001 census, many detailed cross-tabulations were still not released. It is not therefore surprising that India found great challenges in 2001 in enumerating its population of 1.027 billion people. In general, however, it would be fair to say that in India, like most developing countries, the pace of publication of results has improved, making the most recent census much more useful to researchers than in the past. Although much remains to be done to improve the quality of secondary data, development researchers should therefore welcome recent trends. In the long run it is more costly for a developing country not to have the data on which to base policy and investment decisions. Without this information governments have no basis on which to plan the distribution of goods and services to their peoples, and researchers have no marker against which to evaluate the equity and efficacy of development policies.

Some researchers argue against work based on census data and secondary sources since it tends to involve the use of quantitative indicators. They argue that, even if the data could be trusted, human dimensions of development cannot be readily captured in numerical form and that in-depth qualitative research is more effective in extending understanding. No one could disagree with the view that it is easier to use numerical measures of, say, national incomes than of more ethereal concepts such as human development, but without global, national and regional statistics on human dimensions of development it would be all too easy for politicians to focus only on economic growth and to forget that the real end of development is improved human well-being. It therefore remains critical that development-oriented researchers analyse the ever-growing body of census statistics and other secondary data, and hold governments and others in positions of power to account. Secondary data can be used by researchers to reveal many of the consequences of development policies and will often be considered by others interested in evaluating whether governments are acting in an ethical and equitable fashion as more convincing evidence than small-scale survey material (Dorling and Simpson, 1999). For this reason, the last part of the chapter looks briefly at recent depressing trends revealed by the Human Development Index.

A map of the African and Asian countries that had no census in the last ten years (1994–2003) reveals that it is the locations with the poorest political stability and those with the harshest authoritarian regimes which have failed to enumerate their populations (see Figure 27.1). Thus, Afghanistan last had a census in 1979, Lebanon in 1970, Liberia in 1984 and Somalia in 1987. Little better are states like Myanmar and Nigeria, which both claimed to be organizing national censuses in 2005 but which had not had one since 1983 and 1991 respectively. As Table 27.1

shows, the proportion of countries with no recent census is highest in the Middle East and South Asia, with sub-Saharan Africa also weak in producing such data. More encouraging is the increasing number of countries now engaging in publishing census material. No fewer than 18 countries in Africa, Asia and Central and Latin America that held no census during the 1990s have produced population census data since January 2000. This in itself is a very welcome trend, but represents only the tip of a much wider data explosion, with most developing countries during the last decade placing a much greater range of secondary data in the public domain. It is important for the peoples of these countries that the data are analysed and that greater transparency is maintained, even if it forms only one aspect of the array of material studied by development researchers.

This section has provided evidence that the context of census-taking and publication has been changing rapidly in the developing world. Although much remains to be done, unprecedented opportunities exist for development researchers to analyse secondary data and to fail to do so would be to miss a major opportunity to examine the claims of those in power to deliver policies that benefit those whom they govern. Development researchers should continue to press governments and official bodies to be transparent about their activities, one aspect of which is publishing secondary data on a regular basis about the populations that are affected by their policies.

Problems of working with census data in developing countries

In developing countries, as elsewhere, researchers making use of the census immediately face a range of challenges. The first issue that researchers need to be aware of is that the data, simply because it has been collected by a government agency or large organization, may

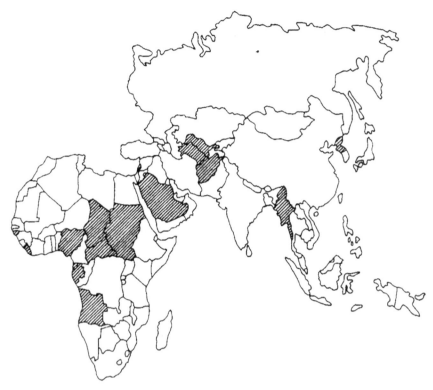

Figure 27.1 Countries in Africa and Asia with no census, 1994–2003 inclusive
Source: Geohive September 2004

not be accurate. This may be for political reasons or it may simply be because of the way questions are worded. The United Nations provides guidance on the design of census materials, and researchers can usefully compare the questions posed in any particular country with those recommended by international bodies (United Nations, 1998). Most census organizations run internal checks on questions that touch on sensitive issues such as income, religion or ethnic identity, but for good reason, people in all countries are suspicious of providing information on these types of topic. Any development researcher using census data therefore needs to think critically about what precisely has been recorded by the census-taker and what respondents might have been thinking as they responded to census questions.

In developing countries, particularly if researchers are looking at historical censuses or if they are interested in the more elderly part of the population, a fundamental problem is that of illiteracy and poor reporting on questions where the respondents may not be sure of the precise answers to questions. A familiar problem, for example, is that of the mis-reporting of age, with older people often not having precise registration documents reporting their year of birth. The net result is age-heaping, with people reporting their ages in round numbers, preferring to state for example that they are 60 or 65 rather than 62 or 63. The resultant heaping of ages will be evident if the researcher prepares an age–sex pyramid. Standard demographic methods exist to smooth age data to an approximation

Table 27.1 Proportion of countries with no census, 1994–2004, by broad region

Middle East/South and Southeast Asia	17.1%
Sub-Saharan Africa	14.0%
East Asia	12.5%
Eastern Europe and Central Asia	7.1%
Latin America, Caribbean and Central America	4.2%

Source: based on data from www.geohive.com

of the age structure that one would expect to find (Hinde, 1998).

Another problem that is widespread in secondary data in developing countries is gender bias in the reporting of key life events. Many countries have a history of widespread undercounting of both female births and also female infant mortality. An interesting treatment of this issue from a development perspective is offered by Kumar et al. (1997) in their analysis of the imbalance of male–female ratios in India. Equally, there is a significant literature on why maternal mortality during childbirth is under-reported as well as established methods for estimating the scale of under-recording of female deaths in government registration systems (Stanton et al., 2002).

Most demographic textbooks provide details on appropriate techniques to check on the quality of census data and to apply standard corrections (Hinde, 1998). Many of these techniques were first developed because of problems with data in developing countries. Where census or government survey data are incomplete, a range of standard statistical methods also exists to estimate the missing data from information that has been reported. There is not space here to dwell in detail on these techniques. The point is only to signal to the researcher using a census from a developing country that it is wise to start by considering the reliability of the data by running simple common-sense checks on the reliability of the variables in the census.

Of course, census data, like all secondary data, reflects the objectives and value systems of the organizations who pay for, design and publish the data. As such they are both somewhat inflexible sources of information relative to the theory-led objectives of most academic researchers as well as being problematic because they are inescapably cultural and political products. As long as the development researcher's starting point is to be aware of this (as well as of their own cultural and political position) there remains much value in analysing census results.

Inflexibility in census data arises because the questions asked by government offices in organizing censuses are seldom the same as those that the researchers would have used and, in addition, the census-takers may be less concerned than the researcher would be in critically evaluating the categories used to collect and later classify the data (White and Jackson, 1995). These problems are magnified in development studies because researchers are often engaging in cross-cultural research and are working in cultures very different from their own (Smith, 2003).

The fact that most countries publish census data for small spatial units, often known as Enumeration Districts (EDs), is particularly useful to geographers and planners. There is, however, a difficulty in using geographical data of this kind that all researchers need to bear in mind. It is the so-called 'ecological fallacy'. The fallacy arises when a researcher makes unjustified causal links based on aggregate statistics for an area, assuming that the data applies to everyone in the area. For example, if the census EDs in a city in the developing world have a high percentage of recent migrants and also have above-average levels of illiteracy, it would be false to assume that migrants necessarily have above-average illiteracy. It could simply be that recent migrants live in areas with lower-cost housing and that poorer families living in low-cost housing also have higher levels of illiteracy.

The census compared with other secondary data sources

Although this chapter has thus far dealt primarily with the national census as a source of data, this forms only one component of secondary data collection. In most states, large quantities of other survey material are produced on a regular basis. Here I focus only on demographic data because of space constraints within the chapter, but development researchers, whatever their particular interest, should explore other official statistics in order to triangulate these with the census picture. Differences may arise for many reasons (e.g. sampling error in survey material, differences of timing, differences in the efficiency of different research tools for data capture, etc.), but this should not be a reason for failing to compare the census picture with other secondary data sources. For example, in studying population change, at least two other key sources exist in most countries. These include the vital registration of births and deaths and large-scale sample surveys such as the World Fertility Survey (WFS) and Demographic and Health Surveys (DHSs). Balk et al. (2004) provide an excellent example of just how powerfully researchers can combine DHS materials with other spatially referenced statistics in West Africa. Unfortunately, registration systems in some developing countries remain weak both in terms of uneven

demographic coverage and also, as discussed above, due to selective under-registration, often of births (female under-registration) and deaths.

Statistical material from censuses, vital registration systems and demographic surveys are usually needed to ensure that contextual data are available to development experts to provide a wider picture than can usually be achieved from an individual researcher's isolated piece of intensive work. It therefore provides a means to interpret trends over time and to generalize about the processes responsible for demographic change. Strong census coverage is important to development-oriented studies because, arguably, censuses provide the best method to relate population data to a wide range of other socio-economic information at a particular point in time for a national or regional population as a whole. This often provides unique opportunities for researching inter-relationships between population and the key drivers of demographic change. Near-universal representation of a population has many advantages, including the possibility of detailed spatial disaggregation, which is of special value to planners and policy-makers. Poor coverage of the population (as happened in the past in, for example, Nigeria) undermines the value of censuses, but fortunately most developing countries have achieved much better and near-complete coverage of their populations in recent years. The continuity of census questions from one census to another is a further strong advantage, affording researchers the opportunity to evaluate trends from decade to decade and permitting the monitoring of long-term change.

Despite these benefits, census pictures of population face the difficulty of quickly becoming dated by comparison with continuously recorded registration data. Inevitably, it also can only offer a temporal snapshot of population relative to ongoing development processes, and for theory-led development

267

studies, the nature of the data collated by government offices seldom matches the precise issues of interest to social theorists. Researchers will find that, like all secondary data, census data are to some degree inflexible, having not been gathered specifically for the purposes of their work. In addition, there is the very real problem that development researchers can seldom check the quality of the data through their own primary research, since the census is not precisely replicable in terms of the date, methods and circumstances of collection. Nevertheless many development researchers would do well to include some questions in their primary fieldwork that are the same as those asked in the census in order to give them some idea as to how their small-scale survey relates to the wider picture provided by the census.

Unlike in the past, virtually all social scientists using secondary population data are now well aware that such statistics are socially and culturally constructed. They reflect the aims, attitudes and values of those who paid for their collection and reproduction, but this in and of itself does not render them worthless to the researcher in development studies. For example, some social theorists criticize the pre-set labels and categories within which data are captured by census-takers (White and Jackson, 1995). In reality, census categories relating to, for example, ethnicity or religion have changed considerably over time, reflecting how those in power have reconstructed labels in relation to their changing understanding of social groups and their behaviour. An interesting example of this is offered by Christopher's (2005) study of changing census definitions within Commonwealth countries over the last 200 years.

Having made a few generalizations about data sources, it is important to add three footnotes. First, it is interesting to consider the relative strengths of census versus registration systems for reporting particular types of demographic data. While registration systems are perhaps the most useful way of monitoring births and deaths over time and space on account, first, of the need for a continuous recording system of these key events and, second, the increasing probability of capturing these essential life events because of population dependency on nationally supported health systems, it is generally recognized that migration events are poorly recorded by registration systems. Even where recording movements of population is mandatory, it is very hard to police continuous registration systems, and large numbers of moves go unrecorded. For research on migration within developing countries, researchers are therefore likely to continue to be dependent on censuses.

Second, it should be noted that it is becoming increasingly possible to link different data sets over time. Not only is it possible to trace individuals and households from one census to another, but it is also possible to link census and registration data (including sometimes hospital registration data). Longitudinal data such as this may still be too expensive for many developing countries, but only through longitudinal analysis can development researchers escape from treating demographic events in space as a cross-section in time. Hopefully, developing countries will follow the more developed nations in linking census and other data sets to provide a richer tapestry of material for researchers to analyse. As longitudinal data increasingly becomes available, development geographers should strive to use these new resources to theorize how population geographies co-exist with other development geographies in the constant reshaping of space–time.

Third, it is important that development researchers recognize that as population data sets become more comprehensive, and as methods for analysing these statistics become more powerful through the use of GIS and other geo-referenced numerical techniques, so too the potential for geo-demographic statistics to be abused by those in power grows. Development experts therefore need

Table 27.2 HIV/AIDS by world region, 2003

Region	Number of adults and children with HIV/AIDS
Sub-Saharan Africa	25,000,000
South/Southeast Asia	6,500,000
Latin America and Caribbean	2,030,000
Eastern Europe and Central Asia	1,300,000
North America	1,000,000
East Asia	900,000
Western Europe	580,000
North Africa and Middle East	480,000
Oceania	32,000
Total	37,800,000

Source: UNAIDS (2004)

to lead debates over research governance and the potential unethical use of demographic information to the detriment of vulnerable population groups (Findlay, 2003).

Global population issues

This is not the place to explore the full range of global population topics that concern development researchers (Findlay and Hoy, 2000). For illustrative purposes only, the focus here is on two interrelated issues: first, the rising toll of the HIV/AIDS pandemic and, second, the setback in human development experienced over the last decade in at least 20 developing countries.

The United Nations Programme on AIDS suggested that over 20 million people have already died of AIDS and more than 37 million people live with the disease. Table 27.2 estimates that about 95 per cent of these are in developing countries. Health statistics show that the effects of the epidemic are very uneven geographically, with sub-Saharan Africa being the most severely affected region (25 million infected people). No less than 7.5 per cent of adults aged 15–49 in sub-Saharan Africa live with HIV/AIDS. At present South Africa is usually identified as having the highest absolute number of infections, but the prevalence rate

(proportion of adults infected) is higher in Botswana, Swaziland, Lesotho and Zimbabwe. Prevalence is also high in the Caribbean, and rates are rising fast in Eastern Europe, Central Asia and much of eastern and southern Asia.

One of the consequences of the global pandemic has been that many developing countries have seen the health gains of the last fifty years being erased (Barnett and Whiteside, 2002). The demographic impact of this tragic pandemic has been a slowing of population growth rates and, in some cases, the emergence of population decline (in Botswana, South Africa and Swaziland). No other infectious disease has been so aggressive in raising the mortality rates of young adults. Life expectancy at birth in South Africa was over 65 years in the early 1990s, but had fallen to less than 57 years by 2000. The selective death of young adults has rapidly reduced the economically active population with adverse effects being most noticeable in rural areas where it has been blamed for exacerbating famine by causing a reduction in agricultural production (Gould and Woods, 2003).

The AIDS pandemic has directly impacted on the main indicators of human development (life expectancy at birth, adult literacy and education enrolment ratios, and GDP perception in purchasing power parity). Of course human development is a much broader

269

Table 27.3 Countries whose Human Development Index dropped between 1980 and 1990, and 1990 and 2002

Period of decline in the HDI	Number of countries showing a decline in HDI	Countries whose HDI declined
1980–90	3	Democratic Republic of Congo Rwanda Zambia
1990–2002	20	Bahamas Belize Botswana Cameroon Central African Republic Congo Democratic Republic of Congo Côte d'Ivoire Kazakhstan Kenya Lesotho Moldova Russian Federation South Africa Swaziland Tajikistan Tanzania Ukraine Zambia Zimbabwe

Source: UNDP, 2004: 132

concept than can be captured by a single index. Nevertheless, it is sobering to reflect on why 20 countries experienced a drop in their Human Development Index in the period 1990–2002 while only three did so in the 1980s. Table 27.3 shows that the countries experiencing crisis are mostly in sub-Saharan Africa, but others are found in the states that emerged from the former Soviet Union.

While the downturn in the former Soviet bloc started in the mid-1980s with a drop in income levels, the reversal in the Human Development Index in the African states is strongly linked with the HIV/AIDS pandemic. Child mortality, for example, increased from 58 to 110 per 1,000 live births in Botswana between 1990 and 2002, with equivalent figures for Zimbabwe being 80 and 123. There

have also been reductions in enrolments in primary education. In the Democratic Republic of Congo, the net primary enrolment ratio dropped from 54 to 35 per cent.

Global population statistics such as these highlight powerful and tragic stories that require much deeper analysis by development researchers than has been possible here. They equally show that some countries appear to be much more active in terms of human development than others, despite the presence of malevolent national and international forces. Bolivia, for example, despite years of instability, has been able to increase its Human Development Index to a level comparable with Guatemala despite having a GDP per capita that is 30 per cent less. Development-oriented researchers in their enthusiasm for small-scale intensive research should not forget the need to also continue to make comparative analysis at a global scale, as a contextual base for evaluating the underlying reasons for differential performances of those global processes shaping the uneven patterns of human development.

Conclusion

The twenty-first century continues to produce rapid changes in the demographic regimes and the quality of life of populations around the world. Development researchers will continue to require high-quality census, registration and survey data to study these trends. More importantly, without reliable population statistics, researchers will find it hard to fulfil the key role of monitoring and evaluating whether those who govern the world's most vulnerable peoples are either doing what they claim in policy terms or saying what they are doing in terms of the equitable and ethical discharge of their duties. Quality population statistics remain a vital tool in development studies, and development-oriented researchers need to maintain their skills in handling and analysing this kind of data.

QUESTIONS FOR DISCUSSION

Discuss the following topics:

1. Studying the questions included and those not posed in a census in itself reveals much to the development researcher.
2. Research based on secondary data is only as valuable as the quality of data cleaning that the researcher has undertaken.
3. Development researchers should actively lobby for more accurate and more regular censuses to be taken in developing countries.
4. Census analysis too often proceeds without adequate consideration of research ethics.
5. Development-oriented researchers have devoted too much time in recent years to small-scale intensive research at the expense of wider contextual analyses using secondary data.

Further reading

UNFPA annually release a publication entitled *The State of World Population* (New York: UNFPA). This is a useful starting point for researchers who simply want quick access to comparative secondary data at national level for many developing countries. It is not for those who wish to work with census material in a particular country.

White, P. (2003), making use of secondary data, in N. Clifford and G. Valentine (eds), *Key Methods in Geography*, London: Sage, provides an excellent introductory treatment for those with a research project who wish to work on census material within a country. He examines why secondary sources are very valuable in providing a basis for comparative analyses relative to well-known measures of deprivation and poverty, measures of spatial unevenness and segregation, established classifications of population groups as well as for correlation and regression of influences on development.

Hinde, A. (1998) *Demographic Methods*, London: Arnold, is an excellent text for researchers seeking to use censuses and other secondary data as the starting point for demographic analysis. This publication points to various United Nations manuals that provide further guidance on how best to estimate from partial data the true nature of population structures in developing countries.

Websites

Useful websites providing easy access to a wide range of census and other demographic material include:

www.geohive.com – a country-by-country profile of the latest demographic census statistics for most countries. Population statistics are available on this site by region and for the major cities. The site also has excellent links to the web pages of most major national census offices.

www.prb.org – this site produces the annual world population datasheet as well as other demographic statistics at national level. It also has numerous sections on HIV/AIDS and reproductive health.

www.un.org/popin – a guide to population information on UN system websites, including a large number of national demographic data sets and UN demographic projections at global and regional level.

www.unicef.org/stats – UNICEF provides a useful site for comparative international development data on a wide range of topics.

www3.who.int/whosis – the World Health Organization has a range of country-level data that may be of interest to medical and health researchers seeking comparative data on developing countries' health profiles.

References

Balk, D., Pullum, A., Stoneygard, A., Greenwell, F. and Neuman, M. (2004) A spatial analysis of childhood mortality in West Africa, *International Journal of Population Geography*, 10: 175–216.

Barnett, T. and Whiteside, A. (2002) *AIDS in the 21st Century*, Basingstoke: Palgrave-Macmillan.

Christopher, A.J. (2005) Race and census in the Commonwealth, *Population, Space and Place*, 11: 103–118.

Dorling, D. and Simpson, L. (eds) (1999) *Statistics in Society*, London: Arnold.

Findlay, A. (2003) Population geographies for the 21st century, *Scottish Geographical Journal* 119: 177–190.

Findlay, A. and Hoy, C. (2000) Global population issues, *Applied Geography*, 20: 207–219.

Gould, W.T.S. and Woods, R. (2003) Population geography and HIV/AIDS, *Scottish Geographical Journal*, 119: 265–282.

Hinde, A. (1998) *Demographic Methods*, London: Arnold.

Kumar, N., Raju, S., Atkins, P. and Townsend, J. (1997) Where angels fear to tread? Mapping women and men in India, *Environment and Planning* A, 29: 2207–2215.

Smith, F. (2003) Working in different cultures, in N. Clifford, and G. Valentine (eds), *Key Methods in Geography*, London: Sage, pp. 179–193.

Stanton, C., Hobcraft, J., Hill, K., Kodjoojbe, N. et al. (2002) Every death counts, *Bulletin of the World Health Organization*, 79: 657–664.

United Nations (1998) *Principles and Recommendations for Population and Housing Censuses (Revision 1)*, Department of Economic and Social Affairs (Series M, No. 67), New York: United Nations.

UNAIDS (2004) *Report on the Global AIDS Epidemic*, New York: UNAIDS.

UNDP (2004) *Human Development Report 2004*, New York: UNDP.

White, P. and Jackson, P. (1995) (Re)theorising population geography, *International Journal of Population Geography*, 21: 51–74.

28

Using the World Wide Web for Development Research

Emma Mawdsley

The problems and potential of using the web in development research   The web as a medium of research   The web as the object of research   The web as a source of information   Cautions and caveats

Introduction

The World Wide Web developed with extraordinary rapidity at the end of the twentieth century, and is now unparalleled in terms of the speed with which an enormous variety of information can be accessed from a multitude of sites. The web is a rich, dynamic and exciting resource for any researcher, but it can have particular attractions for Northern-based students who are working on development issues, where geographical distances and travel costs can be prohibitive compared to study within the domestic context. Here it is not just a helpful or even essential tool when used in conjunction with fieldwork abroad, it can also allow researchers to do 'development research' even if they are, for one reason or another, unable to travel. There are more constraints to the use of the web in many parts of the 'majority world', but it can also be valuable for researchers in or working from the

South, especially where journals, books and official texts are unavailable or expensive.

Email and the web have done far more than provide faster communication and access to information. They have also created a new socio-technical environment, which itself constitutes a field of research, including within the development context. But while raising many exciting possibilities, there are a series of caveats that must be borne in mind when using the web for development research. As well as being subject to the generic cautions that can be raised in relation to any information source (to do with authorial positionality, the dominance of certain languages and points of view, and the degree of credibility), using the web raises a number of more specific concerns. This chapter will first briefly discuss the three main ways in which the web can be used for development research, and then turn to some of the problems and issues for consideration that arise when using the web for development research.

What the web offers to develoment research

The web can contribute to development research in three main ways. First, it can be a *medium of research*, through chat rooms, online surveys, email interviews and so on. Second, it can be the *object of research* – one can explore the role the web plays in development, who is online and what they are saying, and so on. Finally, and most obviously, it is a *source of information*, allowing access to a staggering amount of data.

The web as a medium of research

Over the last decade the web has opened up the opportunity for development researchers to contact people almost instantaneously, across the world, and online research methods are now increasingly being discussed and used (Best and Krueger, 2004; Jones, 1999; Madge and O'Connor, 2004; Mann and Stewart, 2000; Schonlau et al., 2002). Its strengths include the immediacy and relatively cheap costs of web use and email (once the equipment is in place), while problems include extremely uneven access and, for some, the fact that web-based communication is a rather 'impoverished' means of dialogue compared to face-to-face interaction. This section outlines briefly some of the possibilities that have opened up to researchers in terms of interviews, online surveys, focus groups and eliciting personal documents. As we shall see below, there are research projects for which the web is unlikely to be appropriate, such as those which require direct contact with poor, illiterate and rural people, but there are others where the internet can provide a positive advantage. These include research projects looking at extremely sensitive issues, such as the discussion of politics under certain regimes, where some respondents may feel more comfortable with the anonymity email can offer (in Gaza,

or Zimbabwe, for example). Researchers can also talk to people in dangerous zones to which they might otherwise be denied access. In other cases, internet-based research may not be ideal, but it can be the only feasible option, for example if travel is not possible.

The design of 'online methodologies' is subject to all of the 'standard' issues that confront any research project (which are discussed in detail elsewhere in this book). These include the choice of sampling frame, decision over which technique(s) to use, the precise phrasing of questions, which forms of analysis to use, and ethical considerations. However, these must be addressed within the very specific context of the internet. Some of these issues are technical, for example the pros and cons of web-based versus email surveys; using passwords to ensure secure respondent access; and making sure that both Mac and PC users can respond. Others are more 'practical', such as how to make contact with target groups and people, and designing and formulating the questions. There are also profound cultural issues, such as how to phrase explanations or questions in ways that make sense in the local setting. The potential for ambiguity is present in any conversation, but it is especially likely in cross-cultural, second-language exchanges without the advantages of visual cues or demonstrations. Some subjects may be much more socially or religiously difficult to discuss in some cultures (perhaps death or homosexuality), while many are so multidimensional they are difficult even to begin to express fully, or to capture some of their complexity. Email and the web can be more difficult terrains in which to negotiate these issues. Bearing this in mind, the following gives an indication of some of the ways in which the web has opened up the possibilities of distantiated research.

Interviews

Email now allows contact with distant people – say a worker in a small NGO, a researcher, or a member of an environmental group. Some consider email to be a rather 'thin' form of dialogue – the body language and gestures of face-to-face meetings that help us 'interpret' each other and which, ideally, help establish rapport, are absent from email. Others argue that the 'filtering out' of visual cues can encourage a more egalitarian form of communication, and reduce prejudice based on looks, dress, gender and dis(abilities). What is certainly true is that interpersonal skills are still important in email conversations, and that there are ways of promoting trust and someone's 'comfort' with the conversation, including clear-language descriptions of what you are doing and what you want to achieve, and sensitivity to language and the emotions being expressed. To some extent, it is about individuals – some people feel more comfortable and may have more time, privacy and interest in expressing themselves via email than others. Other advantages of email are that it allows people to answer in their own time, and by cutting and pasting, no transcription is needed (the mistakes, abbreviations and emphases are, in a sense, the email equivalent of 'ums' and 'ers' and other natural accompaniments of most conversations).

Online surveys/questionnaires

These can be a great way of accessing information from populations that might otherwise be inaccessible (because of travel costs, for example), but they demand very careful consideration, particularly in terms of sampling frames, identifying respondents, and design. More advanced surveys can demand sophisticated technical know-how.

Online focus groups

These are still a relatively novel methodology, and although they have been used productively (helped by new conferencing software), they raise a host of considerations, particularly the selection of participants, the choice of 'real-time' or 'asynchronous' meetings, setting up guidelines for the group interaction, dealing with time zone differences, differences in computer access and literacy, facilitation over the web, and so on.

Eliciting personal documents

Researchers have, in other contexts, asked respondents to write personal diaries and accounts, something that can also be requested and sent online. Again, there are a set of ethical and practical issues which are generic to the methodology (see, for example, Meth, 2003), as well as considerations specific to the internet – respondents are limited to those who can use and access a computer, and they may have issues of time, expense, privacy and so on.

As with any set of methodologies, a central consideration in these forms of research must be one's ethical obligations to one's respondents. These include a commitment to informed consent, representing respondents' views as fairly and accurately as is possible, protecting anonymity, and 'returning' findings. It is worth remembering that many people working in development (NGO workers, development agency employees, researchers) are often extremely busy. Although it can pay to be persistent, it is important to be sensitive to signs of reluctance to engage or fatigue. Finally, one should always observe 'netiquette' – good manners on the web!

The web as an object of research

The internet is not just another form of communication or location of data, but in itself a new environment. As Mann and Stewart (2000: 7) argue, 'the Internet is both a technological *and* a cultural phenomenon' (emphasis in the original). The internet can also, therefore, be considered as a field site for development researchers. Like every other aspect of development, the internet must be located within the structures and languages of

275

power – it is not a neutral technology, and it can be analysed as a part of the complex politics of domination and resistance. Thus, one can explore issues like the spread and usage of the web, and the ways in which it has affected people's knowledge, choices, social relations, attitudes and abilities (see, for example, Adams and Ghose, 2003; Mercer, 2004). One can also critically evaluate what is on the web – which individuals and organizations write, in which languages, and with what agendas. Diane Stone (2000), for example, has produced a fascinating analysis of the World Bank's 'Global Development Network'.

The web as an object of research is an especially interesting topic at present, given the fact that many governments, NGOs and development agencies are extremely interested in the role that information and communication technologies (ICTs) might play in development. They are investing in and tracking schemes that offer internet access to children, slum dwellers and small farmers, among others. For its supporters, the web offers poor people great new opportunities to join the knowledge economy, and to be connected and informed. The criticisms are more varied. For some, ICTs are broadly positive but not a priority (telephones, schools, roads and health

clinics could all be seen as more important). For others, ICTs represent another battleground, wherein global hegemonic forces seek to induct yet more people and places into the values, structures and processes of neoliberal capitalism. As always, though, there is resistance, with the Zapatistas' intelligent use of the web and email being the best known example. The 'anti-globalization' movement(s) currently make great use of these technologies too.

In terms of research methodologies, a couple of different approaches are suggested here.

(Participant) observation

One can observe (by 'lurking', in internet jargon), take part in, or even initiate various virtual communities – discussion groups, Multi User Domains (MUDs), chat rooms, usenets, electronic salons and so on. In doing so, one can explore internet subcultures and identities, the dominance or absence of certain groups (assuming that one can make some forms of identification), and how they are managed or even 'policed'. One problem can be how to identify discussion groups, even with the use of Google or Yahoo (see Dodge and Kitchin, 2000, for advice).

Box 28.1   Studying South Asian literature

Lisa Lau, a PhD student in the Geography Department at Durham University, analysed novels written in English by South Asian women. As well as a discursive exploration of certain themes within her chosen novels, she was interested in reader responses among 'domestic' (Asian), diasporic (Asian women living abroad) and Western audiences. As a part of her research, she joined an online discussion forum which focused on subjects that affected and interested South Asian women. She sometimes observed, sometimes took part, and sometimes initiated discussions on literary issues. The list members were all women, mostly but not all of South Asian origin, and lived around the world, although the majority were in the USA. For Lisa, it would have been impossible to reach this range of respondents in any other way but through cyberspace. Among other things, she found that:

(Continued)

(Continued)

the Non-Resident Indians living the States were larger in numbers, more vociferous anyway, don't hesitate to speak out and push forward. The Indians from India, for example, hardly get a look in, have much less access to the internet, and the result is that the cyberspaces for South Asian things are dominated by diasporic South Asians who create an image of South Asia that is globally consumed. (Lau, pers. comm., 2004)

Document analysis

The techniques of textual analysis can be applied to websites, allowing researchers to examine the (re)presentation of organizations and movements.

Box 28.2   Researching neo-Malthusianism on the web

As part of her dissertation on the persistence of neo-Malthusian discourses, Carole Segonds, an undergraduate at Birkbeck College (London University), analysed the official web pages of biotechnology companies. She wanted to see if any of them claimed that their contribution to greater *production levels* would help alleviate world hunger, and if so, whether they also mentioned the critical issues of entitlement, distribution or storage. This involved the deconstruction of both text and images to explore their discursive content.

277

The web as a source of information

Information that can be accessed from the web can be categorized in any number of ways, including qualitative and quantitative data, formal (e.g. official organizational websites) and informal (e.g. chat rooms). What follows is by no means comprehensive, or the only way of designating different sources, but it gives an indication of the very wide range of information that is available.

- Many *government* websites offer a wealth of data. As well as facts and figures about population, climate, economic indicators and trends and so on, they may have various maps (political, physical, resources, etc.). Many also explain the formal structures of government – the parliament, ministries, departments, and so on. Some also have policy statements and plans, which can be useful. For example, if someone was researching dams and development in India, one could look up the Ministry of Water Resources. Depending on the political set-up, federal states and other political and administrative sub-units may have their own websites, which may provide more detailed information on regional issues.

- *Political parties* may also have a website, detailing their beliefs, structure and manifestos.

- Multilateral *development agencies*, such as the World Bank, and bilateral development agencies, such as the Department for International Development (DFID), have extensive websites. They detail their histories, mission statements, structures and policies, and often also have research papers and country overviews.

- All of the larger Northern and Southern *non-governmental organizations* (NGOs) now have their own website, and so too do some smaller Southern-based organizations. Again, they set out their mission statements, details on their policies and programmes around the world, and often their annual reports. Many NGOs produce regular publications, which they may also make available through the web. Closely related are various *research bodies, think tanks* and *lobbying organizations*.
- *Clubs* and *organizations*, such as the Centre for Science and Environment in India, have extensive websites, often with information on up-to-date and contentious issues.
- Many *corporations*, domestic and multinational, also have websites, with mission statements and the like.
- A number of *social movements* publicize their causes on the web. Famously, the Zapatistas made great use of the internet in drawing attention to their struggle in the Chiapas region of Mexico. The Friends of the Narmada Bachao Andolan, in India, also has a website (http://www.narmada.org/), which explains the basis of the protests, details the history of the movement and provides updates on recent developments.
- Electronic versions of some *newspapers* and *magazines* are now available on the net. Although some are available only on a subscription basis, others are free, making it possible to read the daily papers from around the world, as well as weekly and fortnightly magazines. Sites like www.samachar.com offer a suite of papers (Indian, in this case), in English and other languages. Often it is only the headlines and bigger articles that are available, but they can be an incredibly useful way of staying in touch with various perspectives on unfolding stories and current issues.

Other elements of the papers – marriage adverts, legal rulings, daily pollution ratings and so on – can also be a useful resource. Most of these newspapers and magazines have links to their electronic archives, although as yet they rarely extend back beyond a few years.

Cautions

Good research requires a critical and reflexive approach to one's sources, recognizing their biases and limitations. The internet shares the generic features of any information source in this respect, but some issues are more pronounced, while others are particular to it.

Perhaps the most obvious issue for development research is the extremely limited reach that the internet has in most parts of the majority world. While the number of internet cafés and even home-based computers is exploding in the metropolitan cities of the world – Delhi, Jakarta, Cape Town – even in these 'islands' it is generally limited to the elites and middle classes. In most of the world's rural hinterlands, telephone lines are rare, never mind computers (although expensive satellite connections have allowed some better-funded NGOs to get connected). As Thabo Mbeki pointed out in 1995, there are more telephones in Manhattan than in all sub-Saharan Africa (and even here, there is an overwhelming concentration in urban areas of South Africa). Even where the terminals and lines are available, the technology may be dated, the connection slow, and the power supply erratic, making web searches especially frustrating. As well as being urban and elite-biased, other exclusions centre on age, gender and language. English accounts for 90 per cent of all internet transactions, and unless the researcher knows the language in question, they are again directed towards English-speakers, who are likely to be elites. These are the 'cyber-geographies' of power, and they must be taken into account when using the internet for development research. There is nothing wrong with doing development research with elites and middle classes – they form an important and very influential section of society within low-income countries. Research projects working with NGO workers, or call-centre workers, or members of environmental clubs, for example, all have much to offer, but for the most part, one is highly unlikely to have direct access to the poor or marginalized.

A second set of problems arises in relation to language. English has been mentioned above, but language is much more than this. Metaphors, sayings and culturally specific forms of expression can, in some circumstances, lead to confusion and misunderstanding on both sides. In a project that this author was involved in, a Ghanaian respondent said of their funding body, 'Your finger is in their mouth'. This would be instantly understood by another Ghanaian (and was understood by Gina Porter, the UK researcher who has worked there for many years), but although I had an idea, I wasn't sure (it meant they were in a position of power over you). Simple concepts and sayings in one's own society can be baffling to others, and without face-to-face contact, this can be accentuated. On a similar note, in some countries first names are quickly used, especially with email, but in other places it is more usual to continue using someone's title (Professor, Dr) or a more honorific term (Madam, Sir). Overall, when conducting interviews, surveys or more informal conversations through the internet, development researchers must be particularly aware of the potential for cross-cultural 'slippages' of language and meaning. This extends to the use of abbreviations (like BTW – by the way), which may be commonly used in the UK, say, but not in Vietnam, and to emoticons (like 'smiley' – :-)), which again may not be in use in other parts of the world.

Finally, when using data collected from the internet, it is important to be aware of the distinction from academic sources (see also Chapter 22 in this volume). Whatever their failings, academic books and journal articles are subject to a process of peer review and editorial oversight. Articles and pieces on the internet can be posted up by anyone with the access and the ability to do so, leading to an enormous range in terms of the 'quality' and integrity of data available. For example, a UK-based extremist Hindu website has recently posted up a number of 'hate' stories about Muslims in Britain and India, presenting these as factually based news reporting. Like any other source of data, the internet must be critically evaluated, and the information triangulated and checked with as many other sources as can be managed.

Conclusions

279

This is the barest introduction to what is an exciting but complex subject, and it cannot do justice to the many problems and possibilities – practical, technical and cultural – of using the web for development research. There are a growing number of specialist and detailed books and articles on this subject, and although most of them are Western-based, and tend to make assumptions about Western conditions, they do offer a lot of important and relevant advice. However, as Clare Madge (pers. comm.) warns, online research methods have to be used very cautiously in a development context. They can easily pass the 'costs' (online time) on to the researched, and result in very biased sample populations (urban, technological, male, etc.). Using the internet for research is not, therefore, an easy option, but one that demands both generic and specific research design and skills, ethical considerations and reflexive contemplation.

QUESTIONS FOR DISCUSSION

1. At the site for Zooknic Internet Intelligence (http://www.zooknic.com/Users/) you can find a whole variety of statistics and maps on the geography of the internet. What can country maps tell you, and what do they obscure?

2. Who writes in English, who writes in other languages, and who can afford to have their websites made available in translation? Take a theme or a country, and see if you can find websites that are only in the local language (can you identify who wrote them?), only in English, and a website which is available in translation (the World Bank?). What does this tell you about the power and geographies of language?

3. Search for an appropriate (open) discussion forum and 'lurk' for a while. Can you identify potential research possibilities – whether in terms of analysing the discussions taking place or by taking a more active role? What are the shortcomings of this approach?

4. Take a theme (say, the Three Gorges Dam) and try to identify as many different institutions, organizations, movements and individuals (journalists, government, corporations, NGOs, etc.) who have statements available on the web on this issue. How do they differ? Who does not have a direct voice through the web (and how are they represented by the other actors)?

5. Try interviewing a friend or a relative via email on a specific subject (this might take several interchanges over a few days or even a couple of weeks). This should be someone who you won't meet in the meantime, but with whom you can get together after the exercise is over. Afterwards, discuss with them the problems and advantages of this method of questioning. How different would it be if you did not already know them?

Further reading

Herring, S. (ed.) (1996) *Computer-mediated Communication: Linguistic, Social and Cross-cultural Perspectives*, Amsterdam: John Benjamins.

Hine, C. (2000) *Virtual Ethnography*, London: Sage.

Jones, S. (ed.) (1999) *Doing Internet Research: Critical Issues and Methods for Examining the Net*, London: Sage.

Mann, C. and Stewart, F. (2000) *Internet Communication and Qualitative Research: A Handbook for Researching Online*, London: Sage.

Schonlau, M., Fricker, R.D. and Elliott, M. (2002) *Conducting Research Surveys via E-mail and the Web*, Santa Monica, CA: Rand.

Useful Journals

The Information Society
Communication Research
Journal of Communication
Internet Research: Electronic Networking Applications and Policy
Journal of Computer-Mediated Communication

Websites

How to cite web references (and every other sort): http://www.unn.ac.uk/central/isd/cite/
On netiquette: http://www.fau.edu/netiquette/net/index.html
Cyber Geography Research: http://www.cybergeography.org/

References

Adams, P.C. and Ghose, R. (2003) India.com: the construction of a space between, *Progress in Human Geography*, 27 (4): 414–437.

Best, S.J. and Krueger, B.S. (2004) *Internet Data Collection: Quantitative Applications in the Social Sciences.* London: Sage.

Dodge, M. and Kitchin, R. (2000) *Mapping Cyberspace.* London: Routledge.

Jones, S. (ed.) (1999) *Doing Internet Research: Critical Issues and Methods for Examining the Net*, London: Sage.

Lau, L. (2004) Virtually positioned: investigating identity and positionality in a case study of South Asian literature in cyberspace, *Interdisciplinary Science Review*, 29 (1): 65–76.

Madge, C. and O' Connor, H. (2004) Online methods in geography education research. *Journal of Geography in Higher Education* 28 (1): 143–152.

Mann, C. and Stewart, F. (2000) *Internet Communication and Qualitative Research: A Handbook for Researching Online*, London: Sage.

Mercer, C. (2004) Engineering civil society: ICTs in Tanzania, *Review of African Political Economy*, 31 (99): 49–64.

Meth, P. (2003) Entries and omissions: using solicited diaries in geographical Research, *Area*, 35 (2): 195–205.

Schonlau, M., Fricker, R.D. and Elliott, M. (2002) *Conducting Research Surveys via E-mail and the Web*, Santa Monica, CA: Rand.

Stone, D. (ed.) (2000) *Banking on Knowledge*: The Genesis of the Global Development Network, London: Routledge.

281

29

Data from International Agencies

Jonathan Rigg

Identifying and categorizing international agencies ● ● Assessing data 'quality'

● ● Gathering statistics by international agencies ● ● Tracing data flows

● ● Sources of data from international agencies ● ● Case study of Lao PDR

What are international agencies?

Conventionally, international organizations are divided into three categories: intergovernmental organizations (IGOs); international non-governmental (non-profit making) organizations (INGOs); and multinational enterprises (MNCs/TNCs). However, according to the job at hand, it may be useful to categorize international organizations in other ways: according to their regional remit (Asia, Africa, Latin America, etc.); their object (refugees, agricultural development, intellectual property, etc.); or their structure (autonomous, semi-autonomous, dependent, etc.). The *Yearbook of International Organizations* lists 5,900 intergovernmental organizations and 38,000 non-governmental organizations (Table 29.1). For the purpose of this discussion, international agencies are seen to fall into the category of IGOs. While important both in themselves and as sources of data, INGOs and

MNCs/TNCs are not considered here. There are three key categories of international (intergovernmental) organization: the agencies of the United Nations; the specialized agencies of the UN; and other major international organizations (see Table 29.2).

Sources and range of data

Most IGOs have statistical departments that aggregate and synthesize statistics and which publish surveys, statistical yearbooks and comparative reviews. Many also provide statistics online and/or permit free download of publications. In terms of the range and accessibility of statistics, those agencies listed in Table 29.3 provide the best and most comprehensive online services. Many also publish annual reports and texts that have become key sources of data and other types of information on development (see Table 29.4). Those with

Table 29.1 Profiles of international organizations

International organization category	Number in Yearbook of International Organizations
Intergovernmental organizations and networks (IGOs)	5,900
International associations (INGOs)	38,000
Universal membership organizations	529
Inter-continental organizations	1,050
Regional (sub-continental) organizations and networks	4,100
Informal, transnational associations and networks	–
Transnational religious orders	850
International funds, foundations and banks	–
Semi-autonomous international bodies	2,700
Internationally-oriented national organizations	4,500

Source: Data from Yearbook of International Organizations, accessed from http://www.uia.org/ organizations/ (12.7.04). See also: http://www.uia.org/statistics/organizations/ytb199.php

the highest profile are the World Bank's *World Development Report*, published annually since 1978, and the UNDP's *Human Development Report* which dates from 1990.

The quantity and quality of data on development have risen and improved enormously over the last few decades. While in the 1960s, from a data point of view, the 'here be dragons' perspective still held for large swathes of the Global South, this is no longer the case. We know a great deal about most countries and this is of central importance in providing the knowledge base that can then permit, for example, the formulation of effective policies and programmes for fighting poverty. The sheer abundance and range of data can, however, create another type of problem: the assumption that with abundance comes accuracy.

Maintaining quality and standardizing data

The General Data Dissemination System (GDDS) was established by the IMF in 1995 with the intention of improving data quality,

identifying needs for data improvement, and providing guidance to member countries in the dissemination of 'comprehensive, timely, accessible, and reliable economic, financial, and socio-demographic statistics ... based on international methodologies' (IMF, n.d.) (see http://dsbb.imf.org/Applications/web/gdds/ gddswhatgdds/, downloaded 12.7.04). There have been a number of other initiatives to improve, expand, deepen and monitor international statistics: the Data Quality Assessment Framework (DQAF), also developed by the IMF with the assistance of the World Bank; the UN's Fundamental Principles of Official Statistics; the Trust Fund for Statistical Capacity Building (TFSCB), an initiative of the World Bank designed 'to strengthen the capacity of statistical systems in developing countries' (TFSCB, n.d.); and Paris21, a consortium of experts, statisticians, policy-makers and international agencies established in 1999 with the aim, again, of raising the capabilities of statistical agencies in the developing world.

Paris21 was established largely because of concerns about the capacity of countries to deliver accurate, robust and timely statistics

283

Table 29.2   Types of International organization

Category	Agencies	Agencies with development remit and online links to statistical divisions
Agencies of the UN (major offices)[1]	UNICEF (United Nations Children's Fund); UNCTAD (United Nations Conference on Trade and Development); UNDP (United Nations Development Programme); UNEP (United Nations Environment Programme); UNHCR (United Nations High Commissioner for Refugees); UNFPA (United Nations Population Fund): WFP (World Food Programme)	UNICEF, UNCTAD, UNDP, UNEP, UNHCR, UNFPA, WFP
United Nations 'Specialized agencies'[2]	FAO (Food and Agriculture Organization of the UN): IAEA (International Atomic Energy Agency); ICAO (International Civil Aviation Organization); IFAD (International Fund for Agricultural Development); ILO (International Labour Organization); IMO (International Maritime Organization); IMF (International Monetary Fund); ITU (International Telecommunication Union); UNESCO (UN Educational, Scientific and Cultural Organization); UNIDO (UN Industrial Development Organization); UPU (Universal Postal Union); World Bank group; WHO (World Health Organization); WIPO (World Intellectual Property Organization); WMO (World Meteorological Organization)	FAO, IFAD, ILO, IMF, UNESCO, UNIDO, World Bank group, WHO
Other major international organizations (selected)	For full list see http://www.uia.org/organizations/	African Development Bank, Arab Fund for Economic and Social Development, Asian Development Bank, Caribbean Development Bank, European Bank for Reconstruction and Development, Inter-American Development Bank, NAFTA Secretariat, Organization for Economic Cooperation and Development (OECD), Organization of American States (OAS), Pan-American Health Organization, Secretariat of the Pacific Community, World Trade Organization (WTO)

Notes:
[1] For a full list and organizational chart, see http://www.unsystem.org/ (downloaded 12.7.04) and http://www.unsystem.org/en/documents/Systemchart27Feb2004webv.pdf (downloaded 12.7.04).
[2] Autonomous organizations with cooperative agreements with UN. See http://www.un.org/Overview/brief6.html (downloaded 12.7.04) for full list and links.

Table 29.3   Selected online data sources and portals

Data sources

ADB (Asian Development Bank): http://www.adb.org/Economics/default.asp

EU: http://europa.eu.int/comm/eurostat/Public/datashop/print-catalogue/EN?
    catalogue=Eurostat&service=about_eurostat

FAO: http://apps.fao.org/default.jsp; http://www.fao.org/es/ess/index_en.asp

IADB: http://www.iadb.org/

ILO: http://www.ilo.org/public/english/bureau/stat/

IMF: http://www.oecd.org/site/0,2865,en_21571361_31596493_1_1_1_1_1,00.html

WHO: http://www.who.int/whr/en/

UN Statistics Division: http://unstats.un.org/unsd/

UN databases: http://www.un.org/databases/index.html

UNESCAP: http://unescap.org/stat/index.asp

UNECLAC: http://www.eclac.org/estadisticas/default.asp?idioma=IN

UNDP: http://www.undp.org/

World Bank group: http://www.worldbank.org/data/

World Bank development indicators: http://publications.worldbank.org/WDI/indicators

WFP: http://www.wfp.org

Portals

The development gateway (World Bank): http://www.developmentgateway.org/node/244175/

Eldis gateway to development information: http://www.eldis.org/

---

in a standardized manner. Since its launch, Paris21 has 'promoted the principle that statistical development is not merely a technical matter, but a development policy issue' (ADB, 2002b: 2). Central to this effort is the notion of data 'quality', which in turn raises the question as to what is meant by data quality, and how it should be assessed. At the national and international levels, different scholars and practitioners have approached this issue in different ways (Table 29.5). To summarize, while 'there is wide agreement on what the subcomponents [of data quality] should be, there is no universal consensus on how to group them under main components' (Elvers and Rosén, 1997: 622). Central, however, are the following eight (AARCTTIC):

- Accuracy and comprehensiveness
- Accessibility
- Relevance
- Coherence and consistency
- Transparency, accountability and impartiality
- Timeliness
- Interpretability
- Clarity

In highlighting these eight components, two questions come to the fore:

- What do users need and how effective are existing systems in meeting these needs?
- What are the trade-offs between the components identified – for example, between timeliness and comprehensiveness?

Tracing data flows: from the international agency to the household

This section traces the layers of control and administration that lie between the sampled household and the aggregate data disseminated by an international agency. The difficulties and challenges of maintaining quality will be addressed, as will the inconsistencies that continue to prevail even after data have been standardized.

Table 29.4   International agencies for development: key texts and data sources

Agency	Development texts/reports	URL
African Development Bank	African Development Report	http://www.afdb.org/knowledge/publications.htm
Asian Development Bank	Asian Development Outlook; Key Indicators of Developing Asian and Pacific Countries	http://www.adb.org/Economics/ default.asp
Food and Agriculture Organization of the UN	The State of Food and Agriculture	http://apps.fao.org/default.jsp; http://www.fao.org/es/ess/index_en.asp
Inter-American Development Bank	IADB Annual Report	http://www.iadb.org/
International Labour Office	Yearbook of Labour Statistics; Bulletin of Labour Statistics	http://www.ilo.org/public/english/bureau/stat/
International Monetary Fund	World Economic Outlook; Finance and Development; IMF Survey	http://www.oecd.org/site/0,2865, en_21571361_31596493_1_1_1_1_1,00.html
World Health Organization	The World Health Report	http://www.who.int/whr/en/
UN Statistics Division	Demographic Yearbook; International Trade Statistics; Statistical Yearbook	http://unstats.un.org/unsd/pubs/
United Nations Economic Commission for Asia and the Pacific	Statistical Indicators for Asia and the Pacific; Economic and Social Survey of Asia and the Pacific	http://unescap.org/stat/index.asp
Economic Commission for Latin America and the Caribbean	Statistical Yearbook for Latin America and the Caribbean	http://www.eclac.org/estadisticas/default.asp?idioma=IN
United Nations Development Programme	Human Development Report	http://www.undp.org/dpa/publications/

Table 29.4   (continued)

Agency	Development texts/reports	URL
World Bank	World Development Report; World Development Indicators; Global Development Finance; The World Bank Atlas	http://publications.worldbank.org/ecommerce/
World Food Programme	Annual Performance Report	http://www.wfp.org

Where do statistics come from? Gathering data by international agencies

The first important point to note is that while data and statistics are often accessed through international agencies, such agencies are not primary data-collection bodies. They rely on national statistical bodies for their data (see http://www.worldbank.org/data/wdi2004/primary-data.pdf for a list of primary data-collection bodies). Thus it is not to the international organizations that we should be looking to appraise the robustness of statistics, but to the national agencies that generate the statistics in the first place.

Notwithstanding the efforts of the IMF, World Bank, various UN agencies and others, using data from different sources can be problematic because of the different methods employed, different definitions, missing data, varying levels of expertise and capability, different timings and different reporting practices. Inconsistencies, in short, are to be expected. Furthermore, it is those countries for which reliable and robust data are most needed – the poorest countries, generally – where these problems are most acute. Even publications from single agencies that try to iron out inconsistencies are never completely successful in this regard. Thus the World

Bank's widely consulted *World Development Indicators* shows discrepancies between editions. At the press launch of the 2004 edition, World Bank economist Martin Ravallion observed:

> Of course, the data are never ideal. They are getting better over time, but there are still continuing concerns. There have been improvements in survey data and in survey data quality and in coverage, but at the same time, as well as producing numbers like this, the Bank is very actively engaged with governments in improving the quality of their data, improving the quality of household surveys, both through our own efforts, through things like the Living Standards Measurement Study in the Bank and through efforts of governments themselves through their own statistical capacity.(http://web.worldbank.org/WBSITE/EXTERNAL/NEWS/0,,contentMDK:20195186~menuPK:34476~pagePK:34370~piPK:34424~theSitePK:4607,00.html, downloaded 12.7.04)

A theme of many studies is the need to standardize the collection and analysis of statistics. This runs from grand, global projects such as the UN's Millennium Development Goals (MDGs) exercise (endorsed in November 2000), through to more modest regional efforts at standardizing and sharing the collection of statistics. Thus, a significant

287

Table 29.5   Indicators and measures of data quality

Study	Focus	Identified measures of facets of quality
Fellegi and Ryten (2000)	Study of the Swiss federal statistical system	Three general questions: How *adaptable* is the system in adjusting to evolving needs? How *effective* is the system in meeting existing needs? How *credible* is the system in terms of quality and objectivity? Addressing these questions requires an assessment of the *solidity* of the legal and institutional environment; the *trustworthiness* of the products; the *resources* at the agencies' disposal; and the *adequacy* of the instruments developed.
Brackstone (1999)	Managing data quality in national statistical offices	'Quality' reflects fitness for use by clients and Blackstone proposes six dimensions of quality: *relevance, accuracy, timeliness, accessibility, interpretability,* and *coherence.*
De Vries (1998)	Performance indicators for national statistical systems	Proposes that there is a strong correlation between the quality of the system in place and the quality of the outputs (i.e. statistics). These link ten principles that come under the headings: *relevance, impartiality and equal access; professionalism; accountability; prevention of misuse; cost-effectiveness; confidentiality; legislation; national coordination; international coordination;* and *international statistical cooperation.*
Holt and Jones (1998)		Authors identify *accuracy, relevance, coherence and consistency, continuity, timeliness, accessibility,* and *revisability* as central to data quality but also note the potential conflicts (and trade-offs) between these principles, for example between data quality and timeliness.
ABS (1998)	Data quality assessment of the Australian Bureau of Statistics	Quality dimensions identified as *accuracy, revisability, timeliness, relevance, comprehensiveness,* and *accessibility.*
Elvers and Rosén (1997)	General study of quality issues for official statistics	User needs are seen as the primary measure of quality. The main components of quality are identified as *contents, accuracy, timeliness, coherence (comparability), availability,* and *clarity.*

Sources: Adapted from the IMF web page 'Approaches to data quality' (http://dsbb.imf.org/Applications/web/dqrs/dqrsapproaches/) using additional material from the source sites for the following papers:
Fellegi and Ryten (2000) http://www.statistik.admin.ch/stat_ch/ber00/peer_review/peer_review.pdf (downloaded 27.7.04)
Brackstone (1999) http://dsbb.imf.org/vgn/images/pdfs/scpap.pdf (downloaded 27.7.04)
De Vries (1998) http://dsbb.imf.org/vgn/images/pdfs/nld.pdf (downloaded 27.7.04)
Elvers and Rosén (1997) http://dsbb.imf.org/vgn/images/pdfs/Encyc.pdf (downloaded 27.7.04)
Holt & Jones (1998) http://dsbb.imf.org/Application/web/dqrs/dqrsapproaches/.

problem in measuring the achievement of the MDGs has been the difficulties connected with compiling the necessary data that lie behind the 48 indicators and which, in turn, inform the 18 targets and eight goals (http://www.adb.org/documents/speeches/2002/sp 2002027.asp). For example, assessing the goal to reduce maternal mortality by three-quarters, and under-five child mortality by two-thirds by 2015 is compromised by the fact that 'there is no reliable data in countries where the problem is thought to be most acute' (UN, 2001: 21). In a speech in 2002, the President of the Asian Development Bank, Tadao Chino, observed:

> The availability of comprehensive data is a prerequisite for designing viable poverty reduction programs. Data are also critical for effective monitoring of progress towards the attainment of the MDGs. In brief, sound data represent a key weapon in the battle against poverty. Despite the collective efforts of DMC [Developing Member Country] governments and the donor community at large, we still lack the availability of comprehensive, reliable and timely statistics. Country capacities to address data gaps and weaknesses need to be augmented. (Chino, 2002)

A case study of Lao PDR

The danger of using data from international agencies is that the origin of the data, and the limitations connected with their collection and analysis, is often shrouded from view. This can be illustrated with reference to the Lao People's Democratic Republic.

Laos's statistical system was established in 1975. It was established as a decentralized system where responsibility for the collection of statistics was devolved to the different ministries, and they in turn devolved authority to provincial departments and district offices. This decentralized system still, in large part, operates. The National Statistics Centre

(NSC) is charged with the task of collecting statistics from line ministries, compiling statistical reports, and conducting censuses and surveys. Despite financial and technical support from Statistics Sweden (through SIDA), the UNDP, World Bank and the Asian Development Bank (ADB), there remain serious weaknesses in the system which compromise the collection of accurate and robust statistics. These fall into three main areas which are, it should be noted, common to many of the world's poorest countries.

First, the human resource base is weak in terms of number and levels of expertise. In 2002 the total number of professionally trained statisticians in the whole of Laos was less than 30 (ADB, 2002a: 2). One of the reasons why, as of 2003, there was still no sample survey system for the collection of socio-economic statistics was simply because of over-stretch in the NSC. At the provincial and district levels, staff usually number between one and three with secondary-level education and some additional but limited training in statistics being the normal level of expertise.

Second, the decentralized system of data collection means that inconsistencies are amplified as ministries and units of responsibility adopt their own systems of collection with little respect for the demands of the centre and the need to be systematic. Weaknesses are particularly acute when units of collection are at the household or enterprise level and relate to such fields as poverty, household economy, gender, farm-level agricultural production, and the labour market. Here quality is low, methods of reporting cumbersome, timeliness compromised, and the utility of such data questionable.

Third, there remains an official culture that regards statistics as sensitive and strategic. Dissemination is often resisted and full disclosure sometimes far from automatic. Moreover, there is evidence that data are manipulated for political and other reasons. The decentralization of authority does not help in this regard.

289

As a paper to the ADB's High Level Forum on Statistical Capacity Building held in 2002 observed: 'The low availability of statistical information [in Laos] for wider consumption is not only a matter of capacity and capability to compile, publish and disseminate statistical information [but] is also a matter of appreciation on the part of the producers of statistics of the benefits of disclosing statistical information' (ADB, 2002b: 7).

The Lao Expenditure and Consumption Survey (LECS)

Most estimates of levels of poverty in Laos are based on the Lao Expenditure and Consumption Survey (LECS). This has been undertaken on three occasions to date, in 1992/93 (LECS I [1995]), 1997/98 (LECS II [1999]), and 2002/03 LECS III (Lao PDR, 1995, 1999). The results of LECS III were released in 2004 (and can be downloaded from http://www.undplao.org/PovertyReduction/ Final%20report%20LECS%203.pdf). Since their inception in the early 1990s, the surveys have been coordinated by the State Planning Committee with technical assistance from Statistics Sweden (particularly), the UNDP, World Bank and ADB.

The first point to note is that data collection is a process that evolves over time, reflecting improvements in national capacity and capability as well as changes in definition and method. Thus, in the Lao case, there are important differences between LECS I and LECS II, and between LECS II and LECS III. LECS I was very limited in coverage and involved the survey of fewer than 3,000 households across 147 villages. LECS II was rather broader in geographical scope and sampled nearly 9,000 households in 450 villages. It was also more comprehensive in terms of the range of data collected. But while LECS II may be more comprehensive and robust, comparing the two surveys is problematic partly because of the very 'improvements'

introduced for LECS II. In short, like is not being compared with like. Furthermore, even LECS II has been criticized both in itself and in the way the data have been used to calculate, for example, levels and distributions of poverty. There are therefore concerns about the comparability and robustness of the LECS I and II data sets.

A second tier of issues arises when the data collected are employed for other purposes, for example to calculate poverty. Using the LECS II data, various agencies and individuals have calculated an assortment of poverty estimates (Figure 29.1). The most dramatic difference in these estimates – which, it should be reiterated, are based on the same data set – is in terms of levels of urban poverty. For the ADB and the UNDP, levels of urban poverty are 27 per cent, while for the World Bank and the Lao government they are between 15 per cent and 18 per cent. This surprising discrepancy is because of the multipliers used to account for differences in the cost of living between urban and rural areas and between provinces. With, in the Lao case, so many people clustering around the poverty line, even a small variation in the multipliers used to equalize costs of living between rural and urban areas can either pull a large number of people into poverty or, alternatively, lift them out of poverty. (Of course this does not change the real living conditions of people, only whether they are assessed as poor, or not.) In an internal review of the World Bank's living standards study for Laos, Van de Walle criticized the methods employed to calculate provincial prices and warned that this 'could easily result in severe mismanagement of regional poverty levels and relativities' (Van de Walle, 2000: 5). There is an equally dramatic difference in regional poverty profiles between the World Bank and Stenflo (SIDA) studies, something that is 'especially worrying' for Van de Walle, indicating a fundamental mistake probably linked to the estimation of prices (Table 29.6). 'Given that both poverty profiles use the same database and the

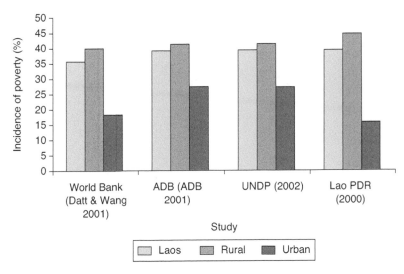

Figure 29.1 Estimates of poverty in Laos using the LECS II data set

Notes on sources: All these estimates are based on the same data set, the LECS II survey. The World Bank assessment was carried out by Datt and Wang (2001), the ADB study (2001) by Kakwani et al. (2001), on which the UNDP (2002) also draws, while the Lao PDR study (Lao PDR, 2000) was financed by the United Nations World Food Programme and undertaken by the National Statistics Centre. Knowles (2002) provides a comparative discussion of the various poverty studies undertaken using the LECS II data.

291

same overall methods', Van de Walle (2000: 6) writes, 'one would expect to find small differences only'.

The point of this discussion is, primarily, to highlight two things. First, often it is not so much how data are collected which is the issue (although, to be sure, this is important), but how raw data are subsequently used. Second, it emphasizes the dangers that the dislocation of the publishing of data by international agencies from its collection by national agencies can create. The assumptions and sometimes arbitrary decisions taken at the national level become lost from view as the data are passed up to international agencies.

Conclusion

At one level it is remarkable what can be accessed with the click of a mouse from the international agencies. The UNDP tells us, for example, that the oral rehydration therapy use rate in the Gambia is 27 per cent, but just 4 per cent in Rwanda; the FAO statistical data base reveals that 6,816 crocodiles and alligators were harvested in Guyana in 2001, and 25,030 in Cambodia; while the World Bank records that 19.4 per cent of births in Laos were attended by a skilled health staff member, but for Thailand this information is not available. The sheer availability of statistics from international agencies raises three particular issues. First, it obscures what we don't know about some countries and some aspects of economy, society and the environment. Second, it also obscures the means and methods by which these statistics reach the international agencies. And third, it sometimes seems to accord a level of accuracy to data which is, if their origins are considered, spurious.

Table 29.6   Laos: poverty headcount by region, 1997–98

	Stenflo (in Knowles1999)	Kakwani et al. (2001)	Datt and Wang (2001)
Laos	39.0	38.6	41.5
Urban	15.0	38.6	36.3
Rural	43.8	41.0	40.0
Vientiane	6.9	12.2	13.7
Urban	n/a	16.7	n/a
Rural	n/a	4.5	n/a
North	52.1	52.5	46.0
Urban	22.9	43.3	21.9
Rural	55.2	53.5	48.6
Centre	29.5	29.6	28.4
Urban	11.4	21.0	15.2
Rural	35.2	32.3	32.6
South	41.2	38.4	39.8
Urban	23.7	35.8	24.0
Rural	43.1	38.6	41.5

Note: Knowles reviews three different analyses of the LECS II data performed by Stenflo (1999, funded by SIDA), Kakwani et al. (2001, funded by the Asian Development Bank), and Datt and Wang (2001, funded by the World Bank).

Source: Knowles (2002)

QUESTIONS FOR DISCUSSION

1. What does 'data quality' mean and how should it be measured or assessed?
2. What are the likely trade-offs between different desired elements comprising data quality?
3. Where does data released by international agencies come from and how is it collected?
4. How reliable are data released by international agencies? What data are likely to be the most reliable?

References and Further reading

ADB (2002a) Country paper: Laos, ADB/PARIS21 High Level Forum on Statistical Capacity Building for ASEAN Countries, Manila, 7–9 November 2002. Available at: http://www.paris21.org/htm/workshop/manila02/Lao_paper.pdf (accessed on 27.7.04).

ADB (2002b) Report of the ADB/Paris21High Level Forum on Statistical Capacity Building for ASEAN Countries, Manila: Economics and Research Department, ADB. Available at: http://www.paris21.org/htm/workshop/manila02/ASEAN_report.pdf (accessed on 27.7.04).

Chino, T. (2002) Opening address to the ADB/Paris21 Joint High Level Forum on Statistical Capacity Building for ASEAN Countries, 7 November 2002, Manila, Philippines. Available at: http://www.adb.org/Documents/Speeches/2002/ms2002129.asp (accessed on 27.7.04).

Datt, G. and Wang, L. (2001) Poverty in Lao PDR: 1992/93 – 1997/98, Washington, DC: World Bank (unpublished document).

Elvers, E. and Rosén, B. (1997) Quality concept for official statistics, in *Encyclopedia of Statistical Sciences*, New York: John Wiley and Sons, pp. 621–629.

IMF (n.d.) What is the General Data Dissemination System (GDDS)? Available at: http://dsbb. imf.org/Applications/web/gdds/gddswhatgdds/ (accessed on 27.7.04).

Kakwani, N., Bounthavy Sisouphanhtong, Phonesaly Souksavath and Dark, Brent (2001) Poverty in Lao PDR, paper presented at the Asia and Pacific Forum on Poverty: Reforming Policies and Institutions for Poverty Reduction, Manila, 5–9 February.

Knowles, J. (2002) Comparative review of 1997–98 Lao PDR poverty profiles, Working Papers on Poverty Reduction No. 1, Vientiane: National Statistics Center, Committee for Planning and Cooperation, Lao PDR.

Lao PDR (1995) *Expenditure and Consumption Survey and Social Indicator Survey (1992–1993)*, Vientiane: National Statistical Centre (July).

Lao PDR (1999) *The Households of Lao PDR: Lao Expenditure and Consumption Survey 1997–98 (LECS 2)*, Vientiane: National Statistical Centre (December).

Lao PDR (2000) An analysis of poverty in Lao PDR, Paper prepared by the National Statistics Center for the United Nations World Food Programme, Vientiane (August).

TFSCB (n.d.) Trust Funds for Statistical Capacity Building, Washington, DC: World Bank. Available at: http://web.worldbank.org/WBSITE/EXTERNAL/DATASTATISTICS/SCBEXTERNAL/0,,content MDK:20100547~menuPK:244204~pagePK:229544~piPK:229605~theSitePK:239427,00.html (accessed on 27.7.04).

UN (2001) *Road Map towards the Implementation of the United Nations Millennium Declaration*, Report of the Secretary-General, New York: United Nations. Available at: http://www.un.org/documents/ga/docs/56/a56326.pdf (accessed on 27.7.04).

UNDP (2002) *National Human Development Report: Lao PDR 2001 – Advancing Rural Development*, Vientiane: UNDP.

Van de Walle, D. (2000) Comments on the Lao PDR poverty analysis, Unpublished World Bank discussion paper, Vientiane, Lao PDR.

293

Part III

Information and Data Collection Methods

(iii) Disseminating Findings/Research

30

Writing an Effective Research Report or Dissertation

Stephen Morse

Writing for an audience, so who are they? ● ● Telling a story: the importance of clear writing and structure ● ● Presenting numerical data ● ● Presenting qualitative data

Introduction

The title of this chapter might be considered somewhat odd given that writing reports in development studies should not be any different from writing research reports in any subject. Indeed, it is probably a safe bet to predict that readers of this book will tend to leave this chapter to last. In part because report writing is the end of a process, but a second, and I suspect more important, reason is that report writing is seen as the hard, boring and tedious bit of the research.

Yet you must always remember that no matter how good the research process, it counts for nothing unless your results are communicated to others. That is how I am interpreting the term 'effective' – the production of a document that 'works' in the sense of presenting the right things but at the same time is easily digested by those meant to assimilate the information and (hopefully!) make some use of it. After all, if you can present your results in such a way that a reader has no difficulty following

the process from background to conclusions, then this maximizes your chances of getting heard, to say nothing of your chances of getting a good mark if the document is assessed!

So how do you make sure that what you have written will be read?

This chapter will provide some advice on how to write an effective research report or dissertation. For more in-depth coverage of the topic the reader is referred to some of the excellent guides such as those listed at the end of the chapter. Availability of these varies from library to library, but the books by Fisher and Holtom (1998), Mauch and Birch (1983), Rudestam and Newton (2001) and Swetnam (2000) are especially recomended. Also, while reports and dissertations differ, I will tend to concentrate more on the latter by assuming that the readership for this book will primarily be students rather than seasoned development professionals. Chapter 31 will focus on the professional dissemination of research findings.

While I will cover a wide range of topics, I will focus on two that in my experience cause the most grief when writing dissertations. The first relates to the structure of the dissertation – what needs to be in there and why? If this is not in place, then no matter how good the research the result can, at worst, appear to be an incoherent mess. The second point has arisen from a frequent observation that while students put a lot of time into collecting and analysing data, they often give little, if any, thought as to how their results will be presented. Badly presented results can cause untold grief for those trying to understand what you have found and may even serve to completely undermine the validity of the research. This is a topic not usually covered in much depth in the literature on writing dissertations.

Writing for an audience: so who are they?

In these days of greater accountability in the research arena, those providing the funds demand milestones of achievement from those they pay to do the research. Indeed, the chances are that the funder has strict guidelines over what should and should not be in the final report. In this case the readership may be quite broad, including personnel of the funding agency, some of whom may be unfamiliar with your research, as well as other researchers working on related projects.

At the other extreme, dissertations are typically a compulsory requirement for an undergraduate or postgraduate degree. Here the readership may be limited to a few (perhaps two) academic assessors, one of whom may well be a supervisor who, while not as familiar with your research as you are, will nonetheless be quite well informed. The second, and even third, assessor will have no prior knowledge of your research and will have to rely solely on what he/she can glean

from the dissertation. Even here remember that other researchers, including students, may want to refer to your work.

It is as well to remind yourself at the start of writing that the majority of readers will have no prior knowledge of what you did. You have to write in such a way that they can fully understand your research.

Do not underestimate how difficult this can be

It can be frustrating to explain things that seem so simple to you because you have lived with the research for months, if not years. Keep reminding yourself that what you see as so clear and obvious may not be to someone else having to read the document for the first time.

Structure: I want to tell you a story…

From here on I will concentrate on dissertations. The 'standard' structure often set out for dissertations is as follows:

Abstract (or Executive Summary)

A brief summary (often restricted in word length to a few hundred words) meant to convey the essence of what was done in the research and the results that were obtained.

Contents page

Use a logical system of numbering the sections of your dissertation. My own favourite is to use a whole number for the main chapter (or section) and decimal points for subsections. Hence the Introduction is '1' and subsections are '1.1', '1.2', etc. The advantage of this system is that tables and figures (diagrams, graphs, maps, photographs and so on are generically referred to as 'figures') can also be numbered to indicate clearly the chapter/section to which they belong. Tables and figures in section 1 are numbered 1.1, 1.2, etc., while those in section 2 are numbered 2.1, 2.2, etc.

Introduction

The introduction sets the scene for the dissertation by briefly stating the context of the research and its main aims and objectives. An 'aim' is broad while objectives are more specific. For example:

> *My broad aim is to explore the economic impact that genetically modified (GM) crops have on resource-poor farmers in South Africa.*

Specific objectives would be:

- to assess the farm-level costs of inputs required by growers of GM cotton (an example of a crop) in the Makhathini Flats, KwaZulu Natal, as well as the yields and revenue they obtain
- to use the information on costs and revenue to explore profitability (expressed as gross margin = revenue − costs) of GM cotton production in this area
- to see what savings (if any) there are in terms of labour for those growing GM cotton compared to those growing conventional (non-GM) varieties.

To each of these objectives we may well have an assumed answer (a best guess on available evidence) which we technically refer to as the 'hypothesis'. For example, we may assume a priori that growers of GM cotton use less insecticide than those growing conventional cotton as previous research from other developing, and indeed developed, countries suggests that this may be the case.

However, remember that with the very best of intentions a research project can start with one set of objectives that have had to 'evolve'. This may be as a result of logistics or because the researcher has discovered other avenues that are more important. For example,

in the GM project above it may emerge that credit supply is a vital element of the whole production system, and what really matters to the farmers and their families is not GM cotton *per se* but issues over access to, and interest rates for, credit. While a deductive purist might decry such flexibility, in development research this is seen as positive.

Literature review

Almost every research topic in development has elements that have been studied by someone else. It is hard, if not impossible, to find something that has not been explored at all. For example, it may be that the methods you intend to use have been employed by someone else, albeit in a different context. While the GM research in South Africa referred to earlier may be the first of its kind on the African continent, and one of a few such studies anywhere in the developing world, there are experiences that can be drawn upon. For example, GM cotton is grown in a number of countries, including the USA, and while the contexts are different, there will nonetheless be some relevance to the South African research. Also, of course, there will be a much longer experience with the impacts of conventional crop varieties or even entirely new crops in South Africa that will have some relevance.

In other words, it is important to set out in a literature review how your research builds upon the work of others. While some have tried, it is very dangerous to argue that a literature review is not necessary 'because no one has ever done anything relevant for my project'.

Methodology

This section sets out the methods used in the research. The rule of thumb is that there should be enough information to allow anyone to repeat your research if they so wish.

Hence make sure that full information is provided for the design of any experiments, derivation of the sampling framework in the case of surveys, and so on.

While in many ways it is the easiest part of the dissertation to write, given that it is largely a factual statement as to what you did, it can be something of a balancing act. There is no point in providing every little detail, but at the same time it is important to show how what you did relates to the objectives set out in the introduction.

Results

This is arguably one of the two most critical sections of any dissertation but at the same time is often confused with that other critical section – the discussion. Some people even prefer to merge these into one. If separated, the results section should be a 'factual' presentation of the main results of the research with no discussion as to what they imply. It may in large part comprise a set of tables and figures with text that elaborates upon the results, perhaps by providing an explanation and a summary of the main points that emerge.

It is important that all tables and figures have a heading and 'stand alone' in the sense that a reader should not have to read the main text of the section in order to understand them. My own preference when writing is to spend time at the very start getting tables and figures right and perhaps annotating them (if needs be) by adding notes regarding what I think are the main conclusions that emerge from them.

Given the importance of the results section, I will return to the presentation of data later in this chapter, but at this point it is also worth mentioning a few other issues that often arise:

- Be careful not to put too much into a table or graph. If too dense, the reader will find them hard to follow and probably won't bother!

- Rotating the rows and columns of a table can make them easier to understand. If in doubt, try it out!
- Space rows and columns so as to keep related information together.
- Do not present the same data as both a table and a graph (as I have done in this chapter to make a point!). Choose one or the other and stick to it.
- Avoid vertical lines in tables and use a minimum of horizontal lines.

These may appear to be minor points, but surprisingly they can make a significant difference in terms of readability. For example, Table 30.1 is adapted from a table published as part of a journal paper (written by myself and two colleagues from the University of Reading, Richard Bennett and Yousouf Ismael). It summarizes the results of a research project conducted in South Africa over three years on the economic impact of a type of GM cotton grown by small-scale farmers. The aims and objectives were pretty much those set out earlier in this chapter. For each of the variables the results are presented for a sample of adopters of GM cotton and non-adopters. The first version of the table (a) makes minimum use of lines and uses blank cells to group related information (such as costs). The second form of the table (b) is identical to the first but with all of the vertical and horizontal lines included and no blank cells. The appearance of table (b) is far more dense and unappealing to digest.

Discussion

Once the results have been presented it is necessary to explain to the reader what they say and imply. Therefore this section has the following aims:

- To articulate the main findings that have arisen from your research.
- To point out what you may have done wrong in terms of methodology, and

Table 30.1 Different ways of presenting the same data: Means and 95 per cent confidence limits (parentheses) of cotton yields, revenue and costs for those smallholder cotton producers not adopting and adopting the GM variety over three growing seasons.

(Figures are in South African Rand (SAR) per ha except yield which is in kg/ha.)

(a) Version of table with spacing between related variables and a minimum of lines

	Cotton growing season					
	1998/1999		1999/2000		2000/2001	
Variable	Non-adopters of GM cotton	Adopters of GM cotton	Non-adopters of GM cotton	Adopters of GM cotton	Non-adopters of GM cotton	Adopters of GM cotton
Yield	452 (26)	738 (118)	264 (23)	489 (68)	501 (81)	783 (93)
Total revenue (yield X price of cotton)	984 (57)	1605 (257)	574 (50)	1064 (148)	1090 (176)	1704 (202)
Seed cost	138 (9)	278 (46)	190 (19)	413 (65)	176 (18)	260 (21)
Pesticide cost	153 (11)	72 (20)	222 (15)	104 (19)	305 (30)	113 (16)
Spray labour cost	77 (6)	38 (11)	108 (7)	49 (9)	135 (13)	45 (7)
Harvest labour cost	113 (7)	184 (30)	66 (6)	122 (17)	125 (20)	196 (23)
Gross margin (revenue − costs)	502 (52)	1033 (207)	−11 (53)	376 (143)	348 (148)	1090 (166)
Gain in gross margin for adopters of GM cotton over non-adopters		531		387		742
Sample size	1196	87	329	112	254	245

	Cotton growing season					
	1998/1999		1999/2000		2000/2001	
Variable	Non-adopters of GM cotton	Adopters of GM cotton	Non-adopters of GM cotton	Adopters of GM cotton	Non-adopters of GM cotton	Adopters of GM cotton
Yield	452 (26)	738 (118)	264 (23)	489 (68)	501 (81)	783 (93)
Total revenue (yield X price of cotton)	984 (57)	1605 (257)	574 (50)	1064 (148)	1090 (176)	1704 (202)
Seed cost	138 (9)	278 (46)	190 (19)	413 (65)	176 (18)	260 (21)
Pesticide cost	153 (11)	72 (20)	222 (15)	104 (19)	305 (30)	113 (16)
Spray labour cost	77 (6)	38 (11)	108 (7)	49 (9)	135 (13)	45 (7)
Harvest labour cost	113 (7)	184 (30)	66 (6)	122 (17)	125 (20)	196 (23)
Gross margin (revenue – costs)	502 (52)	1033 (207)	–11 (53)	376 (143)	348 (148)	1090 (166)
Gain in gross margin for adopters of GM cotton over non-adopters	531		387		742	
Sample size	1196	87	329	112	254	245

whether given your time again you would have done things differently.

- To place your results in context by explaining how they support or disagree with those of others who have worked or are working on related topics.

The first two points are obvious while the last is probably less so. Indeed, I have often read dissertations where there are no references at all to the work of others, even where such work is abundant.

Do not forget the aims and objectives of the research as set out earlier in the dissertation. Some of the discussion needs to relate to these, but can also be wider-ranging.

Conclusion

This is a condensation of all your research into the main outcomes. While at least some of these should address the objectives set out in the introduction, it is also possible for there to be conclusions that do not necessarily equate to any of the objectives, but which nonetheless were important.

References

This is a list of all published works referred to in the dissertation. There can be some confusion with a bibliography. The difference is that a bibliography is, in essence, a sort of recommended reading list, and the items may not necessarily be referred to individually in the main text. There are various systems for presenting references, for example the Harvard system. The university (if it is a dissertation), funder (if it is a funded project) or publisher (if it is a journal or book) will let you know of the particular system they favour.

Whichever referencing system you employ – be consistent!

Also, please remember that the source of all material (quotations, diagrams, data, etc.) must be duly acknowledged if it has been taken from another piece of work. The latter obviously includes copyrighted material such as journal papers and books, but also includes the less obvious sources such as reports, newspapers and even the internet.

Acknowledgements

The acknowledgements may be placed at the start or end of a dissertation, and the guidance provided by the university should specify this. Never forget to thank all of those who have helped you with the research. These may include people who have provided you with direct help (data, advice, etc.), but also those close to you who have had to put up with your virtual absence for weeks, months or even years!

Appendix

The appendix (or appendices if there is more than one) contains additional material. A question often asked is what should be in the main body of a report or in the appendix? It first needs to be stressed that by placing material into an appendix you are implying that it may not necessarily be consulted by a reader in order to gain a full appreciation of the research.

The type of material typically included in appendices is:

- complete transcripts of interviews with key informants
- questionnaire design (including original form and English translation)
- extended summaries of raw data (graphs or tables), but avoid including too much of this
- short explanations of exotic statistical tests if used in the report.

Once you finish writing the dissertation or report always go back to the beginning to see whether your ending matches with your introduction. Most importantly, check that in your discussion/conclusions you have

303

addressed the objectives you set at the start and whether the literature review is still relevant. You would be amazed how many times I've read dissertations that completely fail to address the objectives set out so carefully and in such detail by the author.

The above dissertation structure can be considered a standard one. It reads like any good detective thriller: the crime to be solved, the people and evidence involved and the denouement (i.e. climax as to 'who did it and why?'). It is not meant to straitjacket our thinking and creativity. For example, much research may not have overt hypotheses as such. Inductive research is about 'finding out' in a broad sense, and the research may have evolved into a consideration of different issues from those identified at the start. In development, this style of research has grown with the rise of participatory methods and 'action research', with the 'researcher' almost acting as a facilitator to let a group analyse its own context and what could be done to overcome constraints that it may face. An entirely different structure from the one set out here may be called for.

A jungle of figures

Reports and dissertations often contain tables of data and graphs. These have the great advantage of being able to convey ideas in a way that is very appealing (i.e. visual) and these days are relatively easy to generate with computer software. As the author Frederick Barnard has vividly pointed out:

> One picture is worth ten thousand words

> Frederick R. Barnard in *Printer's Ink*, 8 Dec 1921 retelling a Chinese proverb.

However, tables and graphs can be a double-edged sword if not presented in a way that the reader can follow and understand. The following is a brief discussion of some of the issues involved.

There are many different forms of graph, and the choice largely depends upon the context. A general rule of thumb is to use bar graphs (histograms) for categorical data (i.e. no categories exist between the bars) while line graphs are used when it is implied that categories exist between the points on the horizontal axis. This 'rule' is not universally accepted, however, and some argue strongly that even with categorical data the line graph allows a better comparison. For example, Figure 30.1 is a series of presentations of the yield data in Table 30.1. Given that the data are arranged in categories (season, variable and type of farmer), a histogram would appear to be the most appropriate, and version (a) is just that. However, note how a line graph, as in (b) makes the message even clearer. After all, what we are interested in showing are the differences between the cotton varieties as well as change over season.

When means are presented in tables or graphs it is important to provide some idea of the variation in the data. There are various measures we could use, and the simplest measure of variation is the range (maximum–minimum). In practice we tend to use measures such as confidence limits (CL), standard deviations (SD) and standard errors (SE). In the GM cotton examples given earlier, both Table 30.1 and Figure 30.1 (a) had the means and 95 per cent CLs for each of the variables and sample of farmers, while Figure 30.1 (b) does not include any measure of variation. Opinions vary as to which is the 'best' measure to use. For example, the SD can perhaps be thought of as the purist measure in that it describes variation within a sample and the others are derived in part from it. However, if we employ the SD instead of the CL for the GM cotton data we get Figure 30.1(c). The standard deviation bars are large – so large in fact that for two of the categories the lower end of the SD bar is negative. But what exactly is a negative crop yield? While Figure 30.1(c) does convey the large degree of variation in the data, it does not help us much in making meaningful comparisons between the average yields. Whatever the choice, it is important that you fully understand what these different statistics are measuring.

(a) Histogram of mean yields and 95% confidence limits

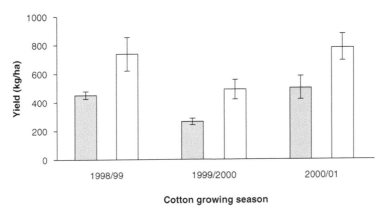

(b) Line graph of mean yields of GM (heavy line) and non-GM (lighter line) cotton varieties

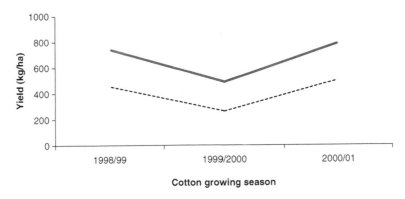

(c) Mean yields and standard deviations

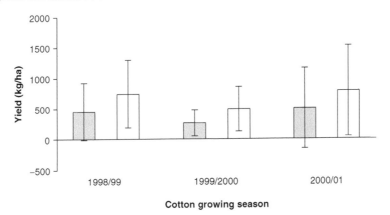

Figure 30.1   Different ways of presenting the same data, lines and variation

Data: Mean yields of GM and non-GM cotton varieties in the Makhathini Flats, South Africa as given in Table 30.1.
In versions (a) and (c) the bar on the left is for the conventional variety while the bar on the right is for
the GM variety.

Remember that even if you have taken statistical advice from an expert, you are still responsible for everything in the dissertation – not the expert!

In this era of political 'spin' it should also be remembered that care needs to be taken with graphical presentation. For example, from the South African research it was possible to explore the labour used to weed the GM and conventional cotton plots. In common with the vast majority of farmers in Africa, all agricultural practices in Makhathini are carried out with human labour – not machinery. In this case, all labour was expressed in terms of cost (SAR/ha) rather than person-days, and Figure 30.2 provides two versions of the same data for weeding labour. Given that the average cost of all inputs measured in the research (labour, seeds and pesticide) was typically of the order of SAR 800/ha, it is perhaps logical to express cost of labour for weeding using this figure as the vertical axis maximum (Figure 30.2(a)). Here it does not look as if there was much of a difference between the varieties, and given that so many other major differences exist, the graph might be a convenient way for us to 'spin' to the reader that we should ignore this variable. But reducing the scale to a maximum of SAR 250/ha (the upper end of the 95 per cent CL for some of the samples) gives a very different picture (Figure 30.2(b)). Here it seems that there are differences, albeit with CLs that overlap. In fact, given the large sample sizes, the cost of labour for weeding was significantly different between adopters and non-adopters in both seasons, although the order is rotated. We never did discover why this should be so. Again, honesty in presentation should always be the best policy.

Counts are a common form of data employed in development reports, and are typically counts of respondents providing a particular answer in a survey. They are often obtained from structured questionnaires, but may also emerge from semi- or unstructured questionnaires as the researcher attempts to categorize certain responses. Such data may or may not be analysed in a formal sense, but if analysed then the typical device employed is the chi-square (or similar) found from the difference between observed counts and expected counts based on some a priori hypothesis. In order to interpret a chi square result it is important to present the expected counts. Without these, interpretation is impossible.

A jungle of pictures and quotes

The typical form of qualitative presentations are pictorial (photographs, drawings, systems diagrams, etc.) or textual. Here I will mention only a few points about quotations. Short quotations only are best handled by 'running' them into the text. For example:

Genewatch, a *'not-for-profit group that monitors developments in genetic technologies from a public interest, environmental protection and animal welfare perspective'* (www.genewatch.org), has been running a series of campaigns against GM food.

Longer quotations are best offset as a separate piece of text. In both cases the quotations need to be demarcated by quotation marks or formatted as italics. The full citation details (author(s) source, website address, page numbers) have to be provided for all quotations. The following is some text written by Sue Mayer (a Director of Genewatch) which provides a very different 'take' on the cotton data presented in this chapter and raises concerns over power which are never far away in the development discourse.

'But it is the developing world that it likely to form the immediate focus of the biotechnology industry's market aspirations. Pushing GM cotton into India as a bridgehead into the vast cotton markets of Asia was one step. South Africa is being used as the way into the African

(a) Using SAR 800/ha as the upper limit of the vertical axis. Doesn't look as if there is much difference between GM and non-GM varieties.

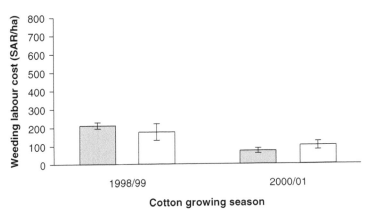

(b) Using SAR 250/ha as the upper limit of the vertical axis. Now there is a difference!

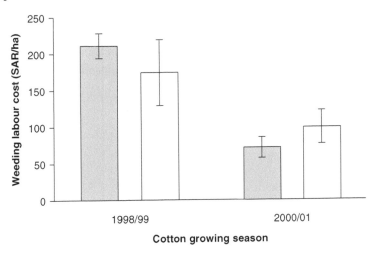

Figure 30.2   Different ways of presenting the same data: the scale effect

Data: Mean cost of weeding labour (SAR/ha) and 95 per cent confidence limits for plots planted to GM and non-GM cotton varieties in the Makhathini Flats, South Africa. In each of the two seasons the bar on the left is for the conventional variety while the bar on the right is for the GM variety.

ontinent. In these countries, it is the voices of small farmers which are more often raised in protest, concerned about the effects on food security that arise from the monopolisation of seed by multinational corporations'.

Sue Mayer (2004)
Extract taken from *Guardian Unlimited* (11 May 2004) accessed at www.guardian.co.uk/ gmdebate/Story/0,2763,1214256,00.html on 14 June.

The Mayer quotation is only four sentences long but you can see the space it has taken. The GM debate is, of course, an extensive one and as a result you could easily fill a 10,000 word dissertation with quotations from individuals and groups on one side of the debate or the other. While this may be tempting, and quotations can undoubtedly liven up a dissertation, too many of them can make the text difficult to read and digest.

Not only can quotations take up space but there are other matters to consider. Even with correct citation there is a limit as to how much can be quoted from a single source before the issue of copyright begins to become significant. Permission has to be sought if a single quote is more than 400 words or if more than 800 words are taken from different places within a single source. The Mayer quote above is 84 words.

In line with my comments over 'spin' with quantitative data, it is as well to remember that the same can equally occur with qualitative data. For example, using an extract from the Mayer piece:

> GM foods do have their benefits, and '*supporters of biotechnology make claims for its ability to provide solutions to world hunger*' (Mayer, 2004). Surely this is something to be applauded by all those anxious to see an end to those intractable problems of poverty and hunger that beset so many people.

In fact, the full extract from which the quotation has been taken reads as follows:

> '*While supporters of biotechnology make claims for its ability to provide solutions to world hunger, those at the sharp end have a different perspective.*'

The extra nine words generate a very different take on the issue! While such 'spin' can be attractive to those wishing to make a case, there are obvious legal dangers implicit in such misinterpretation.

Conclusion

The reporting aspect of any research project is an important dimension that requires careful consideration. Time spent planning the outline of a dissertation is well worthwhile. It is also a painless way of getting over 'writer's block'. Sketching out ideas and plans gets you through that first stage of putting pen to paper or finger to keyboard. Follow this by writing the chapters you know best, and if you are really stuck, then begin with the methodology. Thinking about what you did may help spur you into writing about what you found. Also, do remember that the disserta-tion is but part of your degree – not all of it.

Finally, no matter how dry the research material may seem to be, writing a dissertation is a creative process. If you treat it as a dry and unimaginative exposition, then so will the reader. Write with clarity and flair and use the opportunity to provide answers but also provoke questions. This will help engage the reader and thereby result in an effective dissertation.

QUESTIONS FOR DISCUSSION

1. Discuss how quantitative and qualitative data can be presented so as to bias a discussion (you can use Darrell Huff's book for clues).
2. What are the problems inherent in presenting the outputs from development projects that are participatory or inductive in approach as distinct from having formal objectives and hypotheses?
3. Discuss structures for setting out a dissertation other than the 'standard' structure given in this chapter.

Further reading

Bolker, J. (1998) *Writing Your Dissertation in Fifteen Minutes a Day: A Guide to Starting, Revising and Finishing Your Doctoral Thesis*, New York: First Owl Books.

Fisher, E. and Holtom, D. (1998) *Enjoy Writing Your Science Thesis or Dissertation: A Step-by-Step Guide to Planning and Writing Dissertations*, London: Imperial College Press.

Fitzpatrick, J., Secrist, J. and Wright, D.J. (1998) *Secrets for a Successful Dissertation*, London: Sage.

Glatthorn, A.A. (1998) *Writing the Winning Dissertation: A Step-by-Step Guide*, London: Sage.

Huff, D. (1991) *How to Lie with Statistics*, Harmondsworth: Penguin.

Mauch, J.E. and Birch, J.W. (1983) *Guide to the Successful Thesis and Dissertation: Conception to Publication. A Handbook for Students and Faculty*, New York: M. Dekker.

Rudestam, K.E. and Newton, R.R. (2001) *Surviving Your Dissertation: A Comprehensive Guide to Content and Process*, London: Sage.

Swetnam, D. (2000) *Writing Your Dissertation: How to Plan, Prepare and Present Successful Work*, London: How To Books.

Thomas, R.M. and Brubaker, D.L. (2000) *Theses and Dissertations: A Guide to Planning, Research and Writing*, Westport, CT: Bergin and Garvey.

Walters, D. (1999) *The Readable Thesis: A Guide to Clear and Effective Writing*, Gilsum, NH: Pathway Book Service.

Zerubavel, E. (1999) *The Clockwork Muse: A Practical Guide to Writing Theses, Dissertations and Books*, Cambridge, MA: Harvard University Press.

References

Fisher, E. and Holtom, D. (1998) *Enjoy Writing Your Science Thesis or Dissertation: A Step-by-Step Guide to Planning and Writing Dissertations*, London: Imperial College Press.

Mauch, J.E. and Birch, J.W. (1983) *Guide to the Successful Thesis and Dissertation: Conception to Publication. A Handbook for Students and Faculty*, New York: M. Dekker.

Rudestam, K.E. and Newton, R.R. (2001) *Surviving Your Dissertation: A Comprehensive Guide to Content and Process*, London: Sage.

Swetnam, D. (2000) *Writing Your Dissertation: How to Plan, Prepare and Present Successful Work*, London: How To Books.

31

How is Research Communicated Professionally?

Sally Gainsbury and Cheryl Brown

Reaching out beyond academia • Working out your message and knowing your audience • Writing for a wider audience • Using your own, the mass and the specialist media

It is easy to think that once you have completed writing up your research project into a final dissertation or perhaps even a journal article, that the long process of research design, data collection, analysis and writing is complete. But this is often wrong. You most likely got into researching development through a desire not just to examine the world, but also to change it. And unless you have privileged access to the odd president, the head of a multinational company or of an international financial organization, your best chance to see your painstaking research contribute to social change is to get its message out via the mass media.

Outside academia, most people do not have much time to read. They get most of their information from television, radio, newspapers and magazines; not because they are necessarily disinterested in reading books, academic studies and journal articles, but simply because life and work gets in the way.

As a general rule, the more powerful someone is, the less time they have to read things. If you want your research findings to get to those with the power to change things, you need to learn to become a professional communicator.

And it is not just about getting your research read by those in power. As Joseph Stiglitz has written, the information asymmetry between governments and the people whose interests they purport to serve aids the preservation of unjust and dishonest regimes (Stiglitz, 2002: 27–44). In many political contexts, equipping people with information, or different positions in a debate or even opening up a debate itself, is a vital part of democratic reform and the struggle to re-balance power and resources in a more equitable way.

Much academic research on development could form a worthy contribution to addressing the information asymmetry which underpins, perpetuates and justifies inequality. Yet, confined to the pages of expensively over-priced academic journals,[1] or small lecture rooms, its potential impact is restrained. Until recently, the academic career structure and nature of research funding itself mitigated against academic dissemination beyond schol-arly conferences and journals. Yet ongoing reforms in the UK Research Assessment Exercise (the mechanism through which uni-versities are awarded government funding for their research) and increasing demands from those who fund research that projects engage practitioners as well as scholars, mean that academics have both a moral and contractual obligation to get into the business of profes-sional communication.

Shaping your message

'It's impossible to get the Security Council to read more than two sides of A4', a UN official in New York told an id21 research team a couple of years ago. The bottom line when communicating research outside academia is that your message should be short and to the point. Dispense with the academic jargon and fussy footnotes. You need to see your words as in competition with the other demands on your reader's (or listener's) time. You must catch their interest in the first few lines and then deliver on your promise to tell them something interesting and accessible.

Know your audience

Before thinking about what form of media (the internet, mass media, email, your own newsletter, etc.) may be best for getting your message out, you need to be clear about what your message is. This is not necessarily an easy task. Your main message to other academics – your central thesis, for example – may not be the main message policy-makers, activists and other stakeholders are interested in hearing. You may have written a fantastic Masters

thesis revealing the flaws behind some renowned economist's theory about why cer-tain households systematically fail to move out of chronic poverty. You might even be able to show that the reason for that economist's fail-ure was that the data sets she used to develop her theory were methodologically flawed. It is very likely, however, that few outside academia will care about this. Rather, the primary point for them will be your new theory as to why chronic poverty persists and the suggestions you have for tackling it.

On the other hand, context can be every-thing. This is particularly so when trying to get your research out through the mass media (on which, see further below). If it so happens that the renowned economist with the flawed data has just been appointed to a governmen-tal advisory position, the 'spin' you should put on your research to catch the reader's eye will be altogether different. In other words, dis-semination starts with doing your background research on who you are disseminating to and what they already know about your topic. The following key questions to ask yourself about your audience may help:

311

- What was the last thing they are likely to have read or heard about on your topic? (a World Bank report, a news media report, a political debate?)
- What are the key facts and figures cited in relation to your topic? (How many peo-ple, for example, can be defined as living in 'chronic poverty' in the country/area you are writing about?)
- What are the commonly held myths and presumptions about your topic?
- What are the main political or social debates surrounding your topic? (That poverty is inevitable and necessary in a market society; that there is an important distinction between relative and absolute poverty; that poverty is inherently prob-lematic for social and economic develop-ment, etc.)

Whatever the form of communication you use for getting your research message across, you should aim to structure it around what your readers already know, or think they know. Do not scare the reader off from the start by jumping straight into your own unique and innovative 'take' on the subject. Remind the reader or listener about what they know already and then push their knowledge a little bit further with your new findings and recommendations.

What to leave in, what to leave out and what to do about the caveats?

Once you have decided what your central messages are (you may have a set of different messages, relevant for different audiences), you can start to shape them into a format suitable for your audiences. Whether you choose to disseminate your work through a print newsletter, a website or an email discussion list, your edict should be 'the shorter the better'. If you are writing, your article should ideally be no longer than the initial space you are intending to fill – so one side of A4 if it is in print, or an average computer screen if online or in an email. If you want to go any longer, you will need to demonstrate to your reader that their persistence will be rewarded. Keeping your article short will inevitably mean losing some of your hard-sought detail and discussions, but the important thing at this stage is to catch the interest of the reader and if possible direct them to your longer text where they can explore your research in greater depth.

A major concern many will have at this point is the loss of important caveats. For the purposes of this chapter at least, we can think of the distinction between disseminating your research yourself or through one of the specialist services and disseminating your research through the mass media, as a distinction which largely falls on the extent to which your caveats can be preserved. Although the mass media, by definition, will always enable you to reach a wider audience, the chances of your research reaching that audience with its caveats intact is hugely diminished in comparison with doing it yourself or through a specialist website.

Whatever your chosen medium, however, the fewer caveats your work contains, the more impact it is likely to have. In an 8,000-word article, caveats demonstrate caution, thoughtfulness and clarity. In a 500-word report, they risk undermining your message. It is understandable that you will not want to remove the caveats from your work, but ask yourself if it is possible to make your central points without needing to refer to the element of your argument or data to which the caveat is attached. If you cannot, then obviously the caveats will need to be included (or else the effect really will be to 'dumb down'). If you can avoid them, however, your message may be all the clearer for it.

Telling the story

Once you have decided what your central message is, and the clear arguments, facts and illustrations which strengthen and make up that message, you are ready to shape the message into a narrative which can be easily followed and understood. The format you use will vary depending on your audience and the media you are using. However, the following template[2] can be adapted for anything from a magazine article to a radio script. It focuses on a research report of 500 words (which will fill one A4 page or a full computer screen) which is divided into six sections, as follows:

Headline/Title (maximum of 15 words). This should be arresting, informative and tell the reader precisely what the report is about.

If you are intending to publish this across the world, or somewhere other than your native country, avoid puns or culturally specific references. If your message is aimed at one specific country or region, name it in the title. For example: '*The curse of remoteness: why some African households fail to benefit from economic growth*'[3]

Introductory paragraph (maximum 60 words). This is your chance to 'sell' the research and message to the reader. You need to convince them it is worth spending time reading the rest of the article. State your big central claim here. Doing so will probably also require a summary of the context (often the 'problem') your research addresses. Your aims for this paragraph are to say WHAT is important (your central claim) and WHY it is important (the context). For example: '*Economic growth in some African countries has improved the well-being of the poorest. However, in remote areas poverty remains entrenched. New research argues that Africa's economic growth will not be translated into poverty reduction until the poor are given better access to markets and to basic infrastructure, such as roads.*'

Main paragraphs (1–3 paragraphs). Tell the reader who you are, and what your authority is to make the claims you make (state, for example, your academic institution and the extent of the study you did – that you interviewed 500 people, for example, or have analysed newly available government records). It is important here that you flesh out the claim(s) made in the first paragraph in full; do not disappoint the reader by making claims in the first paragraph you cannot substantiate. Concentrate on telling the reader about your NEW research, rather than going into more detail about background and context. Keep explanations of your methodology to the minimum (say you collected data on x, y and z, but you probably do not need to tell them what

sort of statistical analysis you subjected the data to, or the interview techniques you used, for example).

Bullet points (between 3 and 6). Pull out the main empirical findings of your research and list them in brief, bullet-pointed sentences. Bullet points are particularly good for web publications as they are easier to read. They also break up the text and help the reader remember what has been said.

Concluding paragraph. Use this space to make sure it is clear to your reader WHY your claims and findings are important. Explain where they 'fit' with current practice, policy or orthodoxy. What does your research change? What does it question? What would (or should) be different if those in power knew and understood your claims? You may also like to end this paragraph with a bulleted list of policy implications or lessons.

After you have decided what your central story is, you need to think about the forms of media you will use to disseminate them. Your choice of dissemination media is likely to be determined to a large extent by your available resources. Here we outline three dissemination strategies which are readily available at a low cost.

The internet

Publishing your work on your own website is likely to be the lowest-cost option. If you are based at a university with its own webserver, you will probably be able to host your site for free. If not, many of the well-known web email services also offer free (in return for carrying advertising) or low-cost website hosting and technical support facilities (costs start at around £10 a month). Although the monetary costs of running a site are low, you will

313

need to update your site regularly if you want to keep it relevant.

If you have this time and are *au fait* with website editing software (most of which require little more technical knowledge than your average word-processing package), one particular advantage of a website is that you can use it to inform your audience about the progress of your research as it is still ongoing – perhaps as a way to elicit participation from practitioners or to stimulate discussion. A good example of just such an attempt (on British political research) is www.revolts.co. uk, which is regularly used by journalists, other academics and political activists. Another advantage is that there is theoretically no limit to the amount of material and sources you can publish – photographs, data, audio and visual recordings. You can also make links to the relevant cross-references at a click of a mouse. The ESRC Research Group on Wellbeing in Developing Countries at the University of Bath (www.welldev.org.uk) is a good example of this approach.

The main disadvantage, of course, is that internet access and usage is very low in poor countries. Twenty-nine per cent of the world's internet users are in Europe while only 2 per cent are in Africa. However, the largest percentage of users is in Asia.[4] This said, internet technology is rapidly expanding in these countries as an alternative to expensive printed materials.

A further disadvantage of setting up your own website is that in order to take advantages of the benefits of the World Wide Web (WWW) you will need to ensure your site is registered with the popular search engines, such as Google. The aim of such search engines is to provide an objective ranking of the most relevant sites to specific search criteria. As many sites have a commercial interest, the WWW has become an information marketplace and different sites compete (and it could be said, cheat) to gain the highest search engine ranking. The response from search engines has been to continuously

change their registration processes and ranking criteria (from divining the relevance of your site from a simple analysis of the words upon it to looking at which other sites have links to you, for example). Keeping up with these continual changes is necessary to ensure readers can find your site via the search engines, yet this can be a job in itself.

If you are intending your site to be accessible to users in developing countries, possibly using a slow dial-up connection and an older computer, you will have to make sure your site is quick to load. This means avoiding fancy graphics and large downloads, such as audio files and pictures.

Depending on the nature of your website and where it is hosted, you may need to abide by new disability accessibility rules, such as making your site 'readable' for a blind person using an audio program.[5] If your site is hosted by your university, your institution is likely to have certain stylistic and legal requirements you will have to abide by.

Mass media

One of the most rewarding, but also most risky, approaches to disseminating your research is using the mass media. The strategy can be more risky as you lose control over what happens to your words and research. However the pay-offs are that you potentially reach thousands, if not millions, of people. Another point to remember when engaging with the media is that your engagement need not be a one-off instance. Target quality publications who will aim to represent your research fairly, and stay in touch with the journalists who contact you. That way, you will have a ready-made outlet for the next piece of research you want to disseminate.

The starting point for getting research into the mainstream press is a press or news release. A press release is not a newspaper report; it needs to be even snappier than that. It has to 'sell' the story to the journalist in a matter of seconds (the journalist, in turn, will invariably have to 'sell' the story to his or her editor, to secure the needed column inches or air-time to publish it).

Journalists receive hundreds of news releases every day and most of them end up in the bin so you need to make sure that your 'news' is important and interesting enough to get noticed. The releases need to be written in a style that appeals to journalists and follows certain journalistic conventions, but most importantly, they need to convey a sense of newness and urgency.

In general, there are two reasons why a journalist may be interested in your research:

1   You may have genuinely new news. Your research may have made exciting new discoveries or uncovered shocking truths. Packaged the right way, these may be interesting to journalists.
2   Your research findings may be able to add to an issue (or a country) that is already being discussed on the news agenda.

A good news release is one that gives journalists the details they need to write their story without having to go back to you to fill in the gaps. The release should cover the 'five Ws' – what, where, who, when and why – and one 'H' – how – of news. It should also give a sense of authority: believe it or not, journalists want their stories to be water-tight – their careers and reputation depend on it. They'll want to know who you are, what your qualification is to talk on the issue and who you are funded, employed or supervised by. Note that all of this information needs to go in the body of the press release. Some detail can be added at the end in a section headed 'Notes to editors'.

One way in which journalists convey the authority of their stories is by using quotes.

Ideally, your press release should contain quotes either from you, from the communities (for example) you have been studying, or from some other authoritative individual (the president of a non-governmental organisation, a government department, a politician or a professor, for example). You can either integrate your quotes into the body of text or include two or three stand-alone quotes at the end (Professor Bloggs said: '......'). As journalists need to make sure their stories are different from those in rival newspapers, do not be surprised if they call you up asking you to go over the exact same issues as discussed in the press release: they're just trying to get you to say things in a slightly different way so they can get new quotes.

Beyond the facts, you'll also need to 'sell' to journalists the story behind your research in order for it to get their attention. Your opening paragraph should lead with the stark new statistics, the shocking situation or the new take on an ongoing situation. This might not be the focus of your actual research – it's just the news 'hook' – but the key to using the mass media is to use the news agenda to pull the audience into your broader analysis. For example, a release discussing research on ways of combining refugee relief with development aid began:

> The UNHCR (United Nations High Commission for Refugees) stands accused of subjecting refugees within its African camps to illegal collective punishment by withdrawing food rations for weeks at a time.

While one on the World Bank's thinking on land tenure began:

> The World Bank's World Development Report 2005, due to be published this September, makes recommendations that jeopardize the future of small local businesses in favour of large multinationals.

315

Box 31.1 Key points for writing a press release

- **Length and format**: Keep releases to less than 500 words. Journalists will contact you if they need more information. Ideally, send the release in the body of an email (not as an attachment). Make the 'subject line' as snappy a headline as you would expect to see in a newspaper and avoid giving the recipients the impression that they are one of 300 other journalists who have received the identical release (journalists thrive on 'exclusives').
- **Who to send it to**: Most newspapers give out the email address for their 'news desk' on their website. These are general clearing houses for press releases. It is better to send releases to section editors (most will have a separate editor for economics, social and political affairs, for example). Alternatively, email your release direct to individual journalists whom you know work on areas which your research affects. If you do not know a journalist's email address, call the newspaper's head office and simply ask.
- **Your details**: Include at the end of the email your full contact details, including a mobile or 'out of hours' phone number. You should aim to make yourself readily available during work hours, at least for the day or so after you send out the release.
- **Clearances**: It may be necessary for you to check with your university, funder, supervisor or employer before sending out the press release, especially if you name them within it. They may have special procedures and rules you need to follow before engaging with the mass media.

What happens afterwards?

Some journalists and editors will simply reproduce the press release as an article in their newspaper, although they may call first to check facts or amend quotes. Others will want to call to probe for more information or to get a different spin. If you are nervous or worried about this, ask for their name and number and arrange to call them back in an hour. Use that time to check out their previous work and to gather your own thoughts, and have a copy of your news release to hand to help you remember your key points. If you are still nervous, tell the journalist you want to speak 'off the record' at first and will agree quotes afterwards. (They will email/call you back later to check what you are happy with being quoted on.) But remember that, as a specialist, you are likely to know a lot more about the subject than the journalist, and so you should not be too nervous.

Using existing internet services for research dissemination

Although internet connections are less widespread in the developing world and often expensive, slow and unreliable, for many people it is the only means by which they can access up-to-date development research and is still often much more accessible and cheaper than print journals and books. As discussed above, however, not all websites are automatically recognized by search engines and so potential readers will have no way of finding out they exist. To reach these internet users it is a good idea to 'piggy-back' your research on one of the many online services that have developed over recent years to bring together development research on the internet. These services make it their job to stay abreast of search engines as well as the latest hot topics and debates in development research. They range from huge gateways, where users can search for research on many different topics, to subject-specific sites that are created for communities of specialists (see Box 31.2)

Box 31.2   Multi-topic gateways

One site that aims to make it easier for internet users to find information on development issues is Eldis (www.eldis.org). The site is arranged in resource guides on different subjects but also has a facility for searching by country and keywords. The database is made up of summaries written by the Eldis staff on thousands of online documents, websites, databases and email discussion lists. Although Eldis sources material itself, you can submit your research to their editors for possible inclusion on the site.

If your research isn't already online

The majority of development research portals are designed to direct users to online research, rather than hosting the documents themselves. By contrast, the World Bank's Development Gateway (www.developmentgateway.org) is a website that relies on users to contribute development resources themselves by signing up as members. This is a very simple process and, once subscribed, members can upload reports, documents, news items, website addresses, etc. on any one of over 20 different topics.

Researchers in low- and middle-income countries, who may not have a website to put their research online, can submit their documents to the Global Development Network's website (www.gdnet.org) to be hosted online. To be eligible for this service, the researcher first needs to register with the Global Development Network. As an online community of researchers in developing countries, it also supports its members by providing information on funding opportunities and free access to online journals (see Box 31.3).

Box 31.3   Online communities

Many websites have emerged that respond to the need of specialists worldwide to 'meet' online and contribute their knowledge, and there is a site for almost every subject (e.g. OneFish (www.onefish.org), which brings together research on fisheries and aquatics). These specialist sites tend to require you to register in order to submit material to the website or to access certain areas of the website, such as discussion boards. Registration is often free and enables a community to build up that can freely discuss and share knowledge and resources.

Editorial control

Most of the online services currently available have a relatively relaxed editorial attitude to the content submitted to their site. One exception is id21 (www.id21.org), which attempts to offer the reader expert-produced summaries of selected studies on a range of development topics. Id21 also includes summaries of research that is not necessarily available online. Instead of linking to websites, each summary gives the reference of the original document (with a link to its location online if available) and the contact details of the researcher. Unlike other services, id21 has strict criteria regarding the quality of the research it features and its highlights are approved by the researcher for accuracy before being put online. Because such quality controls are resource-intensive, however, id21 currently restricts itself to providing summaries of only UK-funded research.

Conclusion

Communicating your research beyond academia can be a rewarding way to see your ideas making a difference, even if that 'difference' is just a wider discussion and debate of your subject. But another advantage of mass communication is that doing it makes your research better. Not only do you open your research up to criticism from a wide variety of people with different experiences, but the process of actually putting pen to paper and writing

500 words instead of 5,000 helps you focus your mind on what you *really* want to say and think. In a long essay, it is easy to hide behind jargon and academic shorthand; you can talk comfortably about 'hegemonic discourses' and 'structural constraints' for example. But what does this actually mean? Forcing yourself to write for audiences who do not share your academic canon and paradigm can be an enlightening and rewarding part of the research process itself.

Notes

1. The profits made on some academic journals, which pay for neither the cost of research nor editorial time of the academics who voluntary contribute their time, is an unreported scandal which is only just beginning to receive the political attention it merits.
2. The template is adapted from the id21 Research Highlight style sheet. For more information visit www.id21.org
3. This example is taken from a Research Highlight of the same name published by id21 at www.id21.org/society/s1ael1g2.html. The Highlight was based on 'Land and livelihoods: the politics of land reform in Southern Africa' by Edward Lahiff, *IDS Bulletin*, Vol. 34 No. 3, pp 54–63, July 2003.
4. As cited on www.internetworldstats.com, April 2005.
5. For the UK, see the Disability Rights Commission (www.drc.gov.uk) for the most up-to-date information on the law and recommended practice.

318

QUESTIONS FOR DISCUSSION

1. What policy recommendations or practical changes does your research suggest are necessary and possible?
2. You have two minutes to explain your research to someone who has not studied development. What do you tell them?

(Continued)

(Continued)

3. When you read the paper today, which news stories stuck in your mind the most? What do you remember about them?
4. What are the news and information sources beyond academic publications you trust the most? What is it that makes them authoritative in your view?
5. 'Knowledge is power', wrote Foucault. How can your knowledge empower others?

Further reading

Cottle, S.(ed.) (2003) *News, Public Relations and Power*, London: Sage.

Curran, J. and Seaton, J. (1981) *Power without Responsibility: The Press and Broadcasting in Britain*, London: Fontana.

World Bank (ed.) (2002) *The Right to Tell: The Role of Mass Media in Economic Development*, Washington, DC: The World Bank.

Websites

For a host of websites and internet portals on all aspects of development studies, see http://www.ids.ac.uk/ids/info/index.html

For news with a development and campaign focus, see: www.oneworld.net

One of the most widely used style guides for journalistic writing is *The Economist* guide. The guide gives useful advice on eliminating unnecessary words and adopting a no-nonsense style, although it also betrays the politics of the publication – an interesting demonstration of how political communication can be! see: http://www.economist.com/research/styleGuide/

ESRC Communications Toolkit: http://www.esrcsocietytoday.ac.uk/ESRCInfoCentre/Support/Communications_Toolkit

Reference

Stiglitz, J. (2002) Transparency and government, in The World Bank (ed.), *The Right to Tell: The Role of Mass Media in Economic Development*, Washington, DC: The World Bank, pp. 27–44.

Index

accommodation 18, 80–1
action research 19–20
aerial photography *see* remote sensing
Africa
   photographs 232
   population statistics 269–70
Africa Commission Report 242
agriculture, farm surveys 135–8
AIDS *see* HIV/AIDS
Amazwi Abesifazane 235–8
anthropological case study 184
archives 241–9
   definition 242–3
   ethics 248–9
   interpretation 244
   national archives 245–6
   NGOs 247
   organization of 244–5
   referencing 247–8
   see also literature reviews
atmospheric correction 254, 255
audio diaries 204–5
Australia, participatory video 234

Bangladesh, government research 91
bibliographic searches *see*
   literature reviews
body language 40
body mapping 194
Botswana, local literature 225
Brazil, data collection 66
Burkina Faso, interviews 151
bus stations 134–5

Caribbean, NGO research 96
case studies 184, 200–1
causal flow analysis 195
census data 262–71
Chambers, Robert 14, 15, 191
change, and ethics 28–9
children
   dissemination of research 58–60
   ethical issues 57–8
   hard-to-reach groups 58
   research methods 54–6
   research with 20, 52–60
China, gender relations 46

civil society organizations 107–8
   see also non-governmental organizations
classification, remote sensing 255–6
clothing *see* dress codes
codes of practice, ethics 26
collective action, focus groups 154–6
Colombia, local knowledge 224
commercial activities, urban areas 133–4
communication, and language 39–40
communities
   focus groups 154–6
   impacts of research 18–21, 30, 34–8
   participatory video 233–5
   school studies 81–2
community-based organizations
   (CBOs) 95–8
confidentiality 164, 202–3
conflicts 70–7, 203–4
contentious information 62–8
contexts, and ethics 29
coping strategies 74–5
costs *see* payment
craft-based images 235–8
critical security studies 73
cultural differences 29–30, 40, 63–4, 168–9
cultural identity, researcher 36–7

data collection 131–2
data mining 19
Demographic and Health Surveys (DHSs) 267
Department for International Development (DFID)
   22, 85, 107, 244–5
development agencies, websites 277–8
Development Education Association (DEA) 108
development policy, research on 107
development projects
   conflict areas 71
   ethical implications 28–9
development studies
   and ethnography 180–2
   paradigms 6–9
diaries 56, 197, 200–5
   non-written 204–5
disasters, impact assessment 138–42
dissemination
   internet 313–14
   professional communication 310–19

dissemination *cont.*
  research with children 58–60
  research with government 92
  research report 297–308
dissertation *see* research report
document analysis, internet 277
'do no harm' rule 75–6
drawings, participatory research 197, 226
dress codes 29, 37
'dry season bias' 15

'ecological fallacy' 266–7
educational institutions, working
    with 79–85
Eldis 317
email 274–5
emergency situations 70–7
empiricism 7
English language 83, 174, 278–9
equipment, field surveys 131
ethics 25–32
  archive use 248–9
  codes of practice 26
  definition 25–6
  diaries 202–3
  of fieldwork 13–14, 30–2, 105
  and gender 47
  local knowledge 228
  NGO research 97–8
  online research 275
  participatory research 196
  and power 27–8, 34–5, 47–8, 64–5
  questionnaires 164
  of research methods 122, 123
  and safety 75–6
  working with children 57–8
ethnography 180–7, 226–7, 232

farm surveys 135–8
feminist methodologies 155–6
  see also women
field inventories 131
field mapping 130–1
field surveys 130–42
  urban areas 132–5
fieldwork
  assistants 17–18, 35, 76, 165
  in developing countries 13–22
  equipment 17, 131
  ethics 13–14
  gender awareness 47–8
  guides to 3–4, 14
  logistics 14–15
  preliminary visits 39
  preparing for 14–16, 29, 38
  problems 30–2
  risk assessment 15–16
  timing of 15

Fiji, NGOs 98
film, research tool 232–5
focus groups 153–61
  analysing 160
  children 54–5
  incentives 158–9
  language 175
  logistics 157–60
  online 275
  participatory research 195, 197
  strengths and limitations 155
  women 49
food production, field surveys 135–8
funding, and ethics 27

gardens, food production 136, 137
gatekeepers
  interviews 147–8
  NGOs 99
  and power 35–6
gender
  interpreters 177
  and interviews 148–9
  power relations 44–50
General Data Dissemination System (GDDS) 283
geographic information systems (GIS) 251–2, 256–9
georegistration 254
gifts, to communities 18–19, 30
Global Development Network 317
Goa 65
government departments
  literature 225
  websites 277
  working with 87–92
greed versus grievance 72
'grey literature' 224–5, 244
group interviews *see* focus groups
Guatemala, local knowledge 223–4, 229

hazards, damage assessment 138–41
health research
  census data 269–70
  diaries 203
historical accounts 109
  see also archives
HIV/AIDS research
  census data 269–70
  diaries 203
home country, research in 104–10
Human Development Index 269–70
humanism 7, 8–9
human security agenda 72–4
Hussein, Saddam 177

id21 85, 318
identities
  defining 36–8
  understanding 39

illegal activities 66
images, of development 108–9
India
    census 263
    National Archives 246
indigenous local knowledge 222–9
    accessing 225–7
    importance of 227–8
    limitations 228–9
    sources 223–5
Indonesia, participatory research 192–3
informal sector, surveys 133–4
information and communication technologies
        (ICTs) 109–10, 276
informed consent 26–7, 57
institutional learning 242
international organizations 282–92
internet see World Wide Web
interpreters 145, 165, 172–8
    see also research assistants
interviews 144–51
    accuracy 150–1
    email 274–5
    interviewees 147–8
    participatory research 197
    questionnaires 166–7
    recording 149–50
    time and place 148–9
    types of 144–6
    see also focus groups
inventories 130–42

journal articles
    literature review 211–16
    publishing 310–11
journal-keeping 183

Kenya
    Family Life Training Centres 181, 182
    interviews 145–6
    language 172–3
    schools 83
kit list, fieldwork 17
'knowledge gap' 223

land degradation, field surveys 136–8, 139
land use surveys
    remote sensing 257–9
    urban areas 132–3
language
    and children 54–5
    for communication 39–40, 106, 173
    focus groups 156
    and information control 64
    internet 279
    in schools 83
    see also interpreters

Laos, statistical data 289–92
Liberia, post-conflict 70, 76
libraries, literature reviews 212
literacy, levels of 56
literature, indigenous 223–9
literature reviews 209–20
    analysing 214–15
    literature map 210–11, 218–19
    sources 211–14
    writing up 215–17, 299
    see also archives
local knowledge see indigenous local knowledge
logical positivism 7, 8
Long, Norman 182

Malawi, ethnographic methods 183, 185–6
maps
    field mapping 130–1, 133–4
    literature map 210–11, 218–19
    participatory methods 194
marginalized groups, diaries 204
markets, surveys 135
mass media, for research dissemination 313–15
matrix ranking and scoring 195
memory cloths 235–8
methodology see research methods
Mexico
    gender relations 46–7
    interviews 145, 148
Michaels, Eric 234
migration, census data 268
Millennium Development Goals 83, 85,
        107, 287–9
mobility mapping 194
multi-stage clustering 169–70
Muslim countries 15

Namibia
    ethnography 183
    language 173–4
National Archives, Kew 245
natural disasters 138–42
newspapers, websites 278
New Zealand, participatory video 234
Nigeria, women 20
non-governmental organizations (NGOs) 94–101
    advantages of working with 98–9
    archives 247
    interviews 146, 147
    language use 174
    local literature 224–5
    and politics 97–8, 99–100
    practical guide 100–1
    problems of working with 99–100
    researching 95–8
    websites 278
    see also civil society organizations

observation, participatory research 197
Oxfam 243

Pakistan, working with government 89
Paris 21 283–5
participant observation 180–7
participatory research 189–98
  analysis 195
  with children 53–8
  ethnography 180–7
  focus groups 156–7
  and gender 49–50
  indigenous local knowledge 225–6
  methodology 115–26, 193–8
  rights-based approach 195–6
  tyranny of 193–5
  video 232–5
Participatory Rural Appraisal (PRA) 156–7,
    180, 181, 182–3, 191–3
payment
  to focus groups 158–9
  to interpreters 174–5
  to respondents 19, 58
Peru, participatory methods 193
Philippines
  local literature 225
  photo-essay 231
photocopying 249
photographs
  development images 108–9
  diaries 204–5
  research method 56, 231–2
  sensitivity 65
  urban surveys 134
  see also remote sensing
pilot testing, questionnaires 169
politics, and NGO research
    97–8, 99–100
population studies, censuses 262–71
positionality, of researcher 19
positivism, logical 7, 8
power relations
  and children 57
  and ethics 27–8, 34–6, 47–8, 64–5
  and gender 44–8
  with government 92
  with interpreter 177
  and participatory approaches
    189, 193
  positionality 19
practical value, of research 106
preliminary visits 39
preparation, for fieldwork 16, 29, 38
pre-pilot studies 156
press releases 313–15
primary data, sources 65–6
Public Record Office see National Archives

qualitative research 115–26, 189
  focus groups 153–61
quantitative research 115–26
  tyranny of 189, 190–1
questionnaires 19, 163–70, 190
  for children 55
  design of 165–9
  language of 55
  online 275
  pilot testing 169
  sampling strategy 169–70
  in schools 84–5
quotations, in research report 307

random sampling 169
ranking, participatory research 197
recall, participatory research 197
reconnaissance, urban areas 133
recording
  focus groups 160
  interviews 149–50
referencing
  archives 247–8
  research report 302–3
registration systems, population data 267–8
religion, influence of 29
remote sensing 251–60
  analysis 256–7
  passive and active sensors 252–4
  processing data 254–6
research assistants 17–18, 35, 76, 165
  see also interpreters
research diaries, participatory research 197
researcher
  cultural identity 36–7, 45, 63
  as insider 106
  language skills 172–4
  and participatory methods 192
  and power 19, 27–8, 34–6, 45–6, 64–5
research methods
  comparison of 115–26
  conflict areas 74–5
  ethnography 180–7
  focus groups 154–6
  integrated approach 123–6
  NGO research 96
  sensitive information 66–7
  working with children 54–6
research report 297–308
  data presentation 300, 301–2, 303–7
  quotations 307
  structure 298–303
research results, education 85
resource mapping 194
risk assessment, fieldwork 14–15
risk exposure 74–5
role play 56, 197

safety, and ethics 75–6
sampling frames 132
sampling strategy, questionnaires 169–70
satellite images *see* remote sensing
Save the Children 157
schools
  community-based studies 81–2
  education research 84–5
  as mirrors of development 82–4
  working with 79–85
seasonal and social calendars 195
secondary data 66, 262–71
security-development nexus 71
semi-structured interviews/questionnaires
  144–6, 166
sensitive information 62–8
shock, conflicts 75
Sierra Leone
  community-based organizations (CBOs) 98
  fieldwork 13, 14, 19, 21
snowballing technique, interviews 148
social mapping 194
social movements, websites 278
social network diagrams 194
soil erosion 136–8, 139
Solomon Islands 64
Somalia, focus groups 157–60
South Africa
  action research 19–20
  crafts-based images 235–8
  literature review 210–11, 218–19
  video 233–4
South Asian literature, internet 276–7
stakeholders, participatory research 192
statistical data
  censuses 262–71
  international organizations 282–3, 287–9
  presentation of 303–7
stratified sampling 169
structural adjustment programmes 107
structuralism 7, 8
structured interviews/questionnaires 144–6, 166
Swahili 172–3, 174, 176
systematic sampling 169

Tanzania
  archives 243
  ethnography 183, 184
  language 173, 174
  national archives 246
  schools 82, 83
teachers 81
time, measurement of 168

time transects 195
timing, of fieldwork 15, 148–9
transculturalism 109
translators *see* interpreters
tropical home gardens 136, 137
Tunisia, interviews 146–7

Uganda, research with children 57, 58
United Kingdom, National Archives 245
United Nations Development Programme (UNDP),
  Human Development Report 283
universities, links with 15, 21–2, 80
unstructured interviews/questionnaires
  144–6, 166–7
urban areas, field surveys 132–5

Venezuela 65
video
  diaries 204–5
  research tool 232–5
visual research methods 56, 197, 204–5, 231–9
vulnerability, coping strategies 75

war, diaries 203–4
women
  crafts-based images 237–8
  diaries 203–4
  focus groups 155–6
  participatory methods 193
  research with 20, 45–6, 67
  stereotypes 227
  see also gender
World Bank
  Development Gateway 317
  publications 283, 287
World Fertility Survey (WFS) 267
World Vision 100
World Wide Web 273–80
  cautions 278–9
  international organizations 285–7
  for literature review 212–14
  as medium of research 274–5
  as object of research 275–7
  for research dissemination 313–14, 316–18
  as source of information 277–8
written research methods 56, 197

Zimbabwe
  diaries 204
  ethnographic methods 185
  NGOs 97

Index by Margaret Binns